P9-DNL-660

CHEKHOV
THE MAJOR PLAYS

Ivanov
The Sea Gull
Uncle Vanya
The Three Sisters
The Cherry Orchard

Translated by Ann Dunnigan
With a Foreword by Robert Brustein
and an Afterword by Rosamund Bartlett

SIGNET CLASSICS

To Tamara Daykarhanova
of the Moscow Art Theater,
with gratitude,
A.D.

𝕮

SIGNET CLASSICS
Published by New American Library,
an imprint of Penguin Random House LLC
375 Hudson Street, New York, New York 10014

This book is a publication of New American Library.

First Signet Classics Printing, May 1965
First Signet Classics Printing (Bartlett Afterword), December 2006

Copyright © Ann Dunnigan, 1964
Foreword copyright © Robert Brustein, 1964
Afterword copyright © Rosamund Bartlett, 2006
Penguin Random House supports copyright. Copyright fuels creativity, encourages diverse voices, promotes free speech, and creates a vibrant culture. Thank you for buying an authorized edition of this book and for complying with copyright laws by not reproducing, scanning, or distributing any part of it in any form without permission. You are supporting writers and allowing Penguin Random House to continue to publish books for every reader.

Signet Classics and the Signet Classics colophon are registered trademarks of Penguin Random House LLC.

For more information about Penguin Random House, visit penguinrandomhouse
.com.

ISBN 978-0-451-53037-0

Printed in the United States of America
20   19   18   17   16   15   14   13   12

If you purchased this book without a cover you should be aware that this book is stolen property. It was reported as "unsold and destroyed" to the publisher and neither the author nor the publisher has received any payment for this "stripped book."

Penguin
Random
House

Anton Pavlovich Chekhov (1860–1904) was born in Taganrog, Russia, on the Sea of Azov, the son of a small shopkeeper and the grandson of a serf. At sixteen, he was left to fend for himself while his father fled with the rest of the family to Moscow, escaping a debtors' prison. After finishing school in his native town, Chekhov went to Moscow, where, with the aid of a scholarship, he entered the University to study medicine. To help with the family finances, he started publishing tales, anecdotes, jokes, and articles. By the time he took his medical degree in 1884, writing had become his main interest and occupation. His literary reputation grew with the publication of the book *Motley Stories* (1886). That same year, he made the acquaintance of Alexei Suvorin, owner of the newspaper *New Time*, who invited him to contribute longer tales at a higher rate. In 1888, he was awarded the Pushkin Prize for the collection *In the Twilight*. This and the publication of the long story *The Steppe* marked the beginning of Chekhov's recognition as one of Russia's leading writers. In the years following, he produced his first serious full-length play, *Ivanov* (1887), as well as a steady stream of short stories. The first production of his famous play *The Sea Gull* (1896) was a miserable failure. But in 1898, the play was revived at the Moscow Art Theater and proved a resounding success, as did the Theater's productions of *The Three Sisters* and *The Cherry Orchard*. In 1901, he married the actress Olga Knipper. He died of tuberculosis.

Born in New York City in 1927, **Robert Brustein** is one of the country's preeminent drama critics. He was Dean of the Yale School of Drama from 1966 to 1979 and then became director of the Loeb Drama Center and artistic director of American Repertory Theatre Company at Harvard, where he served until 2002. Among his influential books are *The Third Theatre* and *Dumbocracy in America*.

Rosamund Bartlett is a writer, scholar, translator, and lecture specializing in Russian literature, music, and cultural history. Among her publications are *Tolstoy: A Russian Life*; the Oxford University Press translation of *Anna Karenina*; *Chekhov: Scenes from a Life*; and a Chekhov anthology entitled *About Love and Other Stories*, which was shortlisted for the Weidenfeld European Translation Prize.

Contents

Foreword

Anton Chekhov is the gentlest and the most impersonal of all the great modern dramatists, but there is one sense in which he does align himself on the side of his characters—insofar as they are cultured individuals, constituting the last stronghold of enlightenment against the encroaching mediocrity, vulgarity, and illiteracy of Russian life. For against these forces of darkness—the environment of his plays—he directs a vigorous personal revolt. Chekhov himself was passionately addicted to "culture"—by which he meant not intellectuality (he finds the intelligentsia "hypocritical, false, hysterical, poorly educated, and indolent"), but rather a mystical compound of humanity, decency, kindness, intelligence, education, accomplishment, and will. It is by these standards that he usually measures the worth of human beings. In a long letter to his brother Nikolai, Chekhov begins by accusing him of an "utter lack of culture," and then proceeds to define the characteristics of truly cultured people in a revelatory manner. Such people, he notes, "respect the human personality, and are therefore always forbearing, gentle, courteous, and compliant. They will overlook noise, and cold, and overdone meat, and the presence of strangers in their house. . . . They are sincere and fear untruth like the very devil. . . . They do not make fools of themselves in order to arouse

This is adapted from a chapter in Mr. Brustein's book *Theatre of Revolt*. Printed by permission of the publishers, Little, Brown and Co.—Atlantic Monthly Press.

sympathy. . . . They are not vain. . . . They develop an esthetic sense." Cautioning Nikolai "not to fall below the level of your environment," Chekhov counsels him, "What you need is constant work, day and night, eternal reading, study, willpower."

Chekhov, who had peasant blood himself, foresaw that cultured individuals might arise from any class of society, however humble, but he did not (like Tolstoy) idealize the peasantry, and the crude utilitarianism of the middle class filled him with disgust. If he is aggrieved by any general fact of Russian life, it is the cancerous growth of slovenliness, filth, stupidity, and cruelty among the mass of men; and if he despises the sluggishness and indolence of his upper-class characters, then this is because they, too, are gradually being overwhelmed by the tide, lacking the will to stem it. For if the Russian gentry represents beauty without use, the Russian environment is characterized by use without beauty; and those with the necessary willpower are often utterly without the necessary culture or education. It is this conflict between the cultured upper classes and their stupefying environment—between the forces of light and the forces of darkness—that provides the basic substance of most of Chekhov's plays.

Thus, while David Magarshack, the author of *Chekhov, The Dramatist,** somewhat overstates the case by saying that Chekhov's mature plays are dramas of "courage and hope," he is perfectly right to emphasize the moral purpose behind Chekhov's imitation of reality. Chekhov never developed any program for "life as it should be." His revolt, like that of most great artists, is mainly negative. And it is a mistake to interpret the occasional expressions of visionary optimism that conclude his plays as evidence of "courage and hope" (they are more like desperate defenses against nihilism and despair). Yet it is also wrong to assume that Chekhov shares the pessimism that pervades his plays or the despondency of his defeated characters. Everyone who knew him testified to his gaiety, humor, and buoyancy,

*Gloucester, MA: Peter Smith, 1960.

and if he always expected the worst, he always hoped for the best. Chekhov the realist was required to transcribe accurately the appalling conditions of provincial life without false affirmations or baseless optimism; but Chekhov the moralist has a sneaking belief in change. In short, Chekhov expresses his revolt not by depicting the ideal, which would have violated his sense of reality, and not by merely imitating the real, which would have violated his sense of moral purpose, but by criticizing the real at the same time that he is representing it. He will not comment on reality; he will permit reality to comment on itself. And so it is that while the surfaces of his plays seem drenched with *tedium vitae* and spiritual vapors, the depths are charged with energy and dissent.

These depths are also charged with melodrama. For although this is a mode that Chekhov deplores as unnatural, he smuggles his personal commentary into his plays by means of a hidden melodramatic configuration. Actually, Chekhov uses melodramatic devices all through his career—suicides, duels, attempted murders, love triangles, interrupted love scenes—and, trying to combat his weakness for exciting act curtains, he is constantly working to excise the unnatural from his art. (After *The Cherry Orchard,* he crows triumphantly that there is "not a single pistol shot in it.") On the other hand, all of his mature dramatic works, and especially *The Cherry Orchard,* are constructed on the same melodramatic pattern—the conflict between a despoiler and his victims—while the action of the plays follows the same melodramatic development—the gradual dispossession of the victims from their rightful inheritance.

This external conflict can be more easily observed if we strip away everything extraneous to the (hidden) plot, ignoring for a moment Chekhov's explorations of motive and character. In *The Sea Gull,* Trigorin seduces and ruins Nina; Mme. Arkadina spiritually dispossesses Treplev, her Hamlet-like son. In *Uncle Vanya,* Elena steals Sonya's secret love, Astrov, while Serebryakov robs Sonya of her inheritance and produces in Vanya a soul-killing disillusionment. In *The Three Sisters,* Na-

tasha gradually evicts the Prozorov family from their
provincial house. And in *The Cherry Orchard,* Lopakhin
dispossesses Mme. Ranevskaya and Gayev, taking over
their orchard as acreage for summer cottages. In each
case, the central act of dispossession is symbolized
through some central image, representing what is being
ravished, stolen, or destroyed. In *The Sea Gull,* it is the
bird that Treplev kills, identified with Nina, who is also
destroyed by a man with "nothing better to do." In
Uncle Vanya, it is the forest, "a picture of gradual and
unmistakable degeneration," associated with the lives of
the family, degenerating through sheer inertia. In *The
Three Sisters,* it is the Prozorov house, eventually hol-
lowed out by Natasha as though by a nest of termites.
And in *The Cherry Orchard,* of course, it is the famous
orchard, hacked to pieces by the commercial ax. With
the possible exception of *The Sea Gull,* each play drama-
tizes the triumph of the forces of darkness over the
forces of enlightenment, the degeneration of culture in
the crude modern world.

What prevents us from seeing these melodramatic
configurations is the extraordinary way in which they
have been concealed. Technically, Chekhov's most effec-
tive masking device is to bury the plot (Magarshack's
concept of the "indirect action") so that violent acts and
emotional climaxes occur offstage or between the acts.
In this way, he manages to avoid the melodramatic crisis
and to obscure the external conflict, ducking the event
and concentrating on the denouement. Secondly, Chekhov concludes the action before the conventional melodramatic reversal—the triumphant victory of virtue over
vice; in its place, he substitutes a reversal of his own
invention, in which the defeated characters, shuffling off
the old life, begin to look forward to the new. Most
important, however, he refuses to cast his characters in
conventional hero-villain roles. In the buried plot, Chekhov's despoilers act while his victims suffer; but by sub-
ordinating plot to character, Chekhov diverts our
attention from process to motive and makes us suspend
our judgment of the action.

Chekhov also dilutes the melodramatic pathos by

qualifying our sympathy for the victims. In most cases, they seem largely responsible for whatever happens to them. This is not to say, as some have said, that we do not sympathize with their unhappy lot; we do, but since Chekhov highlights their inertia, irresponsibility, and waste, we also deplore their helpless inability to resist their fate. Carefully balancing pathos with irony, Chekhov avoids the stock responses of conventional theater, deflecting the emphasis from the melodramatic to the natural and the atmospheric, wrapping layers of commonplace detail around extremely climactic events.

And this is precisely the effect that Chekhov aims to achieve. "Let the things that happen onstage," he writes, "be just as complex and yet just as simple as they are in life. For instance, people are having a meal at a table, just having a meal, but at the same time their happiness is being created, or their lives are being smashed up." The placid surface of existence, then, is to be a masking device for his controlled manipulation of human fatality; the trivial course of the daily routine is to disguise his sense of process, development, and crisis. Chekhov is so successful in achieving these goals that English and American critics often condemn his plays as vague, actionless, and formless. They have been blinded by Chekhov's extraordinary atmospheric power and his capacity to evoke, through rhythmic sound effects (scratching pens, guitar music, sneezes, songs, etc.), a poetic illusion of fluid reality.

Beneath this surface, Chekhov's work has the tensile strength of a steel girder, the construction being so subtle that it is almost invisible. And while his characters seem to exist in isolated pockets of vacancy, they are all integral parts of a close network of interlocking motives and effects. Thus, while the dialogue seems to wander aimlessly into discussions of cold samovars, the situation in Moscow, and the temperature of the earth, it is economically performing a great number of essential dramatic functions: revealing character, furthering the action, uncovering the theme, evoking in the spectators a mood identical with that of the characters, and diverting attention from the melodramatic events that are erupting

under the smooth surface of life. Through this original
and inimitable technique, Chekhov manages to exercise
his function both as a realist and as a moralist, and to
express his resistance to certain aspects of modern life
in enduring esthetic form.

All of Chekhov's mature works are masterpieces, but
The Three Sisters perhaps provides the most stunning
example of his dramatic approach. Completed late in
1900, almost four years after *Uncle Vanya*, it was written
mostly in the Crimea, where Chekhov had retired to recu-
perate from the tuberculosis that was soon to prove fatal to
him. One year before, he had published "In the Ravine," a
short story with enough similarities to the play to suggest
that it was a preparatory sketch. The location of the story
is a provincial village called Ukleyevo, so ordinary and
banal that it is identified to visitors as the place "where
the deacon ate all the caviar at the funeral"—nothing
more stimulating has ever happened there. Yet, as usual
with Chekhov, extraordinary events take place in this
commonplace setting. The most important development,
for our purposes, is the progress of the woman, Aksinya—
married to one of the two sons of Tsybukin, an elderly,
generous shopkeeper. Aksinya, contemptuous of the
family, parades wantonly about the town in low-necked
dresses and is openly conducting an affair with a rich
factory owner. When Tsybukin's unmarried son weds a
girl named Lipa—a quiet, frightened, gentle peasant
woman—Aksinya becomes intensely jealous; when Lipa
gives birth to a baby boy, Aksinya scalds it with a ladle
of boiling water, killing both the infant and the hopes of
the family. Instead of being punished, however, Aksinya
continues to flourish in the town, finally turning her
father-in-law and his family out of their own house.

From this story, Chekhov apparently derived his idea
for Natalya Ivanovna, the lustful, ambitious, and preda-
tory woman who eventually disinherits the gentle
Prozorovs—an action played out against the background
of a provincial town so petty, vulgar, and boring that it
has the power to degrade its most cultured inhabitants.
The Three Sisters is richer, more complex, and more ambig-
uous than "In the Ravine"; Chekhov smooths the melodra-

matic wrinkles of the story by toning down the adulterous villainy of Natasha-Aksinya; he enriches the story by adding a military background and transforming the petit-bourgeois Tsybukins into the leisured, upper-class Prozorovs. But the basic outline is the same; and so is Chekhov's careful balancing of the internal and external influences on character, an element of all his mature work. In *Ivanov,* the decline of the hero was mostly determined from within, and Borkin's theory that "it's your environment that's killing you" was rejected as a thoughtless cliché. But in *The Three Sisters,* environment plays a crucial role in the gradual defeat of the central characters, while their own psychological failings are kept relatively muted.

The forces of evil, in fact, are quite inexorable in this work, making the Chekhovian pathos more dominant than usual. Chekhov, according to Stanislavsky, was amazed at the first reading of the play by the Art Theatre, because, in the producer's words, "he had written a happy comedy and all of us considered the play a tragedy and even wept over it." Stanislavsky is probably exaggerating Chekhov's response. Rather than considering it a "happy comedy," he was very careful to call *The Three Sisters* a "drama," the only such classification, as Magarshack notes, among his works. The play is certainly no tragedy, but it is the gloomiest Chekhov ever wrote. Certainly, the author introduces very little of his customary buffoonery. Though the play has its pantaloons, they are too implicated in the events of the house to evoke from us more than occasional smiles: Kulygin, for example, with his genial pedantry and maddening insensitivity to sorrow, is nevertheless a rather pathetic cuckold; and the alcoholic Chebutykin, for all his absurdity, eventually develops into a withdrawn and nihilistic figure. Furthermore, an atmosphere of doom seems to permeate the household, lifted only during brief festive moments; even these are quickly brought to an end by the ominous Natasha. Despite Magarshack's desire to read the play as "a *gay* affirmation of life," there is little that is gay or affirmative about it. Chekhov displays his usual impatience with the delusions of his central characters, but they are more clearly victims than most such figures. And while they undoubtedly are partially responsible for their fates (which explains why Chekhov did not want Stanislavsky's actors to grow maudlin over them), much of the responsibility belongs to Natasha, who represents the dark forces eating away at their lives.

For Natasha is the most malevolent figure Chekhov ever created—a pretentious bourgeois *arriviste* without a single redeeming trait. Everyone emphasizes her vulgarity, vengefulness, and lack of culture, and even Andrei, who leans over backward to be fair, sees in her "a small, blind, sort of thick-skinned animal. In any case, she's not a human being." Natasha is a malignant growth in a benevolent organism, and her final triumph, no matter how Chekhov tries to disguise it, is the triumph of pure evil. Despite the thick texture of the play, then, neatly woven into the tapestry is an almost invisible thread of action: the destruction of the Prozorovs by Natasha. From the moment she enters the house, at the end of Act I, to accept Andrei's proposal of marriage, until she has secured her control at the end of the play, the process of dispossession continues with relentless motion.

It takes place, however, by steady degrees. Andrei has mortgaged the house to the bank in order to pay his gambling debts, but Natasha, a much more dangerous adversary than a bank, takes over from there. Not only has she "grabbed all the money" (presumably the mortgage money), but she is engaged, throughout the play, in shifting the family from room to room, until she has finally shifted them out of the house entirely. Natasha's ambitions proceed under the guise of maternal solicitude and love of order; and never have such qualities seemed so thoroughly repellent. In the second act, she is planning to move Irina into Olga's room so that little Bobik will have a warmer nursery; in the third act, she offers to evict Anfisa, the old family servant, because she has outlived her usefulness (Natasha's unfeeling utilitarianism is among her most inhuman traits); and in the last act—with Olga and Anfisa installed in a government flat and Irina having moved to a furnished room—she is preparing to move Andrei out of his room to make way for baby Sophie. Since Sophie is probably the child of Protopopov, Natasha's lover, the dispossession has been symbolically completed. It will not be long before it is literally completed, and Andrei, the last of the Prozorovs, is ejected from the house altogether.

Chekhov illustrates this process through a careful manipulation of the setting. The first three acts take place in interiors that grow progressively more confined, the third act being laid in the room of Olga and Irina, cramped with people, screens, and furniture. But the last act is laid outdoors. The exterior setting tells the story visually: the family is now out of their own home; Andrei pushes the baby carriage around the house in widening circles; and Protopopov (never seen) is comfortably installed *inside,* in the drawing room with Natasha. Natasha, however, has not yet finished, for she is determined to violate the outdoors as well. Popping out of the house for a moment, she expresses her determination to cut down the fir and maple trees that Tuzenbach admires so much, an act of despoliation that foreshadows a similar act in *The Cherry Orchard.*

The contrast between Natasha and the Prozorovs is demonstrated by the difference in their manners—Natasha's vulgarity is amply documented by her French affectations and her abuse of the servants. An even better contrast is provided during the fire that is raging in town at the beginning of the third act. In this scene, Chekhov sets off Natasha's *arriviste* pretensions against the instinctual humanity of the Prozorovs by comparing their attitudes toward the victims of the conflagration. In accordance with Chekhov's description of the cultured in his letter to Nikolai ("They will overlook . . . the presence of strangers in their house"), the sisters generously offer their hospitality to those without homes, but Natasha is more occupied with fears that her children will catch some disease. When she considers the homeless, she thinks of them as objects to be patronized—"Indeed, we should always be ready to help the poor, that's the duty of the rich"—and talks about joining a committee for the assistance of the victims, that impersonal, dehumanized approach to charity invented by the middle class less out of generosity than out of status-seeking and guilt.

Since the fire is an external crisis introduced to heighten (and at the same time draw attention from) the crisis occurring within, it also illustrates Natasha's destructive tendencies. The fire is closely identified with that conflagration that is destroying the Prozorov household; the fate of the victims anticipates that of the family (they are out on the street); and Natasha symbolically links the two events. As Natasha marches through her room with a candle, Masha suggests this link by saying: "She goes about looking as if it were she who had started the fire." But at the same time that Natasha is a symbolic arsonist, she is also a symbolic fire extinguisher. Always on the lookout for fear something goes wrong, she stalks through the house, snuffing out candles—snuffing, too, all laughter and pleasure in the family. Pleading baby Bobik's health, she puts an end to the Carnival party; for like Serebryakov (who similarly throws cold water on the musical interlude planned by Elena and Sonya in *Uncle Vanya*), she functions to extinguish joy, and to spread gloom and despair.

The conflict between Natasha and the Prozorovs, needless to say, is always kept indistinct. Andrei and the sisters are either too polite or too deeply involved in their own problems to comment much on Natasha's activities, and while she and the family brush each other frequently throughout the play, they never break into open argument. Instead of dramatizing the Prozorovs' relations with Natasha, Chekhov defines them against the background of their surroundings, concentrating on the wasting away of this potentially superior family in a coarse and sordid environment. On the other hand, Natasha is really the personification of this environment—a native of the town who lives in the house—and so both she and the environment are actually related forces converging on the same objects. Thus, the surface and the depths of *The Three Sisters* follow parallel lines of development. The gradual dispossession of the Prozorovs by Natasha is the buried action, while their gradual deterioration in their surroundings proceeds above. In each case, the conflict between culture and vulgarity provides the basic theme.

This conflict is clear from the opening lines of the play, when the three sisters—a doleful portrait in blue, black, and white—first reveal their dissatisfaction with the present by reflecting, nostalgically, on the life of the past. A highly educated Moscow family, the Prozorovs were geographically transplanted eleven years before when their father, a brigadier general, took command of an artillery unit in the provinces. As the action proceeds, Chekhov shows how the family, following the father's death, has tried to adapt to their new surroundings: Olga by teaching school, Masha by marrying the local schoolmaster, Irina by working in a variety of civil jobs, Andrei by marrying Natasha and joining the District Board. All these attempts at assimilation are, however, unsuccessful. And regarding their present life as a kind of involuntary banishment, they are now uncomfortably suspended between their idealization of the past and resentment over their depressing provincial existence.

The past, of course, is closely identified with Moscow, seen through a haze of memory as a city of sun, flowers, refinement, and sensibility—in short, of *culture*—as opposed to the cold, stupidity, and dreariness of their town. Their vision of Moscow, like their hopes of returning, is, of course, delusionary—an idle dream with which we are meant to have little patience—and their endless complaining is neither courageous nor attractive. Still, their shared apprehension of the pettiness, drabness, and conformity of their provincial district is terrifyingly accurate. As Andrei describes it:

Our town has been in existence now for two hundred years, there are a hundred thousand people in it, and not one who isn't exactly like all the others, not one saint, either in the past or in the present, not one scholar, not one artist, no one in the least remarkable who could inspire envy or a passionate desire to imitate him. . . . and an overwhelmingly vulgar influence weighs on the children, the divine spark is extinguished in them, and they become the same pitiful, identical corpses as their fathers and mothers. . . .

In this speech—which may have been intended as an attack on the audience (Chekhov stipulated that Andrei, while speaking it, "must almost threaten the audience with his fists")—Andrei is clearly expressing Chekhov's revolt against the appalling conditions of the provincial town. It is a place in which any man of sensibility is bound to feel "a stranger, and lonely," for it is without culture, without art, without humanity, without excellence; its "overwhelmingly vulgar influence" has the power to brutalize all who live within its circumference. The influence of the town, in its most extreme state, is shown on Chebutykin, who takes refuge from his disillusionment in alcohol and newspapers and from his professional incompetence in a profound nihilism: "Maybe it only appears that we exist, but, in fact, we are not here." For just as the Prozorovs respond to their surroundings by weaving the illusion of Moscow, so Chebutykin responds by declaring that nothing in the world is real, and that "it doesn't matter."

The Prozorovs are aware that the town is brutalizing them, too, which accounts for their growing despair. Masha—dressed in black to illustrate her depression—is perpetually bored; Irina is perpetually tired; Olga suffers from perpetual headaches. As for Andrei, their gifted brother, he trails his life along with no apparent aim, followed by the senile Ferapont, as by an ignominious Nemesis. In this lifeless atmosphere, they are drying up, their culture falling from them like shreds of dead skin—each, in turn, will ask, "Where has it all gone?" For whatever might have made them seem unusual in Moscow is here merely a superfluous layer—useless, unnecessary, and gradually being forgotten. Andrei, carefully trained for a distinguished university career, holds a position in which his education is meaningless. Masha, once an accomplished pianist, now "has forgotten" how to play—just as Chebutykin has "forgotten" his medical training—just as the entire family is forgetting the accomplishments of their hopeful youth. Thus, the Prozorovs alternate between hysteria and despair, their hopes disintegrating in an environment where everything is reduced to zero:

> IRINA [*sobbing*]: Where? Where has it all gone? Where is it? Oh, my God, my God! I have forgotten everything, I've forgotten . . . it's all muddled in my head. . . . I can't remember how to say window or floor in Italian. I'm forgetting everything, every day I forget, and life is slipping by, never to return, never, we shall never go to Moscow. . . . I see that we shall never go. . . .

Life is slipping by, and time, like a cormorant, is devouring hopes, illusions, expectations, consuming their minds, souls, and bodies in its tedious-rapid progress toward death.

While their culture is being forgotten, however, the Prozorovs do try to preserve a pocket of civilization in this dreary wasteland; their house is open to limited forms of intellectual discussion and artistic activity. Generally, the discussions at the Prozorovs' reflect the banality of the surrounding area (Solyony's and Chebutykin's heated argument over *chekhartma* and *cheremsha* is typical), but occasionally, genuine ideas seem to come out of these soirées. Attending the discussions are the Prozorovs' cultural allies, the military officers stationed in town. Chekhov, according to Stanislavsky, looked on the military as "the bearers of a cultural mission, since, coming into the farthest corners of the provinces, they brought with them new demands on life, knowledge, art, happiness, and joy." Masha suggests Chekhov's attitudes when she observes the difference between the crude townspeople and the more refined soldiers: "among civilians generally, there are so many coarse, impolite, ill-bred people," but "in our town the most decent, the most honorable and well-bred people are all in the army." Her attraction to Colonel Vershinin is partially explained by his superior refinement, for he is associated in her mind with the old Muscovite charm and glamour. In part, he probably reminds her of her father (also identified with culture), for he lived on the same street, was an officer in her father's brigade, and has now taken command of her father's old battery. Attracted to educated men (she married Kulygin because she mistakenly thought him "the cleverest of men"), Masha unquestionably finds a suitable intellectual companion in Vershinin; even their courtship reveals their cultural affinities—he hums a tune to which she hums a reply. Magarshack calls this "the most original love declaration in the whole history of the stage"—actually, Congreve's Mirabel and Millamant employ much the same device, when he completes a Lovelace verse that she has begun—but in both cases, the couples signify their instinctual rapport and their superior sophistication to other suitors.

While Masha tries to find expression through an extramarital affair that is doomed to failure, Irina tries to discover a substitute commitment in her work. In this, her spiritual partner, though she doesn't love him, is Tuzenbach, because he too seeks salvation in work, finally, in a Tolstoyan gesture, resigning his commission for a job in a brickyard. Irina's faith in the dignity of labor, however, is gradually destroyed by depressing jobs in a telegraph office and on the Town Council—in this district, work can have no essential meaning or purpose. In the last act, Irina looks forward to "a new life" as a schoolteacher; but we have Olga's enervating academic career as evidence that this "new life" will be just as unfulfilling as the old. And when Tuzenbach is killed in a duel with Solyony (*his* despoiler), even the minor consolations of a loveless marriage are denied her.

Everything, in fact, fails the family in *The Three Sisters.* And as their culture fades and their lives grow grayer, the forces of darkness and illiteracy move in like carrion crows, ready to pick the last bones. There is some doubt, however, whether this condition is permanent. The question the play finally asks is whether the defeat of the Prozorovs has any ultimate meaning: will their suffering eventually influence their surroundings in any positive way? The question is never resolved in the play, but it is endlessly debated by Vershinin and Tuzenbach, whose opinions contrast as sharply as their characters.

Vershinin—an extremely unhappy soul—holds to optimistic theories, while Tuzenbach—inexplicably merry—is more profoundly pessimistic.* This conflict, though usually couched in general terms, is secretly connected with the fate of the Prozorovs. When Masha, for example, declares, "We know a great deal that is useless," Vershinin takes the opportunity to expound his views:

> It seems to me that there is not and cannot be a town so dull and depressing that a clever, educated person would be useless. Let us suppose that among the hundred thousand inhabitants of this town, which, of course, is backward and uncouth, there are only three people such as you. It goes without saying that you cannot vanquish the ignorant masses around you; in the course of your life, little by little, you will have to give way and be lost in that crowd of a hundred thousand; life will stifle you, but all the same you will not disappear, you will not be without influence. After you there may appear perhaps six like you, then twelve, and so on, until finally, your kind will become the majority. In two or three hundred years life on this earth will be unimaginably beautiful, wonderful.

Vershinin, in short—anticipating the eventual transformation of the surrounding area by people like the Prozorovs—believes in the progressive march of civilization toward perfection. And this perfection will be based on the future interrelationship of the benighted mass and the cultured elite ("If, don't you know, we could add culture to the love of work, and love of work to culture.")—a synthesis of beauty and utility.

Tuzenbach, on the other hand, is more skeptical. Seeing no special providence in the fall of a sparrow or

*Chekhov may be dramatizing a paradox here that he once expounded to Lydia Avilova in the course of explaining the alleged gloominess of his themes and characters: "It has always been pointed out to me that somber, melancholy people always write gaily, while the works of cheerful souls are always depressing." Chekhov, like Tuzenbach, is a cheerful soul with a gloomy point of view.

the flight of migratory cranes, he doubts the ability of anyone to influence anything:

> Not only in two or three hundred years, but in a million years, life will be just the same . . . it doesn't change, it remains constant, following its own laws, which do not concern us, or which, in any case, you will never get to know.

Vershinin's view awakens hope that there is some ultimate meaning to life. Tuzenbach's leads to stoicism and tragic resignation. It is the recurrent conflict between the progressive and the static interpretation of history, and its outcome remains insoluble.

In the last act, in fact, both views are recapitulated without being reconciled. The military is leaving the town—a sad departure, because it signifies not only the end of Masha's affair with Vershinin but also the disintegration of the last cultural rampart. Tuzenbach anticipates that "dreadful boredom" will descend upon the town, and Andrei notes (reminding us of Natasha's symbolic role) that "it's as though someone put a hood over it." The end of the Prozorov way of life has almost come. Masha has turned obsessive and hysterical; Olga is installed in a position she loathes; Andrei, likened to an expensive bell that has fallen and smashed, has become hag-ridden and mediocre. Only Irina preserves some hope, but even these hopes are soon to be dashed. The entire family is finally facing the truth: "Nothing turns out as we would have it"—the dream of Moscow will never be realized; the mass of darkness has overwhelmed them. In the requiem that concludes the play, the three sisters meditate on the future, just as, in the beginning of the play, they reflected on the past, while Andrei pushes the carriage, Kulygin bustles, and Chebutykin hums softly to himself.

Their affirmations, showing the strong influence of Vershinin's view of life, are inexplicably hopeful and expectant. Masha expresses her determination to endure; Irina has faith that a "time will come when everyone will know what all this is for"; and Olga affirms that "our sufferings will turn into joy for those who live after us, happiness and peace will come to this earth, and then they will remember kindly and bless those who are living now." The gay band music played by the military evokes in the three sisters the will to live. But the music slowly fades away. Will hope fade away as well? Olga's anxious questioning of life ("If we only knew—if we only knew!") is—as if to suggest this—antiphonally answered by Chebutykin's muttered denials ("It doesn't matter, it doesn't matter!"), the skepticism of Tuzenbach reduced to its most nihilistic form. And on this double note—the dialectic of hope and despair in a situation of defeat— Chekhov's darkest play draws to its close.

In *The Three Sisters,* Chekhov depicts the prostration of the cultured elite before the forces of darkness; in *The Cherry Orchard,* he examines the same problem from a comic-ironic point of view. Written while he was dying and with great difficulty, *The Cherry Orchard* is the most farcical of Chekhov's full-length works, and so it was intended. In 1901, when the play was just beginning to take shape in his mind, he wrote to Olga Knipper: "The next play I write for the Art Theatre will definitely be funny, very funny—at least in intention." The last phrase was probably a sally aimed at Stanislavsky (Chekhov deplored his tendency to turn "my characters into crybabies"), and though Stanislavsky did, in fact, eventually misinterpret *The Cherry Orchard* as a somber study of Russian life, Chekhov always insisted on calling it "not a drama but a comedy; in places almost a farce."

The importance of the comic element in the play suggests that Chekhov is emphasizing the other side of his revolt. Instead of merely evoking sympathy for the victims of the social conflict, he is now satirizing them as well; instead of blackening the character of the despoiler, he is drawing him with a great deal more depth and balance. The change is one of degree—Chekhov has not reversed his earlier position; he has merely modified it— and the dispossession of the victims still evokes strains of pathos that we should not ignore. But in *The Cherry*

Orchard Chekhov is more impatient with his cultured idlers; and their eventual fate seems more fitting and more just.

In all of his plays, on the other hand, Chekhov's revolt remains two-edged, for it is directed both against his leisured characters, too will-less to resist their own liquidation, and also against the dark environment that drags them under. Thus Chekhov's revolt may change in emphasis and attack, but it is always fixed on the fate of the cultured classes in the modern world. This is the great "problem" of his plays—and it is a problem that, in keeping with his artistic creed, he undertakes not to solve but simply to present correctly. Confronting the same world as the other modern dramatists—a world without God and, therefore, without meaning—Chekhov has no remedy for the disease of contemporary life. Ibsen speaks of the importance of one's calling, and Strindberg of resignation. But even Chekhov's panacea of work is ultimately ineffectual before the insupportable fact of death.

Still, despite the bleakness of his vision, Chekhov possesses a deeper humanity than any other modern dramatist. For while he never fails to examine the desperate absurdity of his characters, he never loses sight of the qualities that make them fully alive: "My holy of holies," he writes, "are the human body, health, intelligence, talent, inspiration, love, and the most absolute freedom—freedom from despotism and lies." Chekhov himself embodies these qualities so perfectly that no one has ever been able to write of him without the most profound affection and love; and he, the author, remains the most positive character in his fiction. Because of his hatred of untruth, Chekhov will not arouse false hopes about the future of mankind—but because he is humane to the marrow of his bones, he manages to increase our expectations of the human race. Coupling sweetness of temper with toughness of mind, Chekhov makes his work an extraordinary compound of morality and reality, rebellion and acceptance, irony and sympathy—evoking a singular affirmation even in the darkest despair. There are more powerful playwrights in the modern theater—

artists with greater range, wider variety, more intellectual power—but there are none more warm and generous, and none who bring the drama to a higher
realization of its human role.

—Robert Brustein

Ivanov

———— ∞ ————

A Drama in Four Acts

Characters in the Play

IVANOV, NIKOLAI ALEKSEYEVICH, permanent member of the local Council for Peasant Affairs

ANNA PETROVNA, born Sarah Abramson

SHABELSKY, MATVEI SEMYONOVICH, Count, Ivanov's maternal uncle

LEBEDEV, PAVEL KIRILYCH, president of the District Board

ZINAIDA SAVISHNA, his wife

SASHA, the Lebedevs' daughter, twenty years old

LVOV, YEVGENY KONSTANTINOVICH, a young doctor

BABAKINA, MARFA YEGOROVNA, the young widow of a landowner, daughter of a rich merchant

KOSYKH, DMITRI NIKITICH, an excise officer

BORKIN, MIKHAIL MIKHAILOVICH, a distant relative of Ivanov and steward of his estate

AVDOTYA NAZAROVNA, an old woman of no definite occupation

YEGORUSHKA, a dependent of the Lebedevs

FIRST GUEST

SECOND GUEST

THIRD GUEST

FOURTH GUEST

PYOTR, Ivanov's manservant

GAVRILA, Lebedev's manservant

GUESTS of both sexes

SERVANTS

The action takes place in a district of Central Russia.

Act I

[*The garden of* IVANOV's *estate. On the left is the front of the house with a veranda. One window is open. In front of the veranda there is a broad, semicircular area from which avenues extend center and right. There are garden seats and small tables on the right. A lighted lamp stands on one of the tables. Day is drawing to a close. As the curtain rises a piano and cello duet is heard in the house.* IVANOV *is sitting at a table reading a book.* BORKIN, *wearing big boots and carrying a gun, appears at the back of the garden; he is slightly drunk. Seeing* IVANOV, *he approaches him on tiptoe and, when he reaches him, aims the gun at his face.*]

IVANOV [*seeing* BORKIN, *starts and jumps up*]:   Misha, in the name of God . . . you frightened me. . . . I'm upset as it is, and now you, with your silly tricks . . . [*Sits down.*] You've frightened me and you're delighted. . . .

BORKIN [*guffaws*]:   There, there . . . I'm sorry. [*Sits down beside him.*] I won't do it again, really I won't. . . . [*Takes off his cap.*] Hot! You won't believe it, my dear boy, but I've covered seventeen versts in about three hours . . . I'm worn out. . . . Just feel how my heart's beating. . . .

IVANOV [*reading*]:   All right, later . . .

BORKIN: No, feel it now. [*Takes* IVANOV's *hand and places it on his chest.*] Hear that? Tum-tum-tum-tum-

3

tum. That means I've got heart disease. I might suddenly die at any minute. Look here, will you be sorry if I die?

IVANOV: I'm reading . . . later . . .

BORKIN: No, seriously, will you be sorry if I suddenly die? Nikolai Alekseyevich, will you be sorry if I die?

IVANOV: Stop pestering me!

BORKIN: Tell me, my friend: will you be sorry?

IVANOV: I'm sorry that you smell of vodka. It's disgusting, Misha.

BORKIN [*laughs*]: You really smell it? Amazing. . . . Actually, there's nothing at all amazing about it. In Plesniki I met the examining magistrate and, I must admit, we knocked off about eight glasses. As a matter of fact, drinking is very harmful. . . . Look here, it is harmful, isn't it? Eh? Isn't it?

IVANOV: This is positively unbearable. Understand, Misha, that this mockery——

BORKIN: There, there . . . I'm sorry, I'm sorry! . . . God bless you, you just sit right there now. . . . [*Gets up and walks off.*] Amazing people, you can't even talk to them. [*Comes back.*] Oh, yes! I almost forgot . . . let me have eighty-two rubles!

IVANOV: Why eighty-two rubles?

BORKIN: To pay the workmen tomorrow.

IVANOV: I haven't got it.

BORKIN: Thank you very much! [*Mimics him.*] I haven't got it. . . . But you do know that the workmen have to be paid? . . . Don't they?

IVANOV: I don't know. I have no money today. Wait till the first of the month when I get my salary.

BORKIN: What's the use of talking to such characters! The workmen are coming for their money, not on the first of the month, but tomorrow morning!

IVANOV: Well, what can I do about it now? Go on, kill me, nag me to death. . . . What is this detestable habit you have of badgering me just when I'm reading, writing, or——

BORKIN: I ask you: do the workmen have to be paid or don't they? Ach! What's the use of talking to you! [*Waves his hand.*] That's landlords for you—the hell with them! Landowners . . . scientific farming. . . . Two thousand acres of land—and not a cent in your pocket. . . . It's like having a wine cellar and no corkscrew. . . . See if I don't sell the troika tomorrow! Yes, sir! I sold the oats before they were harvested, and you just see if I don't sell the rye too. [*Striding up and down the stage*] You think I won't do it, don't you? No, sir! That's not the kind of man I am. . . .

[SHABELSKY's *voice through the window: "It's utterly impossible to play with you! . . . You've no more ear than a stuffed fish, and your touch is abominable."*]

ANNA PETROVNA [*appears in the open window*]:   Who was talking here just now? Was it you, Misha? Why are you striding about like that?

BORKIN: Trying to do anything with your *Nicolas, voilà*—is enough to make anyone stride about!

ANNA PETROVNA: Look here, Misha, have some hay brought for the croquet lawn.

BORKIN [*waves his hand*]:   Leave me alone, please . . .

ANNA PETROVNA: Well, now, what does that tone . . .
that tone of voice doesn't suit you at all. If you want
women to love you, don't be cross and don't get high-
and-mighty with them. . . . [*To her husband*] Nikolai,
let's turn somersaults in the hay!

IVANOV: Standing by an open window is bad for you,
Anyuta. Go away, please. . . . [*Shouts.*] Uncle, shut the
window! [*The window is shut.*]

BORKIN: Don't forget that in two days the interest
has to be paid to Lebedev.

IVANOV: I know. I'm going to be at Lebedev's today,
and I'll ask him to wait. . . . [*Looks at his watch.*]

BORKIN: When are you going?

IVANOV: Presently.

BORKIN [*eagerly*]:   Wait a minute, wait! I think today
is Shurochka's birthday. . . . Tch-tch-tch-tch . . . And I
forgot . . . What a memory, eh? [*Capering about.*] I'm
off, I'm off . . . [*Sings.*] I'm off . . . I'll have a swim, chew
some paper, take three drops of spirits of ammonia, and
I'll be a new man! Nikolai Alekseyevich, my dear, my
own, my angel soul, you're always nervous, peevish,
you're perpetually in the doldrums, but, damn it, you
know you and I could do great things together! I'd do
anything for you. . . . You want me to marry Marfusha
Babakina for you? Half the dowry will be yours. . . .
Never mind half, take it all—everything!

IVANOV: Stop talking nonsense.

BORKIN: No, seriously! Do you want me to marry
Marfusha? We'll divide the dowry. . . . But why do I
even talk to you about it? You really don't understand,
do you? [*Mimics him.*] "Stop talking nonsense." You're

a fine man, you're intelligent, but you lack nerve, you know what I mean, a certain drive. If you could just take a swing at something and knock the hell out of it. . . . You're a psychopath, a whiner; if you were a normal man, within a year you'd have a million. For instance, if I had twenty-three hundred rubles right now, in two weeks I'd have twenty thousand. You don't believe me? You think that's nonsense, too? No, it isn't nonsense. . . . Just give me twenty-three hundred rubles, and in one week I'll make twenty thousand for you. On the other side of the river, directly opposite us, Ovsyanov is selling a strip of land for twenty-three hundred rubles. If we buy that strip, both banks of the river are ours. And if both banks belong to us, then, don't you see, we have the right to build a dam. Isn't that so? We'll put up a mill, and as soon as we announce that we want to build a dam, everyone living down the river will kick up a row. And what do we do? *Kommen sie hierher*—if you don't want the dam, it'll cost you money! Understand? The Zarev factory will give us five thousand, Korolkov three thousand, the monastery will give five thousand . . .

IVANOV: That's simply fraud, Misha. . . . If you don't want me to quarrel with you, keep it to yourself.

BORKIN [*sits down at the table*]: Of course! . . . I knew it! You won't do anything yourself, and you tie my hands. . . .

[*Enter* SHABELSKY *and* LVOV.]

SHABELSKY [*coming out of the house with* LVOV]: Doctors are exactly like lawyers, with just this difference: lawyers merely strip you, while doctors strip you and kill you. . . . Present company excepted. [*Sits down on one of the seats.*] Charlatans, exploiters . . . . It may be that in some sort of Arcadia you might come across an exception to the general rule, but . . . in the course of my life I have spent twenty thousand on medical treatment, and I've never met a single doctor who didn't seem to me to be patently a swindler.

BORKIN [*to* IVANOV]: Yes, you do nothing yourself, and you tie my hands. That's why we have no money.

SHABELSKY: As I say, present company excepted. . . . It may be that there are exceptions, however . . . [*Yawns.*]

IVANOV [*closing his book*]: Well, Doctor, what have you to say?

LVOV [*glancing at the window*]: Exactly what I said this morning: she must go to the Crimea at once. [*Paces the stage.*]

SHABELSKY [*bursts out laughing*]: To the Crimea! Misha, why aren't you and I doctors? It's so simple. Some Madame Angot, or Ophelia, say, starts hawking and coughing out of boredom, and you simply take a piece of paper and write out a prescription according to the rules of science: first, a young doctor, then a trip to the Crimea, and, in the Crimea a Tartar——

IVANOV [*to the Count*]: Oh, don't keep going on and on about it! [*To* LVOV] In order to go to the Crimea one must have the means. And suppose I were to find the money—you know that she absolutely refuses to go.

LVOV: Yes, she refuses to go. [*Pause*]

BORKIN: Listen, Doctor, is Anna Petrovna so seriously ill that she has to go to the Crimea?

LVOV [*glancing at the window*]: Yes, she has consumption.

BORKIN: Pssss! That's bad. . . . For some time now, just from the look of her, I've thought she wouldn't last long.

LVOV: But . . . do speak more quietly . . . you can be heard in the house. . . . [*Pause*]

BORKIN [*sighing*]: This life of ours . . . human life is like a flower gloriously blooming in a meadow: along comes a goat, eats it up—no more flower.

SHABELSKY: It's all nonsense, nonsense, nonsense. . . . [*Yawns.*] Nonsense and flimflam. [*Pause*]

BORKIN: Well, my friends, I keep trying to teach Nikolai Alekseyevich here how to make some money. I gave him one marvelous idea, but, as usual, my powder fell on damp ground. You can't get it across. Just look at him, the picture of melancholy, bitterness, anguish, depression, gloom . . .

SHABELSKY [*gets up and stretches*]: You're such a mastermind, always concocting plans for everyone, teaching everyone how to live, but you've never yet taught me anything. . . . Come on, give me an idea, if you're so clever, show me a way out.

BORKIN [*gets up*]: I'm going to have a swim. . . . Good-bye gentlemen. [*To the Count*] There are about twenty different ways out for you. . . . If I were in your shoes, I'd have twenty thousand rubles within a week. [*Starts to go.*]

SHABELSKY [*following him*]: How would you do it? Come on, show me.

BORKIN: There's nothing to show. It's very simple. . . . [*Comes back.*] Nikolai Alekseyevich, give me a ruble!

[IVANOV *gives him the money without a word.*]

BORKIN: *Merci!* [*To the Count*] You're still holding plenty of trumps.

SHABELSKY [*following him*]: Well, what are they?

BORKIN: If I were in your shoes, I'd have thirty thousand within a week, if not more. [*Goes out with the Count.*]

IVANOV [*after a pause*]: Superfluous people, superfluous words, having to answer stupid questions—all this has exhausted me, Doctor, to the point of illness. I've grown so irritable, so short-tempered, harsh, and petty, that I no longer recognize myself. My head aches for days on end, I can't sleep, there's a buzzing in my ears . . . and I positively don't know where to turn . . . I positively do not . . .

LVOV: Nikolai Alekseyevich, I must have a serious talk with you.

IVANOV: Very well.

LVOV: It's about Anna Petrovna. [*Sits down.*] She refuses to go to the Crimea, but she would go with you.

IVANOV [*after a moment's thought*]: It would take a good deal of money for both of us to go. Besides, they wouldn't give me a long enough leave. I've already had one leave this year.

LVOV: Let us assume that this is true. To go on: the most important medicine for the cure of consumption is absolute peace—and your wife never has a moment's peace. She is continually upset by your treatment of her. Forgive me, but I am worried, and I am going to speak frankly. Your conduct is killing her. [*Pause*] Nikolai Alekseyevich, I should like to think better of you!

IVANOV: All that is true, true. . . . I suppose I am dreadfully guilty, but my thoughts are muddled, my soul is in the grip of a kind of apathy, and I am no longer able to understand myself. I don't understand myself or other people. . . . [*Glances at the window.*] Someone may hear us, let us take a walk. [*They get up.*] My dear friend, I should like to tell you everything from the very beginning, but it's a long story, and such a complicated one that if I talked till morning I couldn't finish it. [*They begin to walk.*] Anyuta is a remarkable, an extraordinary woman. . . . She changed her religion for my sake, left her father and mother, gave up wealth, and if I had asked her for a hundred more sacrifices, she would have made them without batting an eye. But, you see, I am in no way remarkable, and I have sacrificed nothing. However, that's a long story. . . . The whole point, my dear Doctor, [*hesitantly*] is that . . . to put it briefly, I was passionately in love with her when I married, and swore that I would love her forever, but . . . five years have passed, she still loves me, but I . . . [*Throws up his hands.*] Here you tell me that she is going to die soon, and I feel neither love nor pity, but only a sort of emptiness and lassitude. To anyone looking at me this must seem appalling; I myself don't understand what is happening within my soul. . . . [*They walk down the avenue.*]

[*Enter* SHABELSKY.]

SHABELSKY [*laughs uproariously as he comes in*]: On my word, he's not a fraud but a thinker, a virtuoso! They ought to put up a monument to him. He's the living combination of every form of corruption in our time: lawyer, doctor, cashkeeper, and pussyfooting poltroon. [*Sits down on the bottom step of the veranda.*] And it seems he never graduated from any school, that's the amazing thing . . . all of which goes to show what a genius of a rogue he would have been had he acquired a little culture, a liberal education! "You could have twenty thousand within a week," he says. "You're holding the ace of trumps in your hand," he says, "your title of count." [*Roars with laughter.*] "Any girl with a dowry will marry you."

[ANNA PETROVNA *opens the window and looks down.*]

SHABELSKY: "You want me to make a match with Marfusha for you?" he says. *Qui est ce que c'est Mar-*

fusha? Oh, it's that Balabalkina . . . Babakalkina . . . the one that looks like a washerwoman.

ANNA PETROVNA: Is that you, Count?

SHABELSKY: What's that?

[ANNA PETROVNA *laughs.*]

SHABELSKY [*with a Jewish accent*]: What you laughing?

ANNA PETROVNA: I was thinking of something you said . . . something you said at dinner, do you remember? A repentant thief, a horse . . . how did it go?

SHABELSKY: A baptized Jew, a repentant thief, an ailing horse—one's worth as much as another.

ANNA PETROVNA [*laughs*]: You can't even make a simple joke without malice. You're a malicious person. [*Seriously*] Joking aside, Count, you are exceedingly malicious. It's tiresome living with you, and painful. You are always querulous, always grumbling, and, according to you, everyone is a good-for-nothing and a scoundrel. Tell me frankly, Count, have you ever had a kind word for anyone?

SHABELSKY: What is this, a cross-examination?

ANNA PETROVNA: I have lived under the same roof with you for five years, and I've never once heard you speak of anyone calmly, without bitterness or mockery. What harm have people done you? Do you really think you're better than everyone else?

SHABELSKY: I don't think so at all. I am just as much of a good-for-nothing, just as much of a swine in a skullcap as anyone. *Mauvais ton,* an old shoe. I'm always running myself down. Who am I? I used to be rich, free, and rather happy, but now . . . I'm a parasite, a hanger-on, an irresponsible buffoon. I show my indignation and contempt for people, and in reply they laugh at me; I laugh, and they sadly shake their heads and say: "The old man's balmy." But more often than not they don't hear me, they don't pay any attention. . . .

ANNA PETROVNA [*quietly*]:   It's screeching again.

SHABELSKY: Who's screeching?

ANNA PETROVNA: The owl. Every evening it screeches.

SHABELSKY: Let it screech. Things can't get any worse than they are. [*Stretching*] Ah, my dear Sarah, if I had won a hundred, or two hundred thousand, I'd have made you sit up and take notice! You wouldn't have seen me again. I'd have left this hole, with its bread of charity, and I wouldn't have set foot here again till Judgment Day.

ANNA PETROVNA: And what would you have done if you had won the money?

SHABELSKY [*after a moment's thought*]:   First of all, I'd have gone to Moscow to hear the Gypsies. Then . . . then I'd have dashed off to Paris. I would have taken an apartment . . . I would have gone to the Russian church. . . .

ANNA PETROVNA: And what else?

SHABELSKY: I'd have sat for whole days at my wife's grave, thinking. I'd have sat by her grave till I dropped dead. My wife was buried in Paris. . . . [*Pause*]

ANNA PETROVNA: This is terribly dull. Shall we play another duet?

SHABELSKY: Very well. Get the music ready.

[ANNA PETROVNA *goes away from the window. Enter*
IVANOV *and* LVOV.]

IVANOV [*appearing in the avenue with* LVOV]:   You
graduated only last year, my friend, you are still young
and vigorous, but I am thirty-five. I have a right to advise
you. Don't marry a Jewess, a neurotic, or a bluestocking,
but choose someone ordinary, colorless, without brilliance, someone who doesn't say an unnecessary word.
In fact, organize your life according to a pattern. The
more colorless and monotonous the background, the better. Don't fight the multitude singlehanded, my boy,
don't tilt at windmills, don't knock your head against a
wall. . . . And God save you from all this scientific farming, these strange schools and passionate speeches. . . .
Crawl into your shell and take care of the little job God
gave you to do. . . . It's more comfortable, honest, and
healthy. As for the life I've lived—how exhausting it has
been! Ah, how exhausting! So many mistakes, injustices,
absurdities! [*Sees the Count, with irritation.*] You're always hanging around, Uncle, you never give me a chance
to talk to anyone alone!

SHABELSKY [*plaintively*]:   Damn it all, there's no place
for me anywhere! [*Jumps up and goes into the house.*]

IVANOV [*shouts after him*]:   Oh, I'm sorry, I'm sorry!
[*To* LVOV] Now, why did I hurt his feelings? I'm absolutely unstrung. I must do something about myself. I
must——

LVOV [*agitated*]:   Nikolai Alekseyevich, I have heard
you out and . . . and, forgive me, I am going to speak
bluntly, without beating about the bush. In your voice,
your intonation, to say nothing of your words, there is
so much callous egotism, such cold, heartless . . . Someone close to you is dying, just because she is close to
you, her days are numbered, and you . . . you can feel
no love for her, you walk about giving advice, showing

off. . . . I can't express myself, I haven't the gift of words, but . . . but I dislike you profoundly!

IVANOV: It may be, it may be that . . . as an outsider you can see more clearly. . . . It's quite possible that you do understand me. . . . I am probably very, very guilty. . . . [*Listens.*] I think the horses are harnessed. I'll go and change. . . . [*Walks toward the house, then stops.*] You don't like me, Doctor, and you don't conceal it. That does you credit. [*Goes into the house.*]

LVOV [*alone*]: I could curse myself! . . . Again I missed the opportunity of talking to him as I ought to. . . . I cannot talk to him calmly! I have only to open my mouth and say one word, and something here [*points to his breast*] begins to suffocate me, to turn over inside me, and my tongue sticks to the roof of my mouth. I despise that Tartuffe, that pompous cheat, with all my heart. . . . There he is, going out . . . and his unfortunate wife's entire happiness is in having him near her; he's the breath of life to her, she begs him to spend just one evening with her, and he . . . he cannot. . . . He, if you please, feels cramped and stifled at home. One evening at home and he'd put a bullet through his head out of boredom. Poor fellow, he needs scope for devising some new abomination. . . . Oh, I know why you go to visit those Lebedevs every evening! I know!

[*Enter* IVANOV, *wearing a hat and coat,* SHABELSKY, *and* ANNA PETROVNA.]

SHABELSKY [*coming out of the house with* IVANOV *and* ANNA PETROVNA]: Really, *Nicolas,* it's inhuman! You go out every night, and we're left here alone. We go to bed at eight o'clock from sheer boredom. It's outrageous, it's not living! And why is it you can go out and we can't? Why?

ANNA PETROVNA: Leave him alone, Count! Let him go, let him——

IVANOV [*to his wife*]: But where could you go, ill as you are? You're sick, and you're not supposed to be out in the air after sunset. . . . Ask the doctor here. You're not a child, Anyuta, you must be reasonable. . . . [*To the Count*] And why should you want to go there?

SHABELSKY: I'd go to the devil in hell, or into the teeth of a crocodile, if I could get away from here. I am bored! I am stupefied with boredom! And everyone is fed up with me. You leave me at home so she won't be lonely, but I worry her to pieces, I drive her crazy!

ANNA PETROVNA: Leave him alone, Count, leave him alone! Let him go if he finds it amusing there.

IVANOV: Anya, why do you take that tone? You know I'm not going there for amusement! I have to talk to them about the promissory note.

ANNA PETROVNA: Why are you justifying yourself? I don't understand! Go along! Who's stopping you?

IVANOV: Oh Lord! Let's not torment each other! Is this really necessary?

SHABELSKY [*plaintively*]: *Nicolas*, my dear boy, do please take me with you! I'll have a look at all those frauds and fools, and it may divert me. You know, I haven't been anywhere since Easter!

IVANOV [*irritably*]: All right, come along! How tired I am of all of you!

SHABELSKY: Yes? *Merci, merci!* [*Gaily takes his arm and leads him aside.*] May I wear your straw hat?

IVANOV: Yes, but hurry, please!

[*The Count runs into the house.*]

IVANOV: How tired I am of all of you! Oh, Lord, what am I saying? Anya, I'm speaking to you in an impossible way. This never used to happen to me. Well, good-bye, Anya, I'll be back by one.

ANNA PETROVNA: Kolya, dear, do stay at home!

IVANOV [*agitated*]: My darling, my poor, unhappy wife, I implore you, do not prevent me from going out in the evening. It is cruel, unfair of me, but permit me this unfairness! I find it unbearably oppressive at home! As soon as the sun goes down I begin to feel depressed. So depressed! Don't ask me why. I myself don't know. I swear to you, I do not know. I'm depressed here, and when I go to the Lebedevs' it's even worse; I come back home, and I'm still depressed, and it's like that all night. . . . I am simply desperate!

ANNA PETROVNA: Kolya . . . if only you would stay at home! Let's sit and talk as we used to. . . . We'll have supper together, and read. . . . We've practiced lots of duets, the old grumbler and I. . . . [*Puts her arms around him.*] Stay! [*Pause*] I don't understand you. This has been going on for a whole year. Why have you changed?

IVANOV: I don't know, I don't know. . . .

ANNA PETROVNA: And why don't you want me to go out with you in the evening?

IVANOV: If you must know, I'll tell you. It's rather cruel, but better to say it. . . . When I am tormented by this depression, I . . . I begin . . . not to love you. And I run away from you at such a time. In short, I have to get out of the house.

ANNA PETROVNA: Depression? I understand, I understand. . . . Do you know what, Kolya? Try to sing, as you used to, to laugh, to get angry. . . . Stay at home, and let's laugh, and have a drink together, and we'll banish your depression in an instant. Do you want me to sing for you? Or shall we sit in the dark in your study, as we used to, and you can talk to me about your

depression. . . . Your eyes are full of suffering! I'll look
into them and weep, and we shall both feel better. . . .
[*Laughs and weeps.*] Or can't we, Kolya? The flowers
return in the spring, but not the joy—is that it? Yes?
Well then, go, go. . . .

IVANOV: Pray for me, Anya! [*Starts to go, stops and
thinks.*] No, I can't! [*Goes out.*]

ANNA PETROVNA: Go. . . . [*Sits down at the table.*]

LVOV [*pacing the stage*]:   Anna Petrovna, you must
make it a rule: as soon as the clock strikes six, go indoors
and stay there till morning. The evening dampness is
bad for you.

ANNA PETROVNA: Yes, sir.

LVOV: Why that "Yes, sir"? I am speaking seriously.

ANNA PETROVNA: But I don't want to be serious.
[*Coughs.*]

LVOV: You see—you're coughing already.

[SHABELSKY, *wearing a hat and coat, comes out of the
house.*]

SHABELSKY: Where's Nikolai? Are the horses ready?
[*Quickly goes up to* ANNA PETROVNA *and kisses her
hand.*] Good night, my charmer! [*Makes a grimace.*] *Gev-
alt!* 'Shcuse plees! [*Goes out quickly.*]

LVOV: Clown!

[*Pause; an accordion is heard in the distance.*]

ANNA PETROVNA: What boredom! The cook and the
coachman are giving a dance, while I . . . I am
deserted. . . . Yevgeny Konstantinovich, why are you
pacing up and down? Come here and sit down!

LVOV: I can't sit still. [*Pause*]

ANNA PETROVNA: They're playing "Greenfinch" in the kitchen. [*Sings.*] "Greenfinch, greenfinch, where have you been? Drinking vodka down on the green." [*Pause*] Doctor, have you got a father and mother?

LVOV: My father's dead, but my mother is still living.

ANNA PETROVNA: Do you miss your mother?

LVOV: I haven't time to miss anyone.

ANNA PETROVNA: The flowers return in the spring, but not the joy. Who said that to me? Why can't I remember? . . . I think it was Nikolai himself who said it. [*Listens.*] The owl is screeching again!

LVOV: Well, let it screech.

ANNA PETROVNA: I am beginning to think that fate has cheated me, Doctor. There are a great many people, perhaps no better than I, who are happy without having had to pay for their happiness. But I have paid for everything, absolutely everything! . . . And so dearly! Why should I have had to pay such terribly high interest? . . . My dear friend, you are always so considerate of me, so tactful, you are afraid to tell me the truth, but do you think I don't know what my illness is? I know perfectly well. However, it's boring to talk about it. . . . [*With a Jewish accent*] 'Shcuse plees! Can you tell funny stories?

LVOV: No, I can't.

ANNA PETROVNA: Nikolai can. . . . I am beginning to be amazed at the unfairness of people; why do they not respond to love with love, and why should truth be answered with lies? Tell me: how long will my father and mother go on hating me? They live about fifty versts from here, but I can feel their hatred day and night, even in my sleep. And what am I to make of Nikolai's depression? He says it's only in the evening that he doesn't love me, when he feels depressed. I understand that, I think it's probably true, but suppose he has stopped loving me altogether! Of course, that's impossible, but—what if he has! No, no, I mustn't even think of it. [*Sings.*] "Greenfinch, greenfinch, where have you been?" . . . [*Shudders.*] What frightening thoughts I have! . . . You have no family of your own, Doctor, and there are a great many things you can't understand. . . .

LVOV: You are amazed. . . . [*Sits down beside her.*] No, it's I who am amazed, amazed at you! Now, explain it to me, help me to understand: how is it that you, an intelligent, honest, almost saintly woman, have allowed yourself to be so brazenly deceived and dragged into this owl's nest? Why are you here? What have you got in common with that cold, heartless—but let's leave your husband out of it—what have you in common with this futile, vulgar environment? Oh, my God! . . . That perpetually grumbling, moth-eaten, lunatic count, that thorough fraud and swindler, Misha, with his hideous face? Explain it to me, what are you doing here? How did you ever come to be here?

ANNA PETROVNA [*laughs*]: You're talking exactly the way he used to talk . . . exactly. . . . Only his eyes are larger, and when he spoke with passion about anything, they glowed like coals. . . . Go on, go on talking!

LVOV [*gets up with a gesture of impatience*]: What's the use? Please go in. . . .

ANNA PETROVNA: You say that Nikolai is this or that, one thing and another. How can you know him? Is it possible to know a man in six months? That is a remarkable man, Doctor, and I am sorry you didn't know him two or three years ago. Now he's depressed, he doesn't talk, he doesn't do anything, but then . . . how fascinating he was! I fell in love with him at first sight. [*Laughs.*] I just looked at him and the trap was sprung! He said: come . . . and I cut myself off from everything; it was just like cutting off dead leaves with a scissors, and I went. . . . [*Pause*] But now it's different. . . . Now he goes to the Lebedevs' to amuse himself with other women, and I . . . I sit in the garden and listen to the owl screech. . . . [*The watchman is heard knocking.*] Doctor, have you any brothers?

LVOV: No.

[ANNA PETROVNA *sobs.*]

LVOV: What is it? What's the matter?

ANNA PETROVNA [*gets up*]:   I can't help it, Doctor, I'm going to go there. . . .

LVOV: Where?

ANNA PETROVNA: There, where he is. . . . I'm going. . . . Please order the horses! [*Runs into the house.*]

LVOV: No, I absolutely refuse to treat people in such circumstances! It's bad enough that they don't pay me anything, but they turn me inside out, besides! . . . No, I refuse! Enough! [*Goes into the house.*]

Act II

[*The reception room in the Lebedevs' house; doors left and right, and one upstage center leading into the garden. Expensive antique furniture. Chandeliers, candelabra, and pictures, all under dust covers.* ZINAIDA SAVISHNA, KO-SYKH, AVDOTYA NAZAROVNA, YEGORUSHKA, GAVRILA, BA-BAKINA, *a maid, and guests—elderly ladies and young girls.* ZINAIDA SAVISHNA *is seated on the sofa; on either*]

*side of her sit elderly ladies in armchairs; the young peo-
ple are sitting on straight chairs. In the background, near
the door leading into the garden, people are playing cards,
among them* KOSYKH, AVDOTYA NAZAROVNA, *and* YEGOR-
USHKA. GAVRILA *stands at the door on the right; the maid
passes a tray of sweets. Throughout the act the guests pass
in and out of the garden and the door on the right.* BA-
BAKINA *enters from door on the right and goes up to*
ZINAIDA SAVISHNA.]

ZINAIDA SAVISHNA [*joyfully*]: Darling Marfa Yegorovna. . . .

BABAKINA: How are you, Zinaida Savishna? Congratulations on your daughter's birthday! [*They kiss.*]
God grant that——

ZINAIDA SAVISHNA: Thank you, darling, I'm so
happy. . . . And how are you?

BABAKINA: Thank you very much. [*Sits down on the
sofa beside her.*] Good evening, you young people!

[*Guests stand up and bow.*]

FIRST GUEST [*laughs*]: Young people . . . as if you
were old.

BABAKINA [*sighing*]: I don't pretend to be young
any more. . . .

FIRST GUEST [*with a deferential laugh*]: Good gracious, what do you mean? You may be a widow, but
you can outshine any young girl. . . .

[GAVRILA *serves tea to* BABAKINA.]

ZINAIDA SAVISHNA [*to* GAVRILA]: Now, why are you
serving it like that? Bring some kind of jam . . . gooseberry, perhaps. . . .

BABAKINA: Don't trouble yourself, thank you very much.

[*Pause*]

FIRST GUEST: Did you come through Mushkino, Marfa Yegorovna?

BABAKINA: No, by way of Zaimishch. The road is better that way.

FIRST GUEST: So it is.

KOSYKH: Two spades.

YEGORUSHKA: Pass.

AVDOTYA NAZAROVNA: Pass.

SECOND GUEST: Pass.

BABAKINA: Lottery tickets, my dearest Zinaida Savishna, have gone way up. Have you ever heard of such a thing: tickets for the first draw are now two hundred and seventy, and for the second they're nearly two hundred and fifty! . . . That never happened before.

ZINAIDA SAVISHNA [*sighs*]: It's all very well for the people with lots of tickets. . . .

BABAKINA: Don't say that, darling; even though the price is high, it is not a profitable way to invest one's capital. The insurance alone would be the death of you.

ZINAIDA SAVISHNA: That's all very well, my dear, but all the same, one keeps hoping. . . . [*Sighs.*] God is merciful . . .

THIRD GUEST: From my point of view, *mesdames,* I contend that at the present time it is vastly unprofitable even to have capital. Interest-bearing securities yield exceedingly small returns, and to invest money is extraordinarily dangerous. As I understand it, *mesdames,* the person with capital finds himself, at the present time, in a more critical condition, *mesdames,* than the person . . .

BABAKINA [*sighs*]:   That is true!

[FIRST GUEST *yawns.*]

BABAKINA: Do you think it's nice to yawn in the presence of ladies?

FIRST GUEST: *Pardon, mesdames,* it was unintentional.

[ZINAIDA SAVISHNA *gets up and goes out through door on the right; there is a prolonged silence.*]

YEGORUSHKA: Two diamonds.

AVDOTYA NAZAROVNA: Pass.

SECOND GUEST: Pass.

KOSYKH: Pass.

BABAKINA [*aside*]:   Lord, what boredom! You could die of it!

[ZINAIDA SAVISHNA *and* LEBEDEV *enter from door on the right.*]

ZINAIDA SAVISHNA [*in a low voice*]:   Why were you sitting out there alone? What a *prima donna!* Sit down here with your guests! [*Sits in her former place on the sofa.*]

LEBEDEV [*yawns*]:   Oh, how we are punished for our sins! [*Seeing* BABAKINA] Goodness gracious, here's our little sugar plum! Our Turkish delight! [*Greets her.*] How is your precious health?

BABAKINA: Thank you very much.

LEBEDEV: Ah, God be praised! . . . God be praised!
[*Sits down in an armchair.*] Well . . . well . . . Gavrila!

[GAVRILA *serves him a small glass of vodka and a glass
of water; he tosses off the vodka and follows it with the
water.*]

FIRST GUEST: To your good health!

LEBEDEV: Good health, indeed! I'm just thankful I'm
still alive! [*To his wife*] Zyuzyushka, where's our birthday baby?

KOSYKH [*plaintively*]: Tell me: now why didn't we
take a single trick? [*Jumps up.*] Eh, why the devil did
we have to lose?

AVDOTYA NAZAROVNA [*jumps up angrily*]: I'll tell
you why, my dear sir: if you don't know the game, then
don't play. What right have you to lead somebody else's
suit? You see, you got stuck with your marinated ace!

[*Both rush forward from behind the table.*]

KOSYKH [*tearfully*]: Please, listen, my friends. . . . I
held the ace, king, queen, and a sequence of eight diamonds, the ace of spades, and only one, you understand,
one little heart, and she, God knows why, couldn't make
a small slam! I bid no trump . . .

AVDOTYA NAZAROVNA [*interrupting*]: I was the one
who bid no trump! You bid two no trump . . .

KOSYKH: This is outrageous! . . . Just let me . . . You
had . . . I had . . . You had. . . . [*To* LEBEDEV] Now,
look here, Pavel Kirilych . . . in diamonds I held the ace,
king, queen, and a sequence of eight——

LEBEDEV [*stops his ears*]:   Leave me out of it, please, leave me out of it. . . .

AVDOTYA NAZAROVNA [*shouts*]:   It was I who bid no trump!

KOSYKH [*fiercely*]:   I'll be cursed and confounded before I ever sit down to play with that old mackerel again. [*Quickly goes out into the garden.*]

[SECOND GUEST *follows him, and only* YEGORUSHKA *is left at the table.*]

AVDOTYA NAZAROVNA: Ugh! . . . he makes my blood boil. . . . Mackerel! . . . Old mackerel yourself!

BABAKINA: Well, you're not exactly sweet-tempered, Grandma.

AVDOTYA NAZAROVNA [*suddenly seeing* BABAKINA, *throws up her hands*]:   My little pet! Here she sits, and I, blind old hen that I am, don't even see her. . . . My little dove. . . . [*Kisses her on the shoulder and sits down beside her.*] What a joy! Let me look at you, my white swan! Tfoo, tfoo, tfoo! May you be safe from the evil eye!

LEBEDEV: She's off again! You'd do better to find her a husband.

AVDOTYA NAZAROVNA: Just see if I don't! Before this old sinner lies in her grave, I'll have her married, and Sanichka, too! . . . Yes, before I'm in my grave. . . . Only where do you find them nowadays, these bridegrooms? Look at them, our marriageable young men, sitting there like wet roosters!

THIRD GUEST: A most unfortunate comparison. From my point of view, *mesdames,* if the young men of today prefer a bachelor existence, it is social conditions, so to say, that are to blame. . . .

LEBEDEV: Now, now, don't start philosophizing. . . . I don't like it. . . .

[*Enter* SASHA.]

SASHA [*going up to her father*]: It's such marvelous weather, and you all sit here in this stuffy room!

ZINAIDA SAVISHNA: Sashenka, don't you see that Marfa Yegorovna is here?

SASHA: I'm sorry. [*Goes up to* BABAKINA *and greets her.*]

BABAKINA: You're getting above yourself, Sashenka, you really are; you haven't once been to see me lately. [*They kiss each other.*] Congratulations, darling!

SASHA: Thank you. [*Sits down beside her father.*]

LEBEDEV: Yes, Avdotya Nazarovna, finding a bridegroom these days is a difficult business. And not only a bridegroom—you can't even get a decent best man to go with him. The youth of today—no offense intended—have somehow gone sour, God help them, they're soft. They don't know how to converse, or dance, or drink properly. . . .

AVDOTYA NAZAROVNA: Come now, they're experts at drinking, just give them——

LEBEDEV: Drinking's no great trick—even a horse can drink. . . . No, it's knowing how to do it properly! In our day, it used to be that you'd grind away in your classes all day long, but as soon as evening came, you'd head for the bright lights and spin like a top till sunrise. . . . You'd dance, amuse yourself with the young ladies, [*with his eye on the vodka, gives himself a flick on the neck*] and all that sort of thing. We used to tell stories and philosophize till our tongues were paralyzed. But today they . . . [*waves his hand*] I don't understand. . . .

They neither love God nor serve the devil. In the whole
district there's only one man that's any good, and he's
married. . . . [*Sighs.*] And it looks as if he's beginning
to lose his mind. . . .

BABAKINA: Who is that?

LEBEDEV: Nikolashka Ivanov.

BABAKINA: Yes, he's a nice man, [*makes a grimace*]
only he's so unhappy!

ZINAIDA SAVISHNA: Well, of course, darling, but how
could he be happy? [*Sighs.*] The poor man, what a mistake he made! He married his Jewess, and then, poor
fellow, after he had counted on her parents giving a
mountain of gold with her, it all turned out quite the
reverse. From the day she changed her religion, her father and mother ceased to recognize her, and put their
curse on her. . . . And he didn't get so much as a kopeck.
Now he's sorry, but, of course, it's too late.

SASHA: Mama, that's not true!

BABAKINA [*vehemently*]:   Shurochka, what do you
mean, not true? Why, everybody knows it! If it were not
for reasons of interest, why should he have married a
Jewess? Aren't there enough Russian girls? He made a
mistake, darling, a mistake! [*Eagerly*] And, Lord, doesn't
he make her smart for it now! It's really funny! Sometimes he comes home after being out somewhere, and
he goes straight to her and says: "Your father and
mother cheated me! Get out of my house!" But where
can she go? Her parents won't take her back; she could
go out as a chambermaid, but she's not accustomed to
working. . . . So he mocks her and torments her till the
Count has to stand up for her. If it weren't for the
Count, he'd have been the death of her long ago. . . .

AVDOTYA NAZAROVNA: And sometimes he locks her up in the cellar—"Eat garlic, you so-and-so!"—and she eats and eats till she starts to get sick.

[*Laughter*]

SASHA: Papa, that's a lie!

LEBEDEV: Well, what does it matter? Let them babble on to their heart's content. . . . [*Shouts.*] Gavrila!

[GAVRILA *serves him vodka and water.*]

ZINAIDA SAVISHNA: So that's how he ruined himself, poor man. His affairs, my dear, are simply going to pieces. . . . If Borkin were not looking after the estate, he and his Jewess would have nothing to eat. [*Sighs.*] And as for us, darling, how we have suffered because of him! . . . Only God knows how we have suffered! Would you believe it, my dear, for three years now he has owed us nine thousand rubles!

BABAKINA [*horrified*]: Nine thousand rubles!

ZINAIDA SAVISHNA: Yes . . . it was my dear Pashenka who made that arrangement. He never knows who you can lend money to and who you can't. I'm not speaking of the capital, you understand—never mind about that—but at least he could pay the interest on time!

SASHA [*hotly*]: Mama, you've gone over this a thousand times already!

ZINAIDA SAVISHNA: What's it got to do with you? Why do you have to stick up for him?

SASHA [*rising*]: How can you be so heartless as to talk that way about a man who has never done you any harm? What did he ever do to you?

THIRD GUEST: Aleksandra Pavlovna, permit me to
say two words! I respect Nikolai Alekseyevich, I have
always considered it an honor to know him, but, speaking *entre nous,* he appears to me to be an adventurer.

SASHA: If that's how you feel, I congratulate you!

THIRD GUEST: As proof of what I say, I present you
with the following fact, which was passed on to me by
his *attaché,* his, so to say, cicerone, Borkin. Two years
ago, at the time of the cattle epidemic, he bought cattle,
insured them——

ZINAIDA SAVISHNA: Yes, yes, yes! I remember that
incident. I was told about it, too.

THIRD GUEST: He insured them, bear that in mind,
then he infected them with the plague and collected
the insurance.

SASHA: Oh, that's all nonsense! Nonsense! No one
bought cattle, and no one infected them! Borkin
trumped up that scheme and then boasted about it
everywhere. When Ivanov learned of it, Borkin had to
beg his forgiveness for two weeks afterward. Ivanov is
guilty of nothing except a weak character, he lacks the
courage to turn that Borkin out. And he's also guilty of
trusting people too much! Everything he had has been
pilfered and plundered: anyone who wanted to could
take advantage of his generosity.

LEBEDEV: Shura, little hothead, that's enough!

SASHA: But why do they talk such nonsense? Oh, it's
all so boring, so boring! Ivanov, Ivanov, Ivanov—there's
no other topic of conversation. [*Goes to the door and
then comes back.*] I am amazed! [*To the young men*] I
am positively amazed at your patience, my friends! Is it
possible that you aren't bored sitting here like this?
Why, even the air is congealed with boredom! Well, say
something, amuse the young ladies, bestir yourselves.

Have you nothing else to talk about besides Ivanov?
Can't you even laugh, sing, dance, or something?

LEBEDEV [*laughs*]: Give it to them, give it to them
good!

SASHA: Listen, then, do me this favor. If you don't
want to dance, or laugh, or sing, if all that bores you,
then I beg you, I implore you, for once in your lives,
just for the fun of it, to amaze or amuse us, summon up
your strength and try, all of you together, to think of
something witty, brilliant, even if it's impertinent or vulgar, so long as it is novel and amusing. Or do something
quite small and barely noticeable, but something just
slightly resembling a heroic feat, so that the young ladies, for once in their lives, can look at you and say:
"Oh!" . . . Listen, you do want to be liked, don't you,
then why don't you try to make us like you? Oh, gentlemen! There is something wrong, wrong, wrong, with all
of you! Just looking at you the flies drop dead and the
lamps begin to smoke. There is something wrong, wrong,
wrong! . . . I've told you a thousand times, and I'll go on
telling you forever that you are all wrong, wrong, wrong!

[*Enter* IVANOV *and* SHABELSKY.]

SHABELSKY [*coming in with* IVANOV *through door on
the right*]: Who's giving a recitation here? You, Shurochka? [*Laughs and shakes hands with her.*] I congratulate you, my angel, God give you long life, and may you
never be born a second time. . . .

ZINAIDA SAVISHNA [*joyfully*]: Nikolai Alekseyevich!
Count!

LEBEDEV: Ah! Who do I see . . . Count! [*Goes to
meet him.*]

SHABELSKY [*seeing* ZINAIDA SAVISHNA *and* BABAKINA,
stretches out his arms]: Two bankers on one sofa! . . .
Lovely to behold! [*Greets them; to* ZINAIDA SAVISHNA.]

How do you do, Zyuzyushka. [*To* BABAKINA] How do you do, little pompon!

ZINAIDA SAVISHNA: I am so glad to see you. You're such a rare visitor here, Count! [*Shouts.*] Gavrila, tea! Please, sit down! [*Gets up and goes out through door on the right and immediately returns, looking extremely preoccupied.*]

[SASHA *takes her former seat;* IVANOV *greets everyone in silence.*]

LEBEDEV [*to* SHABELSKY]: Where did you suddenly appear from? What wind blew you in? This is a surprise! [*Kisses him.*] Count, what a rover you are! That's not the way respectable people behave! [*Takes him by the arm and leads him to front of the stage.*] Why don't you ever come to see us? Angry, or something?

SHABELSKY: And what am I supposed to come on— a broomstick? I have no horses of my own, and Nikolai won't take me with him, he makes me stay home with Sarah, so she won't be lonely. Send your horses for me, then I'll come. . . .

LEBEDEV [*waves his hand*]: Oh, yes! Zyuzyushka would split her seams at the very thought of lending the horses. My dear old friend, you are nearer and dearer to me than anyone! You and I are the only ones left of the old cronies! "In you I love my lost youth and all my former sorrows." . . . Joking aside, it almost makes me cry. [*Kisses the Count.*]

SHABELSKY: Let go, let me go! You smell like a wine cellar.

LEBEDEV: My dear fellow, you can't imagine how I miss my old friends! I could hang myself from boredom! . . . [*Softly*] Zyuzyushka has driven all the decent people away with her moneylending, and now, as

you see, only the Zulus are left . . . all those Doodkins
and Boodkins. . . . Well, let's have some tea. . . .

[GAVRILA *serves tea to the Count.*]

ZINAIDA SAVISHNA [*anxiously*]:   Now, why are you
serving it like that? Bring some kind of jam . . . gooseberry, perhaps. . . .

SHABELSKY [*laughing loudly, to* IVANOV]:   Well, what
did I tell you? [*To* LEBEDEV] I made a bet with him on
the way here that as soon as we arrived Zyuzyushka
would start serving the gooseberry jam. . . .

ZINAIDA SAVISHNA: You still like making fun of people, Count . . . [*Sits down.*]

LEBEDEV: They've put up twenty barrels of it, how
do you think they're going to get rid of it?

SHABELSKY [*sitting down by the table*]:   Still piling up
the money, Zyuzyushka? You must have about a million
by now, eh?

ZINAIDA SAVISHNA [*with a sigh*]:   To an outsider we
may seem to be richer than other people, but where's
the money coming from? It's all talk. . . .

SHABELSKY: Oh, yes, yes . . . we know! We know
what a poor hand you are at that game. . . . [*To* LEBE-
DEV] Pasha, tell the truth, you've piled up a million,
haven't you?

LEBEDEV: I don't know. You have to ask Zyuzyushka. . . .

SHABELSKY [*to* BABAKINA]:   And our plump little
pompon here will soon have a million, too! She grows
prettier and plumper, not just by the day, but by the
hour! That's what it does to have barrels of money . . .

BABAKINA: Thank you very much, Your Excellency, but I don't like being made fun of.

SHABELSKY: My dear little banker, do you think I'm joking? That's simply a cry from the heart. I'm moved to speech by an excess of feeling. . . . I love you and Zyuzyushka infinitely. . . . [*Gaily*] It's sheer rapture! . . . Ecstasy! . . . I cannot look at either of you and remain unmoved. . . .

ZINAIDA SAVISHNA: You haven't changed a bit. [*To* YEGORUSHKA] Yegorushka, put out the candles! Why leave them burning when you're not playing?

[YEGORUSHKA *starts, extinguishes the candles, and sits down.*]

ZINAIDA SAVISHNA [*to* IVANOV]:   Nikolai Alekseyevich, how is your wife's health?

IVANOV: Bad. Today the doctor definitely said that she has consumption. . . .

ZINAIDA SAVISHNA: Really? What a pity! . . . [*Sighs.*] And we are all so fond of her. . . .

SHABELSKY: Nonsense, nonsense, and more nonsense! . . . She hasn't got consumption at all, it's medical quackery, a trick. Aesculapius likes hanging about the house, so he thinks up consumption. It's a good thing the husband's not jealous. [IVANOV *makes a gesture of impatience.*] And so far as Sarah is concerned, I don't trust a single word or gesture of hers. All my life I've distrusted doctors, lawyers, and women. Nonsense, nonsense, charlatanism, and tricks!

LEBEDEV [*to* SHABELSKY]:   You're a strange character, Matvei! You've adopted a sort of misanthropy and you carry it about with you like a child with a new toy. You're a man like any other, but as soon as you start talking, you sound as if you had the pip, or a chronic catarrh.

SHABELSKY: What do you expect me to do, kiss all these swindlers and rogues?

LEBEDEV: Where do you see swindlers and rogues?

SHABELSKY: Well, present company excepted, of course, but . . .

LEBEDEV: There you go with your "but." . . . It's all a front.

SHABELSKY: A front. . . . You're lucky you don't have a philosophy of life.

LEBEDEV: What do you mean, philosophy of life? I just sit here waiting to give up the ghost at any minute. That's my philosophy of life. You and I, brother, are past the age of thinking about a philosophy of life. That's how it is. . . . [*Shouts.*] Gavrila!

SHABELSKY: You've had enough. . . . Take a look at the color of your nose!

LEBEDEV [*drinks*]: Never mind, my friend. . . . I'm not going to my wedding today.

ZINAIDA SAVISHNA: Dr. Lvov hasn't been to see us for a long time. He's quite forgotten us.

SASHA: My aversion. The personification of honesty. He can't ask for a glass of water or light a cigarette without making a show of his extraordinary honesty. Whether he's talking to you or just walking about, it's written all over his face: I am an honest man. He bores me.

SHABELSKY: He's a narrow-minded, stiff-necked leech! [*Mimics.*] "Make way for honest labor!" He goes about squawking like a parrot, thinks he's really a second Dobrolyubov. Anyone who doesn't do the same is a villain. And his views are astounding in their profundity. If a peasant is prosperous and lives like a human being, he's a villain and a kulak. I wear a velvet jacket and have a valet to dress me—I'm a villain and a serf-owner. So honest, so honest that everything's bursting with honesty. He's beside himself with it. I'm almost afraid of him . . . really I am! At any minute he may, out of a sense of duty, give me a rap on the snout, or call me a villain.

IVANOV: I find him awfully tiring, but all the same, I like him; he's extremely sincere.

SHABELSKY: A fine kind of sincerity! He came up to me last night, and for no reason whatever said: "I thoroughly dislike you, Count!" Thank you very much! And all this is not just being simple, it's done for a purpose: his voice trembles, his eyes glow, he shakes in his shoes. . . . He can go to the devil with his wooden sincerity. I'm repulsive to him, odious, that's natural. . . . I am quite aware of it, but why say it to my face? I'm a bad lot, but after all, I do have gray hair. . . . That futile, merciless honesty!

LEBEDEV: Now, now, now! . . . You were young once yourself, you can understand.

SHABELSKY: Yes, I was young and foolish, and in my time I, too, played the role of Chatsky, exposing frauds and scoundrels, but I never in my life called a thief a thief to his face, or mentioned rope in the house of a hanged man. I was properly brought up. But that dim-witted leech of yours—he'd feel he had solved all his problems—he'd be in seventh heaven if only fate would give him a chance—in the name of principle and humanitarian ideals—publicly to give me a rap on the snout or a poke in the ribs.

LEBEDEV: Young people all have their foibles. I had an uncle who was a Hegelian . . . and he used to fill up his house with guests, then after a few drinks, he'd get up on a chair and begin: "You ignoramuses! You are the power of darkness! . . . The dawn of a new life . . ." Ta-ta-ta-ta-ta-ta . . . And he'd go on bawling them out.

SASHA: What did the guests do?

LEBEDEV: Nothing . . . listened and went on drinking. Once, however, I challenged him to a duel . . . my own uncle. It was because of Bacon. As I remember, I was sitting—I hope I can remember it—just where Matvei is sitting now, and my uncle was standing over there, about where Nikolasha is, with poor Gerasim Nilych. . . . Well, sir, Gerasim Nilych had just asked a question and——

[*Enter* BORKIN, *smartly dressed, carrying a parcel. He comes through the door on the right, skipping and singing. There is a hum of approval.*]

YOUNG LADIES: Mikhail Mikhailovich!

LEBEDEV: Mishel   Mishelich!   As   I   live   and breathe. . . .

SHABELSKY: The life of the party!

BORKIN: Here I am! [*Runs up to* SASHA.] Most noble signorina, I make bold to congratulate the universe on the birth of so wondrous a flower as yourself. . . . As a token of my admiration, I have the audacity to present you [*hands her the parcel*] with these fireworks and Roman candles of my own manufacture. May they brighten the night even as you brighten the gloom of this dark realm. [*Bows theatrically.*]

SASHA: Thank you.

LEBEDEV [*to* IVANOV, *laughing loudly*]:   Why don't you get rid of this Judas?

BORKIN [*to* LEBEDEV]: Pavel Kirilych! [*To* IVANOV] My patron. . . . [*Sings.*] *Nicolas voilà,* heigh-de-ho! [*Goes around greeting everyone.*] Most esteemed Zinaida Savishna. . . . Divine Marfa Yegorovna. . . . Venerable Avdotya Nazarovna. . . . His Excellency, the Count. . . .

SHABELSKY [*laughing loudly*]: The life of the party. . . . He no sooner arrives than the air clears. Do you notice it?

BORKIN: Ugh, I'm tired! I think I've said how do you do to everybody, haven't I? Well, what's new, gentlemen? Isn't there something special, something heady? [*Eagerly, to* ZINAIDA SAVISHNA.] Now listen, Mama . . . as I was on my way here . . . [*To* GAVRILA] Bring me some tea, Gavrila, but no gooseberry jam! [*To* ZINAIDA SAVISHNA] As I was on my way here, I saw some peasants stripping the bark off your willow bushes along the river. Why don't you lease out those willow bushes?

LEBEDEV [*to* IVANOV]: Why don't you get rid of this Judas?

ZINAIDA SAVISHNA [*in awe*]: Why, that's true, it never entered my head!

BORKIN [*doing gymnastic exercises with his arms*]: I can't get along without exercise. . . . Mama, how about getting up something a little special? Marfa Yegorovna, I'm in fine fettle . . . I feel exalted! [*Sings.*] "Again I stand before you". . . .

ZINAIDA SAVISHNA: Let's get something going, otherwise everyone will be bored.

BORKIN: Gentlemen, why are you all sitting there with such hangdog expressions? Just like a lot of jurymen in court! . . . Let's have a game. What shall it be? Forfeits, a game of tag, dancing, fireworks?

YOUNG LADIES [*clapping their hands*]: Fireworks, fireworks! [*They run into the garden.*]

SASHA [*to* IVANOV]: Why are you so sad today?

IVANOV: My head aches, Shurochka, and besides, I'm depressed.

SASHA: Let's go into the drawing room.

[*They go out through door on the right. All the others go into the garden except* ZINAIDA SAVISHNA *and* LEBEDEV.]

ZINAIDA SAVISHNA: Now that's what I like—that young man. He hadn't been here two minutes before he'd cheered everybody up. [*Turns down a large lamp.*] As long as they're all out in the garden, there's no use burning good candles. [*Extinguishes the candles.*]

LEBEDEV [*following her*]: Zyuzyushka, we ought to give our visitors a bite to eat. . . .

ZINAIDA SAVISHNA: Just look at all those candles . . . no wonder everybody thinks we're rich. [*Extinguishes them.*]

LEBEDEV [*trailing after her*]: Zyuzyushka, you really ought to give them something to eat. . . . They're young, they must be famished, poor things. . . . Zyuzyushka . . .

ZINAIDA SAVISHNA: The Count didn't finish his glass. What a waste of sugar! [*Goes out through the door on the left.*]

LEBEDEV: Tfoo! [*Goes into the garden.*]

[SASHA *and* IVANOV *enter through the door on the right.*]

SASHA: Everyone has gone into the garden.

IVANOV: That's how things are, Shurochka. In the past I used to work a great deal and think a great deal, and I was never tired; now, however, I do nothing and think about nothing, but I am tired, body and soul. And I am conscience-stricken day and night, I feel deeply guilty, but of what I do not know. And then there is my wife's illness, the lack of money, the constant bickering, gossip, futile talk, and that absurd Borkin. . . . My home has become loathsome to me, and living in it worse than torture. I tell you frankly, Shurochka, even the company of my wife, who loves me, has become unbearable to me. You are an old friend, and you won't be offended by my candor. I came here this evening to be amused, but even in your house I am bored and have a longing to go home. Forgive me, I'll just leave quietly.

SASHA: Nikolai Alekseyevich, I understand you. Your misfortune is that you are lonely. You needed someone near you whom you could have loved, someone who would have understood you. Love alone can renew you.

IVANOV: Come, now, Shurochka! That would be the last straw if a wet rooster like me were to get himself involved in a new love affair! God preserve me from such a misfortune! No, my clever child, it's not a question of romance. I tell you in all honesty, I can bear anything: depression, mental illness, ruin, the loss of my wife, my own premature old age and solitude, but I cannot bear, cannot endure, the contempt I feel for myself. I could die of shame at the thought that I, a healthy, strong man, have turned into some sort of Hamlet, or Manfred, or superfluous man—God only knows what! There are those persons who are flattered at being called Hamlets or superfluous men, but for me it is— ignominious! My pride is outraged, I am weighed down with shame, and I suffer. . . .

SASHA [*jokingly, through tears*]: Nikolai Alekseyevich, let us run away to America!

IVANOV: I feel too indolent to walk so far as the threshold, and you talk of America. . . . [*They go toward the door to the garden.*] Really, Shurochka, living here must be difficult for you! When I look at the people who surround you, I am horrified: who is there here for you to marry? The only hope is that some passing lieutenant or student will abduct you and take you away. . . .

[ZINAIDA SAVISHNA *comes in through door on the left with a jar of jam.*]

IVANOV: Excuse me, Shurochka, I'll join you. . . .

[SASHA *goes into the garden.*]

IVANOV: Zinaida Savishna, I have a favor to ask of you. . . .

ZINAIDA SAVISHNA: What do you want, Nikolai Alekseyevich?

IVANOV [*hesitantly*]: Well, you see, the fact is that my promissory note is due tomorrow. You would greatly oblige me by postponing it, or by allowing me to add the interest to the capital. At the present moment, I have absolutely no money. . . .

ZINAIDA SAVISHNA [*alarmed*]: Nikolai Alekseyevich, but how could I? What sort of procedure is that? No, don't even think of it, and for God's sake, don't torture a poor old woman . . .

IVANOV: I'm sorry, I'm sorry. . . . [*Goes into the garden.*]

ZINAIDA SAVISHNA: Ugh! Good heavens, how he upset me! . . . I'm trembling all over . . . trembling all over. . . . [*Goes out through door on the right.*]

[*Enter* KOSYKH *through the door on the left and crosses the stage.*]

KOSYKH: I held the ace, king, queen, and a sequence of eight diamonds, the ace of spades, and one—one little heart, and she, God knows why, couldn't make a small slam! [*Goes out through door on the right.*]

[*Enter* AVDOTYA NAZAROVNA *and the* FIRST GUEST *from the garden.*]

AVDOTYA NAZAROVNA: I could tear her to pieces, the old skinflint . . . just tear her to pieces! It's no joke, I've been sitting here since five o'clock, and she hasn't offered me so much as a piece of moldy herring! What a house! . . . What a hostess!

FIRST GUEST: And such dreadful boredom—you could take a running jump and knock your head against a wall! What people, God help them! . . . I'm so bored and hungry, I could howl like a wolf and start gnawing on someone.

AVDOTYA NAZAROVNA: I could tear her to pieces, God forgive me!

FIRST GUEST: I'll have a drink, old girl, and be off. Even those prospective brides of yours can't keep me here. How the devil can I think of love when I haven't had a single glass of anything since dinner?

AVDOTYA NAZAROVNA: Let's go and see if we can find——

FIRST GUEST: Sh! . . . Quietly. I think there's some schnapps on the sideboard in the dining room. We'll put the screws on Yegorushka. . . . Sh! . . .

[*They go out through door on the left. Enter* ANNA PETROVNA *and* LVOV *through door on the right.*]

ANNA PETROVNA: Never mind, they'll be glad to see us. There's no one here. They must be in the garden.

LVOV: And why, I should like to know, have you brought me here to this nest of vultures? This is no place for either of us. Honest people can't breathe in such an atmosphere.

ANNA PETROVNA: Now listen to me, Sir Honesty! It's not polite to take a lady out and talk of nothing but your own honesty all the time! You may be honest, but it's boring, to say the least. Never talk to a woman about your virtues, let her discover them for herself. When my Nikolai was your age and in the society of women, he used to do nothing but sing songs and tell fantastic stories, yet everyone knew what sort of man he was.

LVOV: Oh, don't talk to me about your Nikolai, I understand him very well!

ANNA PETROVNA: You're a good man, but you don't understand anything. Let's go into the garden. He never used to say: "I am honest. I can't breathe in such an atmosphere! Nest of vultures! Owl's nest! Crocodiles!" He left the menagerie out of it, and when he felt indignant I never heard anything from him except: "Ah, how unjust I was today!" or "Anyuta, I'm sorry for that man!" That's how he was, while you . . .

[*They go out. Enter* AVDOTYA NAZAROVNA *and* FIRST GUEST *through door on the left.*]

FIRST GUEST: It's not in the dining room, so it must be somewhere in the pantry. We ought to sound out Yegorushka. Let's go through the drawing room.

AVDOTYA NAZAROVNA: I could tear her to pieces! . . .

[*They go out through door on the right.* BABAKINA *and* BORKIN *run in from the garden laughing;* SHABELSKY *trots after them laughing and rubbing his hands.*]

BABAKINA: How boring! [*Laughs loudly.*] How boring! They all just walk about or sit there as if they had swallowed pokers! My very bones are numb with boredom. [*Hopping about*] I have to loosen up!

[BORKIN *seizes her by the waist and kisses her cheek.*]

SHABELSKY [*roars with laughter and snaps his fingers*]: Well, I'll be damned! [*Heaves a sigh.*] In a certain way . . .

BABAKINA: Let go, hands off, you shameless creature, or God knows what the Count will be thinking! Leave me alone!

BORKIN: Angel, my soul's delight, my heart's carbuncle! [*Kisses her.*] Lend me twenty-three hundred rubles!

BABAKINA: No, no, no! . . . That's all very well, but when it comes to money—thank you very much! No, no, no! . . . Oh, now you let go of my hands!

SHABELSKY [*trotting around them*]: Little pompon . . . she has her charms. . . .

BORKIN [*seriously*]: Now, that's enough of that. Let's talk business. We'll discuss things frankly, in a businesslike way. Give me a straight answer, without guile or trickery: yes or no? Listen! [*Points to the Count.*] He needs money, an income of at least three thousand a year. You need a husband. Do you want to be a countess?

SHABELSKY [*laughs*]: What an amazing cynic!

BORKIN: Do you want to be a countess? Yes or no?

BABAKINA [*agitated*]: You're making it up, Misha, honestly. . . . And these things are not done like that, just out of the blue. . . . If the Count would care to . . .

he himself can . . . and . . . and I don't know how this can suddenly, all at once . . .

BORKIN: Now, now, stop putting it on! This is business. . . . Yes or no?

SHABELSKY [*laughing and rubbing his hands*]: Yes, really, now . . . eh? Damn it all, I'd better settle this infamy myself, eh? My little pompon . . . [*Kisses* BABAKI-NA*'s cheek.*] You charmer! . . . Little cucumber!

BABAKINA: Stop, stop, you've completely upset me. Go away, go away! . . . No, don't go!

BORKIN: Be quick! Yes or no? We haven't time to——

BABAKINA: Do you know what, Count? Come and stay at my house for two or three days. . . . It's cheerful there, not like this place. . . . Come tomorrow. . . . [*To* BORKIN] You were joking, weren't you?

BORKIN [*angrily*]: Now who'd want to joke about serious business?

BABAKINA: Stop, stop! . . . Oh, I feel dizzy . . . faint! A countess . . . I'm going to faint . . . I can't stand up. . . .

[BORKIN *and* SHABELSKY *laughingly take her by the arms and, kissing her cheeks, lead her out through the door on the right.* IVANOV *and* SASHA *run in from the garden.*]

IVANOV [*clutching his head in despair*]: It cannot be! Don't, don't Shurochka! Oh, you mustn't!

SASHA [*carried away*]: I love you madly. . . . Without you my life has no meaning, no happiness, no joy! You are everything to me. . . .

IVANOV: Why, why? My God, I don't understand anything. . . . Shurochka, you mustn't!

SASHA: When I was a child you were my only joy; I loved you, loved your very soul as my own, and now . . . I love you, Nikolai Alekseyevich. . . . I'll go with you to the ends of the earth, wherever you want me to go, even to the grave, only let it be soon, for God's sake, otherwise I won't be able to breathe. . . .

IVANOV [*bursting into joyous laughter*]:   What is this? Can it mean beginning life anew? Can it, Shurochka? . . . My joy! [*Draws her to himself.*] My youth! My freshness! . . .

[ANNA PETROVNA *enters from the garden and, seeing her husband and* SASHA, *stops as if transfixed.*]

IVANOV: It means living again? Yes? Working again?

[*They kiss, then look around and see* ANNA PETROVNA.]

IVANOV [*in horror*]:   Sarah!

Act III

[IVANOV's *study. A desk, on which papers, books, official envelopes, knickknacks, and revolvers lie in disorder; near the papers stand a lamp, a decanter of vodka, a plate of herring, pieces of bread, and pickled cucumbers. On the walls there are maps, pictures, rifles, pistols, sickles, riding crops, etc. It is midday.* SHABELSKY *and* LEBEDEV *are sitting on either side of the desk.* BORKIN *sits astride a chair in the middle of the stage.* PYOTR *stands by the door.*]

LEBEDEV: France has a clear and definite policy. . . . The French know what they want. They just want to rip the guts out of the sausage-makers, that's all. But Germany, my friend, is playing a very different tune. Germany has plenty of enemies besides France. . . .

SHABELSKY: Nonsense! In my opinion the Germans are cowards and the French are cowards. They may thumb their noses at each other, but you can be sure it won't go beyond that. They won't fight.

BORKIN: And why fight, I say. What's the use of all these armaments, congresses, and expenditures? You know what I'd do? I'd collect the dogs from all over the country, inject them with a good dose of Pasteur's virus, and then turn them loose in the enemy's territory. They'd all have rabies within a month.

LEBEDEV [*laughs*]: You look at that head and it seems small, but it holds a multitude of great ideas, like fish in the sea.

SHABELSKY: A virtuoso!

LEBEDEV: God bless you, Mishel Mishelich, you make me laugh! [*Stops laughing.*] Well, gentlemen, you go on and on with your military tactics, but never a word about vodka. *Repetatur!* [*Fills three glasses.*] Our good health! [*They eat and drink.*] Herring, I must say, makes the very best of appetizers.

SHABELSKY: Oh, no, pickles are better. . . . Scientists have been thinking about this since the world began, but they haven't come up with anything better than pickled cucumbers. [*To* PYOTR] Pyotr, go and fetch some more pickles, and tell them to fry us four pasties filled with onions. And see that they're hot.

[PYOTR *goes out.*]

LEBEDEV: Caviar also goes well with vodka. But how? You have to know how. . . . You take a quarter of a pound of pressed caviar, two scallions, some olive oil, mix it all together, you know . . . then a little lemon juice over it . . . Terrific! Just the smell of it drives you crazy!

BORKIN: Another nice snack after vodka is fried gudgeons. Only you have to know how to fry them. First, you must clean them, roll them in breadcrumbs, then fry them till they're crisp, so they crackle when you eat them . . . crunch-crunch-crunch. . . .

SHABELSKY: Yesterday at Babakina's we had a fine hors d'oeuvre—white mushrooms.

LEBEDEV: But of course!

SHABELSKY: Only they were prepared in a special way. You know, with onion, bay leaf, and all sorts of spices. When you took the lid off the saucepan, and the steam rose—what a fragrance! Sheer rapture!

LEBEDEV: Well? *Repetatur,* gentlemen! [*They drink.*] Our good health! [*Looks at his watch.*] It looks as if I won't be able to wait for Nikolasha. Time for me to be going. At Babakina's, you say, they're serving mushrooms, but in my house there's not a sign of a mushroom yet. Will you please tell me why the devil you go to Marfutka's so often?

SHABELSKY [*with a nod in* BORKIN's *direction*]:   It's him—he wants me to marry her.

LEBEDEV: Marry? How old are you?

SHABELSKY: Sixty-two.

LEBEDEV: Just the right age to get married. And Marfutka's the right woman for you.

BORKIN: It's not a question of Marfutka, but of Marfutka's assets.

LEBEDEV: What do you want—two skins from one cow?

BORKIN: When he marries her and fattens his pockets, then you'll see how you get two skins from one cow. And you'll be licking your chops!

SHABELSKY: He's serious, you know. That genius is convinced that I'm going to take his advice and marry. . . .

BORKIN: Well, aren't you? You mean you're not sure now?

SHABELSKY: You're out of your mind. When was I ever sure? Pssssss!

BORKIN: Thank you. . . . Thank you very much! So this means you're going to let me down? One minute you're going to marry her, the next minute you're not. . . . God only knows which it is, and I've already given my word! So you're not going to marry her, then?

SHABELSKY [*shrugs his shoulders*]: He's serious. . . . An amazing fellow!

BORKIN [*indignantly*]: In that case, why did you have to get an honest woman all flustered? She's mad to be a countess, she can't sleep or eat. . . . Is that something to joke about? Is that honest?

SHABELSKY [*snaps his fingers*]: All right, then, and what if I commit this infamous deed? Eh? Just to spite them! I'll go ahead and do it. Word of honor. . . . What a joke!

[*Enter* LVOV.]

LEBEDEV: Aesculapius, our deepest respects. [*Gives him his hand and sings.*] "Doctor, our father, save me, I'm scared to death of death. . . ."

LVOV: Nikolai Alekseyevich is not back yet?

LEBEDEV: No, I've been waiting for him myself for more than an hour.

[LVOV *impatiently paces the stage.*]

LEBEDEV: Well, my friend, and how is Anna Petrovna?

LVOV: Bad.

LEBEDEV: May I go and pay my respects?

LVOV: No, please don't. I think she's sleeping. [*Pause*]

LEBEDEV: Nice woman, very appealing. . . . [*Sighs.*] On Shurochka's birthday, when she fainted in our house, I happened to see her face, and I knew then she hadn't long to live, poor thing. But I don't understand what it was that caused her to faint. I ran into the room and there she was on the floor, pale, with Nikolasha on his knees beside her; he was pale, too, and Shurochka stood there with tears streaming down her face. After that happened Shurochka and I were absolutely distracted for a whole week.

SHABELSKY [*to* LVOV]: Tell me, most esteemed priest of science, who was the learned man who discovered that the frequent visits of a young physician are beneficial to ladies suffering from chest complaints? That was a great discovery! Very great, indeed! Would it be considered allopathy or homeopathy?

[LVOV *is about to answer, but makes a contemptuous gesture and goes out.*]

SHABELSKY: What an annihilating look!

LEBEDEV: That damned tongue of yours! Why did you have to hurt his feelings?

SHABELSKY [*querulously*]: And why does he lie? Consumption . . . no hope . . . she'll die. . . . He's lying! I can't stand that!

LEBEDEV: What makes you think he's lying?

SHABELSKY [*gets up and walks back and forth*]: I think it quite unlikely that a living person, for no reason whatsoever, can suddenly die. Let's drop the subject.

[KOSYKH *runs in, out of breath.*]

KOSYKH: Is Nikolai Alekseyevich at home? How do you do? [*Hastily shakes hands with everyone.*] Is he at home?

BORKIN: No, he isn't.

KOSYKH [*sits down, then jumps up*]: In that case, good-bye. [*Drinks a glass of vodka and quickly eats a snack.*] I must run along. . . . Business. . . . I'm worn out. . . . Barely able to stand up. . . .

LEBEDEV: Where did you blow in from?

KOSYKH: From Barabanov's. We played vint all night, only just finished. . . . Lost everything I had. . . . That Barabanov plays like a shoemaker! [*In a tearful voice*] Just listen to this: I held hearts all the time. . . . [*Addresses* BORKIN, *who springs away from him.*] He goes diamonds, I go hearts again, he goes diamonds. . . . Well, I don't take a trick. [*To* LEBEDEV] We play four clubs. I hold the ace, queen, six in my hand, the ace, ten, and three of spades——

LEBEDEV [*stops his ears*]: Spare me, spare me, for Christ's sake, spare me!

KOSYKH [*to the Count*]: Think of it—ace, queen, six of clubs, ace, ten, three of spades——

SHABELSKY [*pushing him away*]: Go away, I don't want to listen!

KOSYKH: And all of a sudden, bad luck: the ace of spades taken in the first round——

SHABELSKY [*snatches up a revolver from the table*]: Get out of here, or I'll shoot!

KOSYKH [*waving his hand*]: What the devil. . . . Can't I even talk to anyone? It's like living in Australia: no common interests, no solidarity . . . everyone living for himself. . . . However, I'd better go . . . it's time. [*Snatches up his cap.*] Time is precious. [*Shakes hands with* LEBEDEV.] I pass!

[*Laughter.* KOSYKH *goes out, colliding with* AVDOTYA NAZAROVNA *in the doorway.*]

AVDOTYA NAZAROVNA [*gives a shriek*]: Curse you, you nearly knocked me off my feet!

ALL: A-a-a-h! The ubiquitous one!

AVDOTYA NAZAROVNA: There they are, and I've been looking all over the house. How do you do, you bright people, good appetite. . . . [*Shakes hands.*]

LEBEDEV: What are you doing here?

AVDOTYA NAZAROVNA: Business, my friend! [*To the Count*] It concerns you, Your Excellency. [*Bows to him.*] I was told to give you her regards and to inquire after your health. . . . And she also instructed me to say, the little doll, that if you don't come to see her this evening, she'll cry her little eyes out. "Take him aside and whisper it secretly into his ear," the little darling said. But why secretly? We're all friends here. And it's not a matter of stealing chickens, it's legal and it's love, and by mutual consent. I never drink, old sinner that I am, but on such an occasion as this—I'll have one!

LEBEDEV: And so will I! [*Pours the drinks.*] You know, old magpie, you wear well. You've been an old woman ever since I've known you—for the last thirty years.

AVDOTYA NAZAROVNA: I've lost count of the years. . . . I buried two husbands, and I'd have married a third, but no one would have me without a dowry. I've had about eight children. . . . [*Takes her glass.*] Well, good luck! We've begun a good job, and, with God's blessing, we'll finish it! They'll live happily ever after, and we can look at them and rejoice. Live in peace and love. . . . [*Drinks.*] That's strong vodka!

SHABELSKY [*laughing loudly, to* LEBEDEV]: You know, the most curious thing of all is that they think I'm serious, as if I . . . Amazing! [*Gets up.*] But what if I were actually to commit this infamous deed, Pasha? Out of spite. . . . There, you old dog, take that! Eh, Pasha?

LEBEDEV: You're talking nonsense, Count. Our business, brother, is to think about kicking the bucket, and as for Marfutka and her assets, you missed your chance a long time ago. . . . Our day has passed.

SHABELSKY: Yes, I'm going to go through with it! Word of honor, I'll do it!

[*Enter* IVANOV *and* LVOV.]

LVOV: I ask you to spare me just five minutes.

LEBEDEV: Nikolasha! [*Goes to meet* IVANOV *and embraces him.*] How are you, my dear friend? I've been waiting a whole hour for you.

AVDOTYA NAZAROVNA [*bows*]: How do you do, my dear.

IVANOV [*acridly*]: Gentlemen, again you have turned my study into a tavern! A thousand times I have asked each and every one of you not to do this.... [*Goes to his desk.*] Look here, you've spilled vodka on my papers ... crumbs ... pickles.... It's disgusting!

LEBEDEV: My fault, Nikolasha, my fault.... Forgive me. I must have a talk with you, my friend, about a very serious matter.

BORKIN: Me too.

LVOV: Nikolai Alekseyevich, may I have a word with you?

IVANOV [*pointing to* LEBEDEV]:   Now he wants me, too. Wait, I'll see you afterwards.... [*To* LEBEDEV] What is it you want?

LEBEDEV: Gentlemen, I want to speak to him confidentially. Please ...

[*The* COUNT *goes out with* AVDOTYA NAZAROVNA; BORKIN *follows, then* LVOV.]

IVANOV: Pasha, you can drink as much as you like, that's your sickness, but I beg you not to make a drunkard of my uncle. He never used to drink. It's bad for him.

LEBEDEV [*alarmed*]:   My dear boy, I didn't know ... I wasn't even aware that ...

IVANOV: If that old baby were to die, God forbid, I'd be the one to feel bad about it, not you.... What is it you want? [*Pause*]

LEBEDEV: You see, my dear friend ... I don't know how to begin, to make it seem less disgraceful.... Nikolasha, I feel ashamed, I'm blushing and stammering, but, my dear boy, put yourself in my place, try to understand that I am helpless, a slave, a milksop.... Forgive me....

IVANOV: Well, what is it?

LEBEDEV: My wife sent me. . . . Do me a favor, be a friend, pay her the interest! You wouldn't believe how she's pestered, nagged, tormented me. Settle up with her, for the love of God!

IVANOV: Pasha, you know I have no money now.

LEBEDEV: I know, I know, but what am I to do? She won't wait. If she protests your promissory note, how can Shurochka and I ever look you in the face?

IVANOV: I myself am ashamed, Pasha, I could sink through the floor, but . . . where am I going to get it? Tell me: where? There's only one thing to do: wait till autumn when I sell the wheat.

LEBEDEV [*shouts*]: She won't wait! [*Pause*]

IVANOV: You're in an awkward, difficult position, but mine is worse. [*Walks up and down, thinking.*] And I can't think of any way . . . I have nothing to sell. . . .

LEBEDEV: You could go and ask Milbakh; after all, he owes you sixteen thousand. [IVANOV *hopelessly waves his hand.*] I'll tell you what, Nikolasha . . . I know you'll quarrel with me about it, but . . . out of respect for an old drunkard . . . As one friend to another . . . Do consider me a friend. . . . We've both been students, liberals. . . . Community of ideas and interests. . . . We both studied at the University of Moscow. . . . Our *Alma Mater*. . . . [*Takes out his wallet.*] I've got a little something laid aside, not a soul in my house knows about it. Take it as a loan. . . . [*Takes out money and puts it on the table.*] Give up your pride and accept it out of friendship. I'd take it from you, on my word. . . . [*Pause*] There it is on the table: eleven hundred rubles. You go and see her today and give it to her yourself. Say: "There you are, Zinaida Savishna, may you choke on it!" Only mind you don't let on that you borrowed it from me—God help you—or Madame Gooseberry-Jam will make it hot for me! [*Scrutinizes* IVANOV's *face.*] There, there, never mind! I was only joking. . . . Forgive me, for Christ's sake! [*Pause*] You're feeling low? [IVANOV *waves his hand.*] Yes, it's a bad business. [*Sighs.*] You're going through a time of trial and tribulation. Man, my dear boy, is like a samovar. He isn't always left to cool on the shelf, now and then he gets some hot coals put into him: psh! . . . psh! The comparison's not worth a damn, but . . . well, I just can't think of anything more clever. . . . [*Sighs.*] Misfortune hardens the soul. I'm not sorry for you, Nikolasha, you'll land on your feet, it'll all come out in the wash, but it hurts me, my boy, and I'm provoked that people . . . Tell me, please, where does all this gossip come from? There's so much gossip going around about you that before you know it, my boy, the assistant prosecutor will be dropping in on you. . . . You're a murderer, an extortioner, a robber. . . .

IVANOV: That's all nonsense. . . . Now I have a headache.

LEBEDEV: That comes from thinking so much.

IVANOV: I'm not thinking.

LEBEDEV: Nikolasha, now you just sneeze at all that and come and see us. Shurochka is fond of you, she understands and appreciates you. She's a fine, honest person, Nikolasha. She doesn't take after her mother or her father, it must have been a passing stranger. . . . Sometimes I look at her, my boy, and I can't believe that a bottle-nosed old drunkard like me has such a treasure. You just drop in and discuss something intellectual with her—it'll cheer you up. She's a true, sincere person. . . . [*Pause*]

IVANOV: Pasha, my dear friend, leave me alone. . . .

LEBEDEV: I understand, I understand. . . . [*Hurriedly looks at his watch.*] I understand. [*Kisses* IVANOV.] Good-bye. I've still got to go to a consecration service at the school. [*Goes to the door and stops.*] She's so clever. . . . Yesterday Shurochka and I were talking about gossip. [*Laughs.*] And she fired off an aphorism: "Papa," she says, "glowworms shine only at night so the night birds can find them and eat them, and good men exist so that gossip and slander may have something to feed on." What do you think of that? A genius! George Sand!

IVANOV: Pasha! [*Stops him.*] What's wrong with me?

LEBEDEV: I've been wanting to ask you about that myself, but to tell you the truth, I felt embarrassed. I don't know, my friend! On the one hand, it seems to me that these various misfortunes have got the best of you, but on the other hand, I know you're not the sort that . . . you can't be overcome by adversity. It's something else, Nikolasha, but what it is—I can't make out.

IVANOV: I don't understand it. It seems to me that either . . . but, no! [*Pause*] You see, this is what I wanted to say. I used to have a workman, Semyon, you remember him. Once, at threshing time, he wanted to show how strong he was before the girls, so he hoisted two sacks of rye onto his back and broke it. He died soon after. It seems to me that I, too, have broken my back. High school, the university, then farming, and projects for schools. . . . My ideas were different from everyone else's, I married differently, I was hotheaded, took risks, threw my money around right and left, I was happier and suffered more than anyone else in the whole district. Those have been my sacks, Pasha. . . . I hoisted a load onto my back, and my back gave way. At twenty we are all heroes, we undertake anything, we can do anything, but by thirty we are exhausted and good for nothing. Tell me, how do you explain such exhaustion? However, perhaps that's not what it is. . . . No, it's not that, it's not that! Go, Pasha, God bless you, you must be fed up with me.

LEBEDEV [*eagerly*]: Do you know what? It's your environment that's getting you down.

IVANOV: That's silly, Pasha, and banal. Go along.

LEBEDEV: It really is silly. I myself can see that it's silly now. I'm going, I'm going! . . . [*Goes out.*]

IVANOV [*alone*]: I'm a rotten, pitiful, worthless man. You would have to be a miserable, worn-out drunkard like Pasha to be able to love and respect me still. My God, how I despise myself! How profoundly I hate my voice, my footsteps, my hands, these clothes, my thoughts. Now, isn't that ridiculous, isn't it shocking? Less than a year ago I was strong and healthy, confident, tireless, impassioned; I worked with my hands, talked so that even the illiterate were moved to tears; I could weep when I saw grief, and feel indignation when I encountered evil. I knew what inspiration was, I knew the charm and poetry of those quiet nights when you sit at your desk and work from sunset to sunrise, or beguile your mind with dreams. I had faith, and I gazed into the future as into my mother's eyes. . . . But now . . . oh, my God! I'm exhausted, I have no faith, and I spend my days and nights in idleness. I can make neither my brain nor my hands and feet obey me. The estate is going to ruin, the forests are groaning under the ax. [*Weeps.*] My land contemplates me like an orphan. I look forward to nothing, regret nothing, my soul trembles in fear of tomorrow. . . . And this business with Sarah? I swore to love her forever, promised her happiness, opened her eyes to a future that she had never even dreamed of. And she believed me. For five years now I've watched her sinking under the burden of her sacrifice, breaking down in the struggle with her conscience, yet, God knows, with never so much as a sidelong glance or a word of reproach to me! . . . And now? I no longer love her. . . . How can it be? Why? What is the reason? I can't understand it. Here she is suffering, her days are numbered, and I, like the worst coward, run away from her pale face, her shrunken chest, her imploring eyes. . . . It's shameful, shameful! [*Pause*] Sasha, a mere girl, is touched by my troubles. She says she is in love with me—me, almost an old man—and I am intoxicated by this, forget everything else in the world, like someone enthralled by music, and I start shouting: "A new life! Happiness!" But the next day I no more believe in the new life and happiness than I do in ghosts. . . . What's wrong with me then? What is this abyss that I am propelling myself into? Where does this weakness come from? What has happened to my nerves? If my poor wife piques my vanity, or a servant displeases me, or my gun misfires, I instantly become rude, bad-tempered, and unlike myself. . . . [*Pause*] I don't understand, I don't, I don't understand! I simply feel like putting a bullet into my head!

[*Enter* LVOV.]

LVOV: I am going to have to speak plainly to you, Nikolai Alekseyevich!

IVANOV: Doctor, if you and I continue to speak plainly day after day, it will be more than human strength can bear.

LVOV: Will you be so good as to hear me out?

IVANOV: I hear you out every day, and up to now I in no way understand you: what exactly do you want of me?

LVOV: I tell you clearly and precisely, and only someone completely heartless could fail to understand, that——

IVANOV: That my wife is about to die—I know; that I am irreparably guilty where she is concerned—that I know, too; that you are an honest, upright man—I also know. What more do you want?

LVOV: Human cruelty fills me with indignation! A woman is dying. She has a father and a mother whom she loves and whom she would like to see before she dies. They know quite well that she will die soon and that she still loves them, but they—the deplorable cruelty of it—as if they wished to astound everyone with their religious integrity, continue to put their curse on her! You are the person for whom she has sacrificed everything—her home, her peace of mind—yet you openly, and with the most obvious intentions, go driving off to those Lebedevs every day.

IVANOV: Oh, I haven't been there for two weeks. . . .

LVOV [*not listening to him*]: With people such as you one has to speak plainly, without beating about the bush, and if you don't care to listen to me, then don't! I am accustomed to calling things by their right names. . . . You want this death so as to be free for new exploits: but even so, wouldn't it be possible for you to wait? If you were to let her die in the natural order of things, instead of killing her off with that undisguised cynicism of yours, do you think you might lose the Lebedev girl and her dowry? If you were to wait, within a year or two you'd manage to turn the head of some other young girl and get hold of her dowry, you prodigious Tartuffe, just exactly as you are doing now. . . . Why are you in such a hurry? Why is it so urgent that your wife should die now, instead of in a month, or in a year?

IVANOV: This is torture. . . . Doctor, you're an exceedingly poor physician if you suppose that a man can control himself indefinitely. It's costing me a terrific effort to keep from replying to your insults.

LVOV: Enough of that! Whom are you trying to fool? Drop this pretense.

IVANOV: You're a clever man: think. According to you, nothing could be simpler than to understand me! Yes? I married Anya for her large dowry. . . . I didn't get the dowry, I missed my aim, and now I am trying to get rid of her so I can marry someone else with a dowry. . . . Yes? How simple and ingenuous! . . . Man is such a simple, uncomplicated machine! No, Doctor; in every one of us there are far too many wheels, screws, and valves for us to be able to judge one another by first impressions, or by two or three external signs. I don't understand you, you don't understand me, and we don't understand ourselves. It is possible to be an excellent doctor—and at the same time to know absolutely nothing about people. Don't be so sure of yourself, admit that I am right.

LVOV: Do you really think that you are so impenetrable and I so lacking in intelligence, that I cannot distinguish baseness from honesty?

IVANOV: Evidently you and I will never see eye to eye. . . . For the last time I ask you, and please answer me without preamble: what exactly do you want of me? What are you after? [*Exasperated*] And with whom have I the honor of speaking: with a prosecuting attorney, or with my wife's physician?

LVOV: I am a physician, and as such, I demand that you alter your behavior. . . . It is killing Anna Petrovna!

IVANOV: But what am I to do—what? If you understand me better than I understand myself, then be specific: what am I to do?

LVOV: At least you could proceed less openly.

IVANOV: Oh, my God! Do you really understand yourself? [*Drinks water.*] Leave me. I am guilty a thousand times over, and I shall answer to God for it, but no one has given you the authority to torture me every day. . . .

LVOV: And who gave you the authority to offend against my idea of justice? You have worn me out and poisoned my soul. Until I found myself in this district, I accepted the existence of people who were stupid, mad, or carried away by their emotions, but I never believed that there were people who criminally, deliberately and knowingly, directed their will toward evil ends. . . . I used to respect and love people, but when I saw you——

IVANOV: I've already heard about that!

LVOV: Have you?

[*Enter* SASHA, *wearing a riding habit.*]

LVOV [*catching sight of her*]: Well, now I hope we thoroughly understand each other! [*Shrugs his shoulders and goes out.*]

IVANOV [*dismayed*]: Shura—you here?

SASHA: Yes, I am here. How are you? You didn't expect me? Why haven't you been to see us for so long?

IVANOV: Shura, for God's sake, this is most imprudent! Your coming here could have a terrible effect on my wife.

SASHA: She won't see me. I came by the back way. I'll go in a minute. I am worried: are you all right? Why haven't you come for so long?

IVANOV: My wife is deeply hurt as it is, she is virtually dying, and you come here! Shura, Shura, this is thoughtless and inhuman!

SASHA: What was I to do? You haven't been to see us for two weeks, and you didn't answer my letters. I've been dreadfully worried. I imagined you here suffering unbearably, ill, dead. Not one night have I been able to sleep in peace. I'll go in a minute. . . . Tell me at least: are you well?

IVANOV: No, I've been torturing myself, and other people torment me continually. . . . I simply cannot endure it! And now you! How unhealthy all this is, how abnormal! Shura, I am so guilty, so guilty!

SASHA: How you love to use frightening and pathetic words! You are guilty? Yes? Guilty? Then tell me, what are you guilty of?

IVANOV: I don't know, I don't know. . . .

SASHA: That's no answer. A sinner ought to know what his sin is. Have you been forging bank notes, or what?

IVANOV: That is not witty!

SASHA: Are you to blame because you no longer love your wife? Perhaps, but a man isn't master of his feelings; you didn't want to fall out of love. Is it your fault that she saw me telling you I loved you? No, you didn't want her to see it——

IVANOV [*interrupting*]: And so forth and so on. . . . Falling in love, falling out of love, not master of my feelings—all platitudes, trite phrases, which do not help. . . .

SASHA: It's tiresome talking to you. [*Looks at a picture.*] How well that dog is painted! Was it done from life?

IVANOV: From life. And this entire romance of ours is also commonplace and trite: he lost heart and got beyond his depth; she appeared, strong, courageous, and extended a helping hand. . . . Beautiful, but true only in novels; in life——

SASHA: In life it's exactly the same.

IVANOV: I see you have a keen understanding of life! My whining inspires you with reverent awe, you imagine that in me you have discovered a second Hamlet; but in my opinion this psychosis of mine, with all its appurtenances, furnishes excellent material for laughter and nothing more! One could laugh till his sides split at my affectations, but you cry "help!" You want to save me, to perform a heroic deed! Ah, how angry I am with myself today. I feel that this state of tension I am in must somehow be resolved. . . . Either I shall break something, or——

SASHA: Exactly, that's just what you need. To break something, smash something, or start shouting. You're angry with me, it was stupid of me to decide to come here. So then, show your indignation, shout at me, stamp your foot. Well? Go on, get angry. . . . [*Pause*] Well?

IVANOV: You're funny.

SASHA: That's perfect. It seems we are smiling. Deign to smile once more.

IVANOV [*laughs*]: I've noticed that when you start trying to save me and teach me some sense, your face becomes terribly naive, and the pupils of your eyes are enlarged, as if you were gazing at a comet. Wait, you have some dust on your shoulder. [*Brushes the dust off her shoulder.*] A man who's naive is a fool. But you women contrive to be naive in such a way that it's charming, and natural, and warm, and not so silly as it might seem. Only what is this habit you all have? As long as a man is healthy, strong, and cheerful, you pay absolutely no attention to him, but as soon as he starts sliding downhill, or playing Lazarus, you hang on his neck. Is it really worse to be the wife of a strong, courageous man than to be the nurse of a whimpering failure?

SASHA: It is worse!

IVANOV: But why? [*Laughs loudly.*] It's good that Darwin didn't get wind of this—he'd have set you straight. You're ruining the human race. Thanks to people like you, there'll soon be nothing but malcontents and psychotics born into the world.

SASHA: There are a lot of things that men don't understand. Every girl is more attracted to a man who is a failure than to one who's a success, because every girl is fascinated by an active love. . . . Do you understand? Active. Man is absorbed in his work, and so love has to take second place. He talks a little with his wife, strolls in the garden and pleasantly passes the time with her, sheds a few tears on her grave—and that's all. But for us—love is life. I love you, which means that I dream of curing you of your depression, of following you to the ends of the earth. . . . When you are on the mountaintop, I am with you; when you are in the abyss, I am there. For me it would be the greatest happiness to spend the whole night copying your papers for you, or watching over you to see that no one wakes you, or just walking with you for a hundred versts or so. I remember once, three years ago at threshing time, you came to our house all covered with dust, sunburnt, and tired out, asking for something to drink. When I brought it to you, there you were on the sofa, sleeping like a log. You slept the whole day in our house, and all that time I was standing outside the door, guarding it so that no one should come in. And how happy I was! The greater the labor, the greater the love, because then, you see, one feels it more strongly.

IVANOV: Active love . . . hm. . . . That's all fantasy, female philosophy, or . . . perhaps that is the way it ought to be. . . . [*Shrugs.*] God knows! [*Gaily*] Shura, on my word, I really am a decent fellow! . . . Judge for yourself: I've always had a weakness for philosophizing, but I've never in my life said: "Our women are corrupted," or "Women have taken the wrong path." I've merely been grateful, and nothing more! Nothing more! My dear, good little girl, how funny you are! And I— I'm just a ludicrous dolt! Day in and day out I go about upsetting decent people, playing Lazarus. [*Laughs.*] Boo-hoo! Boo-hoo! [*Quickly walks away from her.*] But go now, Shura. We've been forgetting ourselves. . . .

SASHA: Yes, it's time I went. Good-bye! I'm afraid your honest doctor, out of a sense of duty, may tell Anna Petrovna that I'm here. Now, listen to me: go to your wife at once and stay with her, stay by her side and don't leave her. . . . If you have to stay a year—then stay a year. If ten years—then stay ten years. Do your duty. Grieve, ask her forgiveness, and weep—all that is as it should be. But the main thing is not to forget your work.

IVANOV: Again I've got a sensation of having eaten a lot of toadstools. Again!

SASHA: Well, God keep you! You don't have to think about me at all! Just send me a line in a week or two— I'll be grateful for that. And I'll write you. . . .

[BORKIN *puts his head in at the door.*]

BORKIN: Nikolai Alekseyevich, may I? [*Seeing Sasha*] Sorry, I didn't even see you. . . . [*Comes in.*] *Bon jour!* [*Bows.*]

SASHA [*embarrassed*]: How do you do?

BORKIN: You've grown plumper, prettier.

SASHA [*to* IVANOV]: Well, I'll be going, Nikolai Alekseyevich. . . . I'm going. [*Goes out.*]

BORKIN: A vision of loveliness! I come on a prosaic matter, and I meet with poetry. . . . [*Sings.*] "You came to me as a bird to the light. . . ."

[IVANOV *paces up and down in agitation.*]

BORKIN [*sitting down*]: She's got something, *Nicolas,* something the others haven't got. Isn't that true? Something special . . . phantasmagorical. . . . [*Sighs.*] As a matter of fact, she's the richest match in the whole district, but Mama's such an old radish no one wants to tie up with her. When she dies, Shurochka will get everything, but until then she'll only give ten thousand, with the ironing board and iron, and expect you to fall on your knees in gratitude. [*Rummages through his pockets.*] Smoke a *De los majores.* Don't you want one? [*Offers his cigar case.*] They're good. . . . You can really smoke these.

IVANOV [*walks up to* BORKIN, *choking with rage*]: Get out of here, at once, and never let me see you in this house again! At once!

[BORKIN *half rises and drops his cigar.*]

IVANOV: Out of here, this instant!

BORKIN: *Nicolas,* what does this mean? Why are you so angry?

IVANOV: Why? Where did you get those cigars? And do you think I don't know where you take the old man every day, and why?

BORKIN [*shrugs his shoulders*]: But what difference does that make to you?

IVANOV: You are such a scoundrel! These infamous schemes you spawn all over the district are giving me a bad name! You and I have nothing in common, and I want you to get out of my house this instant! [*Rapidly paces the floor.*]

BORKIN: I know you're saying all this because you're irritated, so I'm not going to get angry with you. Insult me as much as you like. . . . [*Picks up his cigar.*] But it's high time you dropped the melancholy, you're not a schoolboy——

IVANOV: What did I tell you? [*Trembling*] Are you playing the fool with me?

[*Enter* ANNA PETROVNA.]

BORKIN: Well, here's Anna Petrovna. . . . I'll go. [*Goes out.*]

[IVANOV *stops by his desk and stands with his head down.*]

ANNA PETROVNA [*after a pause*]: Why did she come here just now? [*Pause*] I ask you: why did she come?

IVANOV: Don't ask, Anyuta. . . . [*Pause*] I am deeply guilty. Devise whatever punishment you like, I can stand anything, but don't ask me that. I cannot talk about it.

ANNA PETROVNA [*angrily*]: Why was she here? [*Pause*] Oh, so that's what you are! Now I understand you. At last I see the sort of man you are. Dishonest, base. . . . Remember how you came and lied to me, telling me you loved me. . . . I believed you, I left my father and mother, gave up my religion, and married you. . . . You lied to me about justice, about kindness, about your high-minded plans, and I believed every word——

IVANOV: Anyuta, I never lied to you.

ANNA PETROVNA: I've lived with you five years, I've been miserable and sick, but I've loved you, I never left you for a minute. . . . You have been my idol. And now? Now I know that all this time you have been deceiving me in the most brazen manner. . . .

IVANOV: Anyuta, don't say what isn't true. I made mistakes, yes, but never in my life did I lie to you. . . . You dare not reproach me with that.

ANNA PETROVNA: It's all clear to me now. You married me thinking that my parents would forgive me and give me money. . . . You thought that——

IVANOV: Oh, my God! Anyuta, you are trying my patience. . . . [*Weeps.*]

ANNA PETROVNA: Be quiet! When you saw that there would be no money, you started a new game. . . . Now I recall everything, now I understand. [*Weeps.*] You have never loved me, and you have never been faithful to me . . . never!

IVANOV: Sarah, that is a lie! . . . Say what you like, but don't insult me with lies!

ANNA PETROVNA: You are a base, dishonorable man. . . . You owe Lebedev money, and now, to get out of paying your debt, you're trying to turn his daughter's head and deceive her just as you've deceived me. Isn't that true?

IVANOV [*gasping*]: Be still, for God's sake! I can't answer for myself . . . my anger is choking me . . . I may say something that will wound you. . . .

ANNA PETROVNA: You always brazenly deceived me, and not me alone. . . . You blamed all your disgraceful actions on Borkin, but now I know whose——

IVANOV: Sarah! Be quiet and go, otherwise I shall say something I don't want to say! I can hardly keep myself from saying something horrible, insulting. . . . [*Shouts.*] Be silent, Jewess!

ANNA PETROVNA: I won't be silent. . . . You've deceived me too long for me to be silent now. . . .

IVANOV: So you won't be silent? [*Struggles with himself.*] For God's sake——

ANNA PETROVNA: Now go and deceive the Lebedev girl. . . .

IVANOV: You may as well know, then, that you . . . you are going to die soon. . . . The doctor told me that you would die soon. . . .

ANNA PETROVNA [*sits down, her voice failing her*]: When did he say that? [*Pause*]

IVANOV [*clutching his head*]: How guilty I am! God, how guilty I am! [*Sobs.*]

Act IV

[*About a year later. One of the drawing rooms in the Lebedev house. An arch separates the drawing room from the reception room; doors left and right; antique bronzes, family portraits, festive decorations. There is a piano, a violin on top of it, a cello beside it. During the entire act guests in evening dress come and go.*]

[*Enter* LVOV.]

LVOV [*looking at his watch*]: Five o'clock. I suppose the benediction is about to begin. . . . The benediction, then they'll be off to the wedding. There's a triumph of virtue and justice! He didn't succeed in robbing Sarah, so he tortured her to death and sent her to her grave; now he's found another one. He'll be a hypocrite with this one, too, till he's robbed her, then he'll put her right where poor Sarah is. The same old moneygrubbing story. . . . [*Pause*] He's in seventh heaven now, and he'll live to a ripe old age and die with a clear conscience. . . . No, I'm going to show you up! When I rip off that damned mask of yours and everyone finds out what sort of bird you are, you'll fall head first out of that seventh heaven and into such a pit that the devil himself won't be able to extricate you! I'm an honest man, and it's my duty to come forward and open their eyes. I'll do my duty, and tomorrow I'll get out of this abominable district! [*Growing thoughtful*] But what am I to do? Explain everything to Lebedev? A waste of breath. Challenge him to a duel? Create a scandal? My God, I'm as nervous as a schoolboy, and I've completely lost the ability to reason. What am I to do? Fight a duel?

[*Enter* KOSYKH.]

KOSYKH [*gleefully*]: Yesterday I declared a small slam in clubs, and then I made a grand slam. Only again that Barabanov ruined the whole thing for me. We're playing. I bid no trump. He passes. Two clubs. He passes. I bid two hearts . . . three clubs. . . . And imagine, would you believe it: I declare a slam, but he doesn't show his ace. If the idiot had only shown his ace, I could have made a grand slam in no trump. . . .

LVOV: Excuse me, I don't play cards, and I am therefore unable to share your delight. Will the benediction be soon?

KOSYKH: It should be soon. They're trying to bring Zyuzyushka around. She's howling like a jackal . . . upset about the dowry.

LVOV: But not about her daughter?

KOSYKH: The dowry. And she's bitter. Since he's marrying her daughter he's certainly not going to pay his debt. And you don't protest your own son-in-law's promissory note.

[*Enter* BABAKINA, *all decked out, and walks past* LVOV *and* KOSYKH *with an air of importance;* KOSYKH *bursts out laughing and covers his mouth with his hand.*]

BABAKINA [*glancing back at* KOSYKH]: How stupid!

[KOSYKH *touches her waist with one finger and guffaws.*]

BABAKINA: Peasant! [*Goes out.*]

KOSYKH [*roaring with laughter*]: The woman's absolutely balmy! Until she started thinking about being a countess, she was just a woman, like any other woman, but now you can't go near her. [*Mimics her.*] Peasant!

LVOV [*agitated*]:   Listen, tell me honestly, what is your opinion of Ivanov?

KOSYKH: He's no good. He plays cards like a shoe-maker. Last year, during Lent, do you know what happened? We sit down to a game: I, the Count, Borkin, and Ivanov. I deal——

LVOV [*interrupting*]:   Is he a good man?

KOSYKH: That one? A sharper! Knows all the tricks. He and the Count—two of a kind. They know how to sniff out the game. He hooked the Jewess, lost that trick, and now he's got his nose in Zyuzyushka's coffers. I'll bet you, and may I be thrice-damned if I'm wrong, that within one year he'll have made a beggar of her. He'll be the ruin of Zyuzyushka—and the Count of Babakina. They'll grab the money and live on the fat of the land, just piling it up. Doctor, why are you so pale today? You look awful.

LVOV: It's nothing, I'm all right. I drank too much yesterday.

[*Enter* LEBEDEV *and* SASHA.]

LEBEDEV: We can have a talk in here. [*To* LVOV *and* KOSYKH] Go on, you Zulus, go and join the young ladies in the reception room. We want to talk privately in here.

KOSYKH [*snaps his fingers in admiration as he passes* SASHA]:   What a picture! The queen of trumps!

LEBEDEV: Out you go, cave man, run along!

[LVOV *and* KOSYKH *go out.*]

LEBEDEV: Sit down, Shurochka, that's right. [*Sits down and glances back.*] Now, listen to me attentively and with proper respect. The fact is, your mother instructed me to tell you the following. . . . You understand, I'm not speaking for myself, but on orders from your mother.

SASHA: Papa, don't take so long!

LEBEDEV: Fifteen thousand silver rubles have been made over to you as a dowry. So . . . see that there's no further talk of that! Wait, don't say anything! That's only the blossom, the fruit comes later. Fifteen thousand has been made over to you as a dowry, but, now pay attention: since Nikolai Alekseyevich owes your mother nine thousand, a deduction is being made in your dowry. . . . Well then, besides that——

SASHA: Why are you telling me all this?

LEBEDEV: Your mother's orders!

SASHA: Leave me alone! If you had even the slightest respect for me, or for yourself, you wouldn't permit yourself to talk to me like this. I don't want your dowry. I haven't asked for anything, and I won't.

LEBEDEV: What are you jumping on me for? Gogol's two rats sniffed first and then ran away, but you, you emancipated woman, you don't even sniff before you jump on a person.

SASHA: Leave me alone, don't offend my ears with your petty calculations.

LEBEDEV [*losing his temper*]: Tfoo! Between you and your mother, I'll end by sticking a knife into myself, or cutting somebody's throat! One sets up a hullabaloo, picking and nagging, counting her kopecks day in and day out, and the other—so clever, so humane and emancipated, damn it—can't even understand her own father! I offend her ears! You know, before I came in here to offend your ears, [*points to the door*] out there, I was being drawn and quartered. . . . She can't understand! You've made my head spin, I'm all confused. . . . Well,

I've had enough! [*Goes to the door, then stops.*] I don't like it, I don't like anything about it.

SASHA: What is it you don't like?

LEBEDEV: The whole thing! Everything!

SASHA: What do you mean everything?

LEBEDEV: Am I supposed to sit down before you and make a report? I don't like anything, and I don't even want to see your wedding! [*Goes up to* SASHA *and speaks affectionately.*] Forgive me. Shurochka, maybe your marriage is wise, honest, noble, high-principled, but there's something wrong about it—wrong! It isn't like other marriages. You are young, fresh, clean as a windowpane, and beautiful, while he—he's a widower, he's knocked about, he's worn out. And I don't understand him, that's all. [*Kisses his daughter.*] Shurochka, forgive me, but there's something not quite clean about it. People are talking too much. First there was all that about Sarah dying, then for some reason, he suddenly took it into his head to marry you. . . . [*Quickly*] But I'm just an old woman, an old woman. I've been chattering away like an old crinoline. Don't listen to me. Don't listen to anybody but yourself.

SASHA: Papa, I myself feel that something is wrong . . . wrong, wrong, wrong! If you only knew how miserable I am. It's unbearable! I feel foolish, and afraid to admit it. Papa, darling, say something to encourage me, for God's sake, tell me what to do!

LEBEDEV: What? What's this?

SASHA: I am frightened, as I have never been before! [*Looks around.*] It seems to me that I don't understand him, that I will never understand him. The whole time I've been engaged to him, he has never once smiled, never once looked me straight in the eye. Nothing but perpetual complaining, repentance, hints at some sort of guilt, trembling . . . I'm tired of it. There are even moments when it seems to me that I . . . that I don't love him as much as I ought to. And when he comes here to see us or when he talks to me, I begin to feel bored. What does it all mean, Papa, dear? I'm frightened!

LEBEDEV: My darling, my only child, listen to your old father. Give him up!

SASHA [*shocked*]: What are you saying! What are you saying!

LEBEDEV: I mean it, Shurochka. There'll be a scandal, the tongues will wag throughout the whole district, but better to endure a scandal than to ruin your whole life.

SASHA: Don't say that, Papa, don't say it! I won't listen. One must resist these dark thoughts. He's a good, unhappy, misunderstood man; I will love him, understand him, put him on his feet again. I'm going to do my duty, that's settled!

LEBEDEV: That's not doing your duty, that's psychotic.

SASHA: Enough. I've confessed something to you that I didn't want to confess even to myself. Don't tell anyone. We'll forget it.

LEBEDEV: I don't understand anything. Either I have grown stupid in my old age, or you've all become very clever, but, damn it all, I don't understand anything.

[*Enter* SHABELSKY.]

SHABELSKY: The hell with everybody, including myself! It's revolting!

LEBEDEV: What do you want?

SHABELSKY: No, seriously, I am going to have to do something so outrageous, so low, that everyone will be disgusted, including myself. But I'm going to do it. On my word! I've already told Borkin to announce my nuptials. Everyone else is rotten, so I'll be rotten, too.

LEBEDEV: I'm fed up with you! Listen, Matvei, if you go on talking like this it's going to end in your being taken to the booby hatch, excuse the expression.

SHABELSKY: And in what way is the booby hatch worse than any other place? Do me a favor and take me there now. Do me that favor. Everybody is so low, so petty, insignificant, and dull . . . I'm even disgusting to myself, I don't believe one word I say. . . .

LEBEDEV: You know what, my friend? Put some hemp in your mouth, light it, and breathe fire at everyone. Or, better still, take your hat and go home. There's a wedding going on here, everyone's enjoying himself, and you caw-caw-caw, like a crow. Yes, I mean it. . . .

[SHABELSKY *leans on the piano and sobs.*]

LEBEDEV: Good heavens! . . . Matvei! . . . Count! . . . What's the matter with you? Matyusha, my dear friend . . . my angel. . . . Did I hurt you? Forgive me, old dog that I am. . . . Forgive an old drunkard. . . . Drink a little water. . . .

SHABELSKY: I don't want any.

LEBEDEV: Why are you crying?

SHABELSKY: It's nothing. . . .

LEBEDEV: No, Matyusha, don't lie . . . why? What's the reason?

SHABELSKY: I happened to glance at this cello just now and . . . and it made me think of the little Jewess. . . .

LEBEDEV: Listen to that! What a time to think of her! May the kingdom of heaven be hers, and eternal rest, but this is not the time to think of——

SHABELSKY: I used to play duets with her. . . . A wonderful, splendid woman!

[SASHA *sobs.*]

LEBEDEV: Now, what have you done? That's enough! Oh, Lord, both of them bawling, and I . . . I . . . At least, go somewhere else, the guests will see you!

SHABELSKY: Pasha, when the sun is shining, you can feel cheerful even in a cemetery. And when there's hope, you can be happy even in old age. But I haven't a single hope, not one!

LEBEDEV: Yes, you really are in a bad way. . . . No children, no money, no work. . . . But what can you do about it? [*To* SASHA] And what's the matter with you?

SHABELSKY: Pasha, let me have some money. We'll settle up in the next world. I'll go to Paris and have a look at my wife's grave. I've given away plenty in my lifetime, half my fortune, so I have a right to ask. Besides, I'm asking a friend. . . .

LEBEDEV [*embarrassed*]:   My dear fellow, I haven't a kopeck! However, all right, all right! That is, I don't promise, you understand. . . . Of course, of course! [*Aside*] They've worn me out!

[*Enter* BABAKINA.]

BABAKINA: Now where is my cavalier? Count, how dare you leave me alone? Oo-oo! You dreadful man! [*Raps him on the hand with her fan.*]

SHABELSKY [*with disgust*]: Leave me alone! I detest you!

BABAKINA [*struck dumb*]: What? . . . Why . . .

SHABELSKY: Get away from me!

BABAKINA [*falls into an armchair*]: Oh! [*Weeps.*]

[*Enter* ZINAIDA SAVISHNA, *weeping.*]

ZINAIDA SAVISHNA: Someone's just arrived. . . . The best man, I think. It's time for the benediction. . . . [*Sobs.*]

SASHA [*imploringly*]: Mama!

LEBEDEV: There, now, everyone's bawling! A quartet! That's enough. Turn off the waterworks! Matvei! . . . Marfa Yegorovna! . . . If you keep it up, I . . . I'll start crying, too. . . . [*Weeps.*] Oh, Lord!

ZINAIDA SAVISHNA: If you don't care about your mother, if you won't listen to me . . . then have it your own way . . . I'll give you my blessing.

[*Enter* IVANOV *wearing a dress coat and gloves.*]

LEBEDEV: This is the last straw! What is it?

SASHA: What are you here for?

IVANOV: Forgive me, ladies and gentlemen, permit me to have a word with Sasha alone.

LEBEDEV: This is quite out of order, to come and see the bride before the wedding! It's time you were going to the church!

IVANOV: Pasha, please. . . .

[LEBEDEV *shrugs his shoulders; he,* ZINAIDA SAVISHNA, *the Count and* BABAKINA *go out.*]

SASHA [*severely*]: What do you want?

IVANOV: I am choking with anger, but I'll speak coolly. Listen. Just now, as I was dressing for the wedding, I looked at myself in the mirror, and I saw . . . gray hair on my temples. Shura, I cannot! We must end this senseless comedy before it's too late. . . . You are young, pure, you have your whole life before you, while I——

SASHA: This is not new, I've heard it all a thousand times before, and I'm sick of it! Go to the church, and don't keep everyone waiting.

IVANOV: In just a moment I am going home, and you must tell them there will be no wedding. Explain it to them somehow. It's time we came to our senses. I was playing Hamlet, and you were the noble young woman— but now it's over.

SASHA [*flaring up*]: What sort of tone is that? I won't listen to you!

IVANOV: But I shall say what I have to say.

SASHA: What have you come for? Your whining has become a mockery.

IVANOV: No, I am not whining now. But mockery? Yes, I am mocking. And if I could mock myself a thousand times more violently and make the whole world laugh at me, I would! I saw myself in the mirror, and it was as if a bomb had exploded in my conscience! I began to laugh at myself and nearly went out of my mind with shame. [*Laughs.*] Melancholia! Noble sorrow! Unaccountable anguish! All that's lacking is that I should write poetry. Whining, playing Lazarus, boring everyone to death . . . and then to realize that the vital force of life has been lost forever, that I have grown cankerous, outlived my time, that I've given way to cowardice and am sunk up to my ears in this loathsome melancholy; to realize that when the sun is brightly shining, when even the ants are carrying their burdens and are satisfied with themselves—no thank you! To see some people take you for a charlatan, some pity you, some extend a helping hand, while others—and this is the worst of all—listen in awe to your sighing and look at you as though you were a second Mohammed about to reveal a new religion to them. . . . No, thank God, I still have some pride and conscience! On my way here, I was laughing at myself, and it seemed to me that the birds were laughing at me, that the trees were laughing. . . .

SASHA: This is not anger, it's madness!

IVANOV: Do you think so? No, I'm not mad. Now I see things in their true light, and my mind is as clear as your conscience. We love each other, but our wedding will not take place! I can rave and fume as much as I please, but I have no right to destroy others. I poisoned my wife's last year with my whining. Since you have been my fiancée, you have forgotten how to laugh, and you've grown five years older. And your father, to whom everything in life used to be quite clear, no longer understands people, thanks to me. Wherever I go—whether to a meeting, or hunting, or visiting someone, I bring boredom, despondency, dissatisfaction. Wait, don't interrupt me! I'm being harsh and brutal, but forgive me, my fury is choking me and I cannot speak otherwise. I have never lied about life nor spoken ill of it, but having developed into a grumbler I now disparage life, revile fate, and complain without meaning to, without even being aware of it, and anyone listening to me is infected with my disgust for life and begins to curse it, too. What an attitude! As if I were doing nature a favor by living. Oh, what hell——

SASHA: Stop, now. . . . From all you have been saying it's clear that you're fed up with whining, and it's time to begin a new life! . . . That's splendid!

IVANOV: I see nothing splendid in it. And what sort of new life? I am irretrievably destroyed. It's time we both realized that. A new life!

SASHA: Nikolai, come to your senses! Where is the evidence that you are destroyed? What kind of cynicism is this? No, I don't want to talk or listen. . . . Go to the church!

IVANOV: Destroyed!

SASHA: Don't shout like that, the guests will hear you!

IVANOV: If an intelligent, educated, healthy man starts playing Lazarus and, without any apparent reason, starts going downhill, he'll continue to go down without stopping, and there is no salvation for him! Well, where is my salvation? Where? I can't drink—it gives me a headache; I can't write bad poetry; and to make oblations to my spiritual inertia, and regard it as something elevated—I cannot. Inertia is inertia, weakness is weakness—I have no other names for them. I am ruined, ruined—there can be no argument about it! [*Glances around.*] We may be interrupted. Listen. If you love me, you must help me. Now, this very minute, you must give me up! Quickly——

SASHA: Oh, Nikolai, if you knew how tired you make me! You have worn me out. You are a good intelligent man—think: is it right to give me such problems? There's not a day without some problem—one more difficult than the other. . . . I wanted an active love, but this is a martyred love!

IVANOV: And when you become my wife, the problems will be still more complex. So give me up! Try to understand: you are prompted, not by love, but by the stubbornness of your honest nature. You set yourself the goal of resurrecting the man in me, of saving me, come what may, and it flattered you to feel you were accomplishing a great feat. Now you are ready to give up, but a false emotion prevents you. Try to understand!

SASHA: What a strange, fantastic logic. And can I give you up? How can I? You have no mother, no sister, no friends. . . . You are ruined, you've been robbed of your estate, you are being slandered on all sides. . . .

IVANOV: It was stupid of me to come here, I ought to have done what I intended. . . .

[*Enter* LEBEDEV.]

SASHA [*runs to meet her father*]: Papa, for God's sake—he's burst in here like a lunatic and he's torturing me! He insists that I give him up, he doesn't want to ruin my life. Tell him I don't want his magnanimity! I know what I'm doing!

LEBEDEV: I don't understand anything. . . . What magnanimity?

IVANOV: There will be no wedding.

SASHA: There will be! Papa, tell him there will be a wedding!

LEBEDEV: Wait, wait! . . . Why don't you want the wedding to take place?

IVANOV: I have explained to her why, but she refuses to understand.

LEBEDEV: Don't explain it to her, explain it to me, but so I can understand it. Oh, Nikolai Alekseyevich! May God be your judge! You have so befogged our lives that I feel as if I were living in a wax museum. I look, and I don't understand anything. It's sheer misery. Well, what do you expect an old man to do about it? Shall I challenge you to a duel?

IVANOV: There's no need for a duel. All that's needed is for you to have a head on your shoulders and to understand plain language.

SASHA [*paces the stage in agitation*]: This is awful, awful! He's just like a child!

LEBEDEV: There's nothing left but to throw up your hands. Listen to me, Nikolai. You think all this is intelligent, perceptive, and according to the rules of psychology, but in my opinion it's a disaster and a scandal. Now, for the last time, hear an old man out! This is what I want to tell you: try to calm yourself! Look at things simply, the way other people do. Everything is simple in this world. Ceilings are white, boots are black, sugar is sweet. You love Sasha, she loves you. If you love her—stay; if you don't—go, we'll bear you no grudge. It's as simple as that! You're both healthy, intelligent, right-minded people, and, thank God, you're well-fed and well-clothed. What more do you want? You've no money? That's of no importance! Happiness doesn't depend on money. . . . Of course, I understand . . . your estate is mortgaged, you haven't the money to pay the interest, but I—I'm her father, and I understand. Let her mother do as she likes, and God be with her, if she won't give you any money, she needn't. Shura says she doesn't want the dowry. Principles . . . Schopenhauer . . . that's all nonsense. . . . I've got ten thousand put away in the bank. [*Looks around.*] Not a soul in the house knows about it . . . it was Granny's. That will be for you both. Take it, but on one condition, that you give Matvei a thousand or two. . . .

[*The guests begin to assemble in the reception room.*]

IVANOV: Pasha, this talk is futile. I am acting according to the dictates of my conscience.

SASHA: And I am acting according to the dictates of my conscience. Say what you like, I am not going to give you up. I'll go and call Mama. [*Goes out.*]

LEBEDEV: I don't understand anything.

IVANOV: Listen, my poor fellow. . . . I'm not going to explain to you what I am—honest or base, healthy or psychopathic, I couldn't make you understand. I used to be young, ardent, sincere, intelligent: I loved, hated, and believed differently from other people; I did the work of ten men, and had the hopes of ten men, too; I tilted at windmills, beat my head against a wall; and without judging my strength, without reasoning, and with no knowledge of life, I took up a burden which promptly strained my muscles and broke my back; I lost no time in expending myself in my youth. I was overwrought, drank, worked, did everything without moderation. And tell me, could I have done otherwise? There are so few of us, you see, and so much work to be done! God, how much! And now, how cruelly life, the life I struggled with, is avenging itself on me! I'm used up! At thirty I already had a hangover from life, I'm old, I've put on my dressing gown. With a heavy head, an indolent soul, exhausted, depleted, broken, without faith, without love, without aim, drifting like a shadow among people, I don't know who I am, why I live, or what I want. And it now seems to me that love is senseless, endearments cloying, that work is meaningless, that song and impassioned speeches are trivial and stale. Wherever I go, I bring misery, cold indifference, discontent, and a disgust with life. . . . I am irretrievably ruined! Before you stands a man of thirty-five, already worn out, disillusioned, crushed by his own petty exploits; he burns with shame, mocks at his own weakness. . . . Oh, how my pride rebels in me, I am suffocating with fury! [*Reeling*] Oh, I'm done for. I can't even stand up . . . I have grown so weak. Where is Matvei? Have him take me home.

[*Voices in the reception room: "The best man has arrived!" Enter* SHABELSKY.]

SHABELSKY: Here I am wearing someone else's shabby dress coat . . . without gloves . . . and so they do nothing but sneer, smile insipidly, and make their stupid jokes. . . . Disgusting little people!

[*Enter* BORKIN; *he bursts in, wearing a dress coat with the best man's flower in his buttonhole.*]

BORKIN: Ugh! Now where is he? [*To* IVANOV] They've been waiting for you at the church all this time, and here you are holding a philosophical discussion. What a comedian! You really are a comedian! You know, you aren't supposed to go to the church with the bride, but with me, and then I have to come back to fetch her. Is it possible that you don't know that? You are positively a comedian!

[*Enter* LVOV.]

LVOV [*to* IVANOV]: Oh, you're here! [*In a loud voice*] Nikolai Alekseyevich Ivanov, I wish to state publicly that you are a scoundrel!

IVANOV: I humbly thank you.

[*General embarrassment.*]

BORKIN [*to* LVOV]: Sir, this is contemptible! I challenge you to a duel!

LVOV: Mr. Borkin, I consider it degrading even to speak to you, much less to fight you! As for Mr. Ivanov, he can have satisfaction whenever he wishes.

SHABELSKY: My dear sir, I'll fight you!

SASHA [*to* LVOV]: Why have you done this? Why have you insulted him? Gentlemen, please make him tell me why.

LVOV: Aleksandra Pavlovna, I did not insult him without reason. I came here, as an honest man, in order to open your eyes, and I beg you to hear me out.

SASHA: What can you say? That you're an honest man? The whole world knows it! Rather tell me, in all fairness, whether or not you understand yourself! You came in here just now, like an honest man, and hurled a dreadful insult at him, which nearly killed me; before that, when you were pursuing him like a shadow and interfering with his life, you were convinced that you were fulfilling your duty, that you were an honest man. You meddled with his personal life, slandered and criticized him, whenever possible bombarded me and all his friends with anonymous letters, always thinking you were an honest man. You even thought it was honest—you, a doctor—not to spare his sick wife, and gave her no peace with your suspicions. And no matter what acts of violence or cruelty or meanness you may commit, you'll still think of yourself as an extraordinarily honest and progressive man.

IVANOV [*laughs*]:   This isn't a wedding, it's a parliament! Bravo, bravo. . . .

SASHA [*to* LVOV]:   Now, just think about it: do you understand yourself, or don't you? Obtuse, heartless people! [*Takes* IVANOV's *hand.*] Let's go away from here, Nikolai! Father, let us go!

IVANOV: Where are we to go? Wait, I'll put an end to all this! Youth has awakened in me, the old Ivanov is speaking now! [*Takes out a revolver.*]

SASHA [*screams*]:   I know what he's going to do! Nikolai, for God's sake!

IVANOV: I've been going downhill long enough—now I'll stop! There's a limit to everything! Stand aside! Thank you, Sasha!

SASHA [*shrieks*]:   Nikolai, for God's sake! Stop him!

IVANOV: Leave me alone! [*Runs aside and shoots himself.*]

1887

The Sea Gull

A Comedy in Four Acts

Characters in the Play

ARKADINA, IRINA NIKOLAYEVNA, (Madame Trepleva), an actress

TREPLEV, KONSTANTIN GAVRILOVICH, her son, a young man

SORIN, PYOTR NIKOLAYEVICH, her brother

ZARECHNAYA, NINA MIKHAILOVNA, a young girl, the daughter of a wealthy landowner

SHAMRAYEV, ILYA AFANASYEVICH, a retired lieutenant, Sorin's steward

POLINA ANDREYEVNA, his wife

MASHA, his daughter

TRIGORIN, BORIS ALEKSEYEVICH, a writer

DORN, YEVGENY SERGEYEVICH, a doctor

MEDVEDENKO, SEMYON SEMYONOVICH, a schoolmaster

YAKOV, a workman

A COOK (male)

A HOUSEMAID

The action takes place on Sorin's estate.

Between the third and fourth acts there is an interval of two years.

Act I

[*A section of the park on* SORIN's *estate. A wide avenue, leading away from the spectators into the depths of the park toward a lake, is obstructed by a stage hurriedly put together for amateur theatricals, so that the lake is not visible. There are bushes left and right of the stage. A few chairs, a small table. The sun has just set.*

YAKOV *and other workmen are on the stage behind the curtain; sounds of coughing and hammering are heard.* MASHA *and* MEDVEDENKO *enter from the left, returning from a walk.*]

MEDVEDENKO: Why do you always wear black?

MASHA: I am in mourning for my life. I am unhappy.

MEDVEDENKO: Why? [*Pondering*] I don't understand. . . . You are in good health, and your father, though not rich, is well off. My life is much harder than yours. I get only twenty-three rubles a month, and out of that they take something for the pension fund, but I don't wear mourning.

[*They sit down.*]

MASHA: It isn't a question of money. Even a beggar can be happy.

89

MEDVEDENKO: Yes, in theory, but in practice it's like this: there's me, my mother, my two sisters, and a little brother—on a salary of only twenty-three rubles. People have to eat and drink, don't they? And they need tea and sugar? And tobacco? It's not easy to make ends meet.

MASHA [*glancing toward the stage*]: The performance will begin soon.

MEDVEDENKO: Yes. Nina Zarechnaya is going to act, and the play was written by Konstantin Gavrilovich. They are in love with each other, and today their souls will be merged in the desire to create a single artistic image. But your soul and mine have no common point of contact. I love you, I'm so miserable I can't stay at home, every day I walk six versts here and six versts back, but I get nothing but indifference from you. It's quite understandable. I am without means, I have a large family. . . . Who wants to marry a man who hasn't even got enough to eat?

MASHA: Nonsense. [*Takes a pinch of snuff.*] Your love touches me, but I can't return it, that's all. [*Holding out the snuff box to him*] Have some.

MEDVEDENKO: I don't feel like it. [*Pause*]

MASHA: It's sultry; there'll probably be a thunderstorm tonight. You are always philosophizing or talking about money. You think there's no greater misfortune than poverty, but in my opinion, it's a thousand times easier to be a beggar and wear rags than . . . however, that's something you wouldn't understand. . . .

[SORIN *and* TREPLEV *enter from the right.*]

SORIN [*leaning on a cane*]: For some reason, my boy, I'm not quite myself in the country, and, it stands to reason, I'll never get accustomed to it. I went to bed at ten o'clock last night and woke up at nine this morning feeling as though my brain were stuck to my skull from sleeping so long, and all that sort of thing. [*Laughs.*]

And after dinner I accidentally fell asleep again, and now I'm a complete wreck. I feel as if I were in a nightmare, and . . . so forth and so on. . . .

TREPLEV: You're right, Uncle, you really ought to live in town. [*Catching sight of* MASHA *and* MEDVEDENKO] Look, my friends, when the play begins, we'll call you, but you can't stay here now. I'll have to ask you to go.

SORIN [*to* MASHA]: Maria Ilyinichna, be so good as to ask your papa to have the dog let off its chain, otherwise it howls. My sister was kept awake again the whole night.

MASHA: You'll have to speak to my father yourself. I won't do it, so please don't ask me. [*To* MEDVEDENKO] Let's go!

MEDVEDENKO [*to* TREPLEV]: Then you will let us know before it begins.

[MASHA *and* MEDVEDENKO *go out.*]

SORIN: That means the dog will howl all night again. The trouble is, I've never lived as I wanted to in the country. I used to take a month's leave and come here to rest and all, but as soon as I got here they began to pester me so with all sorts of nonsense that by the next day I was ready to leave. [*Laughs.*] It was always a pleasure to go. . . . Well, now I'm retired, and I have no place to go, and all that. Like it or not, you've got to live. . . .

YAKOV [*to* TREPLEV]: We're going for a swim, Konstantin Gavrilovich.

TREPLEV: Very well, only be in your places in ten minutes. [*Looks at his watch.*] We're going to begin soon.

YAKOV: Yes, sir. [*Goes out.*]

TREPLEV [*looking over the stage*]: There's a theater for you. A curtain, two wings, and beyond that—open space. No scenery at all. There's a clear view to the lake and the horizon. We'll raise the curtain at half past eight, as the moon is rising.

SORIN: Magnificent.

TREPLEV: If Nina is late, then, of course, the whole effect will be spoiled. It's time she was here. Her father and stepmother keep such a close watch over her that it's as hard for her to get out of the house as a prison. [*Straightens his uncle's necktie.*] Your hair and beard are untidy. Maybe you ought to have them trimmed. . . .

SORIN [*combing his beard*]: The tragedy of my life. Even when I was young I used to look as if I had been drinking for days, and all that. The ladies never loved me. [*Sitting down*] Why is my sister in such a bad mood?

TREPLEV: Why? She's bored. [*Sits down beside him.*] And jealous. She's set against me, against the performance, and against my play, because Nina—and not she—is acting in it. She hasn't even read the play, but she already hates it.

SORIN [*laughing*]: You just imagine that, really. . . .

TREPLEV: It actually annoys her that here, on this tiny stage, it will be Nina, and not she, who's a success. [*Looking at his watch*] A psychological curiosity—my mother. Unquestionably talented, intelligent, she can sob over a book, reel off the whole of Nekrasov by heart, nurse the sick like an angel; but just try praising Duse in her presence! Oh, ho! You must praise no one but her; you must write about her, rave about her, go into ecstasies over her acting in *La Dame aux Camélias* or *The Fumes of Life;* but here in the country, where she can't get these opiates, she's bored, bad-tempered, and we are all her enemies, we're all to blame. And she's superstitious—she's afraid of three candles and the number thirteen. And stingy. She has seventy thousand rubles in the bank in Odessa—I know this for a fact—but ask her for a loan and she'll burst into tears.

SORIN: You've got it into your head that your mother doesn't like your play, and now you're upset and all that. Don't worry, your mother adores you.

TREPLEV [*pulling the petals off a flower*]: She loves me—she loves me not; she loves me—she loves me not; she loves me—she loves me not. [*Laughs.*] You see, my mother doesn't love me. Of course not! She wants to live, to love, to wear bright dresses, and here I am, twenty-five years old, a constant reminder that she is no longer young. When I'm not there, she's only thirty-two, but when I am, she's forty-three—and for that she hates me. Besides, she knows I don't accept the theater. She loves the theater, she thinks she is serving humanity and the sacred cause of art, while in my opinion, the theater of today is hidebound and conventional. When the curtain goes up, and, in a room with three walls and artificial light, those great geniuses, those priests of holy art, show me how people eat, drink, love, walk about, and wear their jackets; when from those banal scenes and phrases they try to fish out a moral—some little moral that is easily grasped and suitable for domestic use; when, in a thousand variations, I am served the same thing over and over and over again—then I flee, as Maupassant fled from the Eiffel Tower, which made his brain reel with its vulgarity.

SORIN: We can't do without the theater.

TREPLEV: We need new forms. New forms are needed, and if we can't have them, then we had better have nothing at all. [*Looks at his watch.*] I love my mother, love her very much; but she leads a senseless life, always fussing over that writer of hers, her name constantly bandied about in the papers—I find all that very tiresome. Sometimes the simple egoism of an ordinary mortal makes me regret that I have a mother who's a famous actress, and it seems to me that if she had been an ordinary woman I should have been happier. Uncle, what could be more hopeless and absurd than my position: she's always been surrounded by celebrities—actors, authors—and among them all, I alone was nothing; they tolerated me only because I was her son. Who am I? What am I? I left the university in my third year, because of circumstances, as they say, over which the editors have no control; I have no special talent, no money of my own, and, according to my passport, I am—just a Kiev petty bourgeois. My father, you see, was a petty bourgeois from Kiev, though he was also a well-known actor. So whenever those actors and writers who frequented her drawing room would bestow their gracious attentions on me, I felt their eyes were measuring my insignificance—I could guess their thoughts and I suffered from humiliation.

SORIN: By the way, what sort of man is this writer? I can't make him out. He never opens his mouth.

TREPLEV: He's an intelligent man, simple, and rather melancholy, it seems. Very decent. He's well under forty, and already famous and extremely well off. . . . As for his writing . . . well . . . what shall I say? Charming, shows talent, but . . . after Tolstoy or Zola, you don't feel much like reading Trigorin.

SORIN: But I love writers, my boy. There was a time when I passionately wanted two things: I wanted to get married, and I wanted to become a writer; but I didn't succeed in doing either. Yes . . . even to be a minor writer must be pleasant, and all that sort of thing.

TREPLEV [*listens*]: I hear footsteps. [*Embraces his uncle.*] I can't live without her. . . . Even the sound of her footsteps is beautiful. . . . I am insanely happy! [*Quickly goes to meet* NINA ZARECHNAYA *as she enters.*] My enchantress—my dream!

NINA: I'm not late . . . surely I'm not late . . .

TREPLEV [*kissing her hands*]: No, no, no. . . .

NINA: I've been worried all day, and so frightened! I was afraid Father wouldn't let me come . . . but he just went out with my stepmother. The sky turned red, the moon was beginning to rise, and I kept urging and urging the horse on. . . . [*Laughs.*] But now I'm happy. [*Warmly shakes* SORIN's *hand.*]

SORIN [*laughs*]: Those little eyes look as if they had been shedding tears. . . . Ah-ah! That's not right!

NINA: It's nothing. . . . You see how out of breath I am. I'll have to go in half an hour, we must hurry. I can't stay, I really can't, so don't, for Heaven's sake, detain me. My father doesn't know I'm here.

TREPLEV: It's time to begin, anyhow. I'll go and call the others.

SORIN: I'll go, and all that. I'll go at once. [*Starts off right singing "The Two Grenadiers" then stops.*] Once I began singing like that and the Assistant Prosecutor said to me: "You have a strong voice, Your Excellency." Then he thought a moment and added: "Strong, but revolting."

NINA: My father and his wife won't let me come here. They say it's Bohemian . . . they're afraid I might go on the stage. . . . But I am drawn here to this lake, like a sea gull. . . . My heart is full of you. [*Glances back.*]

TREPLEV: We are alone.

NINA: I think someone is there . . .

TREPLEV: There's no one. . . . [*Kisses her.*]

NINA: What kind of tree is that?

TREPLEV: An elm.

NINA: Why is it so dark?

TREPLEV: Because it's evening, and everything looks darker. Don't go early, please don't.

NINA: I must.

TREPLEV: And if I come to you, Nina? I'll stand all night in the garden, gazing at your window.

NINA: No, you mustn't, the watchman would see you. And Trésor isn't used to you, he would bark.

TREPLEV: I love you.

NINA: Sh-sh!

TREPLEV [*hearing footsteps*]: Who's there? Is that you, Yakov?

YAKOV [*behind the stage*]: Yes, sir.

TREPLEV: Take your places. It's time to begin. The moon is rising, isn't it?

YAKOV: Yes, sir.

TREPLEV: Have you got the methylated spirit? Is the sulfur there? When the red eyes appear, there's got to be a smell of sulfur. [*To* NINA] You'd better go now, everything's ready. Are you nervous?

NINA: Yes, very. It's not so much your mother . . . I'm not afraid of her, but there's Trigorin. . . . I feel ashamed and terrified to act before him. . . . A famous author . . . Is he young?

TREPLEV: Yes.

NINA: What wonderful stories he writes!

TREPLEV [*coldly*]: I don't know, I don't read them.

NINA: It's difficult to act in your play. There are no living characters in it.

TREPLEV: Living characters! One must portray life not as it is, and not as it ought to be, but as it appears in our dreams.

NINA: There's not very much action in the play, only reciting. And I do think a play ought to have love in it. . . .

[*They go behind the stage. Enter* POLINA ANDREYEVNA *and* DORN.]

POLINA ANDREYEVNA: It's getting damp. Go back and put on your galoshes.

DORN: I'm hot.

POLINA ANDREYEVNA: You don't take care of yourself. It's just stubbornness. You're a doctor, and you know perfectly well the damp air is bad for you, but you love making me miserable; you sat out on the veranda all last evening on purpose. . . .

DORN [*softly singing*]: "Never say that youth is wasted . . ."

POLINA ANDREYEVNA: You were so fascinated by your conversation with Irina Nikolayevna . . . you didn't even notice the cold. You may as well confess, you find her attractive. . . .

DORN: I am fifty-five years old.

POLINA ANDREYEVNA: Fiddlesticks! For a man that's not old. You're very well preserved, and you're still attractive to women!

DORN: Well, what do you want me to do about it?

POLINA ANDREYEVNA: You are all ready to fall on your knees before an actress. Every one of you!

DORN [*singing*]:   "Again I stand before you . . ." If society loves artists and treats them differently from . . . merchants, let us say, that is in the nature of things. That's—idealism.

POLINA ANDREYEVNA: Women have always fallen in love with you and hung on your neck. Was that also idealism?

DORN [*shrugging his shoulders*]:   Well . . . there was always a great deal that was fine in their relations to me. What they chiefly loved in me was an excellent physician. Ten or fifteen years ago, you remember, I was the only decent obstetrician in the whole province. And then, I've always been honest.

POLINA ANDREYEVNA [*clasping his hand*]:   My darling!

DORN: Hush—they're coming.

[*Enter* ARKADINA *on* SORIN'S *arm*, TRIGORIN, SHAMRAYEV, MEDVEDENKO, *and* MASHA.]

SHAMRAYEV: In 1873, at the Poltava Fair, she played astoundingly! Sheer delight! Marvelous acting! Would you happen to know where Chadin—the comedian Pavel Semyonovich Chadin—is at present? His Rasplyuev was inimitable, better than Sadovsky's, I assure you, most esteemed lady. Where is he now?

ARKADINA: You keep asking me about antedeluvians. How should I know? [*Sits down.*]

SHAMRAYEV [*sighing*]: Pashka Chadin! Nobody like that now. The theater has declined, Irina Nikolayevna! In the old days there were mighty oaks, but now we see nothing but stumps.

DORN: There are fewer brilliant talents today, that's true, but the general level is much higher.

SHAMRAYEV: I can't agree with you. However, it's a matter of taste. *De gustibus aut bene, aut nihil.*

[TREPLEV *comes out from behind the stage.*]

ARKADINA: My dear son, when is it going to begin?

TREPLEV: In a moment. Please have patience.

ARKADINA: My son! [*reciting from* Hamlet]
  "Thou turn'st mine eyes into my very soul;
  And there I see such black and grainèd spots
  As will not leave their tinct."

TREPLEV [*paraphrasing* Hamlet]: Nay, but to live
      In wickedness, to seek love
      In the depths of sin . . .

[*A horn is sounded behind the stage.*]

TREPLEV: Ladies and gentlemen, we are about to begin! Attention, please! [*Pause*] I shall begin. [*Taps with a stick and recites in a loud voice.*] Oh, you ancient, venerable shades, that float above this lake by night, darken our eyes with sleep, and bring us dreams of what will be two hundred thousand years from now!

SORIN: There'll be nothing two hundred thousand years from now.

TREPLEV: Then let them portray that nothing to us.

ARKADINA: Let them. We are asleep.

[*The curtain rises, revealing a view of the lake; the moon, above the horizon, is reflected in the water;* NINA, *all in white, is seated on a large rock.*]

NINA: Men, lions, eagles, and partridges, horned deer, geese, spiders, silent fish that dwell in the deep, starfish, and creatures invisible to the eye—these and all living things, all, all living things, having completed their sad cycle, are no more. . . . For thousands of years the earth has borne no living creature. And now in vain this poor moon lights her lamp. Cranes no longer wake and cry in meadows, May beetles are heard no more in linden groves. Cold, cold, cold. Empty, empty, empty. Awful, awful, awful. [*Pause*] The bodies of all living creatures having turned to dust, eternal matter has transformed them into stones, water, clouds, and all their souls have merged into one. That great world soul—is I . . . I. . . . In me are the souls of Alexander, of Caesar, Shakespeare, and Napoleon, and of the lowest worm. In me the consciousness of man is merged with the instincts of animals, and I remember all, all, all, and in me each several life is lived anew.

[*Will-o'-the-wisps appear.*]

ARKADINA [*in a low voice*]: There's something decadent about this.

TREPLEV [*reproachfully imploring her*]: Mother!

NINA: I am all alone. Once in a hundred years I open my mouth to speak, my voice echoes dolefully in this void, and no one hears it. . . . And you, pale lights, you do not hear me. . . . The stagnant marsh begets you before dawn, you drift till daybreak without thought, without will, without the throb of life. Fearing lest life should spring up in you, the devil, father of eternal matter, at every instant produces in you a continual interchange of atoms, as in stones and in water, and you are ceaselessly being changed. Within the universe, spirit alone remains constant and unaltered. [*Pause*] Like a prisoner cast into a deep and empty well, I know not where I am or what awaits me. One thing only is not hidden from me: in the cruel, persistent struggle with the devil, the principle of the forces of matter, I am destined to be victorious; then matter and spirit shall merge in glorious harmony, and the kingdom of universal will shall be at hand. But this will come only little by little, after a long, long succession of millennia, when the moon, bright Sirius, and the earth have turned to dust. . . . Until then . . . horror, horror . . . [*Pause; in the background two red spots appear over the lake.*] Behold, my powerful enemy, the devil, approaches. I see his awful, blood-red eyes. . . .

ARKADINA: There's a smell of sulfur. Is that necessary?

TREPLEV: Yes.

ARKADINA [*laughs*]: Oh, it's a stage effect!

TREPLEV: Mother!

NINA: He yearns for man . . .

POLINA ANDREYEVNA [*to* DORN]: You've taken off your hat. Put it on or you'll catch cold.

ARKADINA: The doctor has taken off his hat to the devil, the father of eternal matter.

TREPLEV [*flaring up, loudly*]: The play is over! That's enough! Curtain!

ARKADINA: Why are you angry?

TREPLEV: Enough! Curtain! Bring down the curtain! [*Stamping his foot*] Curtain! [*The curtain falls.*] You must forgive me. I overlooked the fact that only the chosen few can write plays and act in them. I have infringed on a monopoly! To me . . . I . . . [*Tries to continue, then, with a gesture of resignation, goes out left.*]

ARKADINA:　What's the matter with him?

SORIN:　Irina, my dear, you shouldn't wound a young man's pride like that.

ARKADINA:　But what have I said to him?

SORIN:　You've hurt his feelings.

ARKADINA:　He told us himself it was going to be a joke, so I treated it as a joke.

SORIN:　All the same . . .

ARKADINA:　Now it appears he has written a great work! Oh, really! Evidently he got up this performance and fumigated us with sulfur, not as a joke but as a demonstration. . . . He wanted to teach us how one ought to write, and what one ought to act in. After all, this is getting tiresome! These continual sallies at my expense, these gibes, if you please, would try anyone's patience! He's a conceited, capricious boy!

SORIN:　He meant to give you pleasure.

ARKADINA:　Yes? Then why didn't he choose the usual sort of play instead of forcing us to listen to these decadent ravings? I don't mind listening even to raving if it's a joke, but here we have pretensions to new forms, a new era in art. To my way of thinking this has nothing at all to do with new forms, it's simply bad temper.

TRIGORIN:　Everyone writes as he likes and as he can.

ARKADINA:　Let him write as he likes and as he can, so long as he leaves me in peace.

DORN: Jupiter, you grow angry——

ARKADINA: I'm not Jupiter, I'm a woman. [*Lights a cigarette.*] And I'm not angry, I'm merely annoyed that a young man should spend his time in such a tiresome way. I didn't mean to hurt his feelings.

MEDVEDENKO: Nobody has any grounds for separating spirit from matter, for it may be that this very spirit is an aggregation of material atoms. [*Eagerly, to* TRIGORIN] You know, someone ought to write a play describing how we teachers live, and put that on. It's a hard, hard life!

ARKADINA: You may be quite right, but let's not talk about plays or atoms. It's such a lovely evening! Do you hear them singing? [*Listens.*] How pleasant!

POLINA ANDREYEVNA: It's on the other side of the lake.

ARKADINA [*to* TRIGORIN]: Sit here beside me. Ten or fifteen years ago you could hear music and singing on this lake almost every night. There are six country houses here on the lake. I remember the laughter, the noise, the shooting . . . and the love affairs, always love affairs. . . . The *jeune premier* and idol of all six houses was our friend here—[*Nods toward* DORN.] I give you Dr. Yevgeny Sergeyevich. He's fascinating now, but he was irresistible then. . . . Oh, my conscience is beginning to torment me. Why did I hurt my poor boy's feelings? I'm so troubled. [*Loudly*] Kostya! Son! Kostya!

MASHA: I'll go and look for him.

ARKADINA: Please do, my dear.

MASHA [*going to the left*]: Aa-oo! Konstantin Gavrilovich! Aa-oo! [*Goes out.*]

[*Enter* NINA *from behind the stage.*]

NINA: Apparently we're not going on, so I may as well come out. Good evening! [*Kisses* ARKADINA *and* POLINA ANDREYEVNA.]

SORIN: Bravo! Bravo!

ARKADINA: Bravo! Bravo! We were enchanted! With your looks and that marvelous voice, you really cannot remain in the country—it's a sin! I wouldn't be surprised if you have talent. Do you hear? You simply must go on the stage!

NINA: Oh, that is my dream! [*Sighing*] But it will never come true.

ARKADINA: Who knows? But let me present Boris Alekseyevich Trigorin.

NINA: Oh, I'm so glad to . . . [*overcome with embarrassment*] I'm always reading your . . .

ARKADINA [*making her sit down beside them*]: Don't be embarrassed, dear. He's a celebrity, but he has a simple heart. You see, he's embarrassed himself.

DORN: I suppose we may raise the curtain now—it looks rather sinister as it is.

SHAMRAYEV: Yakov, my boy, pull up the curtain.

[*The curtain goes up.*]

NINA [*to* TRIGORIN]: It's a strange play, isn't it?

TRIGORIN: I didn't understand a word, but I enjoyed watching it. You acted with great sincerity. And the scenery was lovely. [*Pause*] I expect there are a lot of fish in that lake.

NINA: Yes.

TRIGORIN: I love to fish. For me there is no greater pleasure than to sit on the bank of a river toward evening watching a float.

NINA: But I should have thought that for anyone who had experienced the joy of creation, no other pleasure could exist.

ARKADINA [*laughing*]: You mustn't talk like that. When people make him pretty speeches, it simply floors him.

SHAMRAYEV: I recall one evening at the opera house in Moscow when the famous Silva took a low C. It so happened that the bass from our church choir was sitting in the gallery, and suddenly—you can imagine our utter amazement—we heard: "Bravo, Silva" from the gallery—but a whole octave lower! Like this: [*in a deep bass*] "Bravo, Silva!" . . . The audience was thunderstruck. [*Pause*]

DORN: The angel of silence has flown over us.

NINA: It's time for me to go. Good-bye.

ARKADINA: Where are you off to? Why so early? We won't let you go.

NINA: Papa is expecting me. . . .

ARKADINA: What a man, really . . . [*Kisses her.*] Well, it can't be helped. I'm so sorry, so sorry to let you go.

NINA: If you only knew how hard it is for me to go!

ARKADINA: Someone ought to see you home, little one.

NINA [*frightened*]: Oh, no, no!

SORIN [*entreating her*]: Do stay!

NINA: I can't, Pyotr Nikolayevich.

SORIN: Just stay for an hour, and all . . . Come, now, do. . . .

NINA [*after a moment's thought, through tears*]: I can't! [*Shakes hands and quickly goes.*]

ARKADINA: A most unfortunate girl, really. They say her mother left her father her entire, enormous fortune, everything, to the last kopeck, and now this girl has nothing; and the father has already made a will leaving it all to his second wife. It's shocking!

DORN: Yes, her papa is a pretty thorough swine, to give him his due.

SORIN [*rubbing his hands to warm them*]: Let us go, too, my friends, it's getting damp. My legs ache.

ARKADINA: It's just like having wooden legs, you can hardly walk. Well, come along, you poor old man. [*Takes his arm.*]

SHAMRAYEV [*offering his arm to his wife*]: Madam?

SORIN: I hear that dog howling again. [*To* SHAMRAYEV] Ilya Afanasyevich, be so good as to have them let it off the chain.

SHAMRAYEV: Can't be done, Pyotr Nikolayevich, I'm afraid of thieves breaking into the barn. I've got millet in there. [*To* MEDVEDENKO, *walking beside him*] Yes, a whole octave lower: "Bravo, Silva!" And not even a singer, mind you, just an ordinary church chorister.

MEDVEDENKO: What salary does a church chorister get?

[*All go out except* DORN.]

DORN [*alone*]: I don't know, perhaps I don't understand these things, or maybe I've gone off my head, but I like the play. There's something in it. When that girl talked of solitude, and afterward when the red eyes of the devil appeared, my hands trembled with excitement. It's fresh, ingenuous. . . . Here he comes, I believe. I'd like to say everything nice I possibly can to him. . . .

[*Enter* TREPLEV.]

TREPLEV: They've all gone.

DORN: I'm here.

TREPLEV: Masha's been hunting all over the park for me. Insufferable creature!

DORN: Konstantin Gavrilovich, I liked your play enormously. It's somewhat strange, and, of course, I haven't heard the end, but even so, it made a strong impression on me. You're a talented man, and you must go on.

[TREPLEV *warmly presses his hand, then impulsively embraces him.*]

DORN: Whew, what a nervous fellow! Tears in your eyes . . . Now, what did I want to say? You took a subject from the realm of abstract ideas. That's as it should be, because a work of art decidedly should express a great idea. Only what is serious can be beautiful. . . . How pale you are!

TREPLEV: So you're telling me—to keep at it?

DORN: Yes. . . . But write only of what is important and eternal. You know, I've lived a varied and discriminating life, I'm satisfied, but if it had ever been my lot to experience the exaltation that comes to artists in their moments of creation, I believe I should have despised this material shell of mine and all that pertains to it, and I'd have soared to the heights, leaving earthly things behind me.

TREPLEV:　Excuse me, where is Nina?

DORN:　And here's another thing. In a work of art there should be a clear, definite idea. You must know what you are writing for, otherwise, if you just move along some esthetic road without a definite aim, you'll be lost and your talent will destroy you.

TREPLEV [*impatiently*]:　Where is Nina?

DORN:　She went home.

TREPLEV [*in despair*]:　What shall I do? I want to see her. . . . I must see her. . . . I'm going . . .

[*Enter* MASHA.]

DORN [*to* TREPLEV]:　Calm yourself, my friend.

TREPLEV:　But all the same I am going. I must go.

MASHA:　Come into the house, Konstantin Gavrilovich. Your mother wants you. She's worried.

TREPLEV:　Tell her I've gone away. And please, all of you, leave me in peace! Leave me alone! Don't keep following me!

DORN:　Come, come, come, my boy . . . you mustn't . . . That's not right.

TREPLEV [*through tears*]:　Good-bye, Doctor. Thank you. . . . [*Goes out.*]

DORN [*sighing*]:　Youth, youth!

MASHA:　When there's nothing else to say, people always say: youth, youth . . . [*Takes a pinch of snuff.*]

DORN [*takes the snuff box from her and flings it into the bushes*]:　That's disgusting! [*Pause*] They seem to be playing there in the house. We'd better go in.

MASHA: Wait.

DORN: What is it?

MASHA: I want to tell you once more . . . I feel like talking . . . [*Agitated*] I don't love my father . . . but I am fond of you. For some reason I feel with all my heart that you are close to me. . . . Help me. Help me, or I'll do something stupid—I'll make a mockery of my life, ruin it. . . . I can't go on. . . .

DORN: What is it? Help you how?

MASHA: I am suffering. No one, no one knows what I am suffering! [*Lays her head on his breast, softly.*] I love Konstantin.

DORN: How nervous you all are! How nervous! And so much love! Oh, that bewitching lake! [*Tenderly*] But what can I do, my child? What? What?

Act II

[*A croquet lawn, flowerbeds. In the background on the right is the house with a large veranda; on the left, the lake, glimmering in the sunlight. It is midday and hot. At the side of the croquet lawn* ARKADINA, DORN, *and* MASHA *are sitting on a bench in the shade of an old linden tree.* DORN *has an open book on his lap.*]

ARKADINA [*to* MASHA]: Come, let's stand up. [*Both get up.*] Side by side. You are twenty-two and I am nearly twice that. Yevgeny Sergeyevich, which of us looks the younger?

DORN: You, of course.

ARKADINA: There you are! And why? Because I work, I feel, I am always on the go, while you stay in the same place all the time, you don't live. . . . And I make it a rule not to look into the future. I never think about old age or death. What is to be, will be.

MASHA: And I feel as if I had been born a long, long time ago; I drag my life behind me like an endless train. . . . Sometimes I haven't the slightest desire to go on living. [*Sits down.*] Of course, that's all nonsense. I ought to shake myself and throw it off.

DORN [*sings softly*]: "Tell her, pretty flowers . . ."

ARKADINA: Besides, I'm as correct as an Englishman. Yes, my dear, I keep myself in hand, as they say. I'm always dressed, and my hair is always *comme il faut.* Do you think I'd permit myself to go out of the house, even here into the garden, in a dressing gown or without my hair being done? Never. That's why I've kept young, because I was never dowdy, never let myself go as some women do. . . . [*Walks up and down the lawn, arms akimbo.*] You see—light as a bird. I could play a girl of fifteen.

DORN: Well, I may as well continue. [*Takes up his book.*] We left off at the corn merchants and the rats.

ARKADINA: Yes, the rats. Go on. [*Sits down.*] No, give it to me, I'll read. It's my turn, anyhow. [*She takes the book and looks for the place.*] And the rats . . . Here it is. . . . [*Reads.*] "And it goes without saying that for society people to pamper novelists and entice them into their own circle is as dangerous as for corn merchants to breed rats in their barns. And yet they are loved. Thus, when a woman has chosen a writer whom she wishes to capture, she lays siege to him by means of compliments, courtesies, and favors. . . ." Well, that may be true of the French, but with us there's nothing like that, we have no set rules. Here, if you please, a woman is generally head over heels in love herself before she sets out to capture a writer. To go no further, take Trigorin and me . . .

[*Enter* SORIN, *leaning on a cane, with* NINA *at his side.* MEDVEDENKO *pushes an empty wheelchair after them.*]

SORIN [*in the caressing tone one uses to a child*]: Yes? We're delighted, aren't we? And we're cheerful today, and all that sort of thing? [*To his sister*] We're delighted! Father and stepmother have gone off to Tver, and now we're free for three whole days.

NINA [*sits down beside* ARKADINA *and embraces her*]: I'm so happy! Now I belong to you.

SORIN [*sits in his wheelchair*]: She's looking very pretty today.

ARKADINA: And very smartly dressed, interesting. . . . There's a clever girl. [*Kisses her.*] But we mustn't praise her too much—it's bad luck. Where is Boris Alekseyevich?

NINA: He's down by the bathhouse, fishing.

ARKADINA: You'd think he'd get sick of it! [*About to go on reading*]

NINA: What is that?

ARKADINA: Maupassant's "On the Water," my dear. [*Reads a few lines to herself.*] Well, the rest is uninteresting and untrue. [*Closes book.*] I'm worried. Tell me, what is the matter with my son? Why is he so sad and so austere? He spends whole days by the lake, and I hardly ever see him.

MASHA: His heart is troubled. [*To* NINA, *timidly*] Please read something from his play.

NINA [*shrugs her shoulders*]: Do you really want me to? It's so uninteresting!

MASHA [*restraining her enthusiasm*]: When he reads anything himself, his eyes glow and his face turns pale. He has a beautiful, sad voice and the manner of a poet.

[SORIN *can be heard snoring.*]

DORN: Good night!

ARKADINA: Petrusha!

SORIN: Eh?

ARKADINA: Are you asleep?

SORIN: Not at all.

[*A pause*]

ARKADINA: You're not having any medical treatment, and that's not right, my dear.

SORIN: I'd be glad to, but the doctor here doesn't want me to.

DORN: Take medicine at sixty!

SORIN: Even at sixty one wants to live.

DORN [*with vexation*]: Ach! Well then, take valerian drops.

ARKADINA: I think it would do him good to take a cure at some mineral spring.

DORN: Well . . . it might. Or it might not.

ARKADINA: And how is one supposed to understand that?

DORN: There's nothing to understand. It's quite clear.

[*A pause*]

MEDVEDENKO: Pyotr Nikolayevich ought to give up smoking.

SORIN: Nonsense.

DORN: No, it's not nonsense. Wine and tobacco rob us of our personalities. After a cigar or a glass of vodka, you are no longer Pyotr Nikolayevich, but Pyotr Nikolayevich plus somebody else; your ego becomes diffused, and you begin to see yourself as a third person—as he.

SORIN [*laughs*]:   It's all very well for you to talk, you have lived your life, but what about me? I served in the Department of Justice for twenty-eight years, but I've never lived, never experienced anything, and so forth and so on, and it's natural that I should feel very much like living. You've had your fill and you don't care any more, so you're inclined to be philosophical, but I want to live, and that's why I drink sherry at dinner and smoke cigars, and all that sort of thing. And there you have it.

DORN: One must take life seriously, but to go in for cures at sixty and to regret that one has not sufficiently enjoyed one's youth is, if you will forgive me, frivolous.

MASHA [*getting up*]:   It must be time for lunch. [*Walking with an indolent, lagging gait*] My foot has gone to sleep. . . . [*Goes out.*]

DORN: Now she'll go and have a couple of glasses before lunch.

SORIN: She's not happy in her personal life, poor thing.

DORN: Ridiculous, Your Excellency!

SORIN: You argue like a man who's had his fill.

ARKADINA: Oh, what could be more boring than this sweet country boredom! It's hot, quiet, nobody does anything, everyone philosophizes. . . . It's good to be with you, my friends, pleasant to listen to you, but . . . to be sitting in a hotel room learning a part—how much better!

NINA [*ecstatically*]: Oh, yes! I understand you!

SORIN: Of course, it's better in town. You sit in your study, the footman lets no one in unannounced, there's a telephone . . . cabs in the streets, and all that sort of thing. . . .

DORN [*sings*]: "Tell her, pretty flowers . . ."

[*Enter* SHAMRAYEV, *followed by* POLINA ANDREYEVNA.]

SHAMRAYEV: Here they are! Good morning! [*Kisses* ARKADINA'*s hand, then* NINA'*s.*] Delighted to see you looking so well. [*To* ARKADINA] My wife tells me that you are planning on driving into town with her today. Is that right?

ARKADINA: Yes, we are planning on it.

SHAMRAYEV: Hm! That's splendid, but how do you intend to travel, most esteemed lady? We're carting the rye today, and all the men are busy. And what horses would you take, may I ask?

ARKADINA: What horses? How should I know what horses!

SORIN: We have carriage horses.

SHAMRAYEV [*growing excited*]: Carriage horses? And where am I to get the collars? Where am I to get the collars? It's amazing! Inconceivable! Most esteemed lady! Excuse me, I have the greatest reverence for your talent, I would give ten years of my life for you, but I cannot let you have the horses!

ARKADINA: And if I have to go? This is a strange state of affairs!

SHAMRAYEV: My dear lady, you don't realize what farming means!

ARKADINA [*flaring up*]: The same old story! In that case I'll leave for Moscow today. Order horses for me from the village, or I'll walk to the station!

SHAMRAYEV [*flaring up*]: In that case, I resign! Find yourself another steward! [*Goes out.*]

ARKADINA: Every summer it's like this, every summer they insult me here! I'll never set foot in this place again!

[*She goes off left in the direction of the bathhouse; a moment later she is seen going into the house, followed by* TRIGORIN *carrying fishing rods and a pail.*]

SORIN [*flaring up*]: This is insolence! It's beyond everything! I'm sick and tired of it . . . and so forth. Have all the horses brought around at once!

NINA [*to* POLINA ANDREYEVNA]: To refuse Irina Nikolayevna, the famous actress! Surely any wish of hers, even the least whim, is more important than your farming? It's simply unbelievable!

POLINA ANDREYEVNA [*in despair*]: What can I do? Put yourself in my position: what can I do?

SORIN [*to* NINA]: Let us go to my sister. . . . We'll all plead with her not to go. Shall we? [*Looking in the direction of* SHAMRAYEV'*s departure*] Insufferable man! Despot!

NINA [*preventing him from getting up*]: Sit still, sit still. . . . We'll wheel you in. . . . [*She and* MEDVEDENKO *push the wheelchair.*] Oh, how dreadful this is!

SORIN: Yes, yes, it is dreadful. . . . But he won't leave. I'll talk to him presently.

[*They go out.* DORN *and* POLINA ANDREYEVNA *are left alone.*]

DORN: People are tiresome. As a matter of fact, what they ought to do is simply to kick your husband out, but instead it will end in that old woman Pyotr Nikolayevich and his sister both begging the man's pardon. You'll see!

POLINA ANDREYEVNA: He's even put the carriage horses into the field. Every day there are these misunderstandings. If you only knew how it upsets me! It's making me ill; you see how I am trembling. I can't endure his coarseness. [*Entreating*] Yevgeny, my dearest, my beloved, let me come to you. Our time is passing, we're not young any more, if only—for the end of our lives, at least—we could stop hiding and lying . . .

DORN: I'm fifty-five; it's too late for me to change my life.

POLINA ANDREYEVNA: I know why you refuse me—because there are other women besides me who are close to you. You can't take them all to live with you. I understand. Forgive me, you are tired of me.

[NINA *appears near the house; she is picking flowers.*]

DORN: No, it's all right.

POLINA ANDREYEVNA: I am tormented by jealousy. Of course, you are a doctor, you can't escape women. I understand. . . .

DORN [*to* NINA, *who has joined them*]: How are things going in there?

NINA: Irina Nikolayevna is crying, and Pyotr Nikolayevich is having an attack of asthma.

DORN [*gets up*]: I'll go and give them both some valerian drops.

NINA [*handing him the flowers*]: For you!

DORN: *Merci bien.* [*Goes toward the house.*]

POLINA ANDREYEVNA [*going with him*]: What pretty flowers! [*Nearing the house, in a choked voice*] Give me those flowers! Give me those flowers!

[*He gives them to her, and she tears them to pieces and flings them away. They go into the house.*]

NINA: How strange to see a famous actress cry, and for such a trivial reason! And isn't it strange that a celebrated author, adored by the public, written about in all the papers, his photograph for sale, his works translated into foreign languages, should spend the whole day fishing, and be delighted that he has caught two chub? I thought that famous people were proud, unapproachable, that they despised the crowd, and that with the luster of their names, and all their glory, they somehow revenged themselves on the world for placing rank and wealth above everything. But here they are crying, fishing, playing cards, laughing, and losing their tempers just like everybody else. . . .

[*Enter* TREPLEV, *without a hat, carrying a gun and a dead sea gull.*]

TREPLEV: Are you alone here?

NINA: Alone. [TREPLEV *lays the sea gull at her feet.*] What does that mean?

TREPLEV: I was so low as to kill this sea gull today. I lay it at your feet.

NINA: What's the matter with you? [*Picks up the sea gull and looks at it.*]

TREPLEV [*after a pause*]: Soon, in the same way, I shall kill myself.

NINA: I hardly know you.

TREPLEV: Yes, ever since I began to feel that I no longer know you. You have changed toward me, your eyes are cold, I'm in your way.

NINA: You've become so irritable lately, and whenever you say anything I can't understand you, it's as if you were talking in symbols. This sea gull, I suppose, is another symbol, but, forgive me, I don't understand. . . . [*Lays the sea gull on the bench.*] I am too simple to understand you.

TREPLEV: This began the evening that my play failed so stupidly. Women never forgive failure. I've burned it all, everything, to the last scrap. If you only knew how unhappy I am! Your coldness is awful, unbelievable. . . . It's as if I had woken up and found that this lake had suddenly dried up or sunk into the earth. You said just now that you are too simple to understand me. Oh, what is there to understand? My play was not liked, you despise my inspiration, you already consider me mediocre, insignificant, like so many others. . . . [*Stamps his foot.*] How well I understand it, how well! I feel as if I had a spike in my brain, may it be damned along with my pride, which is sucking my blood, sucking it like a viper. . . . [*Seeing* TRIGORIN, *who enters reading a book.*] Here comes the real genius, walking like Hamlet—and with a book. [*Mimicking*] "Words, words, words . . ." This sun has hardly reached you, but already you are smiling, your glance is melting in its rays. I won't stand in your way. [*Quickly goes.*]

TRIGORIN [*making a note in his notebook*]: Takes snuff and drinks vodka . . . always in black. The schoolmaster in love with her . . .

NINA: Good morning, Boris Alekseyevich!

TRIGORIN: Good morning. Things have taken an unexpected turn, and it appears we are leaving today. It's not very likely that we shall meet again. I am sorry. I don't often meet young girls . . . youthful and interesting. I've forgotten how it feels to be eighteen or nineteen, I can't picture it very clearly, that's why the young girls in my novels and stories are generally false. I'd like to be in your shoes, if only for an hour, to find out how you think, and, in general, what a pretty young girl is like.

NINA: And I should like to be in your shoes.

TRIGORIN: Why?

NINA: To find out how it feels to be a famous, gifted writer. What does it feel like to be famous? How does it affect you?

TRIGORIN: How? Not at all, I expect. I've never thought about it. [*After a moment's thought*] One of two things: either you exaggerate my fame, or it's . . . just not something that one feels.

NINA: But if you read about yourself in the papers?

TRIGORIN: When they praise me, I'm pleased; when they abuse me, I'm in a bad mood for a couple of days.

NINA: A wonderful world! How I envy you, if you only knew! People's destinies are so different. Some can barely drag out their dull, obscure existences, all very much alike, and all miserable, while others, like you, for example—but you are one in a million—are given a life that is brilliant, interesting, full of meaning. . . . You are fortunate. . . .

TRIGORIN: I? [*Shrugging his shoulders*] Hm . . . You talk of fame, of happiness, of some sort of brilliant, interesting life, but to me all these fine words, if you will forgive me, are like sugar plums—which I never eat. You are very young and very kind.

NINA: Your life is beautiful!

TRIGORIN: What's so good about it? [*Looks at his watch.*] I must get to my writing directly. Excuse me, I haven't time to . . . [*Laughs.*] You've stepped on my pet corn, as they say, and here I am getting excited and rather cross. Well, then, let's talk. We'll talk about my beautiful, brilliant life. . . . Where shall we begin? [*After a moment's thought*] There are such things as fixed ideas, when a man keeps thinking day and night, about the moon, for instance. I have just such a moon. Day and night I am haunted by one thought: I must write, I must write, I must. . . . I have scarcely finished one novel when, for some reason, I have to write another, then a third, and after that a fourth. . . . I write incessantly, at a furious rate, I can't work any other way. What is brilliant and beautiful about that, I ask you? Oh, what a preposterous life! Here I am talking to you, I'm excited, yet not for a moment do I forget that my unfinished novel is waiting for me. I see that cloud, it looks like a grand piano. I think: must remember to put into a story somewhere that a cloud floats by looking like a grand piano. There's a scent of heliotrope. I quickly make a mental note: cloying smell, widow's color, use when describing a summer evening. I catch up every word and phrase we utter, and lock them in my literary storeroom—they may be useful. When I finish work, I hurry off to the theater or go fishing, and there's where I ought to rest and forget, but—no, a great, heavy cannon ball begins rolling around in my head—a new subject for a story; and once more I am pulled back to my desk and have to rush to start writing and writing again. And it's always like that, always; I have no rest from myself, and I feel that I am consuming my own life, that for the sake of the honey I give to someone in a void,

I despoil my finest flowers of their pollen, tear them up, trample on their roots. Do you think I am mad? Do you think my relatives and friends treat me as if I were sane? "What are you scribbling now? What are you going to present us with next?" It's always the same, and I begin to think that these attentions on the part of my friends, all this praise and admiration—is nothing but a sham, that they're deceiving me as one does an invalid; and I sometimes fear that at any moment they may steal up from behind, seize me, and carry me off, like Poprishchin, to a madhouse. As for the years of my youth, my best years, when I was just beginning, my writing was one continuous torture. A minor writer, especially when he has no luck, feels clumsy, awkward, and superfluous; he is nervous, overwrought, he can't resist hanging around people connected with literature and the arts; he is unrecognized, unnoticed, afraid to look anyone straight in the eye—exactly like a man who has a passion for gambling but no money. I'd never seen my readers, but for some reason, I pictured them as unfriendly and suspicious. I was afraid of the public, it terrified me, and whenever a new play of mine was produced, it seemed to me that all the dark-haired people in the audience were hostile and all the fair-haired ones cold and indifferent. Oh, how awful it was! What agony!

NINA: But surely inspiration and the very process of creation have given you moments of exalted happiness?

TRIGORIN: Yes, while I'm writing I enjoy it. And I like reading the proofs, but . . . as soon as it appears in print, I can't bear it, I see that it's all wrong, a mistake, that it ought never to have been written, and I feel vexed and miserable. . . . [*Laughs.*] Then the public reads it: "Yes, charming, clever. . . . Charming but a far cry from Tolstoy"; or, "A fine thing, but Turgenev's *Fathers and Sons* is better." And so it will be to my dying day: charming and clever, charming and clever—nothing more; and when I die my friends will walk by my grave and say: "Here lies Trigorin: a good writer, but Turgenev was better."

NINA: Forgive me, but I give up trying to understand you. You are simply spoiled by success.

TRIGORIN: What success? I have never pleased myself. I don't like myself as a writer. The worst of it is that I'm in some sort of haze and often don't understand what I am writing. . . . I love this water here, the trees, the sky, I have a feeling for nature, it arouses in me a passionate, irresistible desire to write. But, you see, I'm not just a landscape painter, I'm a citizen besides, I love my country and its people, I feel that if I am a writer it is my duty to write about them, about their sufferings, their future, and to write about science, the rights of man, and so on, and so I write about everything, I am hurried, driven from all sides, people get angry at me, I dash back and forth like a fox brought to bay by the hounds; I see that life and science keep moving farther and farther ahead, while I fall farther and farther behind, like a peasant who has missed the train, and, in the end, I feel that I only know how to paint landscapes and in all the rest I am false—false to the marrow of my bones.

NINA: You have worked too hard and you have neither the time nor the inclination to realize your own importance. You may be dissatisfied with yourself, but to others you are a great and wonderful person! If I were such a writer as you, I'd give my whole life to the people, but I should know that the only happiness for them would be in rising to my level, and they would harness themselves to my chariot.

TRIGORIN: My chariot! What am I—Agamemnon? [*They both smile.*]

NINA: For the happiness of being a writer or an actress, I would endure poverty, disillusionment, the hatred of my family; I would live in a garret and eat black bread, suffer dissatisfaction with myself, and the recognition of my own imperfections, but in return I should demand fame . . . real, resounding fame. . . . [*Covers her face with her hands.*] My head is swimming . . . Ough!

[*The voice of* ARKADINA *from the house:* "*Boris Alekseyevich!*"]

TRIGORIN: I am being called . . . to pack, I suppose. But I don't feel like leaving. [*Glances back at the lake.*] Just look—what a paradise! . . . Lovely!

NINA: Do you see the house with the garden on the other side of the lake?

TRIGORIN: Yes.

NINA: It belonged to my mother when she was alive. I was born there. I've spent my whole life by this lake, I know every little island on it.

TRIGORIN: It's lovely here! [*Seeing the sea gull*] And what is this?

NINA: A sea gull. Konstantin Gavrilovich shot it.

TRIGORIN: A beautiful bird. I really don't want to go. Try to persuade Irina Nikolayevna to stay. [*Makes a note in his book.*]

NINA: What are you writing?

TRIGORIN: Just making a note. . . . An idea occurred to me. [*Putting away notebook*] Subject for a short story: a young girl like you lives all her life beside a lake; she loves the lake like a sea gull, and, like a sea gull, is happy and free. A man comes along by chance, sees her, and having nothing better to do, destroys her, just like this sea gull here.

[*A pause;* ARKADINA *appears at the window.*]

ARKADINA: Boris Alekseyevich, where are you?

TRIGORIN: Coming! [*Goes, then looks back at* NINA; *to* ARKADINA *at the window*] What is it?

ARKADINA: We're staying.

[TRIGORIN *goes into the house.*]

NINA [*comes down to the footlights; after a moment's reflection*]: A dream!

Act III

[*The dining room in* SORIN's *house. Doors on the right and left. A sideboard, a medicine cupboard, and, in the middle of the room, a table. A trunk and hat boxes; signs of preparations for departure.* TRIGORIN *is having lunch;* MASHA *is standing by the table.*]

MASHA: I'm telling you all this because you're a writer. You may be able to use it. I tell you honestly: if he had seriously wounded himself, I would not have gone on living another minute. But I have courage, all the same. I've made up my mind to tear this love out of my heart—tear it out by the roots.

TRIGORIN: How are you going to do that?

MASHA: I'm going to get married. To Medvedenko.

TRIGORIN: That's the schoolmaster?

MASHA: Yes.

TRIGORIN: I don't understand the necessity for that.

MASHA: To love without hope . . . to spend whole years waiting for something . . . But when I marry, there'll be no more of that, new cares will stifle the old. Anyhow, it will be a change. Shall we have another?

TRIGORIN: Haven't you had enough?

MASHA: Oh, come! [*Fills their glasses.*] Don't look at me like that. Women drink more often than you imagine. Only a few drink openly as I do, the majority drink in secret. Yes. . . . And it's always vodka or cognac. [*Clinks glasses with him.*] Good luck! You're a very unassuming person, I'm sorry to be parting from you. [*They drink.*]

TRIGORIN: I don't feel like going myself.

MASHA: You should ask her to stay.

TRIGORIN: No, she won't stay now. Her son is behaving most tactlessly. First he shoots himself, and now they say he's going to challenge me to a duel. And what for? He sulks, sneers, preaches new forms. . . . But there's room for all, the old and the new—why elbow?

MASHA: Well, there's jealousy, too. However, that's not my affair.

[*Pause.* YAKOV *crosses from right to left carrying a suitcase;* NINA *comes in and stops near the window.*]

MASHA: My schoolmaster is none too clever, but he's kind, and a poor soul, and he loves me very much. I'm sorry for him. And I'm sorry for his old mother. Well, I wish you all the best. Don't think badly of me. [*Warmly shakes his hand.*] I'm very grateful to you for your friendly interest. Do send me your books, and be sure to autograph them. Only don't write: "To my esteemed friend"; but simply: "To Maria, who doesn't know where she comes from or why she is living in this world." Good-bye! [*Goes out.*]

NINA [*holding out her hand with the fist closed to* TRIGORIN]:   Odd or even?

TRIGORIN: Even.

NINA [*sighing*]:   No. I had only one pea in my hand. I was trying to tell my fortune—whether to go on the stage or not. If only someone would advise me!

TRIGORIN: It's impossible to advise anyone about that. [*A pause*]

NINA: We are parting and . . . perhaps we shall never meet again. Will you take this little medallion as a remembrance? I had it engraved with your initials . . . and on the other side the title of your book, *Days and Nights.*

TRIGORIN: How charming! [*Kisses the medallion.*] An enchanting gift!

NINA: Think of me sometimes.

TRIGORIN: I shall think of you. I shall think of you as you were on that sunny day—do you remember—a week ago, when you were wearing a light dress . . . we were talking . . . and a white sea gull lay there on the bench beside us.

NINA [*pensively*]:   Yes, the sea gull. . . . [*Pause*] We can't talk any more, someone's coming. . . . Let me have two minutes with you before you go, I beg you . . . [*Goes out left.*]

[*At the same moment* ARKADINA *enters right with* SORIN, *who wears a dress coat with a decoration, then* YAKOV, *busy with the luggage.*]

ARKADINA: Stay at home, old man. Are you really up to gadding about visiting people with your rheumatism? [*To* TRIGORIN] Who was it that just went out? Nina?

TRIGORIN: Yes.

ARKADINA: *Pardon,* we interrupted you. . . . [*Sits down.*] I believe I've packed everything. I'm exhausted.

TRIGORIN [*reading the inscription on the medallion*]: *Days and Nights,* page one twenty-one, lines eleven and twelve.

YAKOV [*clearing the table*]: Am I to pack your fishing rods, too?

TRIGORIN: Yes, I shall be wanting them again. But the books you can give away.

YAKOV: Yes, sir.

TRIGORIN [*to himself*]: Page one twenty-one, lines eleven and twelve. What are those lines? [*To* ARKADINA] Are there copies of my books in the house?

ARKADINA: Yes, in my brother's study, in the corner bookcase.

TRIGORIN: Page one twenty-one . . . [*Goes out.*]

ARKADINA: Really Petrusha, you'd better stay at home. . . .

SORIN: You're going away. . . . It will be miserable for me here without you.

ARKADINA: But what is there in town?

SORIN: Nothing special, but all the same . . . [*Laughs.*] There'll be the laying of the cornerstone for the town hall, and all that sort of thing. . . . I'd like to shake myself free of this gudgeon existence, if only for an hour or two. I've been lying around like an old cigarette holder for too long. I've ordered the horses for one o'clock, so we'll be setting off at the same time.

ARKADINA [*after a pause*]:   Come, stay at home, don't be bored . . . and don't catch cold. Look after my son. Take care of him. Guide him. [*Pause*] Here I am going away, and I shall never know why Konstantin tried to shoot himself. I believe that jealousy was the chief reason, and the sooner I take Trigorin away from here the better.

SORIN: How shall I say it? There were other reasons. It's not hard to understand; an intelligent young man living in this remote place in the country, without money, without position, without future. No occupation whatsoever. Ashamed, and afraid of his idleness. I am extremely fond of him, and he's attached to me, but all the same, when it comes to it, he feels superfluous in this house, like a parasite, a hanger-on. It's only natural, his pride. . . .

ARKADINA: He's such a worry to me! [*Pondering*] He might go into the service, perhaps. . . .

SORIN [*begins to whistle, then, irresolutely*]:   It seems to me the best thing would be if you were to . . . give him a little money. In the first place, he ought to be able to dress like a human being, and all that. Just look at him, he's been going around in the same miserable jacket for the last three years, he has no overcoat. . . . [*Laughs.*] Yes, and it wouldn't do him any harm to have a little fun . . . to go abroad, maybe. . . . It doesn't cost much.

ARKADINA: Well . . . I might manage the suit, but as for going abroad . . . No, at the moment I can't even manage the suit. [*Peremptorily*] No, I haven't any money!

[SORIN *laughs.*]

ARKADINA: I haven't!

SORIN [*begins to whistle*]: Quite so. Forgive me, my dear, don't be angry. I believe you. . . . You are a generous, noble-hearted woman.

ARKADINA [*through tears*]: I have no money!

SORIN: If I had any money, naturally, I'd give it to him myself, but I have nothing, not a kopeck. [*Laughs.*] My steward takes my entire pension and spends it on agriculture, cattle raising, beekeeping. . . . And my money all goes for nothing. The bees die, the cattle die, and he never lets me have the horses. . . .

ARKADINA: I do have some money, but I'm an actress, and my costumes alone are enough to ruin me.

SORIN: You are very kind, my dear. . . . I respect you. . . . Yes . . . But something's wrong with me again. . . . [*Staggers.*] I'm dizzy. [*Holds onto the table.*] I feel ill, and all that. . . .

ARKADINA [*alarmed*]: Petrusha! [*Trying to support him*] Petrusha, my dear! [*Calls.*] Help me! Help!

[*Enter* TREPLEV, *his head bandaged, and* MEDVE-DENKO.]

ARKADINA: He's ill!

SORIN: It's nothing, it's nothing. . . . [*Smiles and drinks some water.*] It's passed off already, and so forth. . . .

TREPLEV [*to his mother*]: Don't be frightened, Mother, it's not serious. This often happens to Uncle now. [*To his uncle*] You must lie down for a while, Uncle.

SORIN: For a little while, yes. . . . But I'm going to town all the same. . . . I'll lie down for a bit, and then

I'm going. . . . It stands to reason . . . [*Goes out, leaning on his stick.*]

MEDVEDENKO [*gives him his arm*]:   There's a riddle: what goes on four legs in the morning, on two legs at noon, and on three in the evening? . . .

SORIN [*laughs*]:   Precisely. And on the back at night. Thank you, I can manage alone.

MEDVEDENKO: Come, now, such formality! [*They go out.*]

ARKADINA: How he frightened me!

TREPLEV: It's not good for him to live in the country. He gets depressed. If you'd just have a sudden burst of generosity, Mother, and lend him fifteen hundred or two thousand rubles, he could live a whole year in town.

ARKADINA: I haven't any money. I'm an actress, not a banker. [*A pause*]

TREPLEV: Mother, change my bandage. You do it so well.

ARKADINA [*takes iodoform and a box of bandage material out of the medicine cupboard*]:   The doctor is late.

TREPLEV: He promised to be here at ten, but it's already noon.

ARKADINA: Sit down. [*Takes the bandage off his head.*] You look as if you were wearing a turban. Yesterday some passer-by asked them in the kitchen what nationality you were. . . . But it's almost entirely healed. What's left is the merest trifle. [*Kisses him on the head.*] And no more click-click while I'm away?

TREPLEV: No, Mother, that was a moment of insane despair, when I couldn't control myself. It won't happen again. [*Kisses her hand.*] You have magic fingers. I remember, a long time ago, when you were still playing in the state theater—I was little then—there was a fight in our courtyard, and one of the tenants, a washerwoman, was badly beaten. Do you remember? She was picked up unconscious. . . . You looked after her, took medicines to her, washed her children in the trough. Don't you remember?

ARKADINA: No. [*Puts on a fresh bandage.*]

TREPLEV: Two ballet dancers were living in the same house with us then. . . . They used to come and have coffee with you. . . .

ARKADINA: That I do remember.

TREPLEV: They were so devout. [*Pause*] Lately, these last few days, I have loved you as tenderly and as completely as when I was a child. I have no one left but you now. Only why, why have you succumbed to the influence of that man?

ARKADINA: You don't understand him, Konstantin. He is a very noble character.

TREPLEV: And yet, when he was told I was going to challenge him to a duel, his nobility of character did not prevent him from playing the coward. He is leaving. An ignominious retreat.

ARKADINA: What nonsense! It is I who am asking him to go.

TREPLEV: A very noble character! Here you and I are nearly quarreling over him, and at this very moment he is somewhere in the garden or the drawing room laughing at us . . . developing Nina, trying to convince her once and for all that he's a genius.

ARKADINA: You take delight in saying disagreeable things to me. I respect that man, and I ask you not to speak ill of him in my presence.

TREPLEV: And I don't respect him. You want me to consider him a genius, too, but forgive me, I can't lie, his books make me sick.

ARKADINA: That's envy. There's nothing left for people who lay claim to a talent they haven't got but to disparage real talent. A fine consolation, I must say!

TREPLEV [*ironically*]:   Real talent! [*Wrathfully*] I have more talent than all of you put together, if it comes to that! [*Tears the bandage off his head.*] You, with your hackneyed conventions, have usurped the foremost places in art, and consider nothing genuine and legitimate except what you yourselves do—everything else you stifle and suppress! I do not accept you! I accept neither you nor him!

ARKADINA: You decadent!

TREPLEV: Go back to your charming theater and play in your miserable, worthless plays!

ARKADINA: I have never acted in such plays! Leave me! You're incapable of writing so much as a paltry little vaudeville sketch. You're nothing but a Kiev petty bourgeois! You sponger!

TREPLEV: Miser!

ARKADINA: Beggar!

[TREPLEV *sits down and quietly weeps.*]

ARKADINA: Nonentity! [*Walking up and down in agitation*] Don't cry. You mustn't cry. . . . [*Weeps.*] Don't. . . . [*Kisses him on the forehead, the cheeks, the head.*] My darling child, forgive me. . . . Forgive your sinful mother. Forgive miserable me!

TREPLEV [*embraces her*]: If you only knew! I have lost everything. She does not love me, I can no longer write. . . . All my hopes are gone. . . .

ARKADINA: Don't despair. . . . It will all pass. He's going away now. She will love you again. [*Dries his tears.*] That's enough. Now we have made peace.

TREPLEV [*kisses her hands*]: Yes, Mother.

ARKADINA [*tenderly*]: Make it up with him, too. You don't want a duel. . . . Do you?

TREPLEV: Very well. . . . Only, Mother, don't make me see him. It's too painful . . . it's more than I can bear. . . . [TRIGORIN *comes in.*] There he is. . . . I'm going . . . [*Hurriedly puts dressings in the cupboard.*] The doctor can put on the bandage. . . .

TRIGORIN [*looking through a book*]: Page one twenty-one . . . lines eleven and twelve. . . . Here it is. . . . [*Reads.*] "If ever my life can be of use to you, come and take it."

[TREPLEV *picks up the bandage from the floor and goes out.*]

ARKADINA [*looking at her watch*]: The horses will be here soon.

TRIGORIN [*to himself*]: "If ever my life can be of use to you, come and take it."

ARKADINA: Your things are all packed, I hope?

TRIGORIN: [*impatiently*]: Yes, yes. . . . [*Musing*] Why is it that in this appeal from a pure soul I have a presentiment of sorrow, and it wrings my heart? . . . "If

ever my life can be of use to you, come and take it."
[*To* ARKADINA] Let us stay one more day!

[ARKADINA *shakes her head.*]

TRIGORIN:　Do let us stay!

ARKADINA:　Darling, I know what's keeping you here,
but have some self-control. You're a little intoxicated,
try to be sober.

TRIGORIN:　And you be sober, too, be wise and reasonable, I beg you; look at this like a true friend. . . .
[*Presses her hand.*] You are capable of sacrifice. . . . Be
a friend to me, let me go. . . .

ARKADINA [*violently agitated*]:　Are you so infatuated
with her?

TRIGORIN:　I am attracted to her! Perhaps this is just
what I need.

ARKADINA:　The love of a provincial girl! Oh, how
little you know yourself!

TRIGORIN:　Sometimes people are walking about but
asleep; that's how it is with me now. . . . I am talking
to you, but it's as if I were asleep and dreaming of her.
I am possessed by sweet, wonderful dreams. . . . Let
me go. . . .

ARKADINA [*trembling*]:　No, no. . . . I am just an ordinary woman, you can't talk to me like this. Don't torture
me, Boris . . . it frightens me. . . .

TRIGORIN:　You could be an extraordinary woman if
you wanted to be. A youthful love, alluring, poetic, carrying one off into a world of dreams—the only thing on
earth that can give happiness! I have never known a
love like that. . . . In my youth there wasn't time, I was
always haunting the editors' offices, fighting off

poverty. . . . And now that love has come at last, and is beckoning me. . . . What sense is there in running away from it?

ARKADINA [*furiously*]: You've gone out of your mind!

TRIGORIN: And why not?

ARKADINA: You are all in a conspiracy to torment me today! [*Weeps.*]

TRIGORIN [*clutching his head*]: She doesn't understand! She doesn't want to understand!

ARKADINA: Am I really so old and ugly that you feel no constraint in talking to me about other women? [*Puts her arms around him and kisses him.*] Oh, you madman! My beautiful, wonderful . . . You are the last chapter of my life! [*Falls on her knees.*] My joy, my pride, my bliss. . . . [*Embraces his knees.*] If you leave me, even for one hour, I won't survive it, I'll lose my mind, my wonderful, magnificent one, my master. . . .

TRIGORIN: Someone may come in. [*Helps her to her feet.*]

ARKADINA: Let them, I'm not ashamed of my love for you. [*Kisses his hands.*] My precious, my reckless boy, you want to be mad, but I won't have it, I won't let you. . . . [*Laughs.*] You are mine . . . mine. . . . This brow is mine, these eyes, this lovely, silky hair is mine. . . . You are all mine. You are so talented, so clever, the best of all modern writers, the hope of Russia. . . . You have such sincerity, such simplicity, freshness, such robust humor. . . . In one stroke you can convey the essence of a person or a landscape, your characters are like living people. Oh, it's impossible to read you without delight! You think this is just adulation—that I'm flattering you? Come, look into my eyes . . . look at me. . . . Do I look like a liar? I am the only one who knows how to appreciate you, the only one who tells you the truth, my darling, wonderful one. . . . Will you come with me? Yes? You won't leave me?

TRIGORIN: I have no will of my own . . . I've never had a will of my own. . . . Flabby, soft, always submissive—how can that appeal to a woman? Take me, carry me off, only don't let me go one step away from you. . . .

ARKADINA [*to herself*]: Now he is mine. [*Casually, as if nothing had happened*] But, of course, if you want to, you can stay. I'll go by myself, and you can come later, in a week. After all, why should you hurry?

TRIGORIN: No, we may as well go together.

ARKADINA: As you wish. We'll go together then. . . .

[*A pause;* TRIGORIN *writes in a notebook.*]

ARKADINA: What are you writing?

TRIGORIN: I heard a good expression this morning: "Vestal forest. . . ." It might do for a story. [*Stretches.*] So, we're off? Again the railway carriages, the stations, refreshment bars, the stews, and conversations. . . .

[*Enter* SHAMRAYEV.]

SHAMRAYEV: I have the honor to inform you, with regret, that the horses are here. It is time, most esteemed lady, to leave for the station; the train comes in at five minutes past two. You will do me the favor, Irina Nikolayevna, and not forget to inquire about the actor Suzdaltsev—if he is alive and in good health? There was a time when we used to drink together. . . . He was inimitable in *The Mail Robbery*. And at Elisavetgrad, I remember, the tragedian Izmailov—also a remarkable character—played in the same company with him. Don't

be in a hurry, most esteemed lady, you still have five
minutes. Once, in some melodrama, they were playing
conspirators, and when they suddenly were discovered
and Izmailov was supposed to say: "We're caught in a
trap," he said: "We're traught in a cap." [*Laughs.*] A
cap!

[*While he is speaking,* YAKOV *is busy with the luggage;
a* MAID *brings* ARKADINA's *hat, cloak, parasol, and gloves;
the* COOK *glances in at the door left and a moment later
hesitantly comes in. Enter* POLINA ANDREYEVNA, *then*
SORIN *and* MEDVEDENKO.]

POLINA ANDREYEVNA [*with a small basket*]: Here are
some plums for the journey. . . . They're very sweet.
You may feel like having a little something. . . .

ARKADINA: You are very kind, Polina Andreyevna.

POLINA ANDREYEVNA: Good-bye, my dear! If there
has been anything . . . not quite as it should be, forgive
it. [*Weeps.*]

ARKADINA [*embraces her*]: Everything has been
lovely, everything. Only you mustn't cry.

POLINA ANDREYEVNA: Our time is passing.

ARKADINA: What can we do?

[*Enter* SORIN *in an overcoat with a cape, his hat on,
and carrying a cane; he comes in from door on the left
and crosses the stage.*]

SORIN: Sister, it's time to start, if you don't want to
be late and all that. . . . I'll go and get into the carriage.
[*Goes out.*]

MEDVEDENKO: I'm going to walk to the station to see
you off. I'll be there in no time. . . . [*Goes out.*]

ARKADINA: Good-bye, my dears. . . . If we are alive and well, we'll meet again next summer. . . . [*The* MAID, YAKOV, *and the* COOK *kiss her hand.*] Don't forget me. [*Gives the* COOK *a ruble.*] Here's a ruble for the three of you.

COOK: We humbly thank you, madam. A happy journey to you! We are most grateful.

YAKOV: Godspeed to you!

SHAMRAYEV: You might make us happy with a letter. Good-bye, Boris Alekseyevich!

ARKADINA: Where's Konstantin? Tell him that I'm leaving. I must say good-bye to him. Well, think kindly of me. [*To* YAKOV] I gave a ruble to the cook. It's for the three of you.

[*All go out on the right. The stage is empty. Offstage there are the customary sounds of people being seen off. The* MAID *comes back for the basket of plums on the table and goes out.*]

TRIGORIN [*returning*]: I forgot my stick. It must be out there on the veranda. [*Goes toward the door on the left and meets* NINA *coming in.*] It's you! We are leaving.

NINA: I felt that we should see each other once more. [*Excitedly*] Boris Alekseyevich, I have come to an irrevocable decision, the die is cast, I am going on the stage. Tomorrow I shall no longer be here, I am leaving my father, giving up everything, and beginning a new life. . . . I am going to Moscow . . . like you. . . . We shall see each other there.

TRIGORIN [*glancing back*]: Stay at the Slavyansky Bazaar. . . . Send me word at once . . . Molchanovka, Grokholsky House. . . . I must hurry. . . .

[*A pause*]

NINA: One minute more . . .

TRIGORIN [*in an undertone*]: You are so lovely. . . . Oh, what happiness to think that we shall meet soon! [*She leans on his breast.*] I shall see these wonderful eyes, this inexpressibly beautiful, tender smile . . . this sweet face with its expression of angelic purity. . . . My darling . . . [*A prolonged kiss*]

[*Two years pass between the third and fourth acts.*]

Act IV

[*One of the drawing rooms in* SORIN'S *house, which has been turned into a study by* KONSTANTIN TREPLEV. *Doors right and left leading to other parts of the house, and French windows center leading to the veranda. Besides the usual drawing-room furniture, there is a desk in the right corner, a sofa and a bookcase near the door left, and books lying on window sills and chairs. Evening. A single lamp with a shade is lighted. The room is in semidarkness. Sounds of trees rustling and wind howling in the chimneys. The watchman is tapping. Enter* MEDVE-DENKO *and* MASHA.]

MASHA [*calling*]: Konstantin Gavrilovich! Konstantin Gavrilovich! [*Looking around*] Nobody here. The old man keeps asking: where's Kostya, where's Kostya? . . . He can't live without him. . . .

MEDVEDENKO: He's afraid of being alone. [*Listening*] What terrible weather! Two whole days of it!

MASHA [*turns up the lamp*]: There are waves on the lake . . . tremendous ones.

MEDVEDENKO: It's dark in the garden. We ought to have told them to pull down that stage. It stands there bare and ugly, like a skeleton, and the curtain flaps in the wind. Last night as I walked by I thought I heard somebody crying inside.

MASHA: What next? . . . [*Pause*]

MEDVEDENKO: Let's go home, Masha.

MASHA [*shakes her head*]: I'm going to stay here tonight.

MEDVEDENKO [*imploring*]: Masha, do let us go! The baby may be hungry.

MASHA: Nonsense. Matryona will feed him. [*Pause*]

MEDVEDENKO: It's a shame. . . . Three nights now without his mother.

MASHA: You're becoming tiresome. In the old days you'd at least philosophize a little, but now it's always home and baby, home and baby—that's all I ever hear from you.

MEDVEDENKO: Do come, Masha.

MASHA: Go yourself.

MEDVEDENKO: Your father won't let me have a horse.

MASHA: He will if you ask him.

MEDVEDENKO: Very well. I'll try. Then you'll come tomorrow?

MASHA [*taking snuff*]:   Yes, tomorrow. Don't bother me. . . .

[*Enter* TREPLEV *and* POLINA ANDREYEVNA; TREPLEV *with pillows and a blanket,* POLINA ANDREYEVNA *with sheets and pillow cases; they lay them on the sofa, then* TREPLEV *goes to his desk and sits down.*]

MASHA: What's this for, Mama?

POLINA ANDREYEVNA: Pyotr Nikolayevich asked us to make up a bed for him in Kostya's room.

MASHA: Let me. . . . [*Makes the bed.*]

POLINA ANDREYEVNA [*sighing*]:   Old people are like children. . . . [*Goes to the desk, leans on her elbow and looks at a manuscript. A pause.*]

MEDVEDENKO: Well, I'm going. Good-bye, Masha. [*Kisses his wife's hand.*] Good-bye, Mother. [*Tries to kiss his mother-in-law's hand.*]

POLINA ANDREYEVNA [*with annoyance*]:   Well, go if you're going!

MEDVEDENKO: Good-bye, Konstantin Gavrilovich.

[TREPLEV *gives him his hand without speaking;* MEDVEDENKO *goes out.*]

POLINA ANDREYEVNA [*glancing at the manuscript*]:   Nobody ever thought or dreamed that you'd turn out to be a real author, Kostya. And here you are, God be praised, getting money from the magazines. [*Passing her hand over his hair*] And you've grown handsome. . . . Dear, good Kostya, be a little kinder to my Mashenka!

MASHA [*making the bed*]:   Leave him alone, Mama.

POLINA ANDREYEVNA [*to* TREPLEV]:   She's a good girl. . . . [*Pause*] A woman doesn't ask for much, Kostya, so long as you give her a kind look. I know from myself.

[TREPLEV *gets up from the desk and goes out without speaking.*]

MASHA: Now you've made him angry. Why did you have to pester him?

POLINA ANDREYEVNA: I'm sorry for you, Mashenka.

MASHA: A lot of good that does!

POLINA ANDREYEVNA: My heart aches for you. I see it all, you know, I understand.

MASHA: It's simply nonsense. Hopeless love—there's no such thing except in novels. It's of no consequence. The only thing is you mustn't let yourself go, and always be expecting something, waiting for the tide to turn. . . . When love plants itself in your heart, you have to clear it out. They've promised to transfer my husband to another district. Once we're there, I shall forget it all—I'll tear it out of my heart by the roots.

[*Two rooms away a melancholy waltz is being played.*]

POLINA ANDREYEVNA: Kostya is playing. That means he's depressed.

MASHA [*takes a few waltz steps in silence*]:   The most important thing, Mama, is not to have him constantly before my eyes. If only they give my Semyon his transfer, believe me, within a month I'll have forgotten. It's all nonsense.

[*The door on the left opens and* DORN *and* MEDVEDENKO *wheel in* SORIN.]

MEDVEDENKO: I've got six in my house now. And flour at two kopecks a pound.

DORN: It's a tight squeeze.

MEDVEDENKO: It's all very well for you to laugh. You've got more money than you know what to do with.

DORN: Money? After thirty years of practice, an onerous practice, my friend, when day and night I couldn't call my soul my own, I managed to save only two thousand rubles, and that I've just spent on a holiday abroad. I have nothing.

MASHA [*to her husband*]: Haven't you gone?

MEDVEDENKO [*guiltily*]: Well . . . how can I go when they won't let me have a horse?

MASHA [*with bitter vexation, in an undertone*]: I wish I had never set eyes on you!

[SORIN, *in the wheelchair, remains on the left side of the room;* POLINA ANDREYEVNA, MASHA, *and* DORN *sit down near him;* MEDVEDENKO, *chagrined, moves to one side.*]

DORN: What a lot of changes you have made here . . . this drawing room turned into a study. . . .

MASHA: It's more convenient for Konstantin Gavrilovich to work here. He can go out into the garden and think whenever he feels like it.

[*The watchman is heard tapping.*]

SORIN: Where is my sister?

DORN: She has gone to the station to meet Trigorin. She'll be back soon.

SORIN: If you found it necessary to send for my sister, I must be seriously ill. [*After a brief silence*] It's very odd, I'm seriously ill, yet they don't give me any medicine.

DORN: What do you want? Valerian drops? Soda? Quinine?

SORIN: Now the philosophy begins. Oh, what an infliction! [*Nods his head in the direction of the sofa.*] Has that been made up for me?

POLINA ANDREYEVNA: For you, Pyotr Nikolayevich.

SORIN: Thank you.

DORN [*sings softly*]: "The moon floats in the evening sky . . ."

SORIN: You know, I'd like to give Kostya a subject for a story. It should be called: "The Man Who Wished"—*"L'Homme qui a voulu."* There was a time in my youth when I wished to become a writer—but I didn't. I wanted to speak well, too—and I speak abominably: [*Mimicking himself*] "and all that sort of thing, and so forth and so on . . ." When I used to try to sum anything up I'd drag on and on till I broke out in a perspiration. I wanted to marry—and I never married. I always wanted to live in town—and here I am ending my life in the country, and so forth and so on.

DORN: You wanted to become a Councilor of State—and you became one.

SORIN [*laughs*]: I didn't seek that, it came of itself.

DORN: To express dissatisfaction with life at sixty-two is, you must admit, not very magnanimous.

SORIN: What an obstinate fellow you are! Can't you understand, one wants to live!

DORN: That's frivolous. It's a law of nature that every life must have its end.

SORIN: You argue like a man who's had his fill. You're satisfied, and so nothing means anything to you. You're indifferent to life. But when it comes to dying, you'll be afraid, too.

DORN: The fear of death is an animal fear. . . . One must overcome it. It's reasonable only for those who believe in eternal life and are in terror because of their sins. But, in the first place, you are not religious, and in the second place, what sins have you committed? You served in the department of justice for twenty-five years—that's all.

SORIN [*laughs*]:   Twenty-eight. . . .

[TREPLEV *enters and sits on a stool at* SORIN's *feet.* MASHA *never takes her eyes off him.*]

DORN: We're keeping Konstantin Gavrilovich from his work.

TREPLEV: No, it doesn't matter.

[*A pause*]

MEDVEDENKO: If I may ask, Doctor, which city appealed to you most in your travels?

DORN: Genoa.

TREPLEV: Why Genoa?

DORN: Because of the wonderful street crowds there. You go out of your hotel in the evening, and the street is filled with people. You wander aimlessly up and down, in and out, mingling with the crowd, psychologically entering into its life, and you begin to believe there might actually be a world soul, like the one Nina Zarechnaya acted in your play. By the way, where is she now? How is she getting on?

TREPLEV: All right, I suppose.

DORN: I was told she'd been leading a rather peculiar life. What does that mean?

TREPLEV: It's a long story, Doctor.

DORN: Well, you can make it short.

[*A pause*]

TREPLEV: She ran away from home and had an affair with Trigorin. You knew that, didn't you?

DORN: Yes, I knew that.

TREPLEV: She had a child. The child died. Trigorin got tired of her and resumed his former attachments, as might have been expected. In fact, he had never given them up, but, in his spineless way, had somehow contrived to be everywhere at once. As far as I can make out from what I have heard, Nina's personal life is a complete failure.

DORN: And the stage?

TREPLEV: Even worse, I believe. She made her debut in a summer theater near Moscow, then went to the provinces. At that time I never lost sight of her; wherever she went, I followed. She always attempted big parts, but she acted crudely, tastelessly, with stiff gestures and strident intonations. There were moments when she showed talent—when she uttered a cry or had a dying scene—but those were only moments.

DORN: She does have talent, then?

TREPLEV: It was hard to tell. I suppose she has. I went to see her, but she didn't want to see me, and the maid would never let me in at her hotel. I understood how she felt and didn't insist on a meeting. [*Pause*] What more can I tell you? Afterward, when I had come back home, I received letters from her—clever, warm, interesting letters; she didn't complain, but I felt that she was profoundly unhappy; there was not a line that didn't betray her sick, strained nerves. And her imagination was somewhat distracted. She always signed herself "The Sea Gull." The miller in *The Mermaid* says that he's a raven, and in the same way she kept repeating that she was a sea gull. She's here now.

DORN: What do you mean—here?

TREPLEV: In town, staying at the inn. She's been here for five days. I was on the point of going to see her, but Masha went, and she won't see anyone. Semyon Semyonovich is convinced that he saw her last night after dinner in the fields a couple of versts from here.

MEDVEDENKO: Yes, I did see her. She was walking in the opposite direction, toward town. I bowed to her and asked her why she didn't come to see us. She said she would come.

TREPLEV: She won't. [*Pause*] Her father and stepmother will have nothing to do with her. They've put watchmen everywhere so that she can't even go near the house. [*Goes toward his desk with the doctor.*] How easy it is, Doctor, to be a philosopher on paper, and how difficult in life.

SORIN: She was a charming girl.

DORN: What's that?

SORIN: She was a charming girl, I say. State Councilor Sorin was positively in love with her for a while.

DORN: You old Lovelace!

[SHAMRAYEV's *laugh is heard.*]

POLINA ANDREYEVNA: I think they've come back from the station. . . .

TREPLEV: Yes, I hear Mother.

[*Enter* ARKADINA *and* TRIGORIN *followed by* SHAMRAYEV.]

SHAMRAYEV: We all grow old and weather-beaten under the influence of the elements, but you, most esteemed lady, are still young. . . . Light blouse, sprightly . . . graceful . . .

ARKADINA: That's enough to bring me bad luck, you tiresome man!

TRIGORIN [*to* SORIN]: How do you do, Pyotr Nikolayevich! Still ailing? That's bad! [*Seeing* MASHA, *delighted*] Maria Ilyinichna!

MASHA: You remember me? [*Shakes hands.*]

TRIGORIN: Married?

MASHA: Long ago.

TRIGORIN: Happy? [*Bows to* DORN *and* MEDVEDENKO, *then hesitantly approaches* TREPLEV.] Irina Nikolayevna tells me that you have forgotten the past and are no longer angry.

[TREPLEV *holds out his hand.*]

ARKADINA [*to her son*]: Look, Boris Alekseyevich has brought the magazine with your new story in it.

TREPLEV [*taking the magazine, to* TRIGORIN]: Thank you. You're very kind.

TRIGORIN: Your admirers send their greetings. . . . In Petersburg and Moscow there's a great deal of interest in your work, and I'm always being asked about you. They want to know what you are like, how old you are, whether you are dark or fair. For some reason they all think you are no longer young. And nobody knows your real name, of course, since your work is always published under a pseudonym. You're as mysterious as the Iron Mask.

TREPLEV: Will you be with us long?

TRIGORIN: No, tomorrow I think I'll go to Moscow. I must. I'm in a hurry to finish my novel, and besides, I've promised to give them something for an anthology. In short—the same old story.

[*While they are talking,* ARKADINA *and* POLINA ANDREYEVNA *set up a card table in the middle of the room.* SHAMRAYEV *lights the candles and arranges the chairs. A game of lotto is brought out of the cupboard.*]

TRIGORIN: The weather has not given me a very friendly welcome. There's a cruel wind. If it dies down tomorrow morning I'm going to the lake to fish. And I want to have a look at the garden and the place—do you remember?—where your play was performed. I've got an idea for a story all worked out, I only want to refresh my memory of the place where it is laid.

MASHA [*to her father*]: Papa, please let my husband have a horse! He must go home.

SHAMRAYEV [*mimicking*]: A horse . . . must go home. . . . [*Sternly*] You can see for yourself they've just been to the station. They'll not go out again.

MASHA: But there are other horses. . . . [*Seeing that her father does not answer, makes a gesture of resignation.*] There's no use trying to do anything with you. . . .

MEDVEDENKO: I can walk, Masha. Really . . .

POLINA ANDREYEVNA [*sighing*]: Walk, in such weather. . . . [*Sits down at the card table.*] Come and sit down, friends.

MEDVEDENKO: It's only six versts, after all. . . . Good-bye . . . [*Kisses his wife's hand.*] Good-bye, Mama. [*His mother-in-law reluctantly holds out her hand.*] I shouldn't have troubled anyone, but the baby. . . . [*Bows to them.*] Good-bye. . . . [*Goes out apologetically.*]

SHAMRAYEV: He can walk all right! He's not a general.

POLINA ANDREYEVNA [*taps on the table*]: Please, friends. Let's not lose time, they'll be calling us to supper soon.

[SHAMRAYEV, MASHA, *and* DORN *sit down at the table.*]

ARKADINA [*to* TRIGORIN]:   When the long autumn evenings commence they always play lotto here. Look, it's the same old lotto set we had when Mother used to play with us as children. Don't you want to have a game with us till supper? [*She and* TRIGORIN *sit down at the table.*] It's a dull game, but it's not bad when you get used to it. [*Deals three cards to each.*]

TREPLEV [*turning the pages of the magazine*]:   He's read his own story, but he hasn't even cut the pages of mine. [*Puts the magazine down on his desk, then goes toward the door left; as he passes his mother, kisses her on the head.*]

ARKADINA: What about you, Kostya?

TREPLEV: Sorry, I don't feel like it somehow. . . . I'm going for a walk. [*Goes out.*]

ARKADINA: The stake is ten kopecks. Put it down for me, will you, Doctor?

DORN: Right.

MASHA: Have you all put down your stakes? I begin—twenty-two!

ARKADINA: I have it.

MASHA: Three!

DORN: Right.

MASHA: Did you put down three? Eight! Eighty-one! Ten!

SHAMRAYEV: Not so fast.

ARKADINA: What a reception they gave me in Kharkov! Goodness, my head is still spinning!

MASHA: Thirty-four!

[*A melancholy waltz is played offstage.*]

ARKADINA: The students gave me an ovation . . . three baskets of flowers . . . two garlands, and look. . . . [*Unfastens a brooch and tosses it onto the table.*]

SHAMRAYEV: Now, that is something. . . .

MASHA: Fifty!

DORN: Exactly fifty?

ARKADINA: I had a marvelous costume. . . . You may
say what you like, but I do know how to dress.

POLINA ANDREYEVNA: Kostya is playing. He's depressed, poor boy.

SHAMRAYEV: They've been abusing him in the
newspapers.

MASHA: Seventy-seven!

ARKADINA: He needn't take any notice of that!

TRIGORIN: He has no luck. He never manages to find
a genuine style of his own. There's always something
strange, vague, at times almost resembling a delirium.
And not one living character.

MASHA: Eleven!

ARKADINA [*looking at* SORIN]: Petrusha, are you
bored? [*Pause*] He's asleep.

DORN: The State Councilor sleeps.

MASHA: Seven! Ninety!

TRIGORIN: If I lived in a place like this, by a lake,
do you think I'd write? I should overcome this passion
of mine and do nothing but fish.

MASHA: Twenty-eight!

TRIGORIN: To catch a perch or a bass—what bliss!

DORN: I believe in Konstantin Gavrilovich. He's got something! He's got something! He thinks in images, his stories are vivid, striking, and I am deeply moved by them. It's only a pity that he has no definite purpose. He creates impressions, nothing more, and, of course, you don't get very far on impressions alone. Irina Niko-layevna, are you glad to have a son who's a writer?

ARKADINA: Imagine, I haven't read anything of his yet. There's never time.

MASHA: Twenty-six!

[TREPLEV *quietly enters and goes to his desk.*]

SHAMRAYEV [*to* TRIGORIN]: We've still got that thing of yours here, Boris Alekseyevich.

TRIGORIN: What thing?

SHAMRAYEV: Konstantin Gavrilovich shot a sea gull once, and you told me to have it stuffed for you.

TRIGORIN: I don't remember. [*Musing*] I don't remember.

MASHA: Sixty-six! One!

TREPLEV [*throws open the window and stands listening*]: How dark it is! I don't know why I feel so uneasy.

ARKADINA: Kostya, shut the window, there's a draft.

[TREPLEV *shuts the window.*]

MASHA: Eighty-eight!

TRIGORIN: Ladies and gentlemen, the game is mine.

ARKADINA: Bravo! Bravo!

SHAMRAYEV: Bravo!

ARKADINA: This man is lucky in everything! [*Gets up.*] And now, let's go and have a bite to eat. Our great man has not dined today. After supper we'll go on. [*To her son*] Kostya, leave your manuscript and come have something to eat.

TREPLEV: I don't want to, Mother, I'm not hungry.

ARKADINA: Just as you like. [*Wakes* SORIN.] Petrusha, supper! [*Takes* SHAMRAYEV'*s arm.*] Let me tell you about my reception in Kharkov. . . .

[POLINA ANDREYEVNA *blows out the candles on the table, then she and* DORN *wheel out* SORIN'*s chair. All go out by the door on the left;* TREPLEV *is left alone at his desk.*]

TREPLEV [*preparing to write, reads through what he has already written*]:   I've talked so much about new forms, and now I feel that little by little I myself am falling into a convention. [*Reads.*] "The placards on the fence proclaimed . . ." "A pale face framed by dark hair . . ." Proclaimed . . . framed by dark hair . . . That's banal. [*Scratches out what he has written.*] I'll begin where the hero is awakened by the sound of rain, and throw out all the rest. The description of the moonlit night is long and artificial. Trigorin has worked out a method, it's easy for him. . . . With him a broken bottleneck glitters on the dam and the mill wheel casts a black shadow—and there you have a moonlit night; but with me there's the shimmering light, the silent twinkling of the stars, the distant sounds of a piano dying away on the still, fragrant air. . . . It's agonizing. [*A pause*] Yes, I'm becoming more and more convinced that it's not a question of old and new forms, but that one writes, without even thinking about forms, writes because it pours freely from the soul. [*Someone taps on the window nearest the desk.*] What's that? [*Looks out the window.*] I don't see anything. [*Opens the French windows and peers into the garden.*] Someone ran down the steps. [*Calls.*] Who's there? [*Goes out; he can be heard walking rapidly along the veranda; a moment later returns with* NINA ZARECHNAYA.] Nina! Nina!

[NINA *lays her head on his breast and quietly sobs.*]

TREPLEV [*moved*]:   Nina! Nina! It's you . . . you. . . . It's as though I had a presentiment, all day long my soul has been in terrible torment. [*Takes off her hat and cloak.*] Oh, my precious darling, she has come at last! Don't let us cry, don't!

NINA: There's someone here.

TREPLEV: No one.

NINA: Lock the doors, someone might come in.

TREPLEV: No one will come in.

NINA: I know Irina Nikolayevna is here. Lock the doors.

TREPLEV [*locks the right door, goes to the door left*]:   There's no lock on this one. I'll put a chair against it. [*Puts an armchair against the door.*] Don't be afraid, no one will come in.

NINA [*looking intently into his face*]:   Let me look at you. [*Looking around*] It's warm, cozy. . . . This used to be the drawing room. Am I very much changed?

TREPLEV: Yes. . . . You are thinner, and your eyes have grown bigger. Nina, it seems so strange to be seeing

you. Why wouldn't you let me come to see you? Why
didn't you come sooner? I know you've been here almost a week. . . . I went there several times every day
and stood under your window like a beggar.

NINA: I was afraid you might hate me. Every night I
dream that you are looking at me and don't recognize
me. If you only knew! Ever since I arrived I've been
walking here . . . by the lake. I came near the house
many times, but I couldn't bring myself to come in. Let's
sit down. [*They sit down.*] Let's sit and talk, and talk. . . .
It's nice here, warm and cozy. . . . Listen—the wind!
There's a passage in Turgenev: "Happy the man who on
such a night has a roof over his head, who has a warm
corner of his own." I am a sea gull. . . . No, that's not
it. [*Rubs her forehead.*] What was I saying? Yes . . .
Turgenev . . . "And may the Lord help all homeless
wanderers." . . . It doesn't matter. [*Sobs.*]

TREPLEV: Nina, you're crying again—Nina!

NINA: Never mind, it does me good. . . . I haven't
cried for two years. Yesterday, in the late evening, I
came into the garden to see if our theater was still there.
It's still standing. I began to cry, for the first time in two
years, and I felt relieved, my soul felt clear. See, I'm not
crying now. [*Takes his hand.*] And so you have become
a writer. . . . You are a writer—and I am an actress. . . .
We, too, have been drawn into the whirlpool. . . . I used
to live happily, like a child—I'd wake up in the morning
singing; I loved you and I dreamed of fame . . . and
now? Tomorrow, early in the morning, I must go to Yelets, third class . . . traveling with peasants, and at Yelets
the educated merchants will pester me with their attentions. It's a coarse life.

TREPLEV: Why to Yelets?

NINA: I've accepted an engagement for the whole
winter. It's time I was going.

TREPLEV: Nina, I cursed you, I hated you, I tore up all your letters and photographs, but every minute I was conscious that my soul was bound to yours forever. I can never stop loving you. Ever since I lost you, and my work began to be published, my life has been unbearable—I am miserable. . . . All of a sudden my youth was snatched from me, and now I feel as if I had been living in this world for ninety years. I call to you, I kiss the ground you walked on; wherever I look I see your face, that tender smile that used to shine on me in the best years of my life. . . .

NINA [*confused*]: Why does he talk like that, why does he talk like that?

TREPLEV: I am alone, I have no one's affection to warm me, I am as cold as if I were living in a dungeon, and no matter what I write, it's dry, hard, dark. Stay here, Nina, I implore you, or let me go with you!

[NINA *quickly puts on her hat and cloak.*]

TREPLEV: Nina, why? For God's sake, Nina. . . . [*Looks at her putting on her things.*]

[*A pause*]

NINA: My horses are waiting at the gate. Don't see me off, I'll go by myself. . . . [*Through tears*] Give me some water. . . .

TREPLEV [*gives her a glass of water*]: Where are you going now?

NINA: To town. [*Pause*] Is Irina Nikolayevna here?

TREPLEV: Yes. . . . On Thursday, Uncle was ill and we telegraphed her to come.

NINA: Why do you say you kissed the ground I walked on? I ought to have been killed. [*Leans on the table.*] I'm so tired! If I could rest . . . rest! [*Raising her head*] I am a sea gull. . . . No, that's not it. . . . I'm an actress. Ah, well! [*Hears* ARKADINA *and* TRIGORIN *laughing, listens, then runs to the door on the left and looks through the keyhole.*] So, he's here, too. . . . [*Goes to* TREPLEV.] Well, it doesn't matter. . . . He didn't believe in the theater, he always laughed at my dreams, and gradually I too ceased believing and lost heart. And then there was the anxiety of love, the jealousy, the constant fears for my baby. . . . I grew petty, trivial, my acting was insipid. . . . I didn't know what to do with my hands, I didn't know how to stand on the stage, I couldn't control my voice. You can't imagine what it's like to feel that you are acting abominably. I am a sea gull. No, that's not it. . . . Do you remember, you shot a sea gull? A man came along by chance, saw it, and having nothing better to do, destroyed it. . . . A subject for a short story. . . . No, that's not it. . . . [*Rubs her forehead.*] What was I saying? . . . I was talking about the stage. . . . I'm not like that now. . . . Now I'm a real actress, I act with delight, with rapture, I'm intoxicated when I'm on the stage, and I feel that I act beautifully. And since I have been here, I've been walking, continually walking and thinking . . . and I think and feel that my soul is growing stronger with each day. . . . I know now, I understand, that in our work, Kostya—whether it's acting or writing—what's important is not fame, not glory, not the things I used to dream of, but the ability to endure. To be able to bear one's cross and have faith. I have faith, and it's not so painful now, and when I think of my vocation, I'm not afraid of life.

TREPLEV [*sadly*]: You have found your way, you know where you are going, but I'm still drifting in a chaos of images and dreams, without knowing why it is necessary, or for whom. . . . I have no faith, and I don't know what my vocation is.

NINA [*listening*]: Sh-sh! . . . I'm going. Good-bye. When I become a great actress, come and see me. Promise? And now. . . . [*Presses his hand.*] It's late. I can hardly stand on my feet. . . . I'm exhausted and hungry. . . .

TREPLEV: Stay, I'll give you supper. . . .

NINA: No, no. . . . Don't go with me, I'll go alone. . . .
My horses are not far. . . . So, she brought him with
her? Well, it doesn't matter. When you see Trigorin,
don't say anything to him. . . . I love him. I love him
even more than before. . . . A subject for a short
story . . . I love him, love him passionately,
desperately. . . . How good life used to be, Kostya! Do
you remember? How clear, how pure, warm, and joyous,
and our feelings—our feelings were like tender, delicate
flowers. . . . Do you remember? [*Recites.*] "Men, lions,
eagles, and partridges, horned deer, geese, spiders, silent
fish that dwell in the deep, starfish, and creatures invisible to the eye—these and all living things, all, all living
things, having completed their sad cycle, are no
more. . . . For thousands of years the earth has borne
no living creature. And now in vain this poor moon
lights her lamp. Cranes no longer wake and cry in meadows, May beetles are heard no more in linden
groves." . . . [*Impulsively embraces* TREPLEV *and runs
out through the French windows.*]

TREPLEV [*after a pause*]:   It would be too bad if someone were to meet her in the garden and tell Mother.
That might upset Mother. . . .

[TREPLEV *spends the next few minutes in silence, tearing
up all his manuscripts and throwing them under the desk,
then he unlocks the door on the right and goes out.*]

DORN [*trying to open the door on the left*]:   That's
strange. This door seems to be locked. . . . [*Comes in
and puts the armchair in its place.*] An obstacle race.

[*Enter* ARKADINA, POLINA ANDREYEVNA, *followed by*
YAKOV *carrying bottles, then* MASHA, SHAMRAYEV, *and*
TRIGORIN.]

ARKADINA: Put the red wine, and the beer for Boris
Alekseyevich, here on the table. We'll have our drinks
as we play. Let's sit down, friends.

POLINA ANDREYEVNA [*to* YAKOV]: Bring the tea now, too. [*Lights the candles and sits down at the card table.*]

SHAMRAYEV [*leading* TRIGORIN *to the cupboard*]: Here's that thing I was telling you about. . . . [*Takes a stuffed sea gull from the cupboard.*] Just as you ordered.

TRIGORIN [*looking at the sea gull*]: I don't remember. . . . [*Musing*] I don't remember. . . .

[*There is the sound of a shot offstage right. Everyone jumps.*]

ARKADINA [*alarmed*]: What was that?

DORN: Nothing. Probably something in my medical case exploded. Don't be alarmed. [*Goes out at the door on the right and returns a moment later.*] That's what it was. A bottle of ether blew up. [*Sings.*] "Again I stand before you, enchanted . . ."

ARKADINA [*sitting down at the table*]: Ough, how that frightened me! It reminded me of the time. . . . [*Covers her face with her hands.*] Everything went black for a minute. . . .

DORN [*turning the pages of a magazine, to* TRIGORIN]: There was an article in here a couple of months ago . . . a letter from America, and I wanted to ask you about it . . . [*putting his arm around* TRIGORIN, *leads him down to the footlights*] since I'm very much interested in this question. . . . [*Lowers his voice.*] Get Irina Nikolayevna away from here somehow. The fact is, Konstantin Gavrilovich has shot himself. . . .

1896

Uncle Vanya

—◦◦◦—

Scenes from Country Life

Characters in the Play

SEREBRYAKOV, ALEKSANDR VLADIMIROVICH, a retired professor

ELENA ANDREYEVNA, his wife, aged twenty-seven

SOFYA ALEKSANDROVNA (SONYA), his daughter by his first wife

VOINITSKAYA, MARIA VASILYEVNA, widow of a Privy Councilor, mother of the professor's first wife

VOINITSKY, IVAN PETROVICH, her son

ASTROV, MIKHAIL LVOVICH, a doctor

TELYEGIN, ILYA ILYICH, an impoverished landowner

MARINA, an old nurse

A WORKMAN

The action takes place on the Serebryakov estate.

Act I

[*A garden. Part of the house and veranda can be seen. Under an old poplar tree in the avenue, a table is set for tea. There are chairs and benches, on one of which lies a guitar. Not far from the table there is a swing. It is between two and three o'clock of a cloudy afternoon.* MARINA, *a heavy, slow-moving old woman, is sitting by the samovar knitting a stocking.* ASTROV *walks up and down near her.*]

MARINA [*pouring a glass of tea*]: Have some, my dear.

ASTROV [*reluctantly taking the glass*]: I don't feel like it, somehow.

MARINA: Perhaps you'd like a drop of vodka?

ASTROV: No. I don't drink vodka every day. Besides, it's sultry. [*Pause*] Nurse, how long have we known each other?

MARINA [*pondering*]: How long? Lord, let me see. . . . You came here, to these parts . . . when was it? Sonichka's mother, Anna Petrovna, was still living then. Two winters you came to see us in her time . . . so, it must be eleven years now. [*After a moment's thought*] But it may be even more. . . .

163

ASTROV: Have I changed much since then?

MARINA: A lot. You were young then, and handsome, but you've aged. And you're not quite so good-looking as you used to be. What's more—you take a drop of vodka now.

ASTROV: Yes. . . . In ten years I've become a different man. And what is the reason? I've worked too hard, nurse. I'm on my feet from morning to night, I don't know what rest is, and at night I lie under the blankets afraid I might be dragged out to see a patient. During all the time you have known me, I haven't had a single free day. Why wouldn't I have aged? And life itself is boring, stupid, squalid. . . . It drags you down, this life. You're surrounded by crackpots, nothing but crackpots; you live with them two or three years, and little by little, without even noticing it, you become odd yourself. It's inevitable. [*Twisting his long moustache*] Look at this enormous moustache I've grown. . . . A ridiculous moustache. I've become an eccentric, nurse. . . . I haven't grown stupid yet—my brains, thank God, are still all there—but my feelings are somehow dulled. There is nothing I want, nothing I need, no one I love . . . except you, perhaps. [*Kisses her on the head.*] I had a nurse like you when I was a child.

MARINA: Perhaps you'd like to have something to eat?

ASTROV: No. In the third week of Lent, I went to Malitskoye, there was an epidemic . . . typhus. . . . In the huts people lay on the floor in rows. . . . Filth, stench, smoke, calves among the sick . . . and young pigs, right there. . . . I was on the move all day, didn't sit down or have a morsel of food, and when I got home they still wouldn't let me rest—brought in a switchman from the railroad; I put him on the table to operate, and he went and died under the chloroform. And just when I least wanted it, feeling awoke in me, and I was as conscience-stricken as if I had deliberately killed him. . . . I sat down, closed my eyes—just like this—and I thought: will those who come after us in a hundred or two hundred years, those for whom we are blazing a trail, will they remember and have a kind word for us? No, they won't, nurse!

MARINA: People won't remember, but God remembers.

ASTROV: Thank you for that. That was well said.

[VOINITSKY *comes out of the house; he has had a nap after lunch and looks rumpled; he sits down on a bench and straightens his fashionable necktie.*]

VOINITSKY: Yes. . . . [*Pause*] Yes. . . .

ASTROV: Had a good sleep?

VOINITSKY: Yes . . . very. [*Yawns.*] Ever since the professor and his wife came here to live, life has been out of joint. . . . I sleep at odd hours, eat all sorts of spicy sauces for lunch and dinner, drink wine—all bad for the health! We never used to have a free minute, Sonya and I worked—I can tell you—but now, only Sonya works, while I just sleep, and eat, and drink. . . . It's not good!

MARINA [*shaking her head*]: Everything's topsy-turvy! The professor gets up at noon, and the samovar is kept boiling the whole morning waiting for him. Before they came, we always had dinner by one o'clock, like everybody else, but with them here it's nearly seven. The professor spends the night reading and writing, and suddenly, about two o'clock, he rings. . . . Good gracious, what is it? Tea! And you have to wake people up to start the samovar. Topsy-turvy!

ASTROV: Are they going to stay much longer?

VOINITSKY [*whistles*]: A hundred years. The professor has decided to settle down here.

MARINA: Now you see! The samovar has been on the table for two hours already, and they've gone for a walk.

VOINITSKY: They're coming, they're coming. . . . Don't worry.

[*Voices are heard; from the farther end of the garden come* SEREBRYAKOV, ELENA ANDREYEVNA, SONYA, *and* TELYEGIN, *returning from a walk.*]

SEREBRYAKOV: Beautiful, beautiful. . . . Wonderful views.

TELYEGIN: Remarkable, Your Excellency.

SONYA: We'll go to the plantation tomorrow, Papa. Would you like to?

VOINITSKY: Let's have tea.

SEREBRYAKOV: My friends, be so kind as to have my tea brought to the study. I still have something more that I must do today.

SONYA: You're sure to like it at the plantation. . . .

[ELENA ANDREYEVNA, SEREBRYAKOV, *and* SONYA *go into the house;* TELYEGIN *goes to the table and sits down beside* MARINA.]

VOINITSKY: It's hot, sultry, but our great scholar wears his overcoat and galoshes, and carries an umbrella and gloves.

ASTROV: That shows he takes care of himself.

VOINITSKY: How lovely she is! How lovely! In all my life I've never seen a more beautiful woman.

TELYEGIN: Whether I drive through the meadow, Marina Timofeyevna, walk in the shady garden, or just look at this table, I experience unaccountable bliss! The weather is delightful, the birds are singing, and we live in peace and harmony—what more do we need? [*Accepting a glass of tea*] I am deeply grateful to you!

VOINITSKY [*dreamily*]: Her eyes . . . Wonderful woman!

ASTROV: Tell us something, Ivan Petrovich.

VOINITSKY [*listlessly*]: What can I tell you?

ASTROV: Isn't there anything new?

VOINITSKY: Nothing. Everything's old. I'm the same as I always was, or worse, perhaps, since I've grown lazy and do nothing but mutter like an old grouch. As for my old magpie, *Maman,* she's still babbling about the emancipation of women; with one eye she looks into her grave, and with the other she scans her books of wisdom, seeking the dawn of a new life.

ASTROV: And the professor?

VOINITSKY: The professor, as before, sits in his study writing from morning till far into the night. "With arduous thought and furrowed brow, all our odes we write, and never a word of praise we hear, our labors to requite." I pity the paper! He would do better to write his autobiography. What a magnificent subject! A retired professor, you know, a dry stick, a learned fish . . . with gout, rheumatism, migraine, and a liver swollen with jealousy and envy. . . . This old codfish lives on the estate of his first wife, lives there against his will, only because he can't afford to live in town. He perpetually complains about his misfortunes, though, as a matter of fact, he is extraordinarily lucky. [*Nervously*] Just think how lucky! A theological student, son of a humble sexton, he managed to get his doctor's degree and a professorship; then he became His Excellency, son-in-law of a Senator, and so forth and so on. All that is unimportant, however, but just consider this: a man lectures and writes about art for exactly twenty-five years, and understands exactly nothing about it. For twenty-five years he has been chewing over other men's ideas about realism, naturalism, and all the rest of that nonsense; twenty-five years lecturing and writing about what intelligent people already know and stupid people aren't interested in—which means twenty-five years of milling the wind. And what self-importance! What pretentiousness! He has retired, and not a single living soul knows who he is, he is absolutely unknown; which means that for twenty-five years he has held some other man's job. And look at him: he struts about like a demigod!

ASTROV: Come now, I believe you envy him.

VOINITSKY: I do envy him! And the success he has with women! No Don Juan ever knew such complete success! His first wife, my sister, a beautiful, gentle creature, pure as that blue sky, noble, generous, and with more admirers than he had pupils—loved him as only pure angels can love those as pure and beautiful as themselves. His mother-in-law, my mother, adores him to this day, and to this day he still inspires her with reverent awe. His second wife, beautiful, intelligent—you just saw her—married him when he was already old, gave him her youth, her beauty, her freedom, and brilliance. For what? Why?

ASTROV: Is she faithful to the professor?

VOINITSKY: Unfortunately, yes.

ASTROV: Why unfortunately?

VOINITSKY: Because that sort of fidelity is false from beginning to end. There is a great deal of rhetoric in it, but no logic. To deceive an old husband you can't endure—that's immoral; but to try to stifle your pitiful youth and vital feelings—that is not immoral.

TELYEGIN [*in a tearful voice*]: Vanya, I don't like it when you talk like that. Come now, really. . . . Anyone who would betray a wife or husband is a person, it seems to me, who is not to be trusted, he might betray his country!

VOINITSKY [*with vexation*]: Turn off the fountain, Waffles!

TELYEGIN: Allow me, Vanya. . . . My wife ran away with the man she loved the day after our wedding, the reason being my unprepossessing appearance. But I have never failed in my duty toward her, I love her to this day and am faithful to her; I do what I can to help her, I gave all I had for the education of the children she had by the man she loved. I have been deprived of happiness, but I still have my pride. And she? Her youth is gone, her beauty, in accordance with the laws of nature, has faded, the man she loved is dead. . . . What has she left?

[*Enter* SONYA *and* ELENA ANDREYEVNA, *and, a little later,* MARIA VASILYEVNA *with a book; she sits down and reads; she is served tea and drinks it without looking up.*]

SONYA [*hurriedly, to nurse*]: Nurse, dear, some peasants have come. Go and speak to them, I'll look after the tea. . . . [*Pours tea.*]

[*Nurse goes out,* ELENA ANDREYEVNA *takes her cup of tea and drinks it sitting in the swing.*]

ASTROV [*to* ELENA ANDREYEVNA]: I came here to see your husband. You wrote me that he was very ill, rheumatism and something else, but it seems that he is perfectly well.

ELENA ANDREYEVNA: Last night he was depressed and complained of pains in his legs, but today he is all right. . . .

ASTROV: And I galloped thirty versts at breakneck speed. Well, never mind, it's not the first time. I'll stay till tomorrow to make up for it; at least I shall sleep *quantum satis.*

SONYA: Wonderful! You so seldom stay the night with us. You probably haven't had any dinner, have you?

ASTROV: No, I haven't.

SONYA: Then you'll be able to have dinner with us, too. We never dine much before seven now. [*Drinks tea.*] The tea is cold!

TELYEGIN: The temperature of the samovar has fallen perceptibly.

ELENA ANDREYEVNA: Never mind, Ivan Ivanovich, we'll drink it cold.

TELYEGIN: I beg your pardon . . . I am not Ivan Ivanovich, but Ilya Ilyich . . . Ilya Ilyich Telyegin, or, as some people call me because of my pock-marked face, Waffles. I am Sonichka's godfather, and His Excellency, your husband, knows me quite well. I live here now, on your estate. . . . You may have been so kind as to notice that I have dinner with you every day.

SONYA: Ilya Ilyich is our helper, our right hand. [*Tenderly*] Let me give you some more tea, Godfather.

MARIA VASILYEVNA: Oh!

SONYA: What is it, Grandmother?

MARIA VASILYEVNA: I forgot to tell Aleksandr . . . I'm losing my memory . . . I received a letter today from Kharkov, from Pavel Alekseyevich. . . . He sent his new pamphlet. . . .

ASTROV: Interesting?

MARIA VASILYEVNA: Interesting, but somewhat strange. He is now refuting what he himself was asserting seven years ago. It's dreadful!

VOINITSKY: There's nothing dreadful about that. Drink your tea, *Maman.*

MARIA VASILYEVNA: But I want to talk!

VOINITSKY: For fifty years now we've been talking and talking and reading pamphlets. It's time to stop.

MARIA VASILYEVNA: For some reason you don't like to listen when I talk. Forgive me, Jean, but you have changed so in the last year that I absolutely do not recognize you. . . . You used to be a man of definite convictions, an enlightened personality. . . .

VOINITSKY: Oh, yes! An enlightened personality who never enlightened anybody. . . . You couldn't have made a more venomous joke. I am now forty-seven years old. Up to a year ago I deliberately tried, just as you do, to cloud my vision with all this scholasticism of yours, and not see real life—and I thought I was doing very well. But now, if you only knew! I lie awake nights in rage and resentment that I so stupidly missed the time when I could have had everything that my old age now denies me!

SONYA: Uncle Vanya, that's tiresome!

MARIA VASILYEVNA [*to her son*]: It's as if you were blaming your former principles somehow. . . . It's not they which are to blame, but you yourself. You seem to have forgotten that principles in themselves are nothing, the dead letter. . . . You ought to have been doing things.

VOINITSKY: Doing things? It's not everyone who is capable of being a writing machine, *perpetuum mobile* like your *Herr* Professor.

MARIA VASILYEVNA: What do you mean by that?

SONYA [*imploringly*]: Grandmother! Uncle Vanya! I implore you!

VOINITSKY: I'll be quiet. I'll be quiet and apologize.

[*A pause*]

ELENA VASILYEVNA: It's a fine day today . . . not too hot . . .

[*A pause*]

VOINITSKY: A fine day to hang oneself. . . .

[TELYEGIN *tunes the guitar.* MARINA *walks near the house, calling the chickens.*]

MARINA: Chick, chick, chick . . .

SONYA: What did those peasants come for?

MARINA: The same old thing—that plot of uncultivated land. . . . Chick, chick, chick . . .

SONYA: Which one are you calling?

MARINA: Speckly, she's gone off somewhere with her chicks. . . . The crows might get them. . . . [*Walks away.*]

[TELYEGIN *plays a polka; everyone listens in silence. Enter a* WORKMAN.]

WORKMAN: Is the doctor here? [*To* ASTROV] Please, Mikhail Lvovich, we've come to get you.

ASTROV: Where from?

WORKMAN: From the factory.

ASTROV [*annoyed*]: Much obliged! Well, I'll have to go. . . . [*Looks around for his cap.*] How annoying, damn it. . . .

SONYA: That really is unpleasant. . . . But do come back to dinner.

ASTROV: No, it will be too late. What's the use? [*To* WORKMAN] See here, my good fellow, you might fetch me a glass of vodka. . . . What's the use? [*Finds his cap.*] In one of Ostrovsky's plays there's a man with a large moustache and small abilities. That's me. . . . Well, I have the honor, my friends . . . [*to* ELENA ANDREYEVNA] If you would ever care to look in on me, with Sofya Aleksandrovna here, I'd really be delighted. I have a small estate, about ninety acres in all, but, if it would interest you, there's a model garden and nursery such as you won't find for a thousand versts around. Next to me is the state forestry. . . . The forester is old and always ill, so that, actually, I supervise all the work.

ELENA ANDREYEVNA: Yes, I've been told that you love forests very much. Of course, that can be of great service, but doesn't it interfere with your real vocation? After all, you are a doctor.

ASTROV: Only God knows what our real vocation is.

ELENA ANDREYEVNA: And is it interesting?

ASTROV: Yes, it's interesting work.

VOINITSKY [*ironically*]: Very!

ELENA ANDREYEVNA [*to* ASTROV]: You're still a young man, you don't look more than . . . well, thirty-six, or thirty-seven . . . and it can't be as interesting as you say. Nothing but trees, trees . . . I think that must be monotonous.

SONYA: No, it's extremely interesting. Every year Mikhail Lvovich plants new forests; he's already received a bronze medal and a citation. He makes great efforts to prevent the old forests from being laid waste. If you listen to him, you'll fully agree with him. He says that the forests beautify the earth, that they teach man to understand beauty and induce in him a nobility of mind. Forests temper the severity of the climate. In countries where the climate is mild, less energy is wasted in the struggle with nature, so man is softer and more tender; in such countries the people are beautiful, flexible, easily stirred, their speech is elegant, their gestures graceful. Science and art flourish among them, their philosophy is not somber, and their attitude toward women is full of an exquisite courtesy. . . .

VOINITSKY [*laughing*]: Bravo, bravo! . . . All that is charming, but not very convincing, [*to* ASTROV] and so, my friend, allow me to go on heating my stoves with logs and building my barns with wood.

ASTROV: You can heat your stoves with peat and build your barns with brick. Now I could accept the cutting of wood out of need, but why devastate the forests? The Russian forests are groaning under the ax, millions of trees are being destroyed, the dwellings of wild beasts and birds are despoiled, rivers are subsiding, drying up, wonderful landscapes vanish never to return, and all because lazy man hasn't sense enough to stoop down and pick up fuel from the ground. [*To* ELENA ANDREYEVNA] Isn't that true, my lady? One would have to be a reckless barbarian to burn this beauty in his stove, to destroy what he cannot create. Man is endowed with reason and creative powers so that he may increase what has been given to him, but up to now he has not created but only destroyed. There are fewer and fewer forests, rivers are drying up, wild life is becoming extinct, the climate is ruined, and every day the earth gets poorer and uglier. [*To* VOINITSKY] You give me that ironical look of yours, what I say doesn't seem very serious to you, and . . . and maybe I am just a crank, but when I walk by a peasant's woodland which I have saved from being cut down, or when I hear the rustling of young trees which I have planted with my own hands, I realize that the climate is somewhat in my power, and that if, a thousand years from now, mankind is happy, I shall be responsible for that too, in a small way. When I plant a birch tree and then watch it put forth its leaves and sway in the wind, my soul is filled with pride, and I . . . [*seeing the* WORKMAN *who has brought a glass of vodka on a tray*] however. . . . [*Drinks.*] Time for me to go. All that is very likely my eccentricity, after all. I have the honor. . . . [*Goes toward the house.*]

SONYA [*takes his arm and goes with him*]: When will you come to see us?

ASTROV: I don't know. . . .

SONYA: Not for a whole month again?

[ASTROV *and* SONYA *go into the house;* MARIA VASILY-EVNA *and* TELYEGIN *remain at the table;* ELENA ANDREY-EVNA *and* VOINITSKY *walk toward the veranda.*]

ELENA ANDREYEVNA: Ivan Petrovich, you have behaved abominably again. Did you have to annoy Maria Vasilyevna with your talk of *perpetuum mobile!* And today at lunch you again argued with Aleksandr. How petty that is!

VOINITSKY: What if I detest him!

ELENA ANDREYEVNA: There's no reason to detest Aleksandr; he's just like everyone else. He's no worse than you.

VOINITSKY: If you could see your face, your movements. . . . You are too indolent to live! Oh, how indolent!

ELENA ANDREYEVNA: Ah, both indolent and bored! Everyone abuses my husband, everyone looks at me with pity: poor thing, she has an old husband! This sympathy for me—oh, how I understand it! As Astrov said just now: you all recklessly destroy the forests, and soon there will be nothing left on earth. In the same way you recklessly destroy man, and soon, thanks to you, there will be no fidelity, no purity, no capacity for self-sacrifice, left on earth. Why is it you can never look at a woman with indifference, unless she is yours? It's because—that doctor was right—there's a demon of destruction in every one of you. You spare neither forests, birds, women, nor one another. . . .

VOINITSKY: I don't care for this philosophy! [*Pause*]

ELENA ANDREYEVNA: That doctor has a tired, nervous face. An interesting face. Sonya is evidently attracted to him; she's in love with him, and I understand her. He has visited the house three times since I've been here, but I am shy, and haven't once really talked to him or been nice to him. He must have thought me disagreeable. It's quite possible, Ivan Petrovich, that the reason you and I are such friends is that we are both tiresome, boring people. Tiresome! Don't look at me like that, I don't like it.

VOINITSKY: How else can I look at you, since I love you? You are my joy, my life, my youth! I know the chances of your returning my feelings are slight, even nil, but I don't want anything, just let me look at you, hear your voice——

ELENA ANDREYEVNA: Hush, they might hear you!

[*They walk to the house.*]

VOINITSKY [*following her*]:   Let me speak of my love, don't drive me away . . . that alone will be the greatest happiness for me. . . .

ELENA ANDREYEVNA: This is agonizing . . .

[*They go into the house.* TELYEGIN *strums on the guitar and plays a polka;* MARIA VASILYEVNA *makes notes on the margins of a pamphlet.*]

Act II

[*The dining room in* SEREBRYAKOV'*s house. Night. A watchman can be heard tapping in the garden.* SEREBRYAKOV *is sitting in an armchair in front of an open window, dozing.* ELENA ANDREYEVNA *sits beside him, also dozing.*]

SEREBRYAKOV [*waking up*]: Who is that? Sonya, is it you?

ELENA ANDREYEVNA: It's me.

SEREBRYAKOV: You, Lenochka. . . . This unbearable pain!

ELENA ANDREYEVNA: Your lap robe has fallen to the floor. [*Wraps it around his legs.*] I'll shut the window, Aleksandr.

SEREBRYAKOV: No, I'm suffocating. . . . I dozed off just now and dreamt that my left leg didn't belong to me. I was awakened by an excruciating pain. No, this is not gout, it's more likely rheumatism. What time is it now?

ELENA ANDREYEVNA: Twenty minutes past twelve.

SEREBRYAKOV: In the morning look in the library for Batyushkov. I think we have him.

177

ELENA ANDREYEVNA: Hm?

SEREBRYAKOV: Look for Batyushkov in the morning. I remember we did have him. But why is it so difficult for me to breathe?

ELENA ANDREYEVNA: You're tired. You haven't slept for two nights.

SEREBRYAKOV: They say that Turgenev developed angina pectoris from gout. I'm afraid I may have it. Damnable, disgusting old age! When I grew old, I began to be repulsive to myself. And now, no doubt, you all find it repulsive to look at me.

ELENA ANDREYEVNA: You speak of your old age as if we were to blame for it.

SEREBRYAKOV: And to you, above all, I'm repulsive.

[ELENA ANDREYEVNA *gets up and sits farther away from him.*]

SEREBRYAKOV: Of course, you are right. I am not stupid and I understand. You are young, healthy, beautiful, you want to live, and I'm an old man, almost a corpse. Well? Do you think I don't understand? And, of course, it is stupid of me to go on living. But wait a bit, soon I shall set you all free. I shan't have to drag on much longer.

ELENA ANDREYEVNA: I am exhausted. . . . For God's sake, be quiet.

SEREBRYAKOV: It appears that everyone, thanks to me, is exhausted, bored, wasting his youth, and only I am content and enjoying life. Oh, yes, of course!

ELENA ANDREYEVNA: Do be quiet! You have worn me out!

SEREBRYAKOV: I have worn everybody out. Of course.

ELENA ANDREYEVNA: [*through tears*]: It's unbearable! Tell me, what is it you want from me?

SEREBRYAKOV: Nothing.

ELENA ANDREYEVNA: Then be quiet. I beg you.

SEREBRYAKOV: It's very strange, when Ivan Petrovich starts talking, or that old idiot, Maria Vasilyevna—it's quite all right, everyone listens, but just let me say one word, and everyone begins to feel miserable. Even my voice is repulsive. Well, let us suppose that I am repulsive, that I am an egotist, a despot—haven't I a right to be selfish in my old age? Haven't I earned it? I ask you, haven't I a right to a peaceful old age and a little attention?

ELENA ANDREYEVNA: No one is disputing your rights. [*The window bangs in the wind.*] The wind has come up, I'll shut the window. [*Shuts it.*] It will rain soon. No one disputes your rights.

[*Pause. In the garden the watchman is tapping and singing a song.*]

SEREBRYAKOV: To devote your entire life to learning, to grow accustomed to your own study, to lecture halls, and esteemed colleagues—and suddenly, for no reason whatsoever, to find yourself in this sepulcher, seeing stupid people every day, listening to their trivial conversations. . . . I want to live, I love success, recognition, excitement, and here—it's like being in exile. Every minute to be grieving for the past, watching the success of others, fearing death. . . . I cannot! It's too much for me! And they won't even forgive me my old age!

ELENA ANDREYEVNA: Wait, have patience: in five or six years I'll be old, too.

[*Enter* SONYA.]

SONYA: Papa, you yourself had us send for Dr. Astrov, and now that he's here you refuse to see him. That's not very considerate. We've simply troubled him for nothing——

SEREBRYAKOV: What do I need your Astrov for? He knows as much about medicine as I know about astronomy.

SONYA: We can't summon the entire medical faculty for your gout.

SEREBRYAKOV: I won't even talk to that imbecile.

SONYA: Just as you please. [*Sits down.*] It's all the same to me.

SEREBRYAKOV: What time is it now?

ELENA ANDREYEVNA: Nearly one.

SEREBRYAKOV: I'm suffocating. . . . Sonya, fetch me my drops from the table!

SONYA: Right away. [*Hands him the drops.*]

SEREBRYAKOV [*peevishly*]: Oh, not these! It's no use asking for anything!

SONYA: Please, don't be so fussy. Some people may like it, but be so good as to spare me—I don't! And I haven't the time; I've got to get up early in the morning for the mowing.

[*Enter* VOINITSKY *in a dressing gown and with a candle.*]

VOINITSKY: There's a storm coming up. [*A flash of lightning*] There, you see! Hélène and Sonya, go to bed, I've come to take your place.

SEREBRYAKOV [*alarmed*]: No, no! Don't leave me with him! Don't! He'll talk my head off!

VOINITSKY: But you have to let them rest. It's the second night they've gone without sleep.

SEREBRYAKOV: Let them go to bed, but you go, too. Thank you. I implore you. For the sake of our former friendship, don't protest. We'll talk some other time.

VOINITSKY [*with an ironical grin*]: Our former friendship . . . Former . . .

SONYA: Be quiet, Uncle Vanya.

SEREBRYAKOV [*to his wife*]: My dear, don't leave me with him! He'll talk my head off.

VOINITSKY: Really, this is beginning to be ridiculous.

[*Enter* MARINA *with a candle.*]

SONYA: Nurse dear, you ought to be in bed. It's late.

MARINA: The samovar is still on the table. I can't very well go to bed.

SEREBRYAKOV: Everyone's kept up, everyone's worn out, I alone am blissfully happy.

MARINA [*going up to* SEREBRYAKOV, *tenderly*]: What is it, my dear? Does it hurt? I've got a pain myself in my legs that keeps droning and droning like that. [*Arranges his lap robe.*] It's that old complaint of yours. Vera Petrovna, Sonya's mother, used to be up nights with you, just killing herself. . . . She loved you so much. . . . [*Pause*] Old folks, like little ones, want somebody to feel sorry for them, but nobody feels sorry for the old. [*Kisses* SEREBRYAKOV *on the shoulder.*] Come, my dear, go to bed now. . . . Come along, dovey . . . I'll

give you some linden tea, and warm your feet . . . I'll
say a prayer for you. . . .

SEREBRYAKOV [*moved*]:   Let us go, Marina.

MARINA: I've got a pain in my legs that keeps droning and droning just like that. . . . [*She and* SONYA *lead
him out.*] Vera Petrovna worried herself to death, always
crying. . . . You were just a silly little thing then,
Sonichka. . . . Come along, come my dear . . .

[SEREBRYAKOV, SONYA, *and* MARINA go *out.*]

ELENA ANDREYEVNA: I'm worn out with him. I can
hardly stand up.

VOINITSKY: You with him, and I with myself. I
haven't slept for three nights.

ELENA ANDREYEVNA: There is something very wrong
in this house. Your mother hates everything except her
pamphlets and the professor; the professor is irritable,
he doesn't trust me and is afraid of you; Sonya is angry
at her father, angry at me—she hasn't spoken to me
for two weeks; you hate my husband and are openly
contemptuous of your mother; I am on edge and have
been on the verge of tears twenty times today. . . . There
is something very wrong in this house.

VOINITSKY: Let's drop the philosophy!

ELENA ANDREYEVNA: Ivan Petrovich, you are an educated, intelligent man, and I should think you would understand that the world is being destroyed not by crime
and fire, but by hatred, enmity, all these petty
squabbles. . . . Your business should be not to grumble,
but to reconcile us to one another.

VOINITSKY: First reconcile me to myself! My
darling . . . [*Bends down to her hand.*]

ELENA ANDREYEVNA: Stop it! [*Withdraws her hand.*]
Go away!

VOINITSKY: The rain will be over presently, and everything in nature will be refreshed and breathe easily. Only
I shall not be refreshed by the storm. Day and night, like
an evil spirit, I am haunted by the thought that my life
has been hopelessly wasted. I have no past, it was stupidly
spent on trifles, and the present is awful in its absurdity.
There is my life for you, and my love: what is to be done
with them, what can I do with them? My feeling for you
is dying in vain, like a ray of sunlight that has fallen into
a pit, and I myself am being destroyed.

ELENA ANDREYEVNA: When you talk to me of your
love I feel numb and don't know what to say. Forgive
me, there is nothing I can say to you. [*About to go.*]
Good night.

VOINITSKY [*barring her way*]:   And if you knew how I
suffer from the thought that by my side in this house another life is being destroyed—yours! What cursed philosophy stands in your way? Understand, do understand——

ELENA ANDREYEVNA: [*looking at him intently*]:   Ivan
Petrovich, you are drunk!

VOINITSKY: It may be, it may be. . . .

ELENA ANDREYEVNA: Where is the doctor?

VOINITSKY: In there, in my room . . . he's spending
the night here. It may be, it may be. . . . Anything is
possible!

ELENA ANDREYEVNA: So you've been drinking
today? What is that for?

VOINITSKY: At least it seems like life. . . . Don't prevent me, Hélène!

ELENA ANDREYEVNA: You never used to drink, and you never used to talk so much. . . . Go to bed! I am bored with you.

VOINITSKY [*seizing her hand*]: My darling . . . wonderful one!

ELENA ANDREYEVNA [*annoyed*]: Leave me alone. This is really disgusting. [*Goes out.*]

VOINITSKY [*alone*]: She's gone. . . . [*Pause*] Ten years ago I met her at my sister's house. She was seventeen and I was thirty-seven. Why didn't I fall in love with her then and propose to her? It could so easily have happened. She would have been my wife now. . . . Yes. . . . Now we both should have been awakened by the storm; the thunder would have frightened her, I would have held her in my arms and whispered: "Don't be afraid, I am here." Oh, wonderful thoughts, how lovely . . . I am even laughing . . . but, my God, the thoughts are muddled in my head. . . . Why am I old? Why doesn't she understand me? All that rhetoric and lazy morality, her foolish, lazy ideas about the ruin of the world—all that is utterly hateful to me. [*Pause*] Oh, how I have been cheated! I worshiped that professor, that pitiful gouty creature, I worked like an ox for him! Sonya and I squeezed the last drop out of this estate; like kulaks, we sold vegetable oil, dried peas, cottage cheese, grudging ourselves every morsel of food, trying to save every little kopeck so we could send him thousands of rubles. I was proud of him, proud of his learning, it was the breath of life to me. Everything he wrote or uttered seemed to come from a genius. . . . God! And now? Now he has retired, and the sum total of his life can be seen: not one page of his work will survive him, he is absolutely unknown, he is nothing! A soap bubble! And I have been cheated . . . I see it—senselessly cheated. . . .

[*Enter* ASTROV *in his coat but without a waistcoat or necktie; he is slightly drunk.* TELYEGIN *follows with his guitar.*]

ASTROV: Play!

TELYEGIN: But everyone's asleep!

ASTROV: Play!

[TELYEGIN *plays softly.*]

ASTROV [*to* VOINITSKY]: Are you alone here? No ladies? [*Arms akimbo, softly sings.*] "Gone my hut, gone my fire, the master has no place to retire . . ." The storm woke me up. A fine rain. What time is it?

VOINITSKY: God only knows.

ASTROV: I thought I heard Elena Andreyevna's voice.

VOINITSKY: She was here a moment ago.

ASTROV: A magnificent woman. [*Examines the medicine bottles on the table.*] Medicines . . . what a variety of prescriptions! From Kharkov, from Moscow, from Tula. . . . Every town in Russia must be fed up with his gout. Is he really ill or just pretending?

VOINITSKY: He's ill. [*Pause*]

ASTROV: Why are you so sad today? Feeling sorry for the professor perhaps?

VOINITSKY: Leave me alone.

ASTROV: Or are you in love with the professor's wife?

VOINITSKY: She is my friend.

ASTROV: Already?

VOINITSKY: What does that "already" mean?

ASTROV: A woman can become a man's friend only in this sequence: first an acquaintance, then a mistress, and then a friend.

VOINITSKY: A vulgar philosophy.

ASTROV: What? Yes . . . I must confess, I am becoming a vulgarian. You see, I'm even drunk. As a rule I get drunk like this once a month. When I'm in this state I become arrogant and insolent in the extreme. I don't stop at anything! I undertake the most difficult operations and do them beautifully; I draw up the most far-reaching plans for the future; at such times I don't see myself as a crank, I believe that I am a tremendous boon to mankind—tremendous! . . . At such times I have my own system of philosophy, and all of you, my friends, appear to me to be such insects . . . such microbes. [*To* TELYEGIN] Waffles, play!

TELYEGIN: My dear friend, I'd be glad to, with all my heart, but don't you realize—everyone in the house is asleep!

ASTROV: Play!

[TELYEGIN *softly plays.*]

ASTROV: Let's have a drink. Come on, I think there's still some cognac left. As soon as it's daylight we'll go to my place. Roight? I've got a medical assistant who never says right, but "roight." An awful scoundrel. So, "roight"? [*Seeing* SONYA *come in*] Excuse me, I haven't got my tie on.

[*He goes out hurriedly, followed by* TELYEGIN.]

SONYA: Uncle Vanya, you've been drinking with the doctor again. You're a fine pair! He's always been like that, but why do you have to do it? It's not very becoming at your age.

VOINITSKY: Age has nothing to do with it. When one has no real life, one lives on illusions. It's better than nothing.

SONYA: The hay has all been mowed and with the rain every day, it's rotting, and you occupy yourself with illusions. You've completely neglected the estate. . . . I've been working all alone and I'm tired out. . . . [*Alarmed*] Uncle, you have tears in your eyes!

VOINITSKY: What do you mean, tears? Not at all . . . nonsense. . . . You looked at me just now exactly as your mother used to. My darling . . . [*Eagerly kisses her hands and face.*] My sister . . . my dear sister. . . . Where is she now? If she knew! Ah, if she knew!

SONYA: What? Knew what, Uncle?

VOINITSKY: It's painful . . . it's not right. . . . Never mind. . . . Later. . . . Never mind. . . . I'm going. . . . [*Goes out.*]

SONYA [*knocking at the door*]: Mikhail Lvovich! You aren't asleep, are you? May I see you for a minute?

ASTROV [*through the door*]: At once! [*A moment later comes in, with his tie and waistcoat on.*] What can I do for you?

SONYA: You can drink, if it doesn't disgust you, but, I implore you, don't let my uncle drink. It's bad for him.

ASTROV: Very well. We won't drink any more. [*Pause*] I was just leaving. Signed and sealed. It'll be daylight by the time the horses are harnessed.

SONYA: It's raining. Wait till morning.

ASTROV: The storm is passing us by, we'll just get the fringe of it. I'm going. And please, don't ask me again to see your father. I tell him it's gout—he says it's rheumatism; I ask him to stay in bed—he sits up in a chair. And today he wouldn't even speak to me.

SONYA: He's spoiled. [*Looks into the sideboard.*] Won't you have a bite to eat?

ASTROV: Yes, perhaps.

SONYA: I like having a snack at night. I think there's something in the sideboard. In his time, they say, he was a great success with women, and they spoiled him. Here, have some cheese.

[*They stand at the sideboard eating.*]

ASTROV: I've had nothing to eat all day, only drink. Your father has a difficult character. [*Takes a bottle out of the sideboard.*] May I? [*Drinks a glass.*] There's no one here, so I can speak frankly. You know, I don't think I could live in this house a month—I'd suffocate in this atmosphere. . . . Your father, completely absorbed in his gout and his books, Uncle Vanya with his depression, your grandmother, and, to top it all, your stepmother . . .

SONYA: What about my stepmother?

ASTROV: Everything ought to be beautiful in a human being: face, dress, soul, and thoughts. She is beautiful, there's no denying it, but . . . you know, she does nothing but eat, sleep, walk about, and bewitch us all with her beauty—and that's all. She has no duties, other people work for her. . . . Isn't that so? An idle life cannot be pure. [*Pause*] However, perhaps I am too hard on her. Like your Uncle Vanya, I am dissatisfied with life, and we're both becoming grumblers.

SONYA: Are you really dissatisfied with life?

ASTROV: On the whole, I love life, but our narrow, provincial Russian life . . . I cannot endure. I despise it with all the strength of my soul. As for my own personal life, God knows there is absolutely nothing good in it. You know, when you walk through a forest on a dark night, if you see a small light gleaming in the distance, you don't notice your fatigue, the darkness, the thorny branches lashing your face. . . . I work harder than anyone in the district—you know that—and fate is continually battering me, there are times when I suffer unbearably, but for me there is no small light in the distance. I look forward to nothing, I don't like people. . . . It's been a long time since I've loved anyone.

SONYA: No one?

ASTROV: No one. I have a certain tenderness for your nurse—in memory of old times. The peasants are all alike, undeveloped, living in squalor; and it's hard to get along with the intelligentsia—they tire you out. All of them, all our good friends here, think and feel in a small way, they see no farther than their noses: to put it bluntly, they're stupid. And those who are more intelligent and more outstanding are hysterical, eaten up with analysis and introspection. . . . They whine, they're full of hatred and morbid slander; they sidle up to a man, look at him out of the corners of their eyes, and conclude: "Oh, that one's a psychopath!" or "That one's a windbag!" And when they don't know what label to stick on my forehead, they say: "He's a strange one, very strange!" I love forests—that's strange; I don't eat meat—that's also strange. There's no longer any spontaneous, pure, free attitude to nature or to people. . . . None, none! [*He is about to drink.*]

SONYA [*stopping him*]: No, please, I beg you, don't drink any more.

ASTROV: Why not?

SONYA: It's so unlike you! You are refined, you have such a gentle voice. . . . And more than that, unlike everyone else I know, you are a beautiful person. So why do you want to be like ordinary people who drink and play cards? Oh, don't do it, I implore you! You always say people don't create, but merely destroy what

has been given them from above. Then why, why are
you destroying yourself? You mustn't, you mustn't! I
entreat you, I implore you!

ASTROV [*holds out his hand to her*]:   I won't drink
any more.

SONYA: Give me your word.

ASTROV: Word of honor.

SONYA [*presses his hand warmly*]:   Thank you!

ASTROV: *Basta!* I've come to my senses. You see, I'm
quite sober now, and I'll stay like this to the end of my
days. [*Looks at his watch.*] Well, let's go on: as I was
saying, my time has passed, it's too late for me now. . . .
I've become old, overworked, vulgar, all my feelings are
blunted, and I don't think I could become attached to
anyone. I don't love anyone, and . . . now I never shall.
What still captivates me is beauty. I am not indifferent
to that. I believe, for instance, that if she wanted to,
Elena Andreyevna could turn my head in one day. . . .
But that's not love, of course, that's not affection. . . .
[*Puts his hand over his eyes and shudders.*]

SONYA: What's the matter?

ASTROV: Nothing. . . . In Lent one of my patients
died under chloroform.

SONYA: It's time you forgot about that. [*Pause*] Tell
me, Mikhail Lvovich . . . if I had a friend, or a younger
sister, and you found out that she . . . well, let us say,
loved you, how would you feel about it?

ASTROV [*shrugs his shoulders*]:   I don't know. I probably wouldn't feel anything. I should give her to understand that I couldn't love her . . . and that my mind is
occupied with other things. However, if I'm going, I'd
better go. I'll say good-bye, my dear, or we'll go on

talking till morning. [*Shakes her hand.*] I'll go through the drawing room, if I may, otherwise I'm afraid your uncle may detain me. [*Goes out.*]

SONYA [*alone*]:   He didn't say anything to me. . . . His heart and soul are still hidden from me . . . but why do I feel so happy? [*Laughs for joy.*] I said to him: You are refined, noble, you have such a gentle voice. . . . I wonder if that was out of place? His voice vibrates and caresses . . . I can still feel it in the air. When I said that to him, about a younger sister, he didn't understand. . . . [*Wringing her hands*] Oh, how dreadful it is that I am not beautiful! How dreadful! And I know I'm not beautiful, I know it, I know it! . . . Last Sunday, coming out of church, I heard them talking about me, and one woman said: "She's kind and unselfish, but it's a pity she's so plain. . . ." So plain . . .

[*Enter* ELENA ANDREYEVNA.]

ELENA ANDREYEVNA   [*opens the window*]:   The storm is over. How lovely the air is! [*Pause*] Where's the doctor?

SONYA: He's gone.

ELENA ANDREYEVNA: Sophie!

SONYA: What?

ELENA ANDREYEVNA: How long are you going to go on being cross with me? We haven't done each other any harm. Why should we be enemies? That's enough now. . . .

SONYA: I myself wanted— [*Embraces her.*] I won't be cross any more.

ELENA ANDREYEVNA: Good!

[*Both are agitated.*]

SONYA: Has Papa gone to bed?

ELENA ANDREYEVNA: No, he's sitting in the drawing room. . . . We don't talk to each other for weeks at a time, God knows why. . . . [*Seeing that the sideboard is open*] What's this?

SONYA: Mikhail Lvovich had supper.

ELENA ANDREYEVNA: There's some wine. . . . Let's drink *brüderschaft.*

SONYA: Yes, let's!

ELENA ANDREYEVNA: Out of the same glass. . . . [*Fills it.*] It's better that way. So, now we are friends?

SONYA: Friends. [*They drink and kiss each other.*] I've wanted to make it up for a long time, but I felt somehow ashamed. . . . [*Weeps.*]

ELENA ANDREYEVNA: But why are you crying?

SONYA: I don't know, for no reason.

ELENA ANDREYEVNA: There, there, now. . . . [*Weeps.*] You funny girl, now I'm crying too. . . . [*Pause*] You're angry with me because you think I married your father for money. . . . If you believe in oaths, I'll swear to you that I married him for love. I was attracted to him as a learned, celebrated man. It wasn't real love, it was make-believe, but you see, it seemed real to me at the time. I'm not guilty. But from the very day of our wedding, you haven't stopped accusing me with your intelligent, suspicious eyes.

SONYA: Come, peace, peace! Let's forget it.

ELENA ANDREYEVNA: You mustn't look like that—it's not becoming. You must believe in everyone, otherwise it's impossible to live. [*Pause*]

SONYA: Tell me honestly, as a friend . . . are you happy?

ELENA ANDREYEVNA: No.

SONYA: I knew that. One more question. Tell me frankly—wouldn't you have liked your husband to be young?

ELENA ANDREYEVNA: What a child you are still. Of course I should have! Well, ask me something else, go on. . . .

SONYA: Do you like the doctor?

ELENA ANDREYEVNA: Yes, very much.

SONYA: I look foolish . . . don't I? Though he has gone, I still keep hearing his voice, his footsteps, and when I look at that dark window . . . I can see his face. Let me tell you everything. . . . But I can't talk so loud . . . I feel ashamed. Let's go to my room, we can talk there. Do I seem silly to you? Own up. . . . Tell me something about him.

ELENA ANDREYEVNA: But what?

SONYA: He is clever. . . . He knows how to do things, he can do anything. . . . He heals the sick, he plants forests. . . .

ELENA ANDREYEVNA: It's not a question of forests and medicine. . . . My darling, don't you understand, he has a touch of genius! And do you know what that means? It means daring, freedom of mind, a broad

scope. . . . When he plants a little tree, he is already
imagining what will come of it in a thousand years, already dreaming of the happiness of mankind. Such people are rare, one must love them. . . . He drinks, he
sometimes seems a little coarse—but what harm is there
in that? A man of genius in Russia cannot remain spot-
less. Just think what sort of life that doctor has! Impass-
able mud on the roads, frosts, snowstorms, vast
distances, uncouth, primitive people, poverty and disease
all around him—it would be hard for a man working
and struggling day after day in such an atmosphere to
keep himself sober and pure till the age of forty. . . .
[*Kisses her.*] But I am a tiresome, inconsequential
person. . . . In my music, in my husband's house, in all
my romances—everywhere, in fact, I have been inconsequential. Actually, when you come to think of it, I am
very, very unhappy! [*Paces the stage in agitation.*] There
is no happiness for me in this world. None! Why are
you laughing?

SONYA [*laughs, hiding her face*]: I am so happy . . .
so happy!

ELENA ANDREYEVNA: I feel like playing the piano. . . .
I could play now.

SONYA: Do play! [*Embraces her.*] I can't sleep. . . .
Play something!

ELENA ANDREYEVNA: In a moment. Your father is
not asleep. Music irritates him when he's ill. Go and ask
him. If he doesn't mind, I'll play. Go on . . .

SONYA: Right away. [*Goes out.*]

[*In the garden the watchman is tapping.*]

ELENA ANDREYEVNA: It's a long time since I've
played. I shall play and cry, cry like a fool. [*Through the
window*] Is that you tapping, Yefim?

WATCHMAN'S VOICE: It's me!

ELENA ANDREYEVNA: Don't tap, the master is not well.

WATCHMAN'S VOICE: I'll go at once. [*Whistles.*] Hey, there, Zhuchka! Good dog! Zhuchka! [*Pause*]

SONYA [*returning*]:   We can't!

Act III

[*The drawing room of* SEREBRYAKOV'*s house. Three doors, right, left, and center. Daytime.* VOINITSKY *and* SONYA *are seated;* ELENA ANDREYEVNA *is walking about the stage, preoccupied.*]

VOINITSKY: The *Herr* Professor has graciously expressed the desire that we should all assemble in this room at one o'clock today. [*Looks at his watch.*] A quarter to one. He wishes to make some sort of disclosure to the world.

ELENA ANDREYEVNA: It's probably business. . . .

VOINITSKY: He has no business. He writes nonsense, grumbles, is jealous, and that's all.

SONYA [*reproachfully*]:   Uncle!

VOINITSKY: Well, I'm sorry. [*Points to* ELENA ANDREYEVNA.] Just look at her! She walks about swaying from indolence. Very charming! Very!

ELENA ANDREYEVNA: You keep buzzing, buzzing away all day—don't you get tired of it? [*In misery*] I'm dying of boredom, I don't know what to do.

SONYA [*shrugging her shoulders*]: Isn't there plenty to do? If only you wanted to. . . . .

ELENA ANDREYEVNA: For instance?

SONYA: You could help with running the estate, teach, take care of the sick. Isn't that enough? When you and Papa were not here, Uncle Vanya and I used to go to the market ourselves to sell the flour.

ELENA ANDREYEVNA: I don't know how to do such things. And it's not interesting. Only in idealistic novels do people teach and doctor the peasants, and how can I, for no reason whatever, suddenly start teaching and looking after peasants?

SONYA: I don't see how one can help doing it. Wait a bit, you'll get accustomed to it. [*Embraces her.*] Don't be bored, darling. [*Laughs.*] You're bored, you don't know what to do with yourself, and boredom and idleness are catching. Look: Uncle Vanya does nothing, just follows you about like a shadow, and I left my work and came running in to have a chat with you. I've grown lazy, I can't help it! Dr. Mikhail Lvovich rarely came to visit us before, once a month perhaps, and then it was hard to persuade him, but now he drives over every day; he's deserted both his forests and his medicine. You must be a witch.

VOINITSKY: Why are you languishing? [*With animation*] Come, my darling, my lovely one, be a clever girl! The blood of mermaids flows in your veins, so be a mermaid! Let yourself go for once in your life, fall head over heels in love with some water sprite, and plunge headlong into the deep, so that the *Herr* Professor and all of us just throw up our hands!

ELENA ANDREYEVNA [*angrily*]: Leave me alone! How cruel this is! [*Starts to go.*]

VOINITSKY [*preventing her*]: Come, come, my joy, forgive me . . . I apologize. [*Kisses her hand.*] Peace.

ELENA ANDREYEVNA: You must admit, an angel wouldn't have the patience—

VOINITSKY: As a token of peace and harmony I am going to bring you a bouquet of roses that I gathered for you this morning. . . . Autumn roses—lovely, sad, roses. . . . [*Goes out.*]

SONYA: Autumn roses—lovely, sad, roses. . . . [*Both look out the window.*]

ELENA ANDREYEVNA: Here it is September already. How are we going to live through the winter here? [*Pause*] Where is the doctor?

SONYA: In Uncle Vanya's room. Writing something. I'm glad Uncle Vanya went out, I must talk to you.

ELENA ANDREYEVNA: What about?

SONYA: What about? [*Puts her head on* ELENA ANDREYEVNA*'s breast.*]

ELENA ANDREYEVNA: Come . . . there, there. . . . [*Strokes her hair.*] That's enough.

SONYA: I'm not beautiful.

ELENA ANDREYEVNA: You have beautiful hair.

SONYA: No! [*Turns to look at herself in the mirror.*] No! When a woman is not beautiful, they always say: "You have beautiful hair, you have beautiful eyes." . . . I have loved him for six years now, I love him more than my own mother. Every minute I seem to hear him, feel the pressure of his hand; I watch the door, waiting, thinking he will come in at any moment. And you see,

I keep coming to you to talk about him. He's here every day now, but he doesn't look at me, he doesn't see me. . . . It's such agony! I have no hope at all, none, none! [*In despair*] Oh, God, give me strength. . . . I've been praying all night. . . . I often go up to him, start talking to him, look into his eyes . . . I have no pride left, no strength to control myself. . . . I couldn't help it, yesterday I told Uncle Vanya that I love him. . . . And all the servants know I love him. Everybody knows.

ELENA ANDREYEVNA: And he?

SONYA: No. He doesn't notice me.

ELENA ANDREYEVNA [*musing*]: He's a strange man. . . . Do you know what? Let me speak to him. I'll do it carefully, in a roundabout way. . . . [*Pause*] Yes, really, how much longer can you go on without knowing? Let me!

[SONYA *nods her head in consent.*]

ELENA ANDREYEVNA: Splendid. Either he loves you or he doesn't—that's not difficult to find out. Don't be embarrassed, dear, don't be troubled—I'll question him so tactfully, he won't even be aware of it. All we want to find out is yes or no. [*Pause*] If it's no, he had better stop coming here, hadn't he?

[SONYA *nods her head in agreement.*]

ELENA ANDREYEVNA: It's easier when you don't see him. We won't put it off, I'll speak to him at once. He intended to show me some charts. . . . Go and tell him I want to see him.

SONYA [*in violent agitation*]: You will tell me the whole truth?

ELENA ANDREYEVNA: Yes, of course. After all, it seems to me that the truth, no matter what it is, is not so dreadful as uncertainty. Trust me, little one.

SONYA: Yes, yes . . . I'll tell him you want to see his charts. . . . [*Goes to the door and stops.*] No, uncertainty is better. . . . At least there is hope . . .

ELENA ANDREYEVNA: What did you say?

SONYA: Nothing. [*Goes out.*]

ELENA ANDREYEVNA [*alone*]: There is nothing worse than knowing someone's secret and not being able to help. [*Musing*] He is not in love with her—that's clear, but why shouldn't he marry her? She isn't beautiful, but for a country doctor, and at his age, she would make an excellent wife. She's clever, and so kind, so pure. . . . No, that's wrong, wrong. . . . [*Pause*] I understand that poor girl. In the midst of desperate boredom, with some sort of gray shadows floating around her instead of people, and hearing only the banalities of those who can do nothing but eat, drink, and sleep—he sometimes appears, unlike the rest, handsome, interesting, fascinating, like a bright moon rising in the darkness. . . . To yield to the charm of such a man, to forget oneself . . . It seems that I, too, am somewhat carried away. Yes, I am bored when he's not here, and I smile just thinking of him. . . . Uncle Vanya says I have mermaid's blood in my veins. "Let yourself go for once in your life." . . . Well? Perhaps that's what I ought to do. . . . To fly, free as a bird, away from all of you, away from your sleepy faces and your talk, to forget you even exist in the world. . . . But I'm a coward, timid. . . . My conscience would torment me. . . . He comes here every day, I can guess why, and even now I feel guilty. I am ready to fall on my knees before Sonya, and ask her to forgive me . . . to weep. . . .

[*Enter* ASTROV *with a chart.*]

ASTROV: Good day! [*Shakes hands.*] You wanted to see my handiwork?

ELENA ANDREYEVNA: Yesterday you promised to show me your work. . . . Are you free?

ASTROV: Oh, of course. [*Spreads a map on a card table and fixes it with thumbtacks.*] Where were you born?

ELENA ANDREYEVNA [*helping him*]: In Petersburg.

ASTROV: And where did you study?

ELENA ANDREYEVNA: At the Conservatory.

ASTROV: I don't suppose this will interest you.

ELENA ANDREYEVNA: Why not? It's true, I am not familiar with country life, but I've read a great deal.

ASTROV: I have a table of my own in this house . . . in Ivan Petrovich's room. When I am completely exhausted—to the point of stupefaction—I drop everything and run in here to amuse myself with this thing for an hour or two. Ivan Petrovich and Sofya Aleksandrovna work at their accounts, clicking the abacus, I sit near them at my own table and dabble away—and I feel snug, at peace . . . and the cricket chirps. But I don't permit myself this pleasure very often, once a month. . . . [*Pointing to the map*] Now, look here. This is a map of our district as it was fifty years ago. The dark and light green represent forests; half of the entire area was covered with woodland. The parts that are cross-hatched with red were inhabited by wild goats and elk. I designate both the flora and the fauna here. On this lake there were swans, geese, ducks, and, as the old people say, a powerful lot of birds of all sorts, no end of them; they flew in clouds. Besides villages and hamlets, you can see, scattered here and there, various settlements, small farms, hermitages of the Old Believers, water mills. . . . There were a lot of horned cattle and horses. That's shown in blue. For example, in this district the blue is thick; there were herds of horses here, three to every homestead. [*Pause*] Now let us look lower down. This is how it was twenty-five years ago. Already only one third of the area is woodland. There are no longer

any goats, but there are elk. Both the green and the blue
are paler. And so forth and so on. Now let's go to the
third section: a map of the district as it is today. The
green appears here and there, but in patches, not solid;
the elk are now extinct, the swans, the grouse. . . .
There's not a trace of the settlements, farms, hermitages,
water mills. On the whole it is a picture of gradual and
unmistakable degeneration, which in another ten or fifteen years will be complete. You will say that there are
cultural influences at work, that the old life must naturally give place to the new. Yes, I understand, and if in
place of these devastated forests there were highways,
railroads, if there were factories, mills, schools, and the
people had become healthier, richer, more intelligent—
but, you see, there is nothing of the sort! There are still
the same swamps and mosquitoes in the district, the
same dearth of roads, the same dire poverty, typhus,
diphtheria, fires. . . . We have here a case of degeneration resulting from a struggle for existence that is beyond
man's strength; a degeneration due to stagnation, ignorance, complete lack of understanding, as when a man
who is freezing, hungry, sick, to save what is left of life
for his children, instinctively, unconsciously, grabs at
anything that might satisfy his hunger or warm him, and
in doing so destroys everything without a thought for
tomorrow. . . . And nearly everything has been destroyed; and so far nothing has been created to take its
place. [*Coldly*] But I can see by your face that this
doesn't interest you.

ELENA ANDREYEVNA: But I understand so little of
all this . . .

ASTROV: There's nothing to understand, it's simply
uninteresting.

ELENA ANDREYEVNA: To be quite frank, my thoughts
were elsewhere. Forgive me. I want to put you through
a little interrogation, and I am embarrassed, I don't
know how to begin.

ASTROV: Interrogation?

ELENA ANDREYEVNA: Yes, an interrogation, but . . . a rather innocuous one. Let's sit down. [*They sit down.*] It concerns a certain young person. We'll speak as honest people, as friends, without beating about the bush. We'll have a little talk and then forget about it. Yes?

ASTROV: Yes.

ELENA ANDREYEVNA: It concerns my stepdaughter, Sonya. Do you like her?

ASTROV: Yes, I respect her.

ELENA ANDREYEVNA: Do you like her as a woman?

ASTROV [*after a pause*]: No.

ELENA ANDREYEVNA: One or two more words—and that's the end of it. Have you noticed nothing?

ASTROV: Nothing.

ELENA ANDREYEVNA [*taking his hand*]: You don't love her, I see it in your eyes. . . . She is suffering. . . . Understand that and . . . stop coming here.

ASTROV [*gets up*]: My day is over. . . . Besides, I have no time. . . . [*Shrugs his shoulders.*] When have I got the time? [*Embarrassed*]

ELENA ANDREYEVNA: Ough! What an unpleasant conversation! I am so upset, I feel as though I had been carrying a great weight. Well, thank God, we have finished. Let's forget it, just as if we hadn't talked at all, and—go away now. You're an intelligent man, you understand. . . . [*Pause*] I'm blushing all over. . . .

ASTROV: If you had told me this a month or two ago, I might perhaps have considered it, but now. . . . [*Shrugs his shoulders.*] And if she is suffering, then, of course . . . There is only one thing I don't understand: why did you find this interrogation necessary? [*Looks into her eyes and shakes a finger at her.*] You're a sly one!

ELENA ANDREYEVNA: What does that mean?

ASTROV [*laughing*]: Sly one! Let us assume that Sonya is suffering, I am quite prepared to think it possible, but why this interrogation? [*Preventing her from speaking, with animation*] Please, don't try to look surprised, you know perfectly well why I come here every day. . . . Why, and on whose account, you know very well, indeed. . . . You charming bird of prey, don't look at me like that, I'm no gosling.

ELENA ANDREYEVNA [*bewildered*]: Bird of prey? I don't understand. . . .

ASTROV: A beautiful, fluffy little weasel. . . . You must have victims. Here I've been doing nothing for a whole month, I've dropped everything, and avidly seek you out—and that pleases you enormously . . . enormously! . . . Well then? I am conquered, but you knew that even without an interrogation! [*Folds his arms and bows his head.*] I submit. Here I am, devour me!

ELENA ANDREYEVNA: You are out of your mind!

ASTROV [*laughs sardonically*]: You're timid. . . .

ELENA ANDREYEVNA: Oh, I am not so low—I am not so bad as you think! I swear it! [*About to go*]

ASTROV [*barring her way*]: I'll leave here today, I won't come again, but . . . [*Takes her hand and looks around.*] Where shall we meet? Tell me quickly: where? Someone may come in, tell me quickly. . . . [*Passionately*] What a wonderful, glorious . . . One kiss. . . . Just let me kiss your fragrant hair——

ELENA ANDREYEVNA: I swear to you——

ASTROV [*preventing her from speaking*]: Why swear? You don't have to swear. There's no need for words. . . .

Oh, how beautiful you are! What hands! [*Kisses her hands.*]

ELENA ANDREYEVNA: That's enough now . . . go away. . . . [*Withdraws her hands.*] You are forgetting yourself.

ASTROV: Tell me, tell me! Where shall we meet tomorrow? [*Puts his arms around her waist.*] You see, it's inevitable, we've got to see each other.

[*He kisses her; at that moment* VOINITSKY *comes in with a bouquet of roses and stops in the doorway.*]

ELENA ANDREYEVNA [*not seeing* VOINITSKY]: Have pity on me . . . leave me alone. . . . [*Lays her head on* ASTROV's *chest.*] No! [*Tries to go.*]

ASTROV [*holding her by the waist*]: Come to the plantation tomorrow . . . about two o'clock. . . . Yes? Yes? You will come?

ELENA ANDREYEVNA [*seeing* VOINITSKY]: Let me go! [*In great confusion goes to the window.*] This is awful!

VOINITSKY [*puts the bouquet on a chair; agitatedly wipes his face and neck with a handkerchief*]: Never mind . . . No . . . Never mind . . .

ASTROV [*with bravado*]: The weather today, my dear Ivan Petrovich, is not so bad. It was overcast in the morning, as if it were going to rain, but now the sun is shining. As a matter of fact, it's turned out to be a beautiful autumn . . . and the winter crops are quite promising. [*Rolls up the map.*] The only thing is . . . the days are getting shorter. . . . [*Goes out.*]

ELENA ANDREYEVNA [*quickly going up to* VOINITSKY]: You must try, do your utmost, to see that my husband and I leave here today! Do you hear? Today!

VOINITSKY [*mopping his face*]: What? Oh, yes . . . very well. . . . I saw everything, Hélène, everything . . .

ELENA ANDREYEVNA [*nervously*]:   Do you hear me? I must leave here this very day!

[*Enter* SEREBRYAKOV, SONYA, TELYEGIN, *and* MARINA.]

TELYEGIN: I don't feel so well myself, Your Excellency. It's two days now that I've been ailing. There's something the matter with my head. . . .

SEREBRYAKOV: But where are the others? I don't like this house. It's a perfect labyrinth. Twenty-six enormous rooms, people wander off in all directions and you never can find anyone. [*Rings.*] Ask Maria Vasilyevna and Elena Andreyevna to come here.

ELENA ANDREYEVNA: I am here.

SEREBRYAKOV: Please, ladies and gentlemen, sit down.

SONYA [*going up to* ELENA ANDREYEVNA, *impatiently*]:   What did he say?

ELENA ANDREYEVNA: Later.

SONYA: You are trembling. You're upset. [*Peers into her face searchingly.*] I understand. . . . He said he wouldn't come here anymore. . . . Yes? [*Pause*] Tell me: yes?

[ELENA ANDREYEVNA *nods.*]

SEREBRYAKOV [*to* TELYEGIN]:   One can reconcile oneself to ill health, but what I cannot endure is this regimen of country life. I feel as if I had fallen off the earth and landed on another planet. Sit down, ladies and gentlemen, please. Sonya! [*She does not hear him, but stands with her head lowered, sadly.*] Sonya! [*Pause*] She doesn't hear. [*To* MARINA] You sit down, too, nurse. [*She sits down and starts knitting a stocking*] I beg you, my friends, to lend me your ears, as the saying goes. [*Laughs.*]

VOINITSKY [*agitatedly*]:   Perhaps I'm not needed here. May I go?

SEREBRYAKOV: No, you above all are needed.

VOINITSKY: What do you require of me?

SEREBRYAKOV: Require of you . . . Why are you angry? [*Pause*] If I have done anything to offend you, forgive me, please.

VOINITSKY: Drop that tone. Let's proceed to the business. What is it you want?

[*Enter* MARIA VASILYEVNA.]

SEREBRYAKOV: Here is *Maman.* I'll begin, my friends. [*Pause*] I invited you here, ladies and gentlemen, to announce that the Inspector General is coming. However, joking aside. This is a serious matter. I have called you together, ladies and gentlemen, to ask your help and advice, and, knowing your customary kindness, I hope to be the recipient of it. I am a scholar, a man of letters, and have always been a stranger to practical life. I cannot get along without the guidance of experienced people, and, I beg you, Ivan Petrovich, and you, Ilya Ilyich, and you, *Maman* . . . The fact is, *manet omnis una nox,* in other words, we are all mortal. I am old, ill, and therefore find it timely to settle matters relating to my property, in so far as they concern my family. My life is over now, I am not thinking of myself, but I have a young wife and an unmarried daughter. [*Pause*] To go on living in the country is impossible for me. We are not made for country life. Yet, to live in town on the income we receive from this estate is also impossible. If we were to sell the forest, let us say, that would be an extreme measure, one of which we could not avail ourselves every year. We must seek some means which would guarantee us a permanent, and more or less definite, income. I have thought of one such measure, and I have the honor of submitting it for your consideration. Omitting details,

I shall put it before you in rough outline. Our estate yields on an average of not more than two per cent. I propose to sell it. If we invest the proceeds in interest-bearing securities, we shall receive from four to five per cent, and I believe we might even have a few thousand to spare, which would enable us to buy a small villa in Finland.

VOINITSKY: Wait . . . I think my ears must be deceiving me. Repeat what you said.

SEREBRYAKOV: To invest the money in interest-bearing securities, and with the surplus, whatever may be left, to buy a villa in Finland.

VOINITSKY: Not Finland. . . . You said something besides that.

SEREBRYAKOV: I propose to sell the estate.

VOINITSKY: That was it. You will sell the estate—splendid, a magnificent idea. . . . And what do you propose to do with me and my old mother, and Sonya here?

SEREBRYAKOV: All this we shall discuss in good time. One can't do everything at once.

VOINITSKY: Wait. Evidently, up to now I have been devoid of common sense. Till now I was so stupid as to think that this estate belonged to Sonya. My late father bought the estate as a dowry for my sister. Up to now I have been naive and, not putting a Turkish interpretation on the law, I thought the estate passed from my sister to Sonya.

SEREBRYAKOV: Yes, the estate belongs to Sonya. Who disputes it? I won't decide to sell without Sonya's consent. Besides, what I propose to do is for her benefit.

VOINITSKY: It's inconceivable, inconceivable! Either I've gone out of my mind or . . . or . . .

MARIA VASILYEVNA: Jean, don't contradict Aleksandr. Believe me, he knows better than we do what is right and what is wrong.

VOINITSKY: No, give me some water. [*Drinks water.*] Say what you like. Whatever you like!

SEREBRYAKOV: I don't understand why you excite yourself. I don't say that my plan is ideal. If everybody finds it unsuitable, I am not going to insist. [*Pause*]

TELYEGIN [*embarrassed*]: Your Excellency, I cherish not only a feeling of reverence for learning, but of kinship as well. My brother, Grigory Ilyich's wife's brother—perhaps you know him—Konstantin Trofimovich Lakedemonov, was an M.A. . . .

VOINITSKY: Be quiet, Waffles, we're talking business. . . . Wait . . . later . . . [*to* SEREBRYAKOV] Here, ask him, the estate was bought from his uncle.

SEREBRYAKOV: Indeed, and why should I ask him? What for?

VOINITSKY: The estate was bought at that time for ninety-five thousand rubles. Father paid only seventy thousand and there remained a debt of twenty-five thousand. Now, listen. . . . The estate would never have been bought if I hadn't given up my share of the inheritance in favor of my sister, whom I dearly loved. What's more, I worked like an ox for ten years and paid off the entire debt.

SEREBRYAKOV: I regret that I began this conversation.

VOINITSKY: The estate is free from debt and in good condition only because of my personal efforts. And now that I've grown old, I'm to be kicked out!

SEREBRYAKOV: I do not understand what you are driving at.

VOINITSKY: For twenty-five years I have been managing this estate, I have worked and sent you money like the most conscientious steward, and during all this time you never once thanked me. All this time—both when I was young and now—I've been receiving from you a salary of five hundred rubles a year—a beggarly sum!—and you never once thought of increasing it by so much as a ruble!

SEREBRYAKOV: Ivan Petrovich, how was I to know? I'm not a practical man, I don't understand these things. You could have increased it yourself, as much as you liked.

VOINITSKY: Why didn't I steal? Why don't you all despise me for not stealing? It would have been just, and I wouldn't be a pauper now!

MARIA VASILYEVNA [*sternly*]: Jean!

TELYEGIN [*in agitation*]: Vanya, my friend, don't. . . . don't . . . I'm trembling. . . . Why spoil good relations? [*Kisses him.*] You mustn't.

VOINITSKY: For twenty-five years I have sat here with this mother, buried like a mole within these four walls. . . . All our thoughts and feelings pertained to you alone. Our days were spent talking of you and your work, we were proud of you, we uttered your name with reverence, our nights were wasted reading books and magazines for which I now have the deepest contempt!

TELYEGIN: Don't, Vanya, don't . . . I can't——

SEREBRYAKOV [*wrathfully*]: I don't understand what it is you want.

VOINITSKY: To us you were a being of a higher order . . . we knew your articles by heart. . . . But now my eyes have been opened! I see everything! You write about art, but you understand nothing of art! All your works, which I used to love, are not worth a copper kopeck. You've swindled us!

SEREBRYAKOV: Ladies and gentlemen! Do stop him! I am going!

ELENA ANDREYEVNA: Ivan Petrovich, I insist that you stop talking! Do you hear?

VOINITSKY: I won't stop talking! [*Barring* SEREBRYA-KOV'*s way*] Wait, I haven't finished! You have ruined my life! I haven't lived! Thanks to you, I have destroyed, annihilated, the best years of my life. You are my worst enemy!

TELYEGIN: I cannot . . . I cannot . . . I am going. . . . [*Goes out in great distress.*]

SEREBRYAKOV: What do you want from me? And what right have you to speak to me in that tone? You nonentity! If the estate is yours, then take it, I don't need it!

ELENA ANDREYEVNA: I'm going to get out of this hell, this very instant! [*Screams.*] I can't bear it any longer!

VOINITSKY: My life is over! I was talented, intelligent, self-confident. . . . If I had had a normal life, I might have been a Schopenhauer, a Dostoyevski. . . . Oh, I'm raving! I'm going out of my mind. . . . Mother, I am in despair! Mother!

MARIA VASILYEVNA [*sternly*]: Do as Aleksandr says!

SONYA [*kneels before the nurse and huddles close to her*]: Nurse, dear! Nurse!

VOINITSKY: Mother! What am I to do? No, you needn't speak! I know myself what I must do! [*To* SEREBRYAKOV] You will remember me! [*Goes out through middle door.*]

[MARIA VASILYEVNA *follows him.*]

SEREBRYAKOV: Ladies and gentlemen, what is this, after all? Remove that madman! I cannot live under the same roof with him! He lives there [*pointing to middle door*] almost by my side. . . . Let him move to the village, or into the lodge, or I will move; but remain in the same house with him I cannot.

ELENA ANDREYEVNA [*to her husband*]: We will leave this place today! Arrangements must be made at once.

SEREBRYAKOV: That nonentity!

SONYA [*on her knees, turns to her father; nervously, through tears*]: One must be merciful, Papa! Uncle Vanya and I are so unhappy! [*Controlling her despair*] One must be merciful! Remember, when you were younger, Uncle Vanya and Grandmother used to spend whole nights translating books for you, copying your papers . . . night after night. Uncle Vanya and I have worked without rest, afraid to spend a kopeck on ourselves, we sent everything to you. . . . We earned our daily bread. I'm saying it all wrong, all wrong, but you ought to understand us, Papa. One must be merciful!

ELENA ANDREYEVNA [*in agitation, to her husband*]: Aleksandr, for God's sake, make it up with him . . . I implore you!

SEREBRYAKOV: Very well, I'll discuss it with him. . . . I'm not accusing him of anything, I am not angry, but you will agree that his behavior is strange, to say the least. Very well, I'll go to him. [*Goes out through middle door.*]

ELENA ANDREYEVNA: Be gentle with him, calm him. . . . [*Goes out after him.*]

SONYA [*huddling up to nurse*]: Nurse, dear! Nurse!

MARINA: Never mind, little one. The geese will cackle—then they'll stop. They cackle . . . and stop. . . .

SONYA: Nurse!

MARINA [*stroking her head*]: You're shivering as if it were freezing. There, there, little orphan, God is merciful. A little linden tea, or raspberry tea, and it will pass. . . . Don't grieve, little orphan. . . . [*Looking at the middle door*] Shoo! Go away with your cackling, off with you!

[*A shot is heard offstage, then a scream from* ELENA ANDREYEVNA; SONYA *shudders.*]

MARINA: Oh, you——

SEREBRYAKOV [*runs in, staggering with fright*]: Hold him! Hold him! He's gone mad!

[ELENA ANDREYEVNA *and* VOINITSKY *struggle in the doorway.*]

ELENA ANDREYEVNA [*trying to take the revolver from him*]: Give it to me! Give it to me, I say!

VOINITSKY: Let me go, Hélène! Let me go! [*Freeing himself, runs in and looks around for* SEREBRYAKOV.] Where is he? Ah, there he is! [*Shoots at him.*] Bang! [*Pause*] Missed him! Missed again! Oh, damn, damn! [*Throws the revolver on the floor and sits down exhausted.*]

[SEREBRYAKOV *is stunned;* ELENA ANDREYEVNA *leans against a wall, almost fainting.*]

ELENA ANDREYEVNA: Take me away from here! Take me away, kill me . . . but I cannot stay here!

VOINITSKY [*in despair*]:   Oh, what am I doing! What am I doing!

SONYA [*softly*]:   Nurse! Nurse!

Act IV

[VOINITSKY's *room, which serves both as his bedroom and as an office for the estate. By the window a large table with account books and papers of all sorts; a desk, bookcases, scales. A smaller table for* ASTROV; *on it are paints, drawing materials, and a large portfolio. A bird cage with a starling in it. On the wall a map of Africa, obviously of no use to anyone. An enormous sofa upholstered in oilcloth. To the left, a door leading to other rooms; to the right, a door into the hall, with a mat in front of it, so the peasants do not muddy the floor. An autumn evening. Stillness.*]

[TELYEGIN *and* MARINA *sit facing each other, winding wool.*]

TELYEGIN: You'd better be quick, Marina Timofey-evna, they'll soon be calling us to say good-bye. They've already ordered the horses.

MARINA [*trying to wind faster*]:   There's not much left.

TELYEGIN: They're going to Kharkov . . . going to live there.

MARINA: And it's better so.

TELYEGIN: They've had a fright. . . . Elena Andre-yevna keeps saying: "I won't stay here another hour . . . we must go, we must go. . . . We can stay in Kharkov for a while," she says, "and when we've had a look around, we'll send for our things." . . . They're traveling light. It seems, Marina Timofeyevna, that it was not destined that they should live here . . . not their destiny . . . fatal predestination.

MARINA: And it's better so. All that hubbub they raised a while ago . . . that shooting—shameful!

TELYEGIN: Yes, a subject worthy of the brush of Aivazovsky.

MARINA: I never hoped to see such a thing! [*Pause*] Well, now we'll go back to our old ways. Breakfast by eight, dinner at one, and in the evening we'll sit down to supper; everything in its proper order, the way other people live . . . like Christians. [*With a sigh*] It's been a long time since this old sinner has tasted noodles.

TELYEGIN: Yes, it's been quite a while since they've made noodles. . . . This morning, Marina Timofeyevna, as I was walking through the village, a storekeeper shouted after me: "Hey, you sponger, you!" How that hurt me!

MARINA: Take no notice, my dear. We all live on God. You, Sonya, Ivan Petrovich—none of us sits idle, everybody works. All of us. . . . Where's Sonya?

TELYEGIN: In the garden. She and the doctor are still looking for Ivan Petrovich. They're afraid he may lay hands on himself.

MARINA: And where is the revolver?

TELYEGIN [*in a whisper*]: I hid it in the cellar!

MARINA [*with an ironical smile*]: How we are punished for our sins!

[*Enter* VOINITSKY *and* ASTROV *from outside.*]

VOINITSKY: Leave me alone. [*To* MARINA *and* TELYEGIN] Go away, leave me alone—if only for one hour! I can't bear being watched.

TELYEGIN: At once, Vanya. [*Goes out on tiptoe.*]

MARINA: The geese go: ga-ga-ga! [*Gathers up her wool and goes out.*]

VOINITSKY: Leave me alone!

ASTROV: With the greatest pleasure. I ought to have left here long ago, but, I repeat, I am not leaving until you return what you took from me.

VOINITSKY: I didn't take anything from you.

ASTROV: I am serious—don't keep me waiting. I ought to have gone a long time ago.

VOINITSKY: I did not take anything from you. [*Both sit down.*]

ASTROV: No? Well, I'll wait a little longer, and then, you must forgive me, I shall use force. We'll tie you up and search you. I am speaking quite seriously.

VOINITSKY: As you wish. [*Pause*] I've made such a fool of myself: to have fired twice and missed both times! I shall never forgive myself for this!

ASTROV: If you felt like shooting, you would have done better to have put a bullet into your own head.

VOINITSKY [*shrugging his shoulders*]:   Strange. I attempt to commit a murder, and they don't arrest me, don't bring me to trial, which means that they consider me insane. [*With a bitter laugh*] I am insane, but those who conceal their lack of talent, their stupidity, their utter heartlessness under the guise of a professor, a learned sage—they are not insane. People are not insane who marry old men and then openly deceive them. I saw you, I saw you with your arms around her!

ASTROV: Yes. I had my arms around her, and you know what you can do about it! [*Thumbs his nose.*]

VOINITSKY [*looking at the door*]:   No, it's a mad world that can contain you!

ASTROV: Now that's silly.

VOINITSKY: Well, I'm insane, I'm not responsible, I have a right to say silly things.

ASTROV: That's a stale trick. You're not insane, you're just a crackpot. A clown. There was a time when I regarded every crackpot as sick, abnormal; but now I am of the opinion that it's the normal state of man—to be a crackpot. You're perfectly normal.

VOINITSKY [*covers his face with his hands*]:   I am ashamed! If you only knew how ashamed I am! No pain can be compared to this acute sense of shame. [*Miserably*] It's unbearable! [*Leans on the table.*] What am I to do? What am I to do?

ASTROV: Nothing.

VOINITSKY: Give me something! Oh, my God! I'm forty-seven years old; if I live to be sixty, I've still got thirteen years to live through. It's a long time. How am

I to get through those thirteen years? What shall I do? Oh, try to understand . . . [*convulsively squeezing* ASTROV*'s hand*] if only it were possible to live through the rest of life in some new way! To wake up on a clear, quiet morning and feel that you had begun your life anew, that all the past had been forgotten, had vanished like smoke. [*Weeps.*] To begin a new life . . . Tell me how to begin . . . where to begin. . . .

ASTROV [*sharply*]: Oh, come now! What sort of new life can there be! Our situation—yours and mine—is hopeless.

VOINITSKY: It is?

ASTROV: I'm convinced of it.

VOINITSKY: Give me something. . . . [*Pointing to his heart*] It's consuming me—here!

ASTROV [*shouts angrily*]: Stop it! [*Softening*] Those who will come after us, in two or three hundred years, and who will despise us for having lived our lives so stupidly and insipidly—perhaps they will find a means of happiness, but we . . . There is only one hope for you and me: the hope that when we are sleeping in our graves we may be attended by visions, perhaps even pleasant ones. [*Sighing*] Yes, my friend. In the whole district there were only two decent, cultured men: you and I. But after some ten years of this contemptible, barbarian existence we have been encompassed by it—it has poisoned our blood with its putrid fumes and we have become just such vulgarians as all the rest. [*Briskly*] But don't try to put me off with fine words. Give me back what you took from me.

VOINITSKY: I didn't take anything from you.

ASTROV: You took a bottle of morphine out of my medical traveling case. [*Pause*] Listen, if you really want to make an end of yourself, go into the woods and shoot yourself. But give me back the morphine, or there will be talk, conjectures, people will think I gave it to you. . . . It's enough that I shall have to perform a post-mortem on you. Do you think that would be interesting?

[*Enter* SONYA.]

VOINITSKY: Leave me alone.

ASTROV [*to* SONYA]: Sofya Aleksandrovna, your uncle removed a bottle of morphine from my medical case and he won't give it back to me. Tell him that it's . . . not very clever, after all. Besides, I have no time. I must be going.

SONYA: Uncle Vanya, did you take the morphine? [*Pause*]

ASTROV: He took it. I am certain of that.

SONYA: Give it back. Why do you want to frighten us? [*Tenderly*] Give it back, Uncle Vanya. I am, perhaps, just as unhappy as you are, but I will not fall into despair. I'll bear it, and go on bearing it till my life comes to an end. . . . And you will bear it. [*Pause*] Give it back. [*Kisses his hand.*] My dear, good uncle, give it back, darling! [*Weeps.*] You are kind, have pity on us and give it back. You must bear it, Uncle, you must!

VOINITSKY [*takes the bottle out of his desk and hands it to* ASTROV]: Here, take it! [*To* SONYA] But we must get to work and do something quickly, otherwise I won't be able to bear it . . . I won't. . . .

SONYA: Yes, yes, work. As soon as we see them off, we'll settle down to work. . . . [*Nervously sorts out papers on the table.*] We've neglected everything.

ASTROV [*puts the bottle into his case and tightens the straps*]:   Now I can be on my way.

[*Enter* ELENA ANDREYEVNA.]

ELENA ANDREYEVNA: Ivan Petrovich, are you here? We are leaving now. Go to Aleksandr, he wants to say something to you.

SONYA: Go on, Uncle Vanya. [*Takes* VOINITSKY *by the arm.*] Let's go. You and Papa must be reconciled. It has to be.

[SONYA *and* VOINITSKY *go out.*]

ELENA ANDREYEVNA: I am leaving. [*Gives* ASTROV *her hand.*] Good-bye.

ASTROV: Already?

ELENA ANDREYEVNA: The carriage is waiting.

ASTROV: Good-bye.

ELENA ANDREYEVNA: Today you promised me that you would go away.

ASTROV: I remember. I am leaving presently. [*Pause*] You're frightened? Is it really so dreadful?

ELENA ANDREYEVNA: Yes.

ASTROV: You had better stay! Well? Tomorrow at the plantation . . .

ELENA ANDREYEVNA: No . . . it's all decided. . . . That's why I can look at you so bravely now, because our departure has been settled. . . . One thing I ask of you: think better of me. I should like you to respect me.

ASTROV: Oh! [*With a gesture of impatience*] Do stay, I beg you. You realize . . . with nothing in the world to do, no aim in life, nothing to occupy your mind, that sooner or later you are bound to give way to your feelings—it's inevitable. And it would be better if it happened, not somewhere in Kharkov or Kursk, but here in the lap of nature. . . . At least it's poetic, the autumn is really beautiful. . . . Here there is the plantation, the dilapidated country houses in the style of Turgenev . . .

ELENA ANDREYEVNA: How absurd you are. . . . I am angry with you, and yet . . . I shall remember you with pleasure. You are an interesting, original man. We shall never see each other again, and so, why hide it? I was really a little carried away by you. Well, let's shake hands and part friends. Don't think ill of me.

ASTROV [*shakes hands*]: Yes, you had better go. . . . [*Musing*] You seem to be a good, sincere person, but at the same time there's something rather strange about your whole nature. You came here with your husband, and every one of us who had been working, bustling about trying to create something, had to drop his work and occupy himself with nothing but you and your husband's gout the entire summer. Both of you—he and you—have infected us with your idleness. I was infatuated with you, and have done nothing for a whole month; meanwhile people have been sick, peasants have been pasturing their cattle among my young trees. . . . So, wherever you set foot, you and your husband, you bring ruin. I'm joking, of course, and yet . . . it is strange, and I'm convinced that if you had stayed, the devastation would have been enormous. I should have been done for, and you would not have fared so well either. Go, then. *Finita la commedia!*

ELENA ANDREYEVNA [*takes a pencil from his table and quickly hides it*]: I'm taking this pencil to remember you by.

ASTROV: It's strange somehow. . . . To have known each other, and all at once, for some reason . . . never to see each other again. That's the way with everything in this world. . . . While there's no one here, and before Uncle Vanya comes in with a bouquet, let me . . . kiss you . . . good-bye . . . Yes? [*Kisses her on the cheek.*] There, now . . . all is well. . . .

ELENA ANDREYEVNA: I wish you the best of everything. [*Glancing around*] Well, so be it! For once in my life! [*Impetuously embraces him; they quickly draw apart.*] I must go.

ASTROV: Go quickly. If the carriage is ready, you'd better set off.

ELENA ANDREYEVNA: I think they're coming. [*Both listen.*]

ASTROV: *Finita!*

[*Enter* SEREBRYAKOV, VOINITSKY, MARIA VASILYEVNA *with a book,* TELYEGIN, *and* SONYA.]

SEREBRYAKOV [*to* VOINITSKY]: Let bygones be bygones. After what has happened, I have lived through so much, and thought so much in the course of a few hours, that I believe I could write a whole treatise for the edification of posterity on how one ought to live. I gladly accept your apologies, and I ask you to forgive me, too. Good-bye! [*Kisses* VOINITSKY *three times.*]

VOINITSKY: You shall receive exactly the same amount you formerly received. Everything will be just as it was.

[ELENA ANDREYEVNA *embraces* SONYA.]

SEREBRYAKOV [*kisses* MARIA VASILYEVNA'*s hand*]: Maman . . .

MARIA VASILYEVNA [*kisses him*]: Aleksandr, have another photograph taken and send it to me. You know how dear you are to me.

TELYEGIN: Good-bye, Your Excellency! Don't forget us!

SEREBRYAKOV [*kissing his daughter*]: Good-bye . . . Good-bye, all. [*Offering his hand to* ASTROV] Thank you for the pleasure of your company. . . . I respect your way of thinking, your ardor and enthusiasm, but, permit an old man to add just one observation to his farewell remarks: one must do something, my friends! One must do something! [*Bows to all in general.*] I wish you the best of everything! [*Goes out followed by* MARIA VASILYEVNA *and* SONYA.]

VOINITSKY [*fervently kisses* ELENA ANDREYEVNA's *hand*]: Good-bye . . . Forgive me. . . . We shall never meet again.

ELENA ANDREYEVNA [*moved*]: Good-bye, my dear. [*Kisses him on the head and goes out.*]

ASTROV [*to* TELYEGIN]: Waffles, you might tell them to bring my horses around at the same time.

TELYEGIN: At your service, my dear friend. [*Goes out.*]

[ASTROV *and* VOINITSKY *remain alone.*]

ASTROV [*clearing his paints from the table and putting them in his suitcase*]: Why don't you go and see them off?

VOINITSKY: Let them go, I . . . I cannot. I feel miserable. I must get busy with something as soon as possible. . . . Work, work! [*Rummages among papers on the desk.*]

[*Pause; the sound of harness bells is heard.*]

ASTROV: They've gone. The professor is happy, that's certain. Nothing could ever tempt him to come back here now.

[*Enter* MARINA.]

MARINA: They've gone. [*Sits down in an armchair and knits her stocking.*]

[*Enter* SONYA.]

SONYA: They've gone. [*Wipes her eyes.*] God grant that all will be well with them. [*To her uncle*] Well, Uncle Vanya, let's get busy.

VOINITSKY: Work, work. . . .

SONYA: It's a long, long time since we have sat at this table together. [*Lights the lamp on the table.*] There seems to be no ink. . . . [*Takes the inkwell, goes to the cupboard and fills it.*] But now that they've gone I feel sad.

[*Enter* MARIA VASILYEVNA, *slowly.*]

MARIA VASILYEVNA: They've gone! [*Sits down and becomes absorbed in her reading.*]

SONYA [*sits down at the table and turns the pages of the account book*]: First of all, Uncle Vanya, let's make up the accounts. We've neglected them terribly. Someone sent for his bill again today. You make it out. You do one, I'll do another. . . .

VOINITSKY [*writing*]:   Delivered to . . . Mister . . .

[*Both write in silence.*]

MARINA [*yawns*]:   I'm ready for bye-bye. . . .

ASTROV: It's quiet. . . . Pens scratching . . . crickets chirping. . . . It's warm and cozy. I don't feel like leaving. [*There is the sound of bells.*] They're bringing my horses. . . . Now nothing remains but to say good-bye to you, my friends, to say good-bye to my table—and be off! [*Puts his charts into a portfolio.*]

MARINA: Why so restless? You should stay. . . .

ASTROV: I can't.

VOINITSKY [*writing*]:   Which leaves a debit of two rubles, seventy-five kopecks . . .

[*Enter a* WORKMAN.]

WORKMAN: Mikhail Lvovich, the horses are here.

ASTROV: I heard them. [*Hands him the medical case, suitcase, and portfolio.*] Here, take these. Mind you don't crush the portfolio.

WORKMAN: Yes, sir. [*Goes out.*]

ASTROV: Well . . . [*Starts saying good-bye.*]

SONYA: When shall we see you again?

ASTROV: Not before summer, I expect. Hardly during the winter. . . . Of course, if anything should happen, let me know—I'll come. [*Shakes hands.*] Thank you for your hospitality, your kindness . . . for everything, in fact. [*Goes to nurse and kisses her on the head.*] Good-bye, old woman.

MARINA: So you're leaving without tea?

ASTROV: I don't want any, nurse.

MARINA: Perhaps you'll have a drop of vodka?

ASTROV [*irresolutely*]:   Perhaps . . .

[MARINA *goes out.*]

ASTROV [*after a pause*]:   My trace horse has gone lame for some reason. I noticed it yesterday when Petrushka led him out to water.

VOINITSKY: You must reshoe him.

ASTROV: I'll have to stop at the blacksmith's in Rozhdestvennoye. There's no help for it. [*Goes up to the map of Africa and looks at it.*] Out there in Africa now, I expect the heat must be terrific!

VOINITSKY: Yes, very likely.

[*Enter* MARINA *with a tray on which there is a glass of vodka and a piece of bread.*]

MARINA: Here you are. [ASTROV *drinks the vodka.*] Your good health, my dear. You should have a bit of bread.

ASTROV: No, that'll do. . . . And now, good luck to you all! [*To* MARINA] Don't see me off, nurse. There's no need.

[*He goes out;* SONYA *follows with a candle to see him off;* MARINA *sits down in her armchair.*]

VOINITSKY [*writes*]:   February second, vegetable oil, twenty pounds. . . . February sixteenth, more vegetable oil, twenty pounds. . . . Buckwheat . . . [*Pause*]

[*The sound of bells*]

MARINA: He's gone.

[*Pause*: SONYA *comes back and puts the candle on the table.*]

SONYA: He's gone. . . .

VOINITSKY [*adding on the abacus then writing*]: Total . . . fifteen . . . twenty-five . . .

[SONYA *sits down and writes.*]

MARINA [*yawning*]:   Oh, Lord have mercy . . .

[TELYEGIN *comes in on tiptoe, sits down by the door, and quietly tunes his guitar.*]

VOINITSKY [*to* SONYA, *passing his hand over her hair*]:   My child, how heavy my heart is! Oh, if you only knew how heavy my heart is!

SONYA: What's to be done, we must go on living! [*Pause*] We shall go on living, Uncle Vanya. We shall live through a long, long chain of days and endless evenings; we shall patiently bear the trials fate sends us; we'll work for others, now and in our old age, without ever knowing rest, and when our time comes, we shall die submissively; and there, beyond the grave, we shall say that we have suffered, that we have wept, and have known bitterness, and God will have pity on us; and you and I, Uncle, dear Uncle, shall behold a life that is bright, beautiful, and fine. We shall rejoice and look back on our present troubles with tenderness, with a smile—and we shall rest. I have faith, Uncle, I have fervent, passionate faith. . . . [*Kneeling before him, lays her head on his hand; in a weary voice.*] We shall rest!

[TELYEGIN *softly plays the guitar.*] We shall rest! We shall hear the angels, and see the heavens all sparkling like jewels; we shall see all earthly evil, all our sufferings, drowned in a mercy that will fill the whole world, and our life will grow peaceful, gentle, sweet as a caress. I have faith, I have faith. . . . [*Wipes away his tears with a handkerchief.*] Poor, poor Uncle Vanya, you're crying. . . . [*Through tears*] You have had no joy in your life, but wait, Uncle Vanya, wait. . . . We shall rest. . . . [*Puts her arms around him.*] We shall rest!

[*The* WATCHMAN *taps;* TELYEGIN *plays softly;* MARIA VASILYEVNA *makes notes on the margin of her pamphlet;* MARINA *knits her stocking.*] We shall rest!

The Curtain Falls Slowly

1897

The Three Sisters

A Drama in Four Acts

Characters in the Play

PROZOROV, ANDREI SERGEYEVICH

NATALYA IVANOVNA, his fiancée, later his wife

OLGA
MASHA } his sisters
IRINA

KULYGIN, FYODOR ILYICH, a high-school teacher, husband of Masha

VERSHININ, ALEKSANDR IGNATYEVICH, Lieutenant Colonel, Battery Commander

BARON TUZENBACH, NIKOLAI LVOVICH, Lieutenant

SOLYONY, VASSILY VASSILYEVICH, Staff Captain

CHEBUTYKIN, IVAN ROMANOVICH, Army doctor

FEDOTIK, ALEKSEI PETROVICH, Second Lieutenant

RODAY, VLADIMIR KARLOVICH, Second Lieutenant

FERAPONT, porter of the District Board, an old man

ANFISA, the nurse, an old woman of eighty

The action takes place in a provincial town.

Act I

[*In the* PROZOROVS' *house. A drawing room with columns, beyond which a large reception room is visible. Midday: it is bright and sunny outside. In the reception room a table is being set for lunch.* OLGA, *in the dark blue uniform of a girls' high-school teacher, is correcting exercise books, standing or walking about as she does so;* MASHA, *in a black dress, her hat on her lap, sits reading a book;* IRINA, *in a white dress, stands lost in thought.*]

OLGA: Father died just a year ago today, on the fifth of May—your name day, Irina. It was snowing then, and very cold. I felt as though I should never live through it, and you lay in a dead faint. But now, a year has gone by, and we think of it calmly; you're already wearing white, and your face is radiant. [*The clock strikes.*] The clock was striking then, too. [*Pause*] I remember there was music when Father was carried out, and they fired a salute at the cemetery. He was a general, in command of a brigade, yet there were very few people walking behind his coffin. But then, it was raining. Heavy rain and snow.

IRINA: Why recall it?

[BARON TUZENBACH, CHEBUTYKIN, *and* SOLYONY *appear behind the columns near the table in the reception room.*]

OLGA: It's so warm today we can keep the windows wide open, but the birches are not yet in leaf. . . . Father was given a brigade and left Moscow eleven years ago, and I remember perfectly that by this time, at the beginning of May in Moscow, everything was in bloom, it was warm, all bathed in sunshine. Eleven years have passed, but I remember it all as though we had left there yesterday. Oh, God! This morning I woke up, I saw this flood of sunlight, saw the spring, and joy stirred in my soul, I had a passionate longing to go home again.

CHEBUTYKIN: Like hell he did!

TUZENBACH: Of course, that's nonsense.

[MASHA, *absorbed in her book, softly whistles a tune.*]

OLGA: Don't whistle, Masha. How can you! [*Pause*] Being in school every day, then giving lessons till evening, my head aches continually, and I'm beginning to think like an old woman. In fact, these four years that I've been teaching in the high school, day by day I feel my youth and strength draining out of me. Only one dream keeps growing stronger and stronger . . .

IRINA: To go to Moscow. To sell the house, make an end of everything here, and go to Moscow. . . .

OLGA: Yes! To go to Moscow as soon as possible.

[CHEBUTYKIN *and* TUZENBACH *laugh.*]

IRINA: Brother will probably become a professor; in any case, he won't go on living here. So there's nothing to stop us but poor Masha.

OLGA: Masha will come and spend the whole summer in Moscow every year.

[MASHA *softly whistles a tune.*]

IRINA: God grant it all works out! [*Looking out the window*] The weather is lovely today. I don't know why I feel so lighthearted! This morning I remembered that it was my name day, and suddenly I felt joyful, and thought of our childhood, when Mama was still alive. And I was stirred by such wonderful thoughts . . . such thoughts!

OLGA: You are radiant today, more beautiful than ever. And Masha looks beautiful, too. Andrei would be handsome if he hadn't grown so stout, it doesn't suit him. But I've grown old and terribly thin, probably because I get so cross with the girls at school. Today I am free, I'm at home, and my head doesn't ache, I feel younger than yesterday. I'm only twenty-eight. . . . It's all good, all from God, but it seems to me that if I had married and stayed at home all day, it would have been better. [*Pause*] I should have loved my husband.

TUZENBACH [*to* SOLYONY]: You talk such nonsense I'm tired of listening to you. [*Coming into the drawing room*] I forgot to tell you, our new battery commander, Vershinin, is going to call on you today. [*Sits down at the piano.*]

OLGA: Really? I shall be delighted.

IRINA: Is he old?

TUZENBACH: No, not particularly. Forty or forty-five at most. Seems to be a nice fellow. Not stupid, that's certain. Only he talks a lot.

IRINA: An interesting man?

TUZENBACH: Yes, rather, but there's a wife, a mother-in-law, and two girls. What's more, he's married for the second time. He calls on everyone and tells them he has a wife and two little girls. He'll tell you, too. The wife seems a bit crazy, wears her hair in a long braid like a girl, talks only of lofty matters, philosophizes, and frequently attempts suicide—evidently to make it hot for her husband. I'd have left such a woman long ago, but he puts up with it and merely complains.

SOLYONY [*coming into the drawing room with* CHEBU-TYKIN]: With one hand I can lift only fifty pounds, but with two I can lift a hundred and eighty or even two hundred pounds. From this I conclude that two men are not just twice as strong as one, but three times as strong, or even more. . . .

CHEBUTYKIN [*reading a newspaper as he comes in*]: For falling hair . . . two ounces of naphthaline to half a bottle of spirits . . . dissolve and apply daily. . . . [*Writes in a notebook.*] Must make a note of that. [*To* SOLYONY] So, as I was telling you, you stick a little cork into a bottle and pass a glass tube through it. . . . Then you take a pinch of plain ordinary alum . . .

IRINA: Ivan Romanych, dear Ivan Romanych!

CHEBUTYKIN: What is it, my child, my joy?

IRINA: Tell me, why am I so happy today? It's just as though I were sailing before the wind, with the broad blue sky above, and great white birds floating overhead. Why is that? Why?

CHEBUTYKIN [*kisses both her hands tenderly*]: My little white bird. . . .

IRINA: When I woke up this morning, I got up and washed, and suddenly I felt as though everything in this world was clear to me, and that I knew how one ought to live. Dear Ivan Romanych, I know everything. Man must work, he must toil by the sweat of his brow, no matter who he is, and in this alone lies the meaning and purpose of his life, his happiness, his ecstasy. How good to be a workman who gets up at dawn and breaks stones in the street, or a shepherd, or a schoolmaster teaching children, or an engineer on a railroad. . . . Oh, Lord, to say nothing of man, it's better to be an ox, better to be a mere horse, if only one works, than to be a young woman who wakes up at twelve o'clock, has coffee in bed, and then spends two hours dressing. . . . Oh, how dreadful that is! In the same way that one has a craving for water in hot weather, I have a craving for work. And if I don't get up early and work, you can give me up as a friend, Ivan Romanych.

CHEBUTYKIN: I will, I'll give you up. . . .

OLGA: Father trained us to get up at seven. Now Irina wakes up at seven and lies in bed at least till nine thinking. And she looks so serious! [*Laughs.*]

IRINA: You're used to thinking of me as a little girl, so it seems strange to you when I look serious. I am twenty years old!

TUZENBACH: The longing for work, oh, my God, how well I understand it! I have never in my life worked. I was born in Petersburg, cold, idle Petersburg, into a family that knew nothing of work or worry of any kind. I remember, when I used to come home from cadet school a footman would pull off my boots, I'd make it difficult for him, and my mother would gaze at me with adoration, surprised that others didn't do the same. I was shielded from work. Though I doubt if they succeeded in shielding me completely, I doubt it! The time has come, something tremendous is hanging over our heads, a powerful, invigorating storm is gathering; it is coming, it's already near, and will blow away the indolence, the indifference, the prejudice against work, the rotten boredom of our society. I am going to work, and in another twenty-five or thirty years everyone will work. Everyone!

CHEBUTYKIN: I'm not going to work.

TUZENBACH: You don't count.

SOLYONY: Twenty-five years from now you'll no
longer be here, thank God. In two or three years you'll
die of apoplexy, or I'll lose my temper and put a bullet
through your head, my angel. [*Takes a bottle of scent
out of his pocket and sprinkles his chest and hands.*]

CHEBUTYKIN: As a matter of fact, I never have done
anything. I haven't lifted a finger since the day I left the
university, haven't even read a book, only newspapers....
[*Takes another newspaper out of his pocket.*] Here ... I
know from the newspapers, for instance, that there was a
person called Dobrolyubov, but what he wrote—I don't
know.... [*Sound of knocking on the floor downstairs.*]
There ... I'm being called from downstairs, someone
has come to see me. I'll be right back ... wait. ...
[*Goes out hurriedly, combing his beard.*]

IRINA: He's up to something.

TUZENBACH: Yes. He looked so elated when he went
out that it's obvious he's about to bring you a present.

IRINA: I wish he wouldn't!

OLGA: Yes, it's awful. He's always doing something
foolish.

MASHA: "A green oak by a curved seashore, upon
that oak a golden chain ... upon that oak a golden
chain ..."* [*Gets up, humming softly.*]

OLGA: You're not very cheerful today, Masha.

*The quotation is from the Prologue of *Ruslan and Ludmilla* by
Aleksandr Sergeyevich Pushkin (1799–1837).

[MASHA, *humming, puts on her hat.*]

OLGA: Where are you going?

MASHA: Home.

IRINA: Strange . . .

TUZENBACH: Leaving a name-day party!

MASHA: Never mind . . . I'll come back in the evening. Good-bye, my lovely one. . . . [*Kisses* IRINA.] Once again, I wish you health and happiness. In the old days, when Father was alive, thirty or forty officers used to come to our name-day parties and there was a real racket, but today there's only a man and a half, and it's silent as a desert. . . . I'm going. . . . I'm in the doldrums today, not very cheerful, so don't listen to me. [*Laughing through her tears*] Later we'll have a talk, but good-bye for now, darling, I'll go off somewhere. . . .

IRINA [*annoyed*]:   Oh, you're so . . .

OLGA [*tearfully*]:   I understand you, Masha.

SOLYONY: If a man philosophizes, you'll get philosophy, or at least sophistry, but if a woman, or a couple of women, start philosophizing—it's like pulling taffy!

MASHA: What do you mean by that, you impossibly dreadful man?

SOLYONY: Nothing. He no sooner cried "Alack" than the bear was on his back.

[*A pause*]

MASHA [*to* OLGA, *angrily*]:   Don't bawl!

[*Enter* ANFISA *and* FERAPONT *with a cake.*]

ANFISA: This way, my dear. Come in, your boots are
clean. [*To* IRINA] From the District Board, from
Protopopov—Mikhail Ivanych . . . a cake.

IRINA: Thank you. Thank him for me. [*Takes cake.*]

FERAPONT: How's that?

IRINA [*louder*]:   Thank him for me!

OLGA: Nurse dear, give him some pie. Go along, Ferapont, they'll give you some pie.

FERAPONT: How's that?

ANFISA: Come along, Ferapont Spiridonych, my dear.
Come along . . . [*Goes out with* FERAPONT.]

MASHA: I don't like Protopopov, that Mikhail Pota-
pych, or Ivanych. He shouldn't be invited here.

IRINA: I didn't invite him.

MASHA: Good.

[*Enter* CHEBUTYKIN, *followed by a soldier carrying a
silver samovar; there is a murmur of astonishment and
displeasure.*]

OLGA [*covers her face with her hands*]:   A samovar!
[*Goes out to the table in the reception room.*]

IRINA: Dear Ivan Romanych, what have you done!

TUZENBACH: I told you.

MASHA: Ivan Romanych, you are simply shameless!

CHEBUTYKIN: My dear ones, my darlings, you are all I have, you are dearer to me than anything in the world. I'll soon be sixty, I'm an old man, a lonely, good-for-nothing old man. . . . There's nothing good about me but this love for you, and if it weren't for you, I'd have been dead long ago. . . . [*To* IRINA] My dear child, I have known you since the day you were born . . . I carried you in my arms. . . . I loved your dear mother. . . .

IRINA: But why such expensive presents!

CHEBUTYKIN [*through his tears, angrily*]: Expensive presents! Why, you're completely—[*to the orderly*] Take the samovar in there. . . . [*Mimicking*] Expensive presents . . . [*The orderly carries the samovar into the reception room.*]

ANFISA [*passing through the drawing room*]: My dears, there's a colonel, a stranger! He's already taken off his overcoat, children, he is coming in here. Irinushka, now you be nice and polite. . . . [*Going out*] And it's high time we had lunch. . . . Mercy on us!

TUZENBACH: Vershinin, I suppose.

[*Enter* VERSHININ.]

TUZENBACH: Lieutenant Colonel Vershinin!

VERSHININ [*to* MASHA *and* IRINA]: I have the honor to introduce myself: Vershinin. I am very, very happy to be in your house at last. How you have grown! Ay! Ay!

IRINA: Please sit down. We are delighted to see you.

VERSHININ [*gaily*]: How glad I am, how glad I am! But there were three sisters. I remember—three little girls. The faces I no longer remember, but that your father, Colonel Prozorov, had three little girls, I remember perfectly, I saw them with my own eyes. How time passes! Oh, oh, how time passes!

TUZENBACH: Aleksandr Ignatyevich is from Moscow.

IRINA: From Moscow? You are from Moscow?

VERSHININ: Yes, from Moscow. Your father was a battery commander there, and I was an officer in the same brigade. [*To* MASHA] Your face, now, I do seem to remember.

MASHA: I don't remember you.

IRINA: Olya! Olya! [*Calling into the reception room*] Olya, come here!

[OLGA *comes from the reception room into the drawing room.*]

IRINA: Lieutenant Colonel Vershinin, it turns out, is from Moscow.

VERSHININ: You must be Olga Sergeyevna, the eldest . . . and you are Maria . . . and you are Irina—the youngest. . . .

OLGA: You're from Moscow?

VERSHININ: Yes. I studied in Moscow and went into the service in Moscow. I served there a long time, and at last I have been given a battery here—and have moved here, as you see. I don't exactly remember you, I only remember that there were three sisters. Your father I remember very well; I can close my eyes and see him as plain as life. I used to visit you in Moscow.

OLGA: I thought I remembered everyone, and all at once I—

VERSHININ: My name is Aleksandr Ignatyevich.

IRINA: Aleksandr Ignatyevich, you are from Moscow. . . . What a surprise!

OLGA: You see, we are going to move there.

IRINA: We hope to be there by autumn. It's our native town, we were born there . . . on Old Basmannaya Street. . . . [*They both laugh delightedly.*]

MASHA: Suddenly we see someone from our own town. [*Animatedly*] Now I remember! Olya, you remember, at home they used to talk of "the lovelorn major." You were a lieutenant then, and in love, and for some reason they used to call you major to tease you. . . .

VERSHININ [*laughing*]: Yes, yes . . . "the lovelorn major," that's right. . . .

MASHA: You had only a moustache then. . . . Oh, how much older you look! How much older!

VERSHININ: Yes, when I was called "the lovelorn major," I was still young, I was in love. It's different now.

OLGA: But you haven't a single gray hair. You've grown older, but you're still not old.

VERSHININ: Nevertheless, I am in my forty-third year. Is it long since you left Moscow?

IRINA: Eleven years. But why are you crying, Masha . . . you funny girl? [*Through tears*] I'm starting to cry, too. . . .

MASHA: I'm all right. And what street did you live on?

VERSHININ: On Old Basmannaya.

OLGA: We did, too.

VERSHININ: At one time I lived on Nemyetskaya Street. I used to walk from there to the Krasny Barracks. There's a gloomy-looking bridge on the way, and under the bridge the water roars. It makes a lonely man feel sick at heart. [*Pause*] But here, what a broad, magnificent river! A wonderful river!

OLGA: Yes, except that it's cold. It's cold here, and there are mosquitoes.

VERSHININ: Really! But it's such a fine, healthy, Russian climate. The woods, the river . . . and then there are birch trees here. Sweet, modest birches, of all trees I love them best. It's good to live here. Only it's strange that the railway station is twenty versts away. . . . And no one knows why that is.

SOLYONY: I know why it is. [*Everyone looks at him.*] Because if the station had been near, then it wouldn't have been far, and since it is far, it can't be near.

[*An awkward silence*]

TUZENBACH: You're a wag, Vassily Vassilyich.

OLGA: Now I remember you. I remember.

VERSHININ: I knew your mother.

CHEBUTYKIN: She was a lovely woman . . . God rest her soul.

IRINA: Mama is buried in Moscow.

OLGA: In the Novo-Dyevichy. . . .

MASHA: Imagine, I'm already beginning to forget her face. And we won't be remembered either. We'll be forgotten.

VERSHININ: Yes, we'll be forgotten. Such is our fate, we can do nothing about it. What to us seems serious, significant, highly important—a time will come when it will be forgotten, or seem unimportant. [*Pause*] And it's interesting that now we absolutely cannot know just what will be considered great, important, and what pitiful, absurd. Didn't the discoveries of Copernicus, or, let us say, Columbus, at first seem worthless and absurd, while the shallow nonsense written by some crank appeared to be the truth? And it may be that our present life, to which we are so reconciled, will in time seem strange, inconvenient, stupid, not pure enough, perhaps even sinful. . . .

TUZENBACH: Who can tell? Perhaps our age will be called great and be remembered with respect. Today there are no torture chambers, no executions, no invasions, and yet, how much suffering!

SOLYONY [*in a high-pitched voice*]: Peep, peep, peep. . . . Don't give the Baron his porridge, just let him philosophize a little.

TUZENBACH: Vassily Vassilyich, I beg you to leave me alone. [*Moves to another chair.*] After all, it's boring.

SOLYONY [*in a high-pitched voice*]: Peep, peep, peep. . . .

TUZENBACH [*to* VERSHININ]: The suffering that can be observed today—and there is so much of it—does speak for a certain moral development which our society has attained.

VERSHININ: Yes, yes, of course.

CHEBUTYKIN: You said just now, Baron, that our age will be called great; but people are small, all the same. . . . [*Gets up.*] Look how small I am. It would only be to console me if you called my life a great, understandable thing.

[*Someone is playing a violin offstage.*]

MASHA: That's Andrei, our brother.

IRINA: He's the scholar in the family. He's probably going to be a professor. Papa was a military man, but his son has chosen an academic career.

MASHA: In accordance with Papa's wish.

OLGA: We haven't stopped teasing him all day. He seems to be slightly in love.

IRINA: With a local girl. She'll very likely call on us today.

MASHA: Oh, how she dresses! It's not just that her clothes are ugly and out of style, they're simply awful. A queer, gaudy, yellowish skirt with some sort of vulgar fringe and a red blouse. And such scrubbed, scrubbed cheeks! Andrei's not in love—I can't believe that, after all, he does have taste—he's simply teasing us, fooling. Yesterday I heard that she was marrying Protopopov, the chairman of the District Board. And a very good thing, too. . . . [*At a side door*] Andrei, come here. Just for a minute, dear.

[*Enter* ANDREI.]

OLGA: This is my brother, Andrei Sergeyich.

VERSHININ: Vershinin.

ANDREI: Prozorov. [*Wipes his perspiring face.*] You are our new battery commander?

OLGA: Just imagine, Aleksandr Ignatych is from Moscow!

ANDREI: Yes? Well, I congratulate you; now my little sisters will give you no peace.

VERSHININ: I'm afraid your sisters must be getting tired of me already.

IRINA: Look at the little picture frame Andrei gave me today. [*Shows the frame.*] He made it himself.

VERSHININ [*looking at the frame, not knowing what to say*]: Yes . . . it's quite . . .

IRINA: And you see the frame above the piano, he made that, too.

[ANDREI, *with a gesture of impatience, moves away.*]

OLGA: He's not only a scholar, but he plays the violin and makes all sorts of things out of wood—in fact, he's good at everything. Andrei, don't go! He has a way of always going off. Come here!

[MASHA *and* IRINA *take hold of his hands and, laughing, lead him back.*]

MASHA: Come on, come on!

ANDREI: Leave me alone, please.

MASHA: You're so funny! Aleksandr Ignatyevich used to be called "the lovelorn major," and he didn't mind in the least . . .

VERSHININ: Not in the least.

MASHA: And I'm going to call you the lovelorn violinist!

IRINA: Or the lovelorn professor!

OLGA: He's in love! Andryusha is in love!

IRINA [*clapping her hands*]: Bravo, bravo! Bis! Andryusha is in love!

CHEBUTYKIN [*comes up behind* ANDREI *and puts both arms around his waist*]: For love alone has nature put us in this world! [*Laughs loudly, still holding his newspaper.*]

ANDREI: Come, that's enough, that's enough. [*Wipes his face.*] I haven't slept all night, and now I'm not quite myself, as they say. I read till four o'clock and then went to bed, but it was no use. I kept thinking of one thing and another, and at the crack of dawn the sun simply poured into my bedroom. During the summer, while I'm here, I'd like to translate a book from the English.

VERSHININ: You read English, then?

ANDREI: Yes. Father—God rest his soul—oppressed us with education. It's ridiculous and stupid, but all the same I must confess that after his death I began to fill out, and now, in one year, I've grown fat, as if a weight had been lifted from my body. Thanks to Father, my sisters and I know French, German, and English, and Irina knows Italian besides. But at what a cost!

MASHA: In this town, to know three languages is a needless luxury—not even a luxury, but a sort of super-fluous appendage, like a sixth finger. We know a great deal that is useless.

VERSHININ: Now, there you are! [*Laughs.*] You know a great deal that is useless! It seems to me that there is not and cannot be a town so dull and depressing that a clever, educated person would be useless. Let us suppose that among the hundred thousand inhabitants of this town, which, of course, is backward and uncouth, there are only three people such as you. It goes without saying that you cannot vanquish the ignorant masses around you; in the course of your life, little by little, you will have to give way and be lost in that crowd of a hundred thousand; life will stifle you, but all the same you will not disappear, you will not be without influence. After you there may appear perhaps six like you, then twelve, and so on, until finally, your kind will become the major-ity. In two or three hundred years life on this earth will be unimaginably beautiful, wonderful. Man needs such a life, and so long as it is not here, he must foresee it, expect it, dream about it, prepare for it; and for this he will have to see and know more than his grandfather and father knew. [*Laughs.*] And you complain of knowing a great deal that is useless.

MASHA [*takes off her hat*]: I am staying for lunch.

IRINA [*with a sigh*]: Really, all that ought to have been written down. . . .

[ANDREI *is not to be seen; he has gone out unobserved.*]

TUZENBACH: After many years, you say, life on earth will be beautiful, wonderful. That is true. But in order to take part in it now, even from afar, we must prepare for it, we must work. . . .

VERSHININ [*gets up*]: Yes. . . . What a lot of flowers you have! [*Looking around*] And a splendid apartment. I envy you! All my life I've been hanging about little apartments with two chairs and a sofa, and a stove that always smokes. That's exactly what's been lacking in my life, flowers such as these. . . . [*Rubbing his hands*] Well, nothing can be done about it now.

TUZENBACH: Yes, we must work. You're probably thinking: the German is getting sentimental. But, word of honor, I'm a Russian, I don't even speak German. My father was a member of the Orthodox Church. . . . [*Pause*]

VERSHININ [*walking about the stage*]: I often think: what if one were to begin life over again, but consciously? If one life, which has already been lived, were only a rough draft, so to say, and the other the final copy! Then each of us, I think, would try above everything not to repeat himself, at least he would create a different setting for his life, he would arrange an apartment like this for himself, with flowers and plenty of light. . . . I have a wife and two little girls, but then, my wife is not in good health, and so forth and so on, and . . . well, if I were to begin life over again, I wouldn't marry. . . . No, no!

[*Enter* KULYGIN *in the uniform of a schoolteacher.*]

KULYGIN [*going up to* IRINA]: Allow me to congratulate you on your saint's day, dear sister, and to wish you sincerely, from my heart, good health and everything that can be wished for a girl of your age. And then to offer you this little book as a gift. [*Giving her a book*] The history of our high school, covering fifty years, written by myself. A mere trifle, written because I had nothing better to do, but read it, anyway. Good morning, ladies and gentlemen! [*To* VERSHININ] Kulygin, teacher in the local high school, Aulic Councilor. [*To* IRINA] In this little book you will find a list of all those who have graduated from our high school in the last fifty years. *Feci quod potui, faciant meliora potentes.* [*Kisses* MASHA.]

IRINA: But you gave me this same book at Easter.

KULYGIN: Impossible! In that case, give it back, or better still, give it to the Colonel. Take it, Colonel. Read it some day when you're bored.

VERSHININ: Thank you. [*About to leave*] I am extremely happy to have made your acquaintance. . . .

OLGA: You aren't going? No, no!

IRINA: You must stay for lunch. Please.

OLGA: Please do!

VERSHININ [*bowing*]: I seem to have happened onto a name-day party. Forgive me, I didn't know and have not offered my congratulations. . . . [*Goes with* OLGA *to the reception room.*]

KULYGIN: Today is Sunday, gentlemen, a day of rest, so let us rest, let us enjoy ourselves, each according to his age and position. The carpets ought to be taken up for the summer and put away till winter . . . Persian powder or naphthaline. . . . The Romans were healthy because they knew how to work and knew how to rest, they had *mens sana in corpore sano.* Their life proceeded in accordance with certain forms. Our director says: the chief thing in every life—is its form. That which loses its form comes to an end—and it is the same with our prosaic lives. [*Puts his arm around* MASHA*'s waist, laughing.*] Masha loves me. My wife loves me. . . . And the window curtains, too, along with the carpets. . . . I'm feeling cheerful today, I'm in excellent spirits. Masha, we're to be at the director's house at four o'clock this afternoon. They're organizing a walk for the teachers and their families.

MASHA: I'm not going.

KULYGIN [*hurt*]: Masha dear, why not?

MASHA: We'll discuss it later. . . . [*Angrily*] All right, I'll go, only leave me alone, please. . . . [*Walks away.*]

KULYGIN: And afterward we shall spend the evening at the director's. Despite his poor health, this man tries above everything to be sociable. A superior, noble person. A splendid man. Yesterday after the conference he said to me: "I am tired, Fyodor Ilyich! Tired!" [*Looks at the clock on the wall, then at his watch.*] Your clock is seven minutes fast. Yes, he says, I am tired!

[*Offstage a violin is heard.*]

OLGA: Please come to lunch, my friends. There's a meat pie!

KULYGIN: Ah, Olga, my dear Olga! Yesterday I worked from early morning to eleven o'clock at night, and was tired out, but today I feel happy. [*Going to the table in the reception room*] My dear . . .

CHEBUTYKIN [*puts the newspaper into his pocket and combs his beard*]: A pie? Splendid!

MASHA [*to* CHEBUTYKIN, *sternly*]: Take care: you're not to drink anything today. Do you hear? It's bad for you to drink.

CHEBUTYKIN: Listen to her! I'm past all that. It's two years since I've been on a spree. Anyway, my girl, what does it matter!

MASHA: All the same, don't you dare drink. Don't you dare. [*Angrily, but so that her husband does not hear*] Another of those long, dull evenings at the director's, damn it!

TUZENBACH: If I were in your place I wouldn't go. . . . Very simple.

CHEBUTYKIN: Don't go, my pet.

MASHA: Yes, don't go. . . . This cursed, unbearable life. . . . [*Goes to the reception room.*]

CHEBUTYKIN [*following her*]: Now, now. . . .

SOLYONY [*goes to the reception room*]: Peep, peep, peep. . . .

TUZENBACH: That's enough, Vassily Vassilyich. Drop it!

SOLYONY: Peep, peep, peep. . . .

KULYGIN [*gaily*]: Your health, Colonel! I'm a pedagogue, and one of the family here, Masha's husband. She is kind, very kind. . . .

VERSHININ: I'll have a little of this dark vodka. . . . [*Drinks.*] Your health! [*To* OLGA] It's so good to be here!

[*Only* IRINA *and* TUZENBACH *remain in the drawing room.*]

IRINA: Masha is in a bad humor today. She married at eighteen, when he seemed to her the cleverest of men. But now it's different. He's the kindest, but not the cleverest.

OLGA [*impatiently*]: Andrei, will you please come?

ANDREI [*offstage*]: Coming. [*Enters and goes to the table.*]

TUZENBACH: What are you thinking about?

IRINA: Oh, nothing. I don't like that Solyony of yours, I'm afraid of him. He talks nothing but nonsense. . . .

TUZENBACH: He's a strange man. I am both sorry for him and annoyed by him, but more sorry. I think he's shy. . . . When I'm alone with him, he can be very intelligent and friendly, but in company he's a crude fellow, a bully. Don't go yet, let them get settled at the table. And let me be near you a little while. What are you thinking about? [*Pause*] You are twenty, I am not yet thirty. How many years lie before us, a long, long succession of days, full of my love for you. . . .

IRINA: Nikolai Lvovich, don't talk to me of love.

TUZENBACH [*not listening*]: I have a passionate thirst for life, for struggle, for work, and that thirst is mingled in my soul with my love for you, Irina, and, just because you are beautiful it seems to me that life, too, is beautiful. What are you thinking about?

IRINA: You say life is beautiful. Yes, but what if it only seems so! Life for us three sisters has not been beautiful, it has stifled us, like weeds. . . . Now I have tears in my eyes. I mustn't . . . [*quickly dries her eyes and smiles.*] We must work, work. That's why we're so melancholy and take such a gloomy view of life, because we know nothing of work. We come of people who despised work. . . .

[*Enter* NATALYA IVANOVNA; *she is wearing a pink dress with a green sash.*]

NATASHA: They're already sitting down to lunch . . . I'm late. [*Steals a glance at herself in the mirror and adjusts her dress.*] My hair seems to be all right. . . . [*Seeing* IRINA] Dear Irina Sergeyevna, I congratulate you! [*Gives her a vigorous and prolonged kiss.*] You have such a lot of guests, I really feel awful. . . . How do you do, Baron!

OLGA [*coming into the drawing room*]: Well, here's Natalya Ivanovna. How do you do, my dear! [*Kisses her.*]

NATASHA: Congratulations on the name day. You have so much company, I feel terribly embarrassed. . . .

OLGA: Nonsense, they're all old friends. [*In a shocked undertone*] You're wearing a green sash! My dear, that's not right!

NATASHA [*plaintively*]: Really? But it's not really green, it's more of a neutral color. [*Follows* OLGA *into the reception room.*]

[*Everyone sits down to lunch in the reception room; there is not a soul in the drawing room.*]

KULYGIN: Irina, I wish you a nice fiancé! It's time you married.

CHEBUTYKIN: Natalya Ivanovna, I wish you a nice fiancé, too.

KULYGIN: Natalya Ivanovna already has a fiancé.

MASHA [*strikes her plate with a fork*]: I'll have a little glass of wine. Why not, it's a rosy life, and we only live once!

KULYGIN: Your conduct merits a C minus.

VERSHININ: This is a delicious liquor. What is it made of?

SOLYONY: Cockroaches.

IRINA [*in a wailing tone*]:   Ugh! Ugh! How disgusting!

OLGA: For supper we're having roast turkey and apple pie. Thank goodness, I'll be home all day today, and in the evening—home. You must all come back this evening. . . .

VERSHININ: May I come too?

IRINA: Please do.

NATASHA: They are very informal.

CHEBUTYKIN: For love alone has nature put us in this world. [*Laughs.*]

ANDREI [*angrily*]:   Stop it, please! Don't you ever get tired of it?

[FEDOTIK *and* RODAY *enter with a big basket of flowers.*]

FEDOTIK: Look, they're already at lunch.

RODAY [*loudly, speaking with guttural R's*]:   Really? Yes, they're lunching already.

FEDOTIK: Wait a minute! [*Takes a snapshot.*] One! Wait, just one more! [*Takes another snapshot.*] Two! All over now! [*They pick up the basket and go to the reception room, where they are greeted noisily.*]

RODAY: Congratulations! I wish you everything, everything! The weather today is delightful, absolutely marvelous! I've been out walking all morning with the high-school boys. I teach gymnastics at the high school. . . .

FEDOTIK: You may move now, Irina Sergeyevna, it's all right. [*Taking a snapshot*] You look charming today. [*Takes a top out of his pocket.*] By the way, here's a top. . . . It has an amazing sound. . . .

IRINA: How fascinating!

MASHA: "A green oak by a curved seashore, upon that oak a golden chain . . . upon that oak a golden chain." . . . [*Plaintively*] Why do I keep saying that? This phrase has been haunting me ever since morning. . . .

KULYGIN: Thirteen at the table!

RODAY [*loudly*]: Ladies and gentlemen, can it be that you attach any significance to superstitions? [*Laughter*]

KULYGIN: If there are thirteen at the table it means that someone here is in love. It's not you by any chance, Ivan Romanovich?

CHEBUTYKIN: I'm an old sinner, but why Natalya Ivanovna should be embarrassed I simply cannot understand.

[*Loud laughter;* NATASHA *runs into the drawing room, and* ANDREI *follows her.*]

ANDREI: Come, don't pay any attention! Wait. . . . Stop . . . I beg of you . . .

NATASHA: I feel so ashamed. . . . I don't know what's the matter with me, but they keep making fun of me. I know it was bad manners to leave the table like that, but I can't help it . . . I can't help it. . . . [*Covers her face with her hands.*]

ANDREI: My darling, I beg of you, I implore you, don't be upset. They are only joking, I assure you, it is not meant unkindly. My darling, my beautiful one, they are all kind, goodhearted people, and they are fond of us both. Come over here to the window, they can't see us here. . . . [*Glances around.*]

NATASHA: I'm so unused to being in company!

ANDREI: Oh, youth, wonderful, beautiful youth! My darling, my lovely one, don't be so upset! Believe me, believe me. . . . I feel so happy, my soul is full of love, and ecstasy. . . . Oh, they can't see us! They can't see us! Why, why did I fall in love with you—when did I fall in love—Oh, I don't understand anything. My darling, my lovely, my pure one, be my wife! I love you, love you, as I have never loved anyone before. . . . [*A kiss*]

[*Two officers enter and, seeing the pair kissing, stop in amazement.*]

Act II

[*The same set as Act I. Eight o'clock in the evening. Offstage the faint sound of an accordion being played in the street. There are no lights.* NATALYA IVANOVNA *enters in a dressing gown carrying a candle; she comes in and stops at the door leading to* ANDREI's *room.*]

NATASHA: Andryusha, what are you doing? Reading? Never mind, I was only . . . [*Goes to another door, opens it, and after looking in, closes it.*] If there's a fire anywhere . . .

ANDREI [*enters with a book in his hand*]: What are you doing, Natasha?

NATASHA: Looking to see if there's a fire. . . . It's Carnival Week, and the servants have lost their heads, you have to keep watching to see that nothing happens. Last night at midnight I walked through the dining room, and there was a candle burning. Who lighted it? I couldn't find out. What time is it?

ANDREI: A quarter past eight.

NATASHA: And Olga and Irina are not in yet. They haven't come back. Still hard at work, poor things . . . Olga at the teachers' meeting, Irina at the telegraph office. . . . [*Sighs.*] This morning I said to your sister: "Take care of yourself, Irina, my dear," I said. But she won't listen. A quarter past eight, you say? I'm afraid our Bobik is not at all well. Why is he so cold? Yesterday he was feverish, and today he is cold all over. . . . I'm so afraid!

ANDREI: It's nothing, Natasha. The boy is all right.

NATASHA: Still it's better to keep him on the diet. I'm afraid. And tonight, they say, the maskers will be here around ten o'clock. It would be better if they didn't come, Andryusha.

ANDREI: I really don't know. They've been invited, you see.

NATASHA: This morning the little fellow wakes up and looks at me, and suddenly he smiles; that means he knows me. "Bobik," I say, "good morning! Good morning, darling!" And he laughs. Children understand, they understand very well. So, then, Andryusha, I'll tell them not to let the maskers in.

ANDREI [*irresolutely*]: But that's up to my sisters. This is their household.

NATASHA: Yes, theirs, too. I'll tell them. They are kind. . . . [*Going*] I've ordered clabber for supper. The doctor says you ought to have nothing but clabber, or you'll never get thin. [*Stops.*] Bobik is cold. I'm afraid his room is too chilly for him. We ought to put him in a different room, at least till the warm weather comes. Irina's room, for instance, is just right for a baby; it's dry, and gets sun all day. I must tell her; she could share Olga's room for a while. . . . She's not at home during the day anyhow, she only sleeps here. . . . [*Pause*] Andryushanchik, why don't you say something?

ANDREI: Oh, I was thinking. . . . Besides, I have nothing to say. . . .

NATASHA: Now there was something I wanted to tell you . . . Oh, yes. Ferapont has come from the District Board and is asking for you.

ANDREI [*yawning*]:   Send him in.

[NATASHA *goes out;* ANDREI, *bending over the candle which she has forgotten, reads his book. Enter* FERAPONT: *he wears a tattered old overcoat with the collar turned up, and his ears are wrapped up.*]

ANDREI: Good evening, my friend. What have you to say?

FERAPONT: The Chairman has sent you a book and a paper of some kind. Here. . . . [*Hands him a book and a packet.*]

ANDREI: Thank you. Good. Why have you come so late? It's past eight.

FERAPONT: How's that?

ANDREI [*louder*]:   I say you came late. It's after eight o'clock.

FERAPONT: Indeed it is. When I came here it was still light, but they wouldn't let me see you. The master is busy, they said. Well, then, if you're busy, you're busy. I'm not going any place. [*Thinking that* ANDREI *has asked him something*] How's that?

ANDREI: Nothing. [*Examining the book*] Tomorrow is Friday. There will be no session, but I'll come anyway . . . and do some work. It's dull at home. . . . [*Pause*] My dear old man, how curiously things change, how life deceives us! Today, out of boredom, having nothing to do, I picked up this book—old university lectures—and I felt like laughing. . . . My God, I'm the Secretary of a District Board, the Board of which Protopopov is Chairman; Secretary, and the very most I can hope for—is to become a member of that Board! I, a member of a District Board, I, who dream every night that I am a professor at the University of Moscow, an illustrious scholar of whom all Russia is proud!

FERAPONT: I wouldn't know . . . I don't hear well. . . .

ANDREI: If you could hear well, I probably wouldn't be talking to you. I must talk to someone, but my wife doesn't understand me, and for some reason I'm afraid of my sisters, I'm afraid they'll laugh at me, make me feel ashamed. . . . I don't drink, I don't like taverns, but right now, how I should enjoy sitting in Tyestov's restaurant in Moscow, or in the Bolshoi Moscovsky, my dear man.

FERAPONT: And in Moscow, so a contractor was saying at the Board the other day, some merchants were eating pancakes; one of them, who ate forty, it seems died. It was either forty or fifty. I don't remember.

ANDREI: You sit in a huge room in a Moscow restaurant, you don't know anyone and no one knows you, and yet you don't feel like a stranger. Here you know everyone, everyone knows you, but you're a stranger, a stranger. . . . A stranger and lonely.

FERAPONT: How's that? [*Pause*] And that same contractor was saying—maybe he was lying—that a rope is stretched all the way across Moscow.

ANDREI: What for?

FERAPONT: I wouldn't know. That's what the contractor said.

ANDREI: Nonsense. [*Reads the book.*] Were you ever in Moscow?

FERAPONT [*after a pause*]: Never was. It was not God's will. [*Pause*] Shall I go now?

ANDREI: You may go. Good-bye. [FERAPONT *goes out.*] Good-bye. [*Reading*] Come back and get these papers tomorrow morning. Go along. . . . [*Pause*] He's gone. [*A bell rings.*] Yes, work. . . . [*Stretches and unhurriedly goes to his own room.*]

[*Behind the scenes a nurse sings, rocking the baby to sleep.* MASHA *and* VERSHININ *enter. While they are talking a maid lights the lamp and candles in the reception room.*]

MASHA: I don't know. [*Pause*] I don't know. Of course, a great deal depends on what one is accustomed to. After Father died, for instance, it took us a long time to get used to having no orderlies in the house. But even apart from habit, I have to say it in all fairness. It may not be so in other places, but in our town the most decent, the most honorable and well-bred people, are all in the army.

VERSHININ: I'm thirsty. I'd like some tea.

MASHA [*glancing at the clock*]: They'll bring it soon. I was married when I was eighteen, and I was afraid of my husband because he was a teacher, and I was hardly out of school. In those days he seemed to me terribly learned, clever, and important. But now, unfortunately, it is different.

VERSHININ: Yes. . . . That's how it is.

MASHA: I don't speak of my husband, I've grown used to him, but among civilians generally, there are so many coarse, impolite, ill-bred people. Coarseness upsets and offends me, I suffer when I see that a man is not fine enough, gentle enough, courteous. When I happen to be among teachers, my husband's colleagues, I am simply miserable.

VERSHININ: Yes. . . . But it seems to me that it's all the same whether they're civilians or military men, they're equally uninteresting, in this town at any rate. It's all the same! If you listen to one of the local intelligentsia, either civilian or military, he's sick and tired of everything; either he's sick and tired of his wife, or his home, his estate, or his horses. . . . A Russian is peculiarly given to an exalted way of thinking, but tell me, why is it that in life he falls so short? Why?

MASHA: Why?

VERSHININ: Why is he sick and tired of his children, sick and tired of his wife? And why are his wife and children sick and tired of him?

MASHA: You're not in a very good mood today.

VERSHININ: Perhaps not. I've had no dinner today, nothing to eat since morning. One of my daughters is not very well, and when my little girls are ill, I am seized with anxiety, my conscience torments me for having given them such a mother. Oh, if you could have seen her today! What a worthless creature! We began quarreling at seven o'clock this morning, and at nine I slammed the door and left. [*Pause*] I never talk about this, strangely enough, I complain only to you. [*Kisses her hand.*] Don't be angry with me. Except for you I have no one—no one. . . . [*Pause*]

MASHA: Such a noise in the stove! Just before Father died, there was a wailing in the chimney. There, just like that.

VERSHININ: Are you superstitious?

MASHA: Yes.

VERSHININ: That's strange. [*Kisses her hand.*] You are a splendid, wonderful woman! Splendid, wonderful! It's dark here, but I can see the sparkle of your eyes.

MASHA [*moves to another chair*]: It's lighter here.

VERSHININ: I love you, love you, love you. . . . I love your eyes, your gestures, I dream about them. . . . Splendid, wonderful woman!

MASHA: When you talk to me like that, for some reason, I laugh, though I am frightened. Don't do it any more, I beg you. . . . [*In a low voice*] But, say it anyway, I don't mind. . . . [*Covers her face with her hands.*] I don't mind. Someone is coming, talk about something else. . . .

[IRINA *and* TUZENBACH *come in through the reception room.*]

TUZENBACH: I've got a triple-barreled name—Baron Tuzenbach-Krone-Altshauer—but I'm Russian, Greek Orthodox, like you. There's very little German left in me, perhaps only this patience and stubbornness that I bore you with. Every evening I see you home.

IRINA: How tired I am!

TUZENBACH: And I'll come to the telegraph office and see you home every day, for ten, for twenty years, till you drive me away. . . . [*Delightedly, seeing* MASHA *and* VERSHININ] It's you? Good evening.

IRINA: Here I am, home at last. [*To* MASHA] A lady just came to telegraph her brother in Saratov that her son had died today, and she couldn't remember the address. So she sent it without an address, simply to Saratov. She was crying. And I was rude to her, for no reason whatever. "I haven't got the time," I said. So stupid of me. Are the maskers coming tonight?

MASHA: Yes.

IRINA [*sits down in an armchair*]:   I must rest. I'm tired.

TUZENBACH [*with a smile*]:   When you come from the office you seem so young, so woebegone. . . . [*Pause*]

IRINA: I'm tired. No, I don't like telegraph work, I don't like it.

MASHA: You've grown thinner. . . . [*Whistles.*] And younger; your face is beginning to look like a little boy's.

TUZENBACH: It's the way she wears her hair.

IRINA: I must look for another place, this is not right for me. What I so wanted, what I dreamed of, is the very thing that's lacking. It's work without poetry, without meaning. . . . [*There is a knock on the floor.*] The doctor is knocking. [*To* TUZENBACH] Answer him, dear. I can't . . . I'm too tired. . . .

[TUZENBACH *knocks on the floor.*]

IRINA: He'll come up now. Something must be done about this. Yesterday the doctor and our Andrei were at the club, and they lost again. I hear Andrei lost two hundred rubles.

MASHA [*indifferently*]: Well, what's to be done about it?

IRINA: Two weeks ago he lost, in December he lost. If he would just lose everything quickly, perhaps we'd get away from this town. Oh, my God, I dream of Moscow every night, I'm absolutely like a madwoman. [*Laughs.*] We'll move there in June, that leaves . . . February, March, April, May . . . almost half a year!

MASHA: The only thing is Natasha must not find out about his losses.

IRINA: I don't think she cares.

[CHEBUTYKIN, *who has just got out of bed—he has been resting after dinner—comes into the reception room combing his beard, then sits down at the table and takes a newspaper out of his pocket.*]

MASHA: There he is. . . . Has he paid his rent?

IRINA [*laughs*]: No. Not a kopeck for eight months. He's evidently forgotten.

MASHA [*laughs*]: How important he looks sitting there! [*Everyone laughs; a pause.*]

IRINA: Why are you so quiet, Aleksandr Ignatych?

VERSHININ: I don't know. I'd like some tea. Half my life for a glass of tea! I've eaten nothing since morning. . . .

CHEBUTYKIN: Irina Sergeyevna!

IRINA: What do you want?

CHEBUTYKIN: Come here, please. *Venez ici.* [IRINA *goes and sits down at the table.*] I can't get along without you.

[IRINA *lays out the cards for a game of patience.*]

VERSHININ: Well, if they won't give us tea, let us at least philosophize a little.

TUZENBACH: Yes, let's. What about?

VERSHININ: What about? Let us dream . . . for instance, of the life that will come after us in two or three hundred years.

TUZENBACH: Well? When we're gone, men will fly in balloons, change the style of their coats, discover a sixth sense, perhaps, and develop it, but life will remain just the same—difficult, full of mysteries, and happy. A thousand years from now man will still be sighing: "Ah, how hard life is!"—yet he will fear death, exactly as he does now, and be unwilling to die.

VERSHININ [*after a moment's thought*]:   How shall I put it? It seems to me that everything on earth must change little by little, and is already changing before our eyes. In two or three hundred years, let's say a thousand years—the time doesn't matter—a new, happy life will dawn. We'll have no part in that life, of course, but we are living for it now, working, yes, suffering, and creating it—in that alone lies the purpose of our existence, and, if you like, our happiness.

[MASHA *laughs softly.*]

TUZENBACH: Why are you laughing?

MASHA: I don't know. I've been laughing all day today, ever since morning.

VERSHININ: I was graduated from the same school you were, but I didn't go to the academy; I read a great deal, but I don't know how to select books, and perhaps I don't read the right things, nevertheless, the longer I live, the more I want to know. My hair is turning gray, I'm almost an old man now, but I know so little, oh, so little! Yet it seems to me that what is most important and real, I do know, firmly know. How I should like to prove to you that there is no happiness, that there should not and will not be, for us. . . . We must only work and work, and happiness—that is the lot of our remote descendants. [*Pause*] Not for me, but at least for my descendants and those who come after them. . . .

[FEDOTIK *and* RODAY *appear in the reception room; they sit down and softly sing, strumming the guitar.*]

TUZENBACH: According to you, we are not even to dream of happiness! But what if I am happy!

VERSHININ: You're not.

TUZENBACH [*throwing up his hands and laughing*]: Obviously we don't understand each other. Well, how am I to convince you?

[MASHA *laughs softly.*]

TUZENBACH [*holding up a finger to her*]: Laugh! [*To* VERSHININ] Not only in two or three hundred years, but in a million years, life will be just the same as it always was; it doesn't change, it remains constant, following its own laws, which do not concern us, or which, in any case, you will never get to know. Birds of passage, cranes, for example, fly on and on, and no matter what thoughts, great or small, stray through their heads, they will still go on flying, not knowing where or why. They fly and will go on flying no matter what philosophers spring up among them; and let them philosophize as much as they like, so long as they go on flying. . . .

MASHA: But there is a meaning?

TUZENBACH: A meaning . . . Look, it's snowing. What meaning has that? [*Pause*]

MASHA: It seems to me a man must have some faith, or must seek a faith, otherwise his life is empty, empty. . . .

To live and not know why the cranes fly, why children are born, why there are stars in the sky . . . Either one knows what one lives for, or it's all futile, worthless. [*Pause*]

VERSHININ: In any case, it is a pity youth is over. . . .

MASHA: Gogol says: It's a bore to live in this world, friends!

TUZENBACH: And I say: It's difficult arguing with you, friends! Well, let it go. . . .

CHEBUTYKIN [*reading the newspaper*]: Balzac was married in Berdichev.

[IRINA *hums softly.*]

CHEBUTYKIN: Must make a note of that. [*Writes.*] Balzac was married in Berdichev. [*Reads newspaper.*]

IRINA [*musing as she lays out cards for a game of patience*]: Balzac was married in Berdichev.

TUZENBACH: The die is cast. You know, Maria Sergeyevna, I have sent in my resignation.

MASHA: So I hear. And I see nothing good in that. I don't like civilians.

TUZENBACH: Never mind. . . . [*Gets up*] I'm not good-looking, what sort of a military man do I make, anyhow? Well, it doesn't matter . . . I'm going to work. If for only one day in my life, to work so that I come home in the evening exhausted, fall into bed, and immediately go to sleep. [*Going into the reception room*] Workmen must sleep soundly.

FEDOTIK [*to* IRINA]: I just bought some crayons for you at Pyzhnikov's on Moscow Street. And this little penknife . . .

IRINA: You've got into the habit of treating me as though I were a little girl, but I'm grown up now. . . . [*Gaily takes the crayons and penknife.*] How charming!

FEDOTIK: And I bought a knife for myself . . . look here . . . one blade, another blade, then a third, this to clean your ears, scissors, this to clean your nails . . .

RODAY [*loudly*]: Doctor, how old are you?

CHEBUTYKIN: Me? Thirty-two.

[*Laughter*]

FEDOTIK: Now I'll show you another kind of patience. . . . [*Lays out the cards.*]

[*The samovar is brought in;* ANFISA *attends to it; a little later* NATASHA *comes in and also fusses about the table;* SOLYONY *enters and, after greeting the others, sits down at the table.*]

VERSHININ: Really, what a wind!

MASHA: Yes, I'm tired of winter. I've almost forgotten what summer is like.

IRINA: The game is coming out, I see. We shall go to Moscow.

FEDOTIK: No, it's not. You see, the eight falls on the two of spades. [*Laughs.*] That means you won't go to Moscow.

CHEBUTYKIN [*reading from the newspaper*]: Tsitsikar. Smallpox is raging here.

ANFISA [*going up to* MASHA]: Masha, have some tea, little one. [*To* VERSHININ] If you please, Your Honor . . . excuse me, sir, I have forgotten your name . . .

MASHA: Bring it here, nurse. I'm not going in there.

IRINA: Nurse!

ANFISA: Com-ing!

NATASHA [*to* SOLYONY]: Little babies understand perfectly. "Good morning, Bobik," I said, "good morning, darling!" He looked at me in a very special way. You think that's just a mother talking, but no, no, I assure you! He is an extraordinary child.

SOLYONY: If that child were mine, I would have fried him in a skillet and eaten him. [*Takes his glass, goes into the drawing room and sits in a corner.*]

NATASHA [*covering her face with her hands*]: Rude, ill-bred man!

MASHA: Happy is he who does not notice whether it's summer or winter. It seems to me that if I were in Moscow now, I'd be indifferent to the weather. . . .

VERSHININ: The other day I was reading the diary of a certain French minister, written in prison. The minister had been convicted of fraud. With what rapture and delight he speaks of the birds he sees from his prison window—birds he had never even noticed when he was a minister. Now that he has been released, of course, he'll no more notice them than he did before. In the same way, you won't notice Moscow when you live there. Happiness is something we never have, but only long for.

TUZENBACH [*takes a box from the table*]: But where's the candy?

IRINA: Solyony ate it.

TUZENBACH: All of it?

ANFISA [*serving tea*]: A letter for you, sir.

VERSHININ: For me? [*Takes the letter.*] From my daughter. [*Reads it.*] Yes, of course. . . . Excuse me, Maria Sergeyevna, I'll just slip out. I won't have any tea. [*Gets up, very much disturbed.*] These eternal scenes . . .

MASHA: What is it? Not a secret, is it?

VERSHININ [*softly*]: My wife has taken poison again. I must go. I'll slip out without being noticed. Horribly unpleasant all this. [*Kisses* MASHA's *hand.*] My dear, fine, lovely woman . . . I'll slip out here quietly. . . .

ANFISA: Now where is he going? I've just brought him his tea. . . . Such a——

MASHA [*flaring up*]: Leave me alone! You keep pestering, you give one no peace. . . . [*Goes to the table with her cup.*] I'm sick of you, old woman!

ANFISA: Why are you so annoyed? Darling!

[ANDREI's *voice:* "Anfisa!"]

ANFISA [*mimicking*]: Anfisa! He sits in there . . .

MASHA [*at the table in the reception room, angrily*]: Do let me sit down! [*Disarranges the cards on the table.*] You take up the whole table with your cards. Drink your tea!

IRINA: Mashka, you are cross!

MASHA: If I'm cross then don't talk to me. Leave me alone!

CHEBUTYKIN [*laughing*]: Leave her alone, leave her . . .

MASHA: You're sixty years old, but you're like a little boy, always prattling some damned nonsense.

NATASHA [*sighing*]: Masha, dear, why employ such expressions in your conversation? I tell you frankly, with your attractive appearance you would be simply enchanting in well-bred society if it were not for those words of yours. *Je vous prie, pardonnez moi, Marie, mais vous avez des manières un peu grossières.*

TUZENBACH [*with suppressed laughter*]: Give me . . . give me . . . I think there's some cognac over there. . . .

NATASHA: *Il paraît que mon Bobik déjà ne dort pas,* he's awake. He doesn't seem to be very well today. I must go to him, excuse me. . . . [*Goes out.*]

IRINA: And where has Aleksandr Ignatych gone?

MASHA: Home. Something odd with his wife again.

TUZENBACH [*goes to* SOLYONY *with the decanter of cognac in his hand*]: You're always sitting by yourself, thinking about something—and there's no telling what it is. Come, let's make it up. Let's have some cognac. [*They drink.*] I shall have to play the piano all night tonight—probably play all kinds of trash. . . . So be it!

SOLYONY: Why make it up? I never quarreled with you.

TUZENBACH: You always give me the feeling that something has happened between us. You have a strange character, I must say.

SOLYONY [*declaiming*]: "I am strange, who is not strange! Be not angry, Aleko!"

TUZENBACH: What's Aleko got to do with it? . . . [*Pause*]

SÓLYONY: When I'm alone with someone, it's all right, I'm like anybody else, but in company I'm despondent, timid, and . . . talk all sorts of nonsense. Nevertheless, I am more honest and more noble than many, many others. And I can prove that.

TUZENBACH: I often get angry with you, you're forever trying to pick a quarrel with me when we're in company, but all the same, I like you for some reason. So be it, I'm going to get drunk tonight. Let's drink!

SÓLYONY: Let's drink. [*They drink.*] I have never had anything against you, Baron. But I have the temperament of Lermontov. [*Softly*] I even look a little like Lermontov . . . . so they say. [*Takes a bottle of scent out of his pocket and pours it on his hands.*]

TUZENBACH: I'm sending in my resignation. *Basta!* I've been considering it for five years, and at last I've made up my mind. I'm going to work.

SÓLYONY [*declaiming*]: "Be not angry, Aleko. . . . Forget, forget, thy dreams." . . .

[*While they are talking,* ANDREI *quietly enters with a book and sits down near a candle.*]

TUZENBACH: I'm going to work.

CHEBUTYKIN [*going into the reception room with* IRINA]: And the food, too, was real Caucasian stuff: onion soup, and for the meat course, *chekhartma.*

SÓLYONY: *Cheremsha* is not meat at all, but a plant something like our onion.

CHEBUTYKIN: No, my angel. *Chekhartma* is not an onion, it's roast lamb.

SOLYONY: And I tell you *cheremsha* is an onion.

CHEBUTYKIN: And I tell you *chekhartma* is lamb.

SOLYONY: And I tell you *cheremsha* is an onion.

CHEBUTYKIN: Why should I argue with you? You've never been to the Caucasus, and you've never eaten *chekhartma*.

SOLYONY: I've never eaten it because I can't stand it. *Cheremsha* smells just like garlic.

ANDREI [*imploring*]:   Enough, gentlemen! Please!

TUZENBACH: When are the maskers coming?

IRINA: They promised to be here by nine; that means any minute now.

TUZENBACH [*embraces* ANDREI *and sings*]:   "Oh, my porch, my porch, oh, my new porch." . . .

ANDREI [*dances and sings*]:   "New porch, maple-wood porch" . . .

CHEBUTYKIN [*dances*]:   "Latticework porch!"

[*Laughter*]

TUZENBACH [*kisses* ANDREI]:   What the hell, let's drink. Andryusha, let's drink to our friendship. And I'll go to Moscow with you, Andryusha, to the university.

SOLYONY: Which university? There are two in Moscow.

ANDREI: In Moscow there is one university.

SOLYONY: Two, I tell you.

ANDREI: Make it three. So much the better.

SOLYONY: In Moscow there are two universities. [*There is a murmur and hissing.*] In Moscow there are two universities: the old one and the new one. And if you don't care to listen, if my conversation is irritating to you, I can stop talking. I can even go into another room. [*Goes out through one of the doors.*]

TUZENBACH: Bravo, bravo! [*Laughs.*] Let's get started, friends, I'm going to play! Funny fellow, that Solyony. . . . [*Sits down at the piano and plays a waltz.*]

MASHA [*waltzing by herself*]:   The Baron is drunk, the Baron is drunk, the Baron is drunk . . .

[*Enter* NATASHA.]

NATASHA [*to* CHEBUTYKIN]:   Ivan Romanych! [*Says something to him then quietly goes out.*]

[CHEBUTYKIN *touches* TUZENBACH *on the shoulder and whispers something to him.*]

IRINA: What is it?

CHEBUTYKIN: It's time we were going. Good night.

TUZENBACH: Good night. Time to go.

IRINA: But, look here . . . What about the maskers?

ANDREI [*embarrassed*]:   They're not coming. Don't you see, my dear, Natasha says that Bobik is not very well, and so . . . In any case, I don't know anything about it, and I certainly don't care.

IRINA [*shrugging her shoulders*]:   Bobik is not well!

MASHA: It's not the first time! If they turn us out, I suppose we must go. [*To* IRINA] It's not Bobik that's sick, but she herself . . . here! [*Taps her forehead.*] Common creature!

[ANDREI *goes out through door on the right to his room;* CHEBUTYKIN *follows him. The others say good-bye in the reception room.*]

FEDOTIK: What a pity! I counted on spending the evening, but if the little fellow is sick, then, of course . . . I'll bring him some toys tomorrow. . . .

RODAY [*loudly*]:   I purposely took a nap after dinner today, I thought I'd be dancing all night. Why, it's only nine o'clock!

MASHA: Let's go out into the street, we can talk there and decide what to do.

[*Voices are heard saying: "Good-bye! Good night!" and* TUZENBACH'S *gay laughter. Everyone goes out.* ANFISA *and a maid clear the table and put out the lights. The nurse sings offstage.* ANDREI, *wearing an overcoat and hat, and* CHEBUTYKIN *enter quickly.*]

CHEBUTYKIN: I never had the time to get married, because life just flashed by like lightning, and because I was madly in love with your mother, who was married. . . .

ANDREI: One shouldn't marry. One shouldn't, because it's boring.

CHEBUTYKIN: That may be so, but what about loneliness? You may philosophize as much as you like, but loneliness is a terrible thing, my boy. . . . Though, as a matter of fact . . . of course, it really doesn't matter.

ANDREI: Let's go quickly.

CHEBUTYKIN: What's the hurry? We have time.

ANDREI: I'm afraid my wife might stop me.

CHEBUTYKIN: Oh!

ANDREI: I'm not going to play tonight, I shall just look on. I don't feel well. . . . What shall I do, Ivan Romanych, for shortness of breath?

CHEBUTYKIN: Why ask me! I don't remember, my boy. Don't know.

ANDREI: Let's go through the kitchen.

[*They go out. There is a ring, then another ring; voices are heard, and laughter.* IRINA *enters.*]

IRINA: What is it?

ANFISA [*in a whisper*]:   The maskers!

[*A ring*]

IRINA: Tell them, nurse dear, that there's no one at home. They must excuse us.

[ANFISA *goes out.* IRINA *paces the room, deep in thought: she is perturbed.* SOLYONY *enters.*]

SOLYONY [*puzzled*]:   Nobody here. . . . Where is everyone?

IRINA: They've gone home.

SOLYONY: Strange. Are you alone here?

IRINA: Alone. [*Pause*] Good-bye.

SOLYONY: I behaved without sufficient restraint just now, tactlessly. But you are not like the rest of them, you are superior and pure, you see the truth. . . . You alone can understand me. I love you, deeply, infinitely love you. . . .

IRINA: Good-bye! Go away!

SOLYONY: I cannot live without you. [*Following her*] Oh, my bliss! [*Through tears*] Oh, happiness! Magnificent, wonderful, amazing eyes, such as I have never seen in another woman. . . .

IRINA [*coldly*]: Stop it, Vassily Vassilyich!

SOLYONY: For the first time I speak to you of love, and it is as though I were not on this earth, but on another planet. [*Rubs his forehead.*] Well, it's all one. Love cannot be forced, to be sure. . . . But there must be no happy rivals. . . . There must not be . . . I swear to you by all that's holy, I will kill any rival. . . . Oh, wonderful one!

[NATASHA *passes with a candle.*]

NATASHA [*peeps in at one door, then another, and passes by the door leading into her husband's room*]: Andrei is there. Let him read. Excuse me, Vassily Vassilyich, I didn't know you were here, I'm in my dressing gown. . . .

SOLYONY: It's all one. Good-bye! [*Goes out.*]

NATASHA: You are tired, my poor, dear girl! [*Kisses* IRINA.] You ought to go to bed a little earlier.

IRINA: Is Bobik asleep?

NATASHA: He's asleep. But he's restless. By the way, dear, I keep meaning to speak to you, but either you are out or I have no time . . . I think the nursery Bobik is in now is cold and damp. And your room is so nice for a baby. My own dearest, do move in with Olya for a while!

IRINA [*not understanding*]: Where?

[*A troika with bells is heard driving up to the house.*]

NATASHA: You and Olya will be in one room for the time being, and Bobik will be in your room. He's such a darling! Today I said to him: "Bobik, my own! My own baby!" And he looked up at me with his dear little eyes. [*A ring*] That must be Olga. How late she is!

[*The maid comes up to* NATASHA *and whispers in her ear.*]

NATASHA: Protopopov? What a queer man! Protopopov has come to invite me to go for a drive with him in his troika. [*Laughs.*] How strange these men are! . . . [*A ring*] Someone has come. Maybe I'll go for a little ride, just for a quarter of an hour. . . . [*To the maid*] Tell him I'll be right there. [*A ring*] The bell . . . It must be Olga. [*Goes out.*]

[*The maid runs out;* IRINA *sits lost in thought;* KULYGIN *and* OLGA *enter, followed by* VERSHININ.]

KULYGIN: How do you like that! They said you were going to have a party.

VERSHININ: Strange, when I left a little while ago, half an hour or so, they were expecting the maskers. . . .

IRINA: They have all gone.

KULYGIN: Has Masha gone, too? Where did she go? And why is Protopopov downstairs waiting in a troika? Who is he waiting for?

IRINA: Don't ask questions. . . . I'm tired.

KULYGIN: Well, Miss Caprice . . .

OLGA: The meeting just ended. I'm exhausted. Our headmistress is ill, and I am to take her place. My head, my head aches, my head . . . [*Sits down.*] Andrei lost two hundred rubles at cards last night. . . . The whole town is talking about it. . . .

KULYGIN: Yes, the meeting tired me, too. [*Sits down.*]

VERSHININ: My wife just took it into her head to frighten me, she almost poisoned herself. It's all right now, and I'm glad, it's a relief. . . . So, we are to go? Very well, then, I wish you good night. Fyodor Ilyich, let's go somewhere together. I cannot stay at home, I absolutely cannot. . . . Come along!

KULYGIN: I'm tired. I'm not coming. [*Gets up.*] I'm tired. Has my wife gone home?

IRINA: I expect so.

KULYGIN [*kisses* IRINA's *hand*]:   Good-bye. Tomorrow and the day after we can rest the whole day. Good night! [*Going*] I do want some tea. I counted on spending the evening in pleasant company, and—*O, fallacem hominum spem!* Accusative case exclamatory. . . .

VERSHININ: Well, then, I'll go by myself. [*Goes out with* KULYGIN, *whistling.*]

OLGA: My head aches, my head . . . Andrei has lost . . . the whole town is talking . . . I'll go and lie down. [*Going*] Tomorrow I shall be free. . . . Oh, Lord, how pleasant that is! Free tomorrow, free the day after. . . . My head aches, my head . . . [*Goes out.*]

IRINA [*alone*]:   They have all gone. No one is here.

[*In the street an accordion is heard; the nurse sings a song.*]

NATASHA [*crosses the reception room in a fur coat and cap, followed by the maid*]:   I'll be back in half an hour. I'm just going for a little drive. [*Goes out.*]

IRINA [*left alone, with longing*]:   Moscow! Moscow! To Moscow!

Act III

[OLGA's *and* IRINA's *room. To the left and right are beds with screens around them. It is past two o'clock in the morning. Offstage a fire alarm is ringing for a fire that has been going on for some time. It can be seen that no one in the house has gone to bed.* MASHA *is lying on a sofa dressed, as usual, in black. Enter* OLGA *and* ANFISA.]

ANFISA: They're sitting below now, under the stairs. . . . I said to them: "Come upstairs," I said, "you can't sit there like that." They're crying. "Papa," they say, "we don't know where Papa is. God forbid he's burned!" What an idea! And there are people in the yard . . . they're without clothes, too.

OLGA [*taking clothes out of the wardrobe*]:   Take this gray dress . . . and this one . . . the blouse, too. . . . And take this skirt, nurse. . . . My God, what a thing to have happened! Kirsanovsky Street has burned to the ground, apparently. . . . Take this . . . and this. . . . [*Tossing clothes into her arms*] The poor Vershinins had a fright. . . . Their house nearly burned down. They'll have to spend the night here . . . we can't let them go home. . . . Everything was burned at poor Fedotik's, there's nothing left. . . .

ANFISA: You'd better call Ferapont, Olyushka, I won't be able to carry——

OLGA [*rings*]: Nobody comes when I ring. . . . [*At the door*] Come here, whoever is there! [*Through the open door a window can be seen, reflecting the glow of the fire; a fire engine is heard passing the house.*] What a horror this is! And how tiring!

[*Enter* FERAPONT.]

OLGA: Here, take these things downstairs. . . . The Kolotilin young ladies are down there, under the staircase . . . give it to them. And this, too. . . .

FERAPONT: Yes, miss. In 1812 Moscow burned down, too. Oh, good Lord! The French were surprised.

OLGA: Go along now.

FERAPONT: Yes, miss.

OLGA: Nurse, dear, give them everything. We don't need anything, give it all away, nurse. . . . I'm tired, I can hardly stand up. . . . We mustn't let the Vershinins go home. . . . The little girls can sleep in the drawing room, and Aleksandr Ignatych downstairs at the Baron's. . . . Fedotik, too, at the Baron's, or let him stay with us in the reception room. . . . The doctor, as if on purpose, got drunk, terribly drunk, and we can't put anyone in with him. Vershinin's wife in the drawing room, too. . . .

ANFISA [*exhausted*]: Olyushka, dear, don't send me away! Don't send me away!

OLGA: You're talking nonsense, nurse. Nobody's sending you away.

ANFISA [*laying her head on* OLGA*'s breast*]: My own, my treasure, I work, I work hard. . . . When I get feeble everybody will say: go away! And where will I go? I'm eighty, going on eighty-two. . . .

OLGA: Sit down, nurse dear. . . . You're tired, you poor thing. . . . [*Seats her in a chair.*] Rest, my dear. How pale you are!

[*Enter* NATASHA.]

NATASHA: They're saying we should form a committee at once to aid the victims of the fire. Why not? It's a fine idea. Indeed, we should always be ready to help the poor, that's the duty of the rich. Bobik and Sofochka are fast asleep, sleeping as if nothing had happened. We've got such a lot of people everywhere, no matter where you turn, the house is full. There's influenza in town now, I'm afraid the children might catch it.

OLGA [*not listening to her*]: You don't see the fire from this room, it's peaceful here. . . .

NATASHA: Yes . . . I suppose I'm all disheveled. [*In front of the mirror*] They say that I've gained weight . . . but it's not true! Not at all! Masha's sleeping, exhausted, poor thing. . . . [*To* ANFISA, *coldly*] Don't you dare sit down in my presence! Stand up! Get out of here! [ANFISA *goes out; a pause.*] Why you keep that old woman, I cannot understand!

OLGA [*taken aback*]: Excuse me, but I cannot understand . . .

NATASHA: She's of no use here. She's a peasant, she should live in the country. . . . What pampering! I like order in a house! There shouldn't be any useless servants in a house! [*Pats* OLGA's *cheek.*] Poor dear, you're tired! Our headmistress is tired! When my Sofochka grows up and goes to high school, I'll be afraid of you.

OLGA: I shan't be the headmistress.

NATASHA: You'll be elected, Olechka. That's settled.

OLGA: I shall refuse. I cannot . . . I haven't the strength for it. . . . [*Drinks water.*] You were so rude to nurse just now. . . . You must excuse me, but I am in no condition to endure . . . I just can't stand it.

NATASHA [*agitated*]: Forgive me, Olya, forgive me . . . I didn't mean to upset you.

[MASHA *gets up, takes her pillow, and goes out angrily.*]

OLGA: You must understand, my dear . . . perhaps we were brought up in a peculiar way, but I cannot bear that. Such an attitude oppresses me, I feel ill, simply sick at heart!

NATASHA: Forgive me, forgive me. . . . [*Kisses her.*]

OLGA: Any rudeness, even the slightest, even a tactless word, upsets me. . . .

NATASHA: I often talk too much, that's true, but you must agree, my dear, that she could just as well live in the country.

OLGA: She has been with us for thirty years.

NATASHA: But now she can't work any more! Either I don't understand, or you don't want to understand me. She is incapable of working, she just sleeps or sits.

OLGA: Then let her sit.

NATASHA [*astonished*]: What do you mean, let her sit? She's a servant, isn't she? [*Through tears*] I don't understand you, Olya. I have a nurse, I have a wet nurse, we have a maid and a cook . . . what do we keep that old woman for? What for?

[*The fire alarm is heard offstage.*]

OLGA: I have aged ten years tonight.

NATASHA: We must come to an understanding, Olya. You are at school—I am at home; you're doing the teaching—I'm doing the housekeeping. And if I say anything about the servants, then I know what I'm talking about; I-know-what-I-am-talk-ing-about. And by tomorrow that old thief, that old hag, [*stamping her foot*] that old witch, will be gone! Don't you dare cross me! Don't you dare! [*Recovering herself*] Really, if you don't move downstairs, we shall always be quarreling. It's awful.

[*Enter* KULYGIN.]

KULYGIN: Where is Masha? It's time to go home. They say the fire is subsiding. [*Stretches.*] Only one section burned down, in spite of the fact that there was a wind; at first it looked as if the whole town was on fire. [*Sits down.*] I'm worn out. Olechka, my dear . . . I often think, if it hadn't been for Masha, I'd have married you, Olechka. You are very good. . . . I'm exhausted. [*Listens.*]

OLGA: What is it?

KULYGIN: Just tonight the doctor had to go on a drinking spree, he's terribly drunk. Just tonight! [*Gets up.*] I think he's coming in here now. . . . Do you hear? Yes, he's coming. . . . [*Laughs.*] Such a fellow, really. . . . I'll hide. [*Goes to the cupboard and stands in the corner.*] What a rascal!

OLGA: He hasn't been drinking for two years, and now all of a sudden he's gone and got drunk. [*Goes with* NATASHA *to the back of the room.*]

[CHEBUTYKIN *comes in; walking as though sober, without staggering, he crosses the room, stops, looks around, then goes to the washstand and begins to wash his hands.*]

CHEBUTYKIN [*sullenly*]: The hell with 'em . . . all of 'em. . . . They think I'm a doctor, that I know how to cure any kind of sickness, I know absolutely nothing, forgot everything I knew, I remember nothing, absolutely nothing. [OLGA *and* NATASHA *go out, unnoticed by him.*] The hell with 'em. Last Wednesday I treated a woman in Zasyp—she died, and it's my fault she died. Yes . . . I used to know a thing or two twenty-five years ago, and now I remember nothing. Nothing. Maybe I'm not even a man, and am just pretending I have arms, and legs, and a head; maybe I don't even exist, and only imagine I'm walking about, eating, sleeping. [*Weeps.*] Oh, if only I didn't exist! [*Stops weeping, sullenly.*] Damn it all. . . . The other day there was a conversation at the club; they were talking about Shakespeare, Voltaire. . . . Never read them, never read them at all, but I tried to look as if I had. And others did the same. Vulgar! Cheap! And that woman I killed Wednesday came to my mind . . . it all came back to me, and in my soul I felt crooked, vile, loathsome . . . and I went out and got drunk. . . .

[*Enter* IRINA, VERSHININ, *and* TUZENBACH; TUZENBACH *is wearing a fashionable new civilian suit.*]

IRINA: Let's sit here. No one will come in here.

VERSHININ: If it weren't for the soldiers, the whole town would have burnt down. Brave boys! [*Rubs his hands with pleasure.*] Salt of the earth! Ah, what a fine lot!

KULYGIN [*going up to them*]: What's the time, gentlemen?

TUZENBACH: Going on four. It's getting light.

IRINA: Everyone's sitting in the reception room, nobody goes. And that Solyony of yours is sitting there, too. . . . [*To* CHEBUTYKIN] You ought to go to bed, Doctor.

CHEBUTYKIN: I'm all right . . . thanks. . . . [*Combs his beard.*]

KULYGIN [*laughs*]: You're tipsy, Ivan Romanych! [*Claps him on the shoulder.*] Good boy! *In vino veritas,* as the ancients used to say.

TUZENBACH: Everyone is asking me to arrange a concert for the benefit of the victims of the fire.

IRINA: But who is there to——

TUZENBACH: It could be arranged, if we wanted to. Maria Sergeyevna plays the piano beautifully, in my opinion.

KULYGIN: She does play beautifully.

IRINA: She's forgotten how by now. She hasn't played for three years . . . or perhaps four.

TUZENBACH: Here in this town, absolutely nobody understands music, not a soul; but I do understand it, and I assure you, on my honor, that Maria Sergeyevna plays magnificently, almost with genius.

KULYGIN: You're right, Baron. I love Masha very much. She's lovely.

TUZENBACH: To be able to play so superbly, and at the same time to realize that nobody, nobody understands you. . . .

KULYGIN [*sighs*]: Yes. . . . But would it be proper for her to take part in a concert? [*Pause*] Of course, I know nothing about it, my friends. Perhaps it would even be a good thing. I must admit, our director is a fine man, in fact, a very fine man, most intelligent, but he holds certain views. . . . To be sure, it is none of his affair, nevertheless, if you like, I might have a word with him about it.

[CHEBUTYKIN *picks up a china clock and examines it.*]

VERSHININ: I got covered with dirt at the fire; I look disgraceful. [*Pause*] Yesterday I happened to hear that our brigade might be transferred somewhere far from here. Some say to Poland, others—to Chita.

TUZENBACH: I heard that, too. Well? The town will be quite deserted.

IRINA: And we shall go away!

CHEBUTYKIN [*drops the clock, which smashes*]: Smashed to smithereens!

[*Pause; everyone is upset and embarrassed.*]

KULYGIN [*picking up the pieces*]:   To break such an expensive thing—oh, Ivan Romanych, Ivan Romanych! You get minus zero for conduct.

IRINA: That was Mama's clock.

CHEBUTYKIN: Maybe . . . Mama's, so it was Mama's. Maybe I didn't break it, and it only appears to have been broken. Maybe it only appears that we exist, but, in fact, we are not here. I don't know anything. Nobody knows anything. [*At the door*] Where are your eyes? Natasha is having a little romance with Protopopov, and you don't see it. There you sit, not seeing what's before you, and Natasha is having a little romance with Protopopov. . . . [*Sings.*] "May I offer you this fig?" . . . [*Goes out.*]

VERSHININ: Yes. . . . [*Laughs.*] How strange all this is, really. [*Pause*] When the fire broke out, I ran home as fast as I could; when I got there I saw that our house was safe and sound and in no danger, but my two little girls were standing in the doorway in their underwear, their mother not there, people bustling about, dogs and horses rushing by, and the children's faces full of alarm, terror, entreaty, and I don't know what; it wrung my heart to see those faces. My God, I thought, what will these little girls have to go through in the course of a long life! I picked them up and ran, still thinking the same thing: what more will they have to live through in this world! [*Fire alarm; a pause*] When I got here I found their mother here, shouting, furious.

[MASHA *enters with a pillow and sits down on the sofa.*]

VERSHININ: When my little girls were standing in the doorway in their underwear, the street red with the blaze, and the noise terrible, I thought that something of the sort must have happened many years ago, when the enemy made a sudden raid, plundering, burning. . . . And yet, what a difference between things as they are and as they were. When a little more time has passed, say, two or three hundred years, then people will look at our present-day life with horror and contempt, and all this will seem awkward, difficult, very uncertain and strange. Oh, what a life that is going to be, what a life! [*Laughs.*] Forgive me, here I am philosophizing again. Please let me go on, my friends. I have a terrific longing to philosophize, now that I am in the mood for it. [*Pause*] It seems everyone is asleep. And so I say: what a life that will be! Try to imagine it. . . . At the present time there are only three of your sort in this town, but in generations to come there will be more and more, a time will come when everything will change to your way, people will live like you, but then later, you, too, will be outmoded, people will appear who will be better than you. . . . [*Laughs.*] I am in a very special mood today. [*Laughs.*] I want desperately to live. . . . [*Sings.*] "To love at every age we yield, and fruitful are its pangs."* [*Laughs.*]

MASHA: Tram-tam-tam . . .

*This is from the Chaikovsky opera *Eugene Onegin*.

VERSHININ: Tam-tam . . .

MASHA: Tra-ra-ra . . .

VERSHININ: Tra-ta-ta . . .

[*Laughter. Enter* FEDOTIK.]

FEDOTIK [*dances*]: Burned down, burned down! All burnt to the ground! [*Laughs.*]

IRINA: What sort of a joke is that! Has everything burnt?

FEDOTIK [*laughs*]: Absolutely everything. There's nothing left. My guitar's burnt, my photography equipment's burnt, and all my letters. . . . Even the little notebook I meant to give you—burnt.

[*Enter* SOLYONY.]

IRINA: No, please go, Vassily Vassilyich. You can't stay here.

SOLYONY: Why is it that the Baron can stay and I can't?

VERSHININ: We must go, really. How's the fire?

SOLYONY: Dying down, they say. Yes, it seems decidedly odd that the Baron can stay and I can't. [*Takes out a bottle of scent and sprinkles himself.*]

VERSHININ: Tram-tam-tam.

MASHA: Tram-tam.

VERSHININ [*laughs, to* SOLYONY]: Let us go into the reception room.

SOLYONY: Ve-ry well, we'll make a note of that. This moral could be made more clear, but might provoke the geese, I fear. . . . [*Fixing his gaze on* TUZENBACH] Peep, peep, peep. . . . [*Goes out with* VERSHININ *and* FEDOTIK.]

IRINA: How that Solyony has smoked up the room. . . . [*Puzzled*] The Baron is asleep! Baron! Baron!

TUZENBACH [*waking up*]: I really am tired. . . . The brickyard . . . I'm not talking in my sleep, as a matter of fact, I intend to begin work at the brickyard soon. It's already been discussed. [*To* IRINA, *tenderly*] You are so pale, beautiful, enchanting. . . . To me it seems your paleness brightens the dark air like light. . . . You are sad, you're dissatisfied with life. . . . Oh, come with me, let us go away and work together!

MASHA: Nikolai Lvovich, I wish you'd go.

TUZENBACH [*laughing*]: Are you here? I didn't see you. [*Kisses* IRINA's *hand.*] Good-bye, I'm going. . . . As I look at you now, I recall how once, a long time ago on your name day, you talked of the joy of work, and you were so gay, so confident. . . . What a happy life I dreamed of then! Where is it? [*Kisses* IRINA's *hand.*] There are tears in your eyes. Go to bed, it's growing light . . . the morning has begun. . . . If only I could give my life for you!

MASHA: Nikolai Lvovich, do go! Really, now. . . .

TUZENBACH: I am going. . . . [*Goes out.*]

MASHA [*lying down*]: Are you asleep, Fyodor?

KULYGIN: Eh?

MASHA: You had better go home.

KULYGIN: My dear Masha, my precious Masha. . . .

IRINA: She's exhausted. You ought to let her rest, Fedya.

KULYGIN: I'll go directly. . . . My dear, lovely wife . . . I love you, my one and only. . . .

MASHA [*irascibly*]: *Amo, amas, amat, amamus, amatis, amant.*

KULYGIN [*laughs*]: Yes, really, she's remarkable. You have been my wife for seven years, but it seems as if we'd been married only yesterday. Word of honor. Yes, really, you are a remarkable woman. I am content, content, content!

MASHA: Bored, bored, bored. . . . [*Sits up.*] I cannot get it out of my mind. . . . Simply revolting. It's there, like a nail in my head, I can't remain silent. I mean about Andrei. . . . He's mortgaged this house to the bank and his wife got hold of all the money; and after all, the house doesn't belong to him alone, but to the four of us! This is something he ought to realize, if he's a decent man.

KULYGIN: Why bother, Masha? What is it to you? Andryusha owes money to everyone, I'm sorry for him.

MASHA: It's revolting anyhow. [*Lies down.*]

KULYGIN: We're not poor. I work, I teach at the high school and give private lessons . . . I'm just a plain, honest man. . . . *Omnia mea mecum porto,* as they say.

MASHA: I don't want anything, but the injustice of it revolts me. [*Pause*] Go along, Fyodor.

KULYGIN [*kisses her*]: You're tired; rest for half an hour, and I'll sit out there and wait for you. Sleep. . . . [*Going*] I am content, content, content. [*Goes out.*]

IRINA: Yes, how shallow our Andrei has become, how dull and old he's grown living with that woman! There was a time when he was preparing for a professorship, and yesterday he boasted of having at last become a member of the District Board. He, a member of the Board, and Protopopov the Chairman. . . . The whole town is laughing and talking about it, and he's the only one who neither sees nor knows anything. . . . And here everyone else has been running to the fire, while he sits in his room taking not the slightest notice. He just plays his violin. [*Nervously*] Oh, it's awful, awful, awful! [*Weeps.*] I can't, I can't bear it any longer! I can't, I can't . . .

[OLGA *enters and begins tidying up her dressing table.*]

IRINA [*sobs loudly*]: Turn me out, turn me out, I can't bear any more!

OLGA [*alarmed*]: What is it, what is it? Darling!

IRINA [*sobbing*]: Where? Where has it all gone? Where is it? Oh, my God, my God! I have forgotten everything, I've forgotten . . . it's all muddled in my head. . . . I can't remember how to say window or floor in Italian. I'm forgetting everything, every day I forget, and life is slipping by, never to return, never, we shall never go to Moscow . . . I see that we shall never go. . . .

OLGA: Darling, darling. . . .

IRINA [*trying to control herself*]: Oh, I am miserable . . . I can't work, I won't work. Enough, enough! I've been a telegraph clerk, and now I have a job in the office of the Town Council, and I loathe and despise every single thing they give me to do. . . . I'm nearly twenty-four already, I've been working a long time, and my brain is drying up, I've grown thin and old and ugly, and there is nothing, nothing, no satisfaction of any kind, and time is passing, and I feel that I'm moving away from the real, beautiful life, moving farther and farther into some sort of abyss. I am in despair, and why I am alive, why I haven't killed myself before now, I don't know. . . .

OLGA: Don't cry, my little one, don't cry. . . . It hurts me.

IRINA: I'm not crying, I'm not crying. . . . That's enough. . . . There, I'm not crying any more. Enough . . . enough!

OLGA: Darling, I'm speaking to you as a sister, as a friend, if you want my advice, marry the Baron!

[IRINA *weeps quietly.*]

After all, you respect him, you value him highly. . . . It's true, he's not good-looking, but he's so honest, so pure. . . . You see, one doesn't marry for love, but to do one's duty. At least, that's what I think, and I would marry without love. I'd marry anyone who asked me, so long as he was a decent man. I'd even marry an old man. . . .

IRINA: I kept thinking that we'd move to Moscow, and there I'd meet my true love, I dreamed of him, I loved him. . . . But it all turned out to be foolishness, just foolishness. . . .

OLGA [*embracing her*]: My dear, lovely sister, I understand it all; when Baron Nikolai Lvovich left the army and came to see us in civilian clothes, he seemed to me so homely that I actually began to cry. . . . He said: "Why are you crying?" How could I tell him! But if it were God's will that he should marry you, I'd be happy. That, you see, would be a different matter, quite different.

[NATASHA, *carrying a candle, enters from the door on the right and crosses the stage without speaking.*]

MASHA [*sitting up*]: She goes about looking as if it were she who had started the fire.

OLGA: Masha, you are silly. The silliest one in the family—is you. Forgive me for saying so. [*Pause*]

MASHA: My dear sisters, I want to confess. My soul is in torment. I shall confess to you, and then never again to anyone. . . . I'll tell you right now. [*Softly*] It is my secret, but you must know everything . . . I cannot remain silent. . . . [*Pause*] I love, love . . . I love that man. . . . You saw him just now. . . . Well, there it is. In short, I love Vershinin.

OLGA [*goes behind her screen*]: Stop that. I can't hear you, anyway.

MASHA: What am I to do! [*Clutching her head*] At first I thought him strange, then I felt sorry for him . . . then I began to love him . . . to love everything about him, his voice, his words, his misfortunes, his two little girls. . . .

OLGA [*behind the screen*]: I'm not listening. Whatever silly things you may say, it doesn't matter, I shan't hear them.

MASHA: Oh, Olya, you're the one that's silly. I love him—such is my fate. Such is my destiny. . . . And he loves me. . . . All this is frightening. Isn't it? Is it wrong? [*Takes* IRINA *by the hand, drawing her to her.*] Oh, my darling . . . how are we going to live our life, what will become of us? . . . When you read it in a novel it just seems stale, and all so clear, but when you fall in love yourself, you begin to see that nobody knows anything, that each of us has to resolve everything for himself. . . . My darlings, my sisters . . . I have confessed to you, now I'll be silent. . . . I shall now be like Gogol's madman. . . . Silence . . . silence. . . .

[*Enter* ANDREI, *followed by* FERAPONT.]

ANDREI [*angrily*]: What do you want? I don't understand.

FERAPONT [*in the doorway, impatiently*]: I've told you ten times already, Andrei Sergeyevich.

ANDREI: In the first place, I am not Andrei Sergeyevich to you but Your Honor.

FERAPONT: The firemen, Your Honor, are asking permission to drive through the garden to the river. Otherwise they have to go round and round—a downright nuisance.

ANDREI: All right. Tell them all right. [FERAPONT *goes out.*] I'm fed up with them. Where's Olga? [OLGA *comes out from behind the screen.*] I've come to ask you to give me the key to the cupboard, I've lost mine. You've got one, the little key. [OLGA *gives him the key without speaking;* IRINA *goes behind her screen; a pause.*] What an enormous fire! It's beginning to die down now. Hang it all, that Ferapont made me lose my temper and I said something stupid to him. . . . Your Honor. . . . [*Pause*] Why don't you speak, Olya? [*Pause*] It's time you dropped this nonsense and gave up sulking for no reason. . . . You're here, Masha, Irina's here, well, that's fine—let's have it out, once and for all. What are you holding against me? What is it?

OLGA: Let it rest, Andryusha. Tomorrow we'll have a talk. [*Agitated*] What an agonizing night!

ANDREI [*very much confused*]: Don't be upset. I'm asking you quite calmly: what are you holding against me? Tell me frankly.

[VERSHININ's *voice:* "*Tram-tam-tam!*"]

MASHA [*in a loud voice, getting up*]: Tra-ta-ta! [*To* OLGA] Good-bye, Olya, God bless you. [*Goes behind screen and kisses* IRINA.] Sleep well. . . . Good-bye, Andrei. Leave them now, they're tired out. . . . You can have it out tomorrow. . . . [*Goes out.*]

OLGA: Yes, really, Andryusha, let's put it off until tomorrow. . . . [*Goes behind her screen.*] It's time to go to sleep.

ANDREI: I'll just say it and then go. Right now. . . . In the first place, you have something against Natasha, my wife, and I've been aware of this from the very day of my wedding. Natasha is a fine, honest person, straightforward and noble—that is my opinion! I love and respect my wife, you understand, I respect her, and I insist that others respect her, too. I repeat, she is an honest, noble person, and all your grievances, if you will forgive me, are mere caprice. [*Pause*] In the second place, you seem to be angry because I am not a professor, engaged in academic work. But I serve on the District Board, and I consider this service just as high and sacred as serving science. I am a member of the District Board and I am proud of it, if you want to know. . . . [*Pause*] In the third place . . . I have something else to say . . . I mortgaged the house without asking your permission. . . . In this I am guilty, yes, and I ask you to forgive me. I was forced to do it because of my debts . . . thirty-five thousand rubles. . . . I am no longer gambling, I gave it up some time ago, but the chief thing I can say to justify myself is that you girls . . . you receive a pension, while I had no . . . emoluments, so to say. . . . [*Pause*]

KULYGIN [*at the door*]: Masha not here? [*Alarmed*] Where could she be? That's strange . . . [*Goes out.*]

ANDREI: They won't listen. Natasha is a superior, honest person. [*Paces the stage in silence, then stops.*] When I married, I thought we should be happy . . . all of us, happy . . . but, my God! [*Weeps.*] My dear sisters, my darling sisters, don't believe me, don't believe me. . . . [*Goes out.*]

KULYGIN [*at the door, anxiously*]:   Where is Masha? Isn't she here? What an extraordinary business! [*Goes out.*]

[*Fire alarm; the stage is empty.*]

IRINA [*behind the screen*]:   Olya! Who is that knocking on the floor?

OLGA: It's the doctor, Ivan Romanych. He's drunk.

IRINA: What a troubled night! [*Pause*] Olya! [*Looks out from behind the screen.*] Have you heard? The brigade is going to be taken from us, transferred to some place far away.

OLGA: That's only a rumor.

IRINA: We shall be left alone then. . . . Olya!

OLGA: Well?

IRINA: Darling, dearest, I do respect and value the Baron, he is a fine man—I'll marry him, I am willing, only let us go to Moscow! I implore you, let us go! There's nothing in the world better than Moscow! Let us go! Olya! Let us go!

Act IV

[*The old garden of the* PROZOROV *house. At the end of a long avenue of fir trees, the river is seen; on the other side of the river, a wood. To the right is the veranda of the house; there, on the table, bottles and glasses have been set out; apparently they have just been drinking champagne. It is twelve o'clock noon. From time to time people from the street cross the garden on their way to the river; four or five soldiers pass by walking rapidly.*

CHEBUTYKIN, *in an amiable mood, which he maintains throughout the act, sits in an easy chair in the garden, waiting to be called; he wears a military cap and carries a stick.* IRINA, TUZENBACH, *and* KULYGIN, *with a decoration around his neck and no moustache, stand on the veranda saying good-bye to* FEDOTIK *and* RODAY, *who are descending the steps; both officers are in field uniform.*]

TUZENBACH [*kisses* FEDOTIK]: You're a good fellow, we got on well together. [*Kisses* RODAY.] Once again . . . good-bye, my dear boy!

IRINA: Till we meet again!

FEDOTIK: It's not till we meet again, but good-bye, we shall never see each other again!

KULYGIN: Who knows! [*Wipes his eyes, smiles.*] Here I am, crying, too.

IRINA: Some day we shall run across one another.

FEDOTIK: In ten or fifteen years, perhaps? By then we shall hardly recognize one another, we'll greet each other coldly. . . . [*Takes a snapshot.*] Stand still. . . . Once more, for the last time.

RODAY [*embraces* TUZENBACH]:   We shall not see each other again. . . . [*Kisses* IRINA*'s hand.*] Thank you for everything, for everything!

FEDOTIK [*vexed*]:   Do wait a bit!

TUZENBACH: Please God we'll meet again. But write to us. Be sure to write.

RODAY [*glancing at the garden*]:   Good-bye, trees! [*Shouts.*] Yoo-hoo! [*Pause*] Good-bye, echo!

KULYGIN: I'm afraid you'll get married there in Poland. . . . Your Polish wife will embrace you and say: "Kokhany!" [*Laughs.*]

FEDOTIK [*looking at his watch*]:   We have less than an hour. Solyony is the only one out of our battery going on the barge, we're with the rank and file. Three battery divisions are going today, three more tomorrow—then peace and quiet will descend upon the town.

TUZENBACH: And the most dreadful boredom.

RODAY: Where is Maria Sergeyevna?

KULYGIN: Masha is in the garden.

FEDOTIK: We'll go and say good-bye to her.

RODAY: Good-bye, I must go, or I shall begin to cry. [*Quickly embraces* TUZENBACH *and* KULYGIN, *and kisses* IRINA*'s hand.*] It's been splendid living here. . . .

FEDOTIK [*to* KULYGIN]:   This is a souvenir for you . . . a notebook with a little pencil. . . . We'll go this way to the river. . . . [*As they go off, both look back.*]

RODAY [*shouts*]:   Yoo-hoo!

KULYGIN [*shouts*]:   Good-bye!

[*At the rear of the stage* FEDOTIK *and* RODAY *meet* MASHA *and bid her good-bye; she walks off with them.*]

IRINA: They are gone. . . . [*Sits on the bottom step of the veranda.*]

CHEBUTYKIN: They forgot to say good-bye to me.

IRINA: Well, what about you?

CHEBUTYKIN: I forgot, too, somehow. However, I'll see them soon, I'm leaving tomorrow. Yes . . . only one more day. In a year I'll be retired, I'll come back here and spend the rest of my life near you. . . . Only one little year left before I get my pension. . . . [*Puts one newspaper into his pocket and takes out another.*] I'll come here to you and change my life radically . . . I'll be such a quiet, well- . . . well-behaved, agreeable man . . .

IRINA: Yes, you really ought to change your life, my dear. You really should, somehow.

CHEBUTYKIN: Yes. I feel that. [*Softly sings.*] "Ta-ra-ra boom-de-ay . . . sit on the curb I may . . ."

KULYGIN: Incorrigible Ivan Romanych! Incorrigible!

CHEBUTYKIN: You ought to have taken me in hand. Then I'd have been reformed.

IRINA: Fyodor has shaved off his moustache. I can't bear to look at him!

KULYGIN: Why?

CHEBUTYKIN: I could tell you what your physiognomy looks like now, but I won't.

KULYGIN: Well! It's the accepted thing, *modus vivendi.* Our director shaved off his moustache, and as soon as I became an inspector, I shaved mine off, too. Nobody likes it, but I don't care. I am content. With a moustache or without a moustache, I am equally content. . . . [*Sits down.*]

[*At the rear of the stage* ANDREI *is wheeling a baby carriage with a sleeping child in it.*]

IRINA: Dear, dear Ivan Romanych, I'm dreadfully worried. You were on the boulevard yesterday, tell me what happened there.

CHEBUTYKIN: What happened? Nothing. Nothing worth talking about. [*Reads newspaper.*] It doesn't matter!

KULYGIN: What they are saying is that Solyony and the Baron met yesterday on the boulevard near the theater——

TUZENBACH: Stop it! Now why, really . . . [*With a wave of his hand, goes into the house.*]

KULYGIN: Near the theater . . . Solyony began badgering him, and the Baron wouldn't stand for it and said something that offended him. . . .

CHEBUTYKIN: I don't know. It's all nonsense.

KULYGIN: In a certain seminary a teacher wrote "nonsense" on a composition, and the pupil, thinking it was written in Latin, read "consensus. . . ." [*Laughs.*] Terribly funny. They say that Solyony is in love with Irina and has conceived a hatred for the Baron. . . .

That's understandable. Irina is a very pretty girl. She even resembles Masha, the same pensiveness. Only you, Irina, have a gentler disposition. Though Masha, too, has a very fine disposition. I love my Masha.

[*At the rear of the garden, offstage:* "Aa-oo! Yoo-hoo!"]

IRINA [*shudders*]: Somehow everything frightens me today. [*Pause*] I have all my things ready, after dinner I shall send them off. The Baron and I are getting married tomorrow, leaving tomorrow for the brickyard, and the day after tomorrow I'll be at the school, a new life begins. God will help me somehow! When I passed my teacher's examination, I wept for joy, for pure bliss. . . . [*Pause*] The cart will soon be here for my things. . . .

KULYGIN: That's all very well, only it doesn't seem to be quite serious. Nothing but ideas and not enough seriousness. However, I wish you well with all my heart.

CHEBUTYKIN [*moved*]: My delightful, lovely . . . my darling. . . . You've gone so far, I can't catch up to you. I've been left behind, like a bird of passage that has grown old and cannot fly. Fly away, my dears, fly away, and God be with you! [*Pause*] It was a mistake, Fyodor Ilyich, to shave off your moustache.

KULYGIN: That'll do! [*Sighs.*] Well, today the military are leaving, and everything will go on again as of old. No matter what they say, Masha is a good, honest woman, I love her very much and am thankful for my fate. . . . Different people have different destinies. . . . Here in the excise office there is a certain clerk, Kozyryov. He went to school with me, and was expelled from the fifth class in high school because he simply could not understand *ut consecutivum*. Now he lives in great poverty, he's ill, and whenever we meet I say to him: "Greetings, *ut consecutivum!*" "Yes," he says, "exactly, *consecutivum*," and then he coughs. . . . And here I've been lucky all my life, I'm happy. I've even been awarded the Order of Stanislav, Second Degree, and now I am teaching others that *ut consecutivum.* Of course, I'm a clever man, cleverer than a great many other people, but happiness does not consist in that. . . .

[*In the house "The Maiden's Prayer" is being played on the piano.*]

IRINA: Tomorrow evening I shall not be hearing that "Maiden's Prayer," and I shan't be meeting Protopopov. . . . [*Pause*] Protopopov is sitting there in the drawing room, he came again today. . . .

KULYGIN: The headmistress is not here yet?

IRINA: No. They have sent for her. If only you knew how hard it has been for me to live here alone, without Olya. . . . She lives at the high school, as headmistress, she's busy all day long, but I am alone, I'm bored, I have nothing to do, and the very room I live in is hateful to me. . . . So I have made up my mind: if I am not destined to be in Moscow, then so be it. It is fate. There is nothing to be done. . . . It is all God's will, that is the truth. Nikolai Lvovich proposed to me. . . . Well? I thought it over and made up my mind. He is a good man, it is really amazing how good he is. . . . And suddenly it was as if my soul had grown wings, I rejoiced and grew light-hearted, and again I had a longing for work, for work. . . . Only something happened yesterday, some sort of mystery is hanging over me. . . .

CHEBUTYKIN: Consensus. Nonsense.

NATASHA [*at the window*]: The headmistress!

KULYGIN: The headmistress has arrived. Let us go! [*Goes into the house with* IRINA.]

CHEBUTYKIN [*reads the newspaper, softly singing to himself*]: "Ta-ra-ra boom-de-ay . . . sit on the curb I may . . ."

[MASHA *approaches; in the background* ANDREI *is pushing the baby carriage.*]

MASHA: There he sits, just sits . . .

CHEBUTYKIN: What?

MASHA [*sits down*]: Nothing. . . . [*Pause*] Did you love my mother?

CHEBUTYKIN: Very much.

MASHA: And did she love you?

CHEBUTYKIN [*after a pause*]: That I no longer remember.

MASHA: Is my man here? That's how our cook Marfa used to speak of her policeman: my man. Is my man here?

CHEBUTYKIN: Not yet.

MASHA: When you have to take your happiness in snatches, in bits, and then lose it, as I am losing it, you gradually coarsen, grow bitter. . . . [*With her hand on her breast*] I'm seething here inside. . . . [*Gazing at AN-DREI, who is pushing the baby carriage*] Look at Andrei, our little brother. . . . All our hopes vanished. Thousands of people raised the bell, a great deal of money and effort were expended, and suddenly it fell and was shattered. All at once, without rhyme or reason. That's how it was with Andrei. . . .

ANDREI: And when will they finally quiet down in the house? Such noise!

CHEBUTYKIN: Soon. [*Looks at his watch.*] My watch is an old-fashioned one, it strikes. . . . [*Winds his watch, it strikes.*] The first, second, and fifth batteries leave at one o'clock sharp. [*Pause*] And tomorrow I go.

ANDREI: For good?

CHEBUTYKIN: I don't know. Perhaps I'll come back in a year. . . . Though, who knows. . . . It doesn't matter. . . .

[*Somewhere in the distance a harp and violin are heard.*]

ANDREI: The town will be empty. As if covered with a hood. [*Pause*] Something happened yesterday near the theater; everyone is talking about it, but I don't know what it was.

CHEBUTYKIN: Nothing. Foolishness. Solyony began picking on the Baron and he lost his temper and insulted him, and it finally got to the point where Solyony had to challenge him to a duel. [*Looks at his watch.*] It's probably time now. . . . At half-past twelve in the Crown forest, the one we see from here, on the other side of the river. . . . Piff-paff! [*Laughs.*] Solyony imagines that he is Lermontov, he even writes verses. A joke's a joke, but this is the third duel for him.

MASHA: For whom?

CHEBUTYKIN: Solyony.

MASHA: And for the Baron?

CHEBUTYKIN: What about the Baron? [*Pause*]

MASHA: My thoughts are in a tangle. . . . All the same, I tell you, it shouldn't be allowed. He might wound the Baron, or even kill him.

CHEBUTYKIN: The Baron is a good fellow, but one Baron more or less—what does it matter? Let them! It doesn't matter! [*Beyond the garden a shout: "Aa-oo! Yoo-hoo!"*] You can wait. That's Skvortsov, the second, shouting. He's in a boat.

ANDREI: In my opinion, to take part in a duel or to be present at one, even in the capacity of a doctor, is simply immoral.

CHEBUTYKIN: It only seems so. . . . We are not here, there is nothing in the world, we do not exist, but merely seem to exist. . . . And it really doesn't matter!

MASHA: Talk, talk, all day long nothing but talk. . . . [*Going*] To live in such a climate, where you keep thinking it's going to snow at any minute, and then on top of it these conversations. . . . [*Stopping*] I'm not going into the house, I cannot go in there. . . . When Vershinin comes, let me know. . . . [*Goes down the avenue.*] The birds of passage are in flight already. . . . [*Looks up.*] Swans or geese. . . . My dear, happy birds. . . . [*Goes out.*]

ANDREI: Our house will be empty. The officers are leaving, you are going, sister is getting married, and I shall be left alone in the house.

CHEBUTYKIN: And your wife?

[FERAPONT *enters with some documents.*]

ANDREI: A wife is a wife. She's honest, good . . . well, kind, but for all that, there's something in her that reduces her to the level of a small, blind, sort of thick-skinned animal. In any case, she's not a human being. I am speaking to you as to a friend, the only person to whom I can open my heart. I love Natasha, it's true, but sometimes she seems to me extremely vulgar, and then I feel lost, and I don't understand why, for what reason, I love her so, or at least, did love her. . . .

CHEBUTYKIN [*gets up*]: I'm going away tomorrow, my boy, perhaps we shall never see each other again, so here's my advice to you. Put on your hat, you know, take up a walking stick, and be off . . . walk out, leave, without looking back. And the farther you go the better.

[SOLYONY *crosses the back of the stage with two officers; seeing* CHEBUTYKIN, *he turns toward him; the officers walk on.*]

SOLYONY: Doctor, it's time! Half-past twelve. [*Greets* ANDREI.]

CHEBUTYKIN: In a moment. I'm fed up with the lot of you. [*To* ANDREI] If someone asks for me, Andryusha, say I'll be back presently. . . . [*Sighs.*] Oh-ho-ho!

SOLYONY: He no sooner cried "Alack" than the bear was on his back. [*Walks off with him.*] Why are you quacking, old man?

CHEBUTYKIN: Come on!

SOLYONY: How do you feel?

CHEBUTYKIN [*angrily*]: Like a pig in clover.

SOLYONY: The old man upsets himself needlessly. I shall indulge myself a bit, I'll simply shoot him like a snipe. [*Takes out scent and sprinkles his hands.*] I've used up a whole bottle today, but they still smell. My hands smell like a corpse. [*Pause*] Yes-s. . . . Remember the poem? "And he, rebellious, seeks the storm, As if in storms lay peace."

CHEBUTYKIN: Yes. He no sooner cried "Alack" than the bear was on his back. [*Goes out with* SOLYONY.]

[*Cries of "Yoo-hoo" and "Aa-oo" are heard.* ANDREI *and* FERAPONT *come in.*]

FERAPONT: Papers to sign . . .

ANDREI [*nervously*]: Leave me alone! Leave me alone! I beg of you! [*Walks away with the baby carriage.*]

FERAPONT: What are papers for, if not to be signed? [*Goes to the back of the stage.*]

[*Enter* IRINA *and* TUZENBACH, *wearing a straw hat;* KU-LYGIN *crosses the stage calling: "Aa-oo, Masha! Aa-oo!"*]

TUZENBACH: That seems to be the only man in town who's glad the officers are leaving.

IRINA: It's understandable. [*Pause*] Our town is going to be empty now.

TUZENBACH: Dear, I'll be back shortly.

IRINA: Where are you going?

TUZENBACH: I must go into town . . . to see my comrades off.

IRINA: That's not true. . . . Nikolai, why are you so distracted today? [*Pause*] What happened yesterday near the theater?

TUZENBACH [*with a gesture of impatience*]: I'll come back in an hour and be with you again. [*Kisses her hands.*] My beloved. . . . [*Looks into her face.*] It's five years now that I have loved you, and I still can't get used to it, and you seem always more beautiful to me. What lovely, wonderful hair! What eyes! Tomorrow I shall carry you off, we'll work, and be rich, and my dreams will come true. You shall be happy. There is only one thing, only one: you do not love me!

IRINA: That is not within my power! I'll be your wife, faithful and obedient, but it's not love, I can't help it! [*Weeps.*] I have never in my life been in love. Oh, how I have dreamed of love, dreamed of it for a long time now, day and night, but my soul is like a fine piano that is locked, and the key lost. [*Pause*] You look troubled.

TUZENBACH: I haven't slept all night. There is nothing in my life so terrible as to frighten me, only that lost key racks my soul and will not let me sleep. . . . Tell me something. . . . [*Pause*] Tell me something. . . .

IRINA: What? What shall I say? What?

TUZENBACH: Something.

IRINA: Don't! Don't! [*Pause*]

TUZENBACH: What trifles, what silly little things in life will suddenly, for no reason at all, take on meaning. You laugh at them just as you've always done, consider them trivial, and yet you go on, and you feel that you haven't the power to stop. Oh, let's not talk about that! I feel elated, I see these fir trees, these maples and birches, as if for the first time, and they all gaze at me with curiosity and expectation. What beautiful trees, and, in fact, how beautiful life ought to be with them! [*A shout of: "Aa-oo! Yoo-hoo!"*] I must go, it's time. . . . There's a tree that's dead, but it goes on swaying in the wind with the others. So it seems to me that if I die, I'll still have a part in life, one way or another. Good-bye, my darling. . . . [*Kisses her hands.*] The papers you gave me are on my table, under the calendar.

IRINA: I am coming with you.

TUZENBACH [*alarmed*]: No, no! [*Quickly goes, then stops in the avenue.*] Irina!

IRINA: What?

TUZENBACH [*not knowing what to say*]: I didn't have any coffee this morning. Ask them to make me some. [*Quickly goes out.*]

[IRINA *stands lost in thought, then goes to the back of the stage and sits down on the swing.* ANDREI *comes in with the baby carriage;* FERAPONT *appears.*]

FERAPONT: Andrei Sergeyevich, the papers aren't mine, you know, they're official papers. I didn't make them up.

ANDREI: Oh, where is it, where has it all gone, my past, when I was young, gay, clever, when I dreamed and thought with grace, when my present and my future were lighted up with hope? Why is it that when we have barely begun to live, we grow dull, gray, uninteresting, lazy, indifferent, useless, unhappy. . . . Our town has been in existence now for two hundred years, there are a hundred thousand people in it, and not one who isn't exactly like all the others, not one saint, either in the past or in the present, not one scholar, not one artist, no one in the least remarkable who could inspire envy or a passionate desire to imitate him. . . . They just eat, drink, sleep, and then die . . . others are born and they, too, eat, drink, sleep, and to keep from being stupefied by boredom, they relieve the monotony of life with their odious gossip, with vodka, cards, chicanery, and the wives deceive their husbands, while the husbands lie and pretend not to see or hear anything, and an overwhelmingly vulgar influence weighs on the children, the divine spark is extinguished in them, and they become the same pitiful, identical corpses as their fathers and mothers. . . . [*Angrily, to* FERAPONT] What do you want?

FERAPONT: How's that? Papers to sign.

ANDREI: I'm fed up with you.

FERAPONT [*handing him the papers*]: The porter from the municipal treasury was saying just now . . . it seems, he says, in Petersburg this winter they had two hundred degrees of frost.

ANDREI: The present is loathsome, but then, when I think of the future, how good it is! I begin to feel so lighthearted, so free: and in the distance a light begins to dawn, I see freedom, I see how I and my children will be liberated from idleness, from kvas, from goose

with cabbage, from after-dinner naps, from base
parasitism . . .

FERAPONT: Two thousand people were frozen, it
seems. They say everyone was terrified. It was either in
Petersburg or Moscow, I don't remember.

ANDREI [*seized with a feeling of tenderness*]: My dear
sisters, my wonderful sisters! [*Through tears*] Masha,
my sister . . .

NATASHA [*in the window*]: Who's talking so loud out
there? Is that you, Andryusha? You'll wake up Sofochka. *Il ne faut pas faire du bruit, la Sofie est dormée
déjà. Vous êtes un ours.* [*Getting angry*] If you want to
talk, then give the baby carriage to someone else to
wheel. Ferapont, take the carriage from your master!

FERAPONT: Yes, ma'am. [*Takes the carriage.*]

ANDREI [*shamefacedly*]: I'm talking quietly.

NATASHA [*behind the window, caressing her little
boy*]: Bobik! Little mischief! Naughty Bobik!

ANDREI [*examining papers*]: Very well, I'll look
through them and sign what's necessary, and you can
take them back to the Board. . . . [*Goes into the house
reading papers;* FERAPONT *pushes the baby carriage to the
rear of the garden.*]

NATASHA [*behind window*]: Bobik, what's Mama's
name? Darling, darling! And who is this? This is Auntie
Olya. Say hello to Auntie Olya!

[*Two street musicians, a man and a girl, play on the
violin and harp;* VERSHININ, OLGA, *and* ANFISA *come out
of the house and listen in silence for a moment;* IRINA
approaches.]

IRINA: Our garden's like a public thoroughfare; people keep walking and driving through it. Nurse, give those musicians something.

ANFISA [*gives money to the musicians*]: Go along and God bless you, good people. [*The musicians bow and leave.*] Poor things! You don't go around playing like that if you're well-fed. [*To* IRINA] Good day, Arisha! [*Kisses her.*] Ee-e, little one, what a life I am having! What a life! Living at the high school in a government apartment with Olyusha—that's what God has granted me in my old age. Never in my life have I lived like this, sinner that I am. . . . A big government apartment, a whole room to myself, my own bed. All at government expense. I wake up in the night and—oh, Lord, Mother of God, there's not a happier person in the world!

VERSHININ [*looking at his watch*]: We shall be leaving directly, Olga Sergeyevna. Time to be off. [*Pause*] I wish you everything, everything. . . . Where is Maria Sergeyevna?

IRINA: She's somewhere in the garden . . . I'll go and look for her.

VERSHININ: Please be so kind. I must hurry.

ANFISA: I'll go look for her, too. [*Calls.*] Mashenka, aa-oo! [*Goes with* IRINA *to the rear of the garden.*] Aa-oo, aa-oo!

VERSHININ: All things come to an end. Here we are parting. [*Looks at his watch.*] The town gave us a sort of lunch, we had champagne, the Mayor made a speech, I ate and listened, but in my heart I was here with you. . . . [*Looks around the garden.*] I've grown attached to you.

OLGA: Shall we meet again some day?

VERSHININ: Probably not. [*Pause*] My wife and the
two little girls will remain here for another month or
two; please, if anything happens, or if they need
anything . . .

OLGA: Yes, yes, of course. You needn't worry.
[*Pause*] By tomorrow there won't be a single officer or
soldier in town; it will all be a memory, and for us, of
course, a new life will begin. . . . [*Pause*] Nothing ever
happens the way we want it to. I didn't want to be a
headmistress, and yet I became one. It means we are
not to be in Moscow . . .

VERSHININ: Well . . . thank you for everything. . . .
Forgive me if anything was not quite . . . I have talked
so much, far too much—forgive me for that, too, and
don't think badly of me. . . .

OLGA [*drying her eyes*]: Oh, why doesn't Masha
come. . . .

VERSHININ: What more can I say to you in parting?
What can I philosophize about? . . . [*Laughs.*] Life is
hard. It presents itself to many of us as desolate and
hopeless, and yet, one must admit that it keeps getting
clearer and easier, and the day is not far off when it will
be wholly bright. [*Looks at his watch.*] Time for me to
go, it's time! Formerly mankind was occupied with wars,
filling its entire existence with campaigns, invasions, con-
quests, but now all that has become obsolete, leaving a
great void, with nothing to fill it; humanity is passionately seeking something, and, of course, will find it. Ah,
if only it would come soon! [*Pause*] If, don't you know,
we could add culture to the love of work, and love of
work to culture. [*Looks at his watch.*] I really must
go. . . .

OLGA: Here she comes.

[*Enter* MASHA. OLGA *walks off and stands a little to one side so as not to interfere with their leave-taking.*]

MASHA [*looking into his face*]:   Good-bye . . . [*A prolonged kiss*]

OLGA: Come, come . . .

[MASHA *sobs violently.*]

VERSHININ: Write to me. . . . Don't forget! Let me go . . . it's time. . . . Olga Sergeyevna, take her, I must go now . . . I'm late. . . . [*Deeply moved, he kisses* OLGA's *hand, then embraces* MASHA *again and quickly goes out.*]

OLGA: Come Masha! Stop, darling. . . .

[*Enter* KULYGIN.]

KULYGIN [*embarrassed*]:   Never mind, let her cry, let her . . . My good Masha, my kind Masha . . . you are my wife and I am happy, no matter what. . . . I don't complain, I make not a single reproach . . . Olga here is my witness. . . . We'll begin again to live as we used to, and I won't say a single word to you, nor make any allusion . . .

MASHA [*restraining her sobs*]:   "A green oak by a curved seashore, upon that oak a golden chain . . . upon that oak a golden chain." . . . I'm going out of my mind. . . . "A green oak . . . by a curved seashore . . ."

OLGA: Calm yourself, Masha . . . calm yourself. . . . Give her some water.

MASHA: I'm not crying any more. . . .

KULYGIN: She's not crying any more . . . she is good. . . .

[*The faint sound of a gunshot is heard in the distance.*]

MASHA: "A green oak by a curved seashore, upon that oak a golden chain." . . . A green cat . . . a green oak . . . I'm mixing it up. . . . [*Drinks the water.*] My life is a failure . . . I want nothing now. . . . I'll be calm in a moment. . . . It doesn't matter. . . . What does that mean, "by a curved seashore"? Why do those words keep running through my head? My thoughts are all tangled.

[*Enter* IRINA.]

OLGA: Calm yourself, Masha. Come, that's a good girl. Let's go in.

MASHA [*angrily*]: I'm not going in there. [*Sobs, but instantly stops herself.*] I'm not going into that house any more, I won't go. . . .

IRINA: Let us sit down together, even if we don't talk. You know, I am going away tomorrow. . . . [*Pause*]

KULYGIN: Yesterday I took this beard and moustache away from a boy in the third grade. . . . [*Puts on the beard and moustache.*] I look like the German teacher. . . . [*Laughs.*] Don't I? Those boys are funny. . . .

MASHA: You really do look like your German.

OLGA [*laughs*]: Yes.

[MASHA *weeps.*]

IRINA: Don't, Masha.

KULYGIN: Very much like him . . .

[*Enter* NATASHA.]

NATASHA [*to the maid*]: What? Mr. Protopopov will sit with Sofóchka, and Andrei Sergeyich can wheel Bobik. So much bother with children. . . . [*To* IRINA] You're going away tomorrow, Irina—such a pity! Stay at least another week. [*Catching sight of* KULYGIN, *utters a shriek; he laughs and takes off the moustache and beard.*] Oh, you—really, you frightened me! [*To* IRINA] I've grown so used to you—do you think parting from you will be easy for me? I'll have Andrei and his violin moved into your room—he can saw away in there!—and we'll put Sofóchka in his room. Marvelous, wonderful child! What an adorable little girl! Today she looked at me with such eyes and said—"Mama"!

KULYGIN: A fine child, that's true.

NATASHA: So tomorrow I shall be all alone here. [*Sighs.*] First of all I shall have this avenue of fir trees cut down, then that maple. . . . It's so unsightly in the evening. . . . [*To* IRINA] That sash doesn't suit you at all, dear . . . it's not in good taste. You need something a little brighter. And then I'll have flowers planted everywhere—flowers, flowers—and it will be fragrant. . . . [*Severely*] What's a fork doing here on the bench? [*Going into the house, to the maid*] What's a fork doing here on the bench, I'd like to know? [*Shouting*] Hold your tongue!

KULYGIN: She's off again!

[*A band plays a military march offstage; everyone listens.*]

OLGA: They are leaving.

[*Enter* CHEBUTYKIN.]

MASHA: Our friends are going. Well . . . a happy journey to them! [*To her husband*] We must go home. . . . Where are my hat and cape?

KULYGIN: I took them into the house. . . . I'll get them right away.

OLGA: Yes, now we can all go home. It's time.

CHEBUTYKIN: Olga Sergeyevna!

OLGA: What is it? [*Pause*] What is it?

CHEBUTYKIN: Nothing . . . I don't know how to tell you. . . . [*Whispers in her ear.*]

OLGA [*shocked*]: It's not possible!

CHEBUTYKIN: Yes . . . what a business! . . . I'm worn out, completely exhausted, I don't want to talk any more. . . . [*Irritably*] Besides, it doesn't matter!

MASHA: What has happened?

OLGA [*puts her arms around* IRINA]: This is a terrible day. . . . I don't know how to tell you, my darling . . .

IRINA: What is it? Tell me quickly, what is it? For God's sake! [*Weeps.*]

CHEBUTYKIN: The Baron has just been killed in a duel.

IRINA [*quietly weeping*]: I knew it, I knew it. . . .

CHEBUTYKIN [*sits down on a bench at the rear of the stage*]: I'm worn out. . . . [*Takes a newspaper out of his pocket.*] Let them cry . . . [*Softly sings.*] "Ta-ra-ra boom-de-ay, sit on the curb I may." . . . As if it mattered!

[*The three sisters stand close to one another.*]

MASHA: Oh, listen to that music! They are leaving us, one has gone for good, forever; we are left alone to begin our life over again. We must live. . . . We must live. . . .

IRINA [*lays her head on* OLGA*'s breast*]: A time will come when everyone will know what all this is for, why there is all this suffering, and there will be no mysteries; but meanwhile, we must live . . . we must work, only work! Tomorrow I shall go alone, and I shall teach in the school, and give my whole life to those who need it. Now it is autumn, soon winter will come and cover everything with snow, and I shall go on working, working. . . .

OLGA [*embracing both her sisters*]: The music plays so gaily, so valiantly, one wants to live! Oh, my God! Time will pass, and we shall be gone forever, we'll be forgotten, our faces will be forgotten, our voices, and how many there were of us, but our sufferings will turn into joy for those who live after us, happiness and peace will come to this earth, and then they will remember kindly and bless those who are living now. Oh, my dear sisters, our life is not over yet. We shall live! The music is so gay, so joyous, it seems as if just a little more and we shall know why we live, why we suffer. . . . If only we knew, if only we knew! [*The music grows softer and softer;* KULYGIN, *cheerful, smiling, brings the hat and cape;* ANDREI *pushes the baby carriage with Bobik in it.*]

CHEBUTYKIN [*softly sings*]: "Ta-ra-ra boom-de-ay, sit on the curb I may." . . . It doesn't matter! It doesn't matter!

OLGA: If we only knew, if we only knew!

1900

The Cherry Orchard

A Comedy in Four Acts

Characters in the Play

RANEVSKAYA, LYUBOV ANDREYEVNA, a landowner

ANYA, her daughter, seventeen years old

VARYA, her adopted daughter, twenty-four years old

GAYEV, LEONID ANDREYEVICH, Madame Ranevskaya's brother

LOPAKHIN, YERMOLAI ALEKSEYEVICH, a merchant

TROFIMOV, PYOTR SERGEYEVICH, a student

SEMYONOV-PISHCHIK, BORIS BORISOVICH, a landowner

CHARLOTTA IVANOVNA, a governess

YEPIKHODOV, SEMYON PANTELEYEVICH, a clerk

DUNYASHA, a maid

FIRS, an old valet, eighty-seven years old

YASHA, a young footman

A STRANGER

THE STATIONMASTER

A POST-OFFICE CLERK

GUESTS, SERVANTS

The action takes place on Madame Ranevskaya's estate.

Act I

[*A room that is still called the nursery. One of the doors leads into* ANYA's *room. Dawn; the sun will soon rise. It is May, the cherry trees are in bloom, but it is cold in the orchard; there is a morning frost. The windows in the room are closed. Enter* DUNYASHA *with a candle, and* LOPAKHIN *with a book in his hand.*]

LOPAKHIN: The train is in, thank God. What time is it?

DUNYASHA: Nearly two. [*Blows out the candle.*] It's already light.

LOPAKHIN: How late is the train, anyway? A couple of hours at least. [*Yawns and stretches.*] I'm a fine one! What a fool I've made of myself! Came here on purpose to meet them at the station, and then overslept. . . . Fell asleep in the chair. It's annoying. . . . You might have waked me.

DUNYASHA: I thought you had gone. [*Listens.*] They're coming now, I think!

LOPAKHIN [*listens*]: No . . . they've got to get the luggage and one thing and another. [*Pause*] Lyubov Andreyevna has lived abroad for five years, I don't know what she's like now. . . . She's a fine person. Sweet-tempered, simple. I remember when I was a boy of fifteen, my late father—he had a shop in the village then—

gave me a punch in the face and made my nose bleed. . . . We had come into the yard here for some reason or other, and he'd had a drop too much. Lyubov Andreyevna—I remember as if it were yesterday—still young, and so slender, led me to the washstand in this very room, the nursery. "Don't cry, little peasant," she said, "it will heal in time for your wedding. . . ." [*Pause*] Little peasant . . . my father was a peasant, it's true, and here I am in a white waistcoat and tan shoes. Like a pig in a pastry shop. . . . I may be rich, I've made a lot of money, but if you think about it, analyze it, I'm a peasant through and through. [*Turning pages of the book*] Here I've been reading this book, and I didn't understand a thing. Fell asleep over it. [*Pause*]

DUNYASHA: The dogs didn't sleep all night: they can tell that their masters are coming.

LOPAKHIN: What's the matter with you, Dunyasha, you're so . . .

DUNYASHA: My hands are trembling. I'm going to faint.

LOPAKHIN: You're much too delicate, Dunyasha. You dress like a lady, and do your hair like one, too. It's not right. You should know your place.

[*Enter* YEPIKHODOV *with a bouquet; he wears a jacket and highly polished boots that squeak loudly. He drops the flowers as he comes in.*]

YEPIKHODOV [*picking up the flowers*]: Here, the gardener sent these. He says you're to put them in the dining room. [*Hands the bouquet to* DUNYASHA.]

LOPAKHIN: And bring me some kvas.

DUNYASHA: Yes, sir. [*Goes out.*]

YEPIKHODOV: There's a frost this morning—three degrees—and the cherry trees are in bloom. I cannot approve of our climate. [*Sighs.*] I cannot. Our climate is not exactly conducive. And now, Yermolai Alekseyevich, permit me to append: the day before yesterday I bought myself a pair of boots, which, I venture to assure you, squeak so that it's quite infeasible. What should I grease them with?

LOPAKHIN: Leave me alone. You make me tired.

YEPIKHODOV: Every day some misfortune happens to me. But I don't complain, I'm used to it, I even smile.

[DUNYASHA *enters, serves* LOPAKHIN *the kvas.*]

YEPIKHODOV: I'm going. [*Stumbles over a chair and upsets it.*] There! [*As if in triumph.*] Now you see, excuse the expression . . . the sort of circumstance, incidentally. . . . It's really quite remarkable! [*Goes out.*]

DUNYASHA: You know, Yermolai Alekseich, I have to confess that Yepikhodov has proposed to me.

LOPAKHIN: Ah!

DUNYASHA: And I simply don't know. . . . He's a quiet man, but sometimes, when he starts talking, you can't understand a thing he says. It's nice, and full of feeling, only it doesn't make sense. I sort of like him. He's madly in love with me. But he's an unlucky fellow: every day something happens to him. They tease him about it around here; they call him Two-and-twenty Troubles.

LOPAKHIN [*listening*]:   I think I hear them coming . . .

DUNYASHA: They're coming! What's the matter with me? I'm cold all over.

LOPAKHIN: They're really coming. Let's go and meet them. Will she recognize me? It's five years since we've seen each other.

DUNYASHA [*agitated*]:   I'll faint this very minute . . . oh, I'm going to faint!

[*Two carriages are heard driving up to the house.* LO-PAKHIN *and* DUNYASHA *go out quickly. The stage is empty. There is a hubbub in the adjoining rooms.* FIRS *hurriedly crosses the stage leaning on a stick. He has been to meet* LYUBOV ANDREYEVNA *and wears old-fashioned livery and a high hat. He mutters something to himself, not a word of which can be understood. The noise off-stage grows louder and louder. A voice: "Let's go through here. . . ." Enter* LYUBOV ANDREYEVNA, ANYA, CHAR-LOTTA IVANOVNA *with a little dog on a chain, all in travel-ing dress;* VARYA *wearing a coat and kerchief;* GAYEV, SEMYONOV-PISHCHIK, LOPAKHIN, DUNYASHA *with a bundle and parasol; servants with luggage—all walk through the room.*]

ANYA: Let's go this way. Do you remember, Mama, what room this is?

LYUBOV ANDREYEVNA [*joyfully, through tears*]:   The nursery!

VARYA: How cold it is! My hands are numb. [*To* LY-UBOV ANDREYEVNA] Your rooms, both the white one and the violet one, are just as you left them, Mama.

LYUBOV ANDREYEVNA: The nursery . . . my dear, lovely nursery. . . . I used to sleep here when I was little. . . . [*Weeps.*] And now, like a child, I . . . [*Kisses her brother,* VARYA, *then her brother again.*] Varya hasn't

changed; she still looks like a nun. And I recognized
Dunyasha. . . . [*Kisses* DUNYASHA.]

GAYEV: The train was two hours late. How's that?
What kind of management is that?

CHARLOTTA [*to* PISHCHIK]: My dog even eats nuts.

PISHCHIK [*amazed*]: Think of that now!

[*They all go out except* ANYA *and* DUNYASHA.]

DUNYASHA: We've been waiting and waiting for
you. . . . [*Takes off* ANYA's *coat and hat.*]

ANYA: I didn't sleep for four nights on the road . . .
now I feel cold.

DUNYASHA: It was Lent when you went away, there
was snow and frost then, but now? My darling! [*Laughs
and kisses her.*] I've waited so long for you, my joy, my
precious . . . I must tell you at once, I can't wait another minute. . . .

ANYA [*listlessly*]: What now?

DUNYASHA: The clerk, Yepikhodov, proposed to me
just after Easter.

ANYA: You always talk about the same thing. . . .
[*Straightening her hair*] I've lost all my hairpins. . . . [*She
is so exhausted she can hardly stand.*]

DUNYASHA: I really don't know what to think. He
loves me—he loves me so!

ANYA [*looking through the door into her room, tenderly*]: My room, my windows . . . it's just as though I'd
never been away. I am home! Tomorrow morning I'll
get up and run into the orchard. . . . Oh, if I could only

sleep! I didn't sleep during the entire journey, I was so tormented by anxiety.

DUNYASHA: Pyotr Sergeich arrived the day before yesterday.

ANYA [*joyfully*]: Petya!

DUNYASHA: He's asleep in the bathhouse, he's staying there. "I'm afraid of being in the way," he said. [*Looks at her pocket watch.*] I ought to wake him up, but Varvara Mikhailovna told me not to. "Don't you wake him," she said.

[*Enter* VARYA *with a bunch of keys at her waist.*]

VARYA: Dunyasha, coffee, quickly . . . Mama's asking for coffee.

DUNYASHA: This very minute. [*Goes out.*]

VARYA: Thank God, you've come! You're home again. [*Caressing her.*] My little darling has come back! My pretty one is here!

ANYA: I've been through so much.

VARYA: I can imagine!

ANYA: I left in Holy Week, it was cold then. Charlotta never stopped talking and doing her conjuring tricks the entire journey. Why did you saddle me with Charlotta?

VARYA: You couldn't have traveled alone, darling. At seventeen!

ANYA: When we arrived in Paris, it was cold, snowing. My French is awful. . . . Mama was living on the fifth floor, and when I got there, she had all sorts of Frenchmen and ladies with her, and an old priest with a little book, and it was full of smoke, dismal. Suddenly I felt sorry for Mama, so sorry. I took her head in my arms and held her close and couldn't let her go. Afterward she kept hugging me and crying. . . .

VARYA [*through her tears*]: Don't talk about it, don't talk about it. . . .

ANYA: She had already sold her villa near Mentone, and she had nothing left, nothing. And I hadn't so much as a kopeck left, we barely managed to get there. But Mama doesn't understand! When we had dinner in a station restaurant, she always ordered the most expensive dishes and tipped each of the waiters a ruble. Charlotta is the same. And Yasha also ordered a dinner, it was simply awful. You know, Yasha is Mama's footman; we brought him with us.

VARYA: I saw the rogue.

ANYA: Well, how are things? Have you paid the interest?

VARYA: How could we?

ANYA: Oh, my God, my God!

VARYA: In August the estate will be put up for sale.

ANYA: My God!

[LOPAKHIN *peeps in at the door and moo's like a cow.*]

LOPAKHIN: Moo-o-o! [*Disappears.*]

VARYA [*through her tears*]: What I couldn't do to him! [*Shakes her fist.*]

ANYA [*embracing* VARYA, *softly*]: Varya, has he proposed to you? [VARYA *shakes her head.*] But he loves you. . . . Why don't you come to an understanding, what are you waiting for?

VARYA: I don't think anything will ever come of it. He's too busy, he has no time for me . . . he doesn't even notice me. I've washed my hands of him, it makes me miserable to see him. . . . Everyone talks of our wedding, they all congratulate me, and actually there's nothing to it—it's all like a dream. . . . [*In a different tone.*] You have a brooch like a bee.

ANYA [*sadly*]: Mama bought it. [*Goes into her own room; speaks gaily, like a child.*] In Paris I went up in a balloon!

VARYA: My darling is home! My pretty one has come back!

[DUNYASHA *has come in with the coffeepot and prepares coffee.*]

VARYA [*stands at the door of* ANYA'S *room*]: You know, darling, all day long I'm busy looking after the house, but I keep dreaming. If we could marry you to a rich man I'd be at peace. I could go into a hermitage, then to Kiev, to Moscow, and from one holy place to another. . . . I'd go on and on. What a blessing!

ANYA: The birds are singing in the orchard. What time is it?

VARYA: It must be after two. Time you were asleep, darling. [*Goes into* ANYA'S *room.*] What a blessing!

[YASHA *enters with a lap robe and a traveling bag.*]

YASHA [*crosses the stage mincingly*]: May one go through here?

DUNYASHA: A person would hardly recognize you, Yasha. Your stay abroad has done wonders for you.

YASHA: Hm. . . . And who are you?

DUNYASHA: When you left here I was only that high—[*indicating with her hand*]. I'm Dunyasha, Fyodor Kozoyedov's daughter. You don't remember!

YASHA: Hm. . . . A little cucumber! [*Looks around, then embraces her; she cries out and drops a saucer. He quickly goes out.*]

VARYA [*in a tone of annoyance, from the doorway*]: What's going on here?

DUNYASHA [*tearfully*]: I broke a saucer.

VARYA: That's good luck.

ANYA: We ought to prepare Mama: Petya is here. . . .

VARYA: I gave orders not to wake him.

ANYA [*pensively*]: Six years ago Father died, and a month later brother Grisha drowned in the river . . . a pretty little seven-year-old boy. Mama couldn't bear it and went away . . . went without looking back. . . . [*Shudders.*] How I understand her, if she only knew! [*Pause*] And Petya Trofimov was Grisha's tutor, he may remind her. . . .

[*Enter* FIRS *wearing a jacket and a white waistcoat.*]

FIRS [*goes to the coffeepot, anxiously*]: The mistress will have her coffee here. [*Puts on white gloves.*] Is the coffee ready? [*To* DUNYASHA, *sternly.*] You! Where's the cream?

DUNYASHA: Oh, my goodness! [*Quickly goes out.*]

FIRS [*fussing over the coffeepot*]: Ah, what an addlepate! [*Mutters to himself.*] They've come back from

Paris. . . . The master used to go to Paris . . . by carriage. . . . [*Laughs.*]

VARYA: What is it, Firs?

FIRS: If you please? [*Joyfully*] My mistress has come home! At last! Now I can die. . . . [*Weeps with joy.*]

[*Enter* LYUBOV ANDREYEVNA, GAYEV, *and* SEMYONOV-PISHCHIK, *the last wearing a sleeveless peasant coat of fine cloth and full trousers.* GAYEV, *as he comes in, goes through the motions of playing billiards.*]

LYUBOV ANDREYEVNA: How does it go? Let's see if I can remember . . . cue ball into the corner! Double the rail to center table.

GAYEV: Cut shot into the corner! There was a time, sister, when you and I used to sleep here in this very room, and now I'm fifty-one, strange as it may seem. . . .

LOPAKHIN: Yes, time passes.

GAYEV: How's that?

LOPAKHIN: Time, I say, passes.

GAYEV: It smells of patchouli here.

ANYA: I'm going to bed. Good night, Mama. [*Kisses her mother.*]

LYUBOV ANDREYEVNA: My precious child. [*Kisses her hands.*] Are you glad to be home? I still feel dazed.

ANYA: Good night, Uncle.

GAYEV [*kisses her face and hands*]: God bless you. How like your mother you are! [*To his sister*] At her age you were exactly like her, Lyuba.

[ANYA *shakes hands with* LOPAKHIN *and* PISHCHIK *and goes out, closing the door after her.*]

LYUBOV ANDREYEVNA: She's exhausted.

PISHCHIK: Must have been a long journey.

VARYA: Well, gentlemen? It's after two, high time you were going.

LYUBOV ANDREYEVNA [*laughs*]:   You haven't changed, Varya. [*Draws* VARYA *to her and kisses her.*] I'll just drink my coffee and then we'll all go. [FIRS *places a cushion under her feet.*] Thank you, my dear. I've got used to coffee. I drink it day and night. Thanks, dear old man. [*Kisses him.*]

VARYA: I'd better see if all the luggage has been brought in.

LYUBOV ANDREYEVNA: Is this really me sitting here? [*Laughs.*] I feel like jumping about and waving my arms. [*Buries her face in her hands.*] What if it's only a dream! God knows I love my country, love it dearly. I couldn't look out the train window, I was crying so! [*Through tears*] But I must drink my coffee. Thank you, Firs, thank you, my dear old friend. I'm so glad you're still alive.

FIRS: The day before yesterday.

GAYEV: He's hard of hearing.

LOPAKHIN: I must go now, I'm leaving for Kharkov about five o'clock. It's so annoying! I wanted to have a good look at you, and have a talk. You're as splendid as ever.

PISHCHIK [*breathing heavily*]:   Even more beautiful. . . . Dressed like a Parisienne. . . . There goes my wagon, all four wheels!

LOPAKHIN: Your brother here, Leonid Andreich, says I'm a boor, a moneygrubber, but I don't mind. Let him talk. All I want is that you should trust me as you used to, and that your wonderful, touching eyes should look at me as they did then. Merciful God! My father was one of your father's serfs, and your grandfather's, but you yourself did so much for me once, that I've forgotten all that and love you as if you were my own kin—more than my kin.

LYUBOV ANDREYEVNA: I can't sit still, I simply cannot. [*Jumps up and walks about the room in great excitement.*] I cannot bear this joy. . . . Laugh at me, I'm silly. . . . My dear little bookcase . . . [*Kisses bookcase.*] my little table . . .

GAYEV: Nurse died while you were away.

LYUBOV ANDREYEVNA [*sits down and drinks coffee*]: Yes, God rest her soul. They wrote me.

GAYEV: And Anastasy is dead. Petrushka Kosoi left me and is now with the police inspector in town. [*Takes a box of hard candies from his pocket and begins to suck one.*]

PISHCHIK: My daughter, Dashenka . . . sends her regards . . .

LOPAKHIN: I wish I could tell you something very pleasant and cheering. [*Glances at his watch.*] I must go directly, there's no time to talk, but . . . well, I'll say it in a couple of words. As you know, the cherry orchard is to be sold to pay your debts. The auction is set for August twenty-second, but you need not worry, my dear, you can sleep in peace, there is a way out. This is my plan. Now, please listen! Your estate is only twenty versts from town, the railway runs close by, and if the cherry orchard and the land along the river were cut up into lots and leased for summer cottages, you'd have, at the very least, an income of twenty-five thousand a year.

GAYEV: Excuse me, what nonsense!

LYUBOV ANDREYEVNA: I don't quite understand you, Yermolai Alekseich.

LOPAKHIN: You will get, at the very least, twenty-five rubles a year for a two-and-a-half-acre lot, and if you advertise now, I guarantee you won't have a single plot of ground left by autumn, everything will be snapped up. In short, I congratulate you, you are saved. The site is splendid, the river is deep. Only, of course, the ground must be cleared . . . you must tear down all the old outbuildings, for instance, and this house, which is worthless, cut down the old cherry orchard——

LYUBOV ANDREYEVNA: Cut it down? Forgive me, my dear, but you don't know what you are talking about. If there is one thing in the whole province that is interesting, not to say remarkable, it's our cherry orchard.

LOPAKHIN: The only remarkable thing about this orchard is that it is very big. There's a crop of cherries every other year, and then you can't get rid of them, nobody buys them.

GAYEV: This orchard is even mentioned in the *Encyclopedia*.

LOPAKHIN [*glancing at his watch*]: If we don't think of something and come to a decision, on the twenty-second of August the cherry orchard, and the entire estate, will be sold at auction. Make up your minds! There is no other way out, I swear to you. None whatsoever.

FIRS: In the old days, forty or fifty years ago, the cherries were dried, soaked, marinated, and made into jam, and they used to——

GAYEV: Be quiet, Firs.

FIRS: And they used to send cartloads of dried cherries to Moscow and Kharkov. And that brought in money! The dried cherries were soft and juicy in those days, sweet, fragrant. . . . They had a method then . . .

LYUBOV ANDREYEVNA: And what has become of that method now?

FIRS: Forgotten. Nobody remembers. . . .

PISHCHIK: How was it in Paris? What's it like there? Did you eat frogs?

LYUBOV ANDREYEVNA: I ate crocodiles.

PISHCHIK: Think of that now!

LOPAKHIN: There used to be only the gentry and the peasants living in the country, but now these summer people have appeared. All the towns, even the smallest ones, are surrounded by summer cottages. And it is safe to say that in another twenty years these people will multiply enormously. Now the summer resident only drinks tea on his porch, but it may well be that he'll take to cultivating his acre, and then your cherry orchard will be a happy, rich, luxuriant——

GAYEV [*indignantly*]: What nonsense!

[*Enter* VARYA *and* YASHA.]

VARYA: There are two telegrams for you, Mama. [*Picks out a key and with a jingling sound opens an old-fashioned bookcase.*] Here they are.

LYUBOV ANDREYEVNA: From Paris. [*Tears up the telegrams without reading them.*] That's all over. . . .

GAYEV: Do you know, Lyuba, how old this bookcase is? A week ago I pulled out the bottom drawer, and what do I see? Some figures burnt into it. The bookcase was made exactly a hundred years ago. What do you think of that? Eh? We could have celebrated its jubilee. It's an inanimate object, but nevertheless, for all that, it's a bookcase.

PISHCHIK: A hundred years . . . think of that now!

GAYEV: Yes . . . that is something. . . . [*Feeling the bookcase*] Dear, honored bookcase, I salute thy existence, which for over one hundred years has served the glorious ideals of goodness and justice; thy silent appeal to fruitful endeavor, unflagging in the course of a hundred years, tearfully sustaining through generations of our family, courage and faith in a better future, and fostering in us ideals of goodness and social consciousness. . . .

[*A pause*]

LOPAKHIN: Yes . . .

LYUBOV ANDREYEVNA: You are the same as ever, Lyonya.

GAYEV [*somewhat embarrassed*]: Carom into the corner, cut shot to center table.

LOPAKHIN [*looks at his watch*]: Well, time for me to go.

YASHA [*hands medicine to* LYUBOV ANDREYEVNA]: Perhaps you will take your pills now.

PISHCHIK: Don't take medicaments, dearest lady, they do neither harm nor good. Let me have them, honored lady. [*Takes the pill box, shakes the pills into his hand, blows on them, puts them into his mouth, and washes them down with kvas.*] There!

LYUBOV ANDREYEVNA [*alarmed*]: Why, you must be mad!

PISHCHIK: I've taken all the pills.

LOPAKHIN: What a glutton!

[*Everyone laughs.*]

FIRS: The gentleman stayed with us during Holy Week . . . ate half a bucket of pickles. . . . [*Mumbles.*]

LYUBOV ANDREYEVNA: What is he saying?

VARYA: He's been muttering like that for three years now. We've grown used to it.

YASHA: He's in his dotage.

[CHARLOTTA IVANOVNA, *very thin, tightly laced, in a white dress with a lorgnette at her belt, crosses the stage.*]

LOPAKHIN: Forgive me, Charlotta Ivanovna, I haven't had a chance to say how do you do to you. [*Tries to kiss her hand.*]

CHARLOTTA [*pulls her hand away*]: If I permit you to kiss my hand you'll be wanting to kiss my elbow next, then my shoulder.

LOPAKHIN: I have no luck today. [*Everyone laughs.*] Charlotta Ivanovna, show us a trick!

LYUBOV ANDREYEVNA: Charlotta, show us a trick!

CHARLOTTA: No. I want to sleep. [*Goes out.*]

LOPAKHIN: In three weeks we'll meet again. [*Kisses* LYUBOV ANDREYEVNA's *hand.*] Good-bye till then. Time to go. [*To* GAYEV] Good-bye. [*Kisses* PISHCHIK.] Good-bye. [*Shakes hands with* VARYA, *then with* FIRS *and* YASHA.] I don't feel like going. [*To* LYUBOV ANDRE-YEVNA] If you make up your mind about the summer cottages and come to a decision, let me know; I'll get you a loan of fifty thousand or so. Think it over seriously.

VARYA [*angrily*]: Oh, why don't you go!

LOPAKHIN: I'm going, I'm going. [*Goes out.*]

GAYEV: Boor. Oh, pardon. Varya's going to marry him, he's Varya's young man.

VARYA: Uncle dear, you talk too much.

LYUBOV ANDREYEVNA: Well, Varya, I shall be very glad. He's a good man.

PISHCHIK: A man, I must truly say . . . most worthy. . . . And my Dashenka . . . says, too, that . . . says all sorts of things. [*Snores but wakes up at once.*] In any case, honored lady, oblige me . . . a loan of two hundred and forty rubles . . . tomorrow the interest on my mortgage is due. . . .

VARYA [*in alarm*]: We have nothing, nothing at all!

LYUBOV ANDREYEVNA: I really haven't any money.

PISHCHIK: It'll turn up. [*Laughs.*] I never lose hope. Just when I thought everything was lost, that I was done for, lo and behold—the railway line ran through my land . . . and they paid me for it. And before you know it, something else will turn up, if not today—tomorrow. . . . Dashenka will win two hundred thousand . . . she's got a lottery ticket.

LYUBOV ANDREYEVNA: The coffee is finished, we can go to bed.

FIRS [*brushing* GAYEV'*s clothes, admonishingly*]: You've put on the wrong trousers again. What am I to do with you?

VARYA [*softly*]: Anya's asleep. [*Quietly opens the window.*] The sun has risen, it's no longer cold. Look, Mama dear, what wonderful trees! Oh, Lord, the air! The starlings are singing!

GAYEV [*opens another window*]: The orchard is all white. You haven't forgotten, Lyuba? That long avenue there that runs straight—straight as a stretched-out strap; it gleams on moonlight nights. Remember? You've not forgotten?

LYUBOV ANDREYEVNA [*looking out the window at the orchard*]: Oh, my childhood, my innocence! I used to sleep in this nursery, I looked out from here into the orchard, happiness awoke with me each morning, it was just as it is now, nothing has changed. [*Laughing with joy*] All, all white! Oh, my orchard! After the dark, rainy autumn and the cold winter, you are young again, full of happiness, the heavenly angels have not forsaken you. . . . If I could cast off this heavy stone weighing on my breast and shoulders, if I could forget my past!

GAYEV: Yes, and the orchard will be sold for our debts, strange as it may seem. . . .

LYUBOV ANDREYEVNA: Look, our dead mother walks in the orchard . . . in a white dress! [*Laughs with joy.*] It is she!

GAYEV: Where?

VARYA: God be with you, Mama dear.

LYUBOV ANDREYEVNA: There's no one there, I just imagined it. To the right, as you turn to the summer-house, a slender white sapling is bent over . . . it looks like a woman.

[*Enter* TROFIMOV *wearing a shabby student's uniform and spectacles.*]

LYUBOV ANDREYEVNA: What a wonderful orchard! The white masses of blossoms, the blue sky——

TROFIMOV: Lyubov Andreyevna! [*She looks around at him.*] I only want to pay my respects, then I'll go at once. [*Kisses her hand ardently.*] I was told to wait until morning, but I hadn't the patience.

[LYUBOV ANDREYEVNA *looks at him, puzzled.*]

VARYA [*through tears*]: This is Petya Trofimov.

TROFIMOV: Petya Trofimov, I was Grisha's tutor. . . .
Can I have changed so much?

[LYUBOV ANDREYEVNA *embraces him, quietly weeping.*]

GAYEV [*embarrassed*]: There, there, Lyuba.

VARYA [*crying*]: Didn't I tell you, Petya, to wait till
tomorrow?

LYUBOV ANDREYEVNA: My Grisha . . . my little
boy . . . Grisha . . . my son. . . .

VARYA: What can we do, Mama dear? It's God's
will.

TROFIMOV [*gently, through tears*]: Don't, don't. . . .

LYUBOV ANDREYEVNA [*quietly weeping*]: My little
boy dead, drowned. . . . Why? Why, my friend? [*In a
lower voice.*] Anya is sleeping in there, and I'm talking
loudly . . . making all this noise. . . . But Petya, why do
you look so bad? Why have you grown so old?

TROFIMOV: A peasant woman in the train called me
a mangy gentleman.

LYUBOV ANDREYEVNA: You were just a boy then, a
charming little student, and now your hair is thin—and
spectacles! Is it possible you are still a student? [*Goes
toward the door.*]

TROFIMOV: I shall probably be an eternal student.

LYUBOV ANDREYEVNA [*kisses her brother, then* VAR-
YA]: Now, go to bed. . . . You've grown older too,
Leonid.

PISHCHIK [*follows her*]: Well, seems to be time to sleep. . . . Oh, my gout! I'm staying the night. Lyubov Andreyevna, my soul, tomorrow morning . . . two hundred and forty rubles. . . .

GAYEV: He keeps at it.

PISHCHIK: Two hundred and forty rubles . . . to pay the interest on my mortgage.

LYUBOV ANDREYEVNA: I have no money, my friend.

PISHCHIK: My dear, I'll pay it back. . . . It's a trifling sum.

LYUBOV ANDREYEVNA: Well, all right, Leonid will give it to you. . . . Give it to him, Leonid.

GAYEV: Me give it to him! . . . Hold out your pocket!

LYUBOV ANDREYEVNA: It can't be helped, give it to him. . . . He needs it. . . . He'll pay it back.

[LYUBOV ANDREYEVNA, TROFIMOV, PISHCHIK, *and* FIRS *go out.* GAYEV, VARYA, *and* YASHA *remain.*]

GAYEV: My sister hasn't yet lost her habit of squandering money. [*To* YASHA] Go away, my good fellow, you smell of the henhouse.

YASHA [*with a smirk*]: And you, Leonid Andreyevich, are just the same as ever.

GAYEV: How's that? [*To* VARYA] What did he say?

VARYA: Your mother has come from the village; she's been sitting in the servants' room since yesterday, waiting to see you. . . .

YASHA: Let her wait, for God's sake!

VARYA: Aren't you ashamed?

YASHA: A lot I need her! She could have come tomorrow. [*Goes out.*]

VARYA: Mama's the same as ever, she hasn't changed a bit. She'd give away everything, if she could.

GAYEV: Yes. . . . [*A pause*] If a great many remedies are suggested for a disease, it means that the disease is incurable. I keep thinking, racking my brains, I have many remedies, a great many, and that means, in effect, that I have none. It would be good to receive a legacy from someone, good to marry our Anya to a very rich man, good to go to Yaroslav and try our luck with our aunt, the Countess. She is very, very rich, you know.

VARYA [*crying*]: If only God would help us!

GAYEV: Stop bawling. Auntie's very rich, but she doesn't like us. In the first place, sister married a lawyer, not a nobleman . . . [ANYA *appears in the doorway.*] She married beneath her, and it cannot be said that she has conducted herself very virtuously. She is good, kind, charming, and I love her dearly, but no matter how much you allow for extenuating circumstances, you must admit she leads a sinful life. You feel it in her slightest movement.

VARYA [*in a whisper*]: Anya is standing in the doorway.

GAYEV: What? [*Pause*] Funny, something got into my right eye . . . I can't see very well. And Thursday, when I was in the district court . . .

[ANYA *enters.*]

VARYA: Why aren't you asleep, Anya?

ANYA: I can't get to sleep. I just can't.

GAYEV: My little one! [*Kisses* ANYA's *face and hands.*] My child. . . . [*Through tears*] You are not my niece, you are my angel, you are everything to me. Believe me, believe . . .

ANYA: I believe you, Uncle. Everyone loves you and respects you, but, Uncle dear, you must keep quiet, just keep quiet. What were you saying just now about my mother, about your own sister? What made you say that?

GAYEV: Yes, yes. . . . [*Covers his face with her hand.*] Really, it's awful! My God! God help me! And today I made a speech to the bookcase . . . so stupid! And it was only when I had finished that I realized it was stupid.

VARYA: It's true, Uncle dear, you ought to keep quiet. Just don't talk, that's all.

ANYA: If you could keep from talking, it would make things easier for you, too.

GAYEV: I'll be quiet. [*Kisses* ANYA's *and* VARYA's *hands.*] I'll be quiet. Only this is about business. On Thursday I was in the district court, well, a group of us gathered together and began talking about one thing and another, this and that, and it seems it might be possible to arrange a loan on a promissory note to pay the interest at the bank.

VARYA: If only God would help us!

GAYEV: On Tuesday I'll go and talk it over again. [*To* VARYA] Stop bawling. [*To* ANYA] Your mama will talk to Lopakhin; he, of course, will not refuse her. . . . And as soon as you've rested, you will go to Yaroslav to the Countess, your great-aunt. In that way we shall be working from three directions—and our business is in the hat. We'll pay the interest, I'm certain of it. . . . [*Puts a candy in his mouth.*] On my honor, I'll swear by anything you like, the estate shall not be sold. [*Excitedly*] By my happiness, I swear it! Here's my hand on it, call me a worthless, dishonorable man if I let it come to auction! I swear by my whole being!

ANYA [*a calm mood returns to her, she is happy*]: How good you are, Uncle, how clever! [*Embraces him.*] Now I am at peace! I'm at peace! I'm happy!

[*Enter* FIRS.]

FIRS [*reproachfully*]: Leonid Andreich, have you no fear of God? When are you going to bed?

GAYEV: Presently, presently. Go away, Firs. I'll . . . all right, I'll undress myself. Well, children, bye-bye. . . . Details tomorrow, and now go to sleep. [*Kisses* ANYA *and* VARYA.] I am a man of the eighties. . . . They don't think much of that period today, nevertheless, I can say that in the course of my life I have suffered not a little for my convictions. It is not for nothing that the peasant loves me. You have to know the peasant! You have to know from what——

ANYA: There you go again, Uncle!

VARYA: Uncle dear, do be quiet.

FIRS [*angrily*]: Leonid Andreich!

GAYEV: I'm coming, I'm coming. . . . Go to bed. A clean double rail shot to center table. . . . [*Goes out;* FIRS *hobbles after him.*]

ANYA: I'm at peace now. I would rather not go to Yaroslav, I don't like my great-aunt, but still, I'm at peace, thanks to Uncle. [*She sits down.*]

VARYA: We must get some sleep. I'm going now. Oh, something unpleasant happened while you were away.

In the old servants' quarters, as you know, there are only the old people: Yefimushka, Polya, Yevstignei, and, of course, Karp. They began letting in all sorts of rogues to spend the night—I didn't say anything. But then I heard they'd been spreading a rumor that I'd given an order for them to be fed nothing but dried peas. Out of stinginess, you see. . . . It was all Yevstignei's doing. . . . Very well, I think, if that's how it is, you just wait. I send for Yevstignei . . . [*yawning*] he comes. . . . "How is it, Yevstignei," I say, "that you could be such a fool. . . ." [*Looks at* ANYA.] She's fallen asleep. [*Takes her by the arm.*] Come to your little bed. . . . Come along. [*Leading her*] My little darling fell asleep. Come. . . . [*They go.*]

[*In the distance, beyond the orchard, a shepherd is playing on a reed pipe.* TROFIMOV *crosses the stage and, seeing* VARYA *and* ANYA, *stops.*]

VARYA: Sh! She's asleep . . . asleep. . . . Come along, darling.

ANYA [*softly, half-asleep*]: I'm so tired. . . . Those bells . . . Uncle . . . dear . . . Mama and Uncle . . .

VARYA: Come, darling, come along. [*They go into* ANYA's *room.*]

TROFIMOV [*deeply moved*]: My sunshine! My spring!

Act II

[*A meadow. An old, lopsided, long-abandoned little chapel; near it a well, large stones that apparently were once tombstones, and an old bench. A road to the* GAYEV *manor house can be seen. On one side, where the cherry orchard begins, tall poplars loom. In the distance a row of telegraph poles, and far, far away, on the horizon, the faint outline of a large town, which is visible only in very fine, clear weather. The sun will soon set.* CHARLOTTA, YASHA, *and* DUNYASHA *are sitting on the bench;* YEPIKHODOV *stands near playing something sad on the guitar. They are all lost in thought.* CHARLOTTA *wears an old forage cap; she has taken a gun from her shoulder and is adjusting the buckle on the sling.*]

CHARLOTTA [*reflectively*]: I haven't got a real pass-port, I don't know how old I am, but it always seems to me that I'm quite young. When I was a little girl, my father and mother used to travel from one fair to another giving performances—very good ones. And I did the *salto mortale* and all sorts of tricks. Then when Papa and Mama died, a German lady took me to live with her and began teaching me. Good. I grew up and became a governess. But where I come from and who I am—I do not know. . . . Who my parents were—perhaps they weren't even married—I don't know. [*Takes a cucumber out of her pocket and eats it.*] I don't know anything. [*Pause*] One wants so much to talk, but there isn't any-one to talk to . . . I have no one.

YEPIKHODOV [*plays the guitar and sings*]: "What care I for the clamorous world, what's friend or foe to me?" . . . How pleasant it is to play a mandolin!

DUNYASHA: That's a guitar, not a mandolin. [*Looks at herself in a hand mirror and powders her face.*]

YEPIKHODOV: To a madman, in love, it is a mandolin. . . . [*Sings.*] "Would that the heart were warmed by the flame of requited love . . ."

[YASHA *joins in.*]

CHARLOTTA: How horribly these people sing! . . . Pfui! Like jackals!

DUNYASHA [*to* YASHA]: Really, how fortunate to have been abroad!

YASHA: Yes, to be sure. I cannot but agree with you there. [*Yawns, then lights a cigar.*]

YEPIKHODOV: It stands to reason. Abroad everything has long since been fully constituted.

YASHA: Obviously.

YEPIKHODOV: I am a cultivated man, I read all sorts of remarkable books, but I am in no way able to make out my own inclinations, what it is I really want, whether, strictly speaking, to live or to shoot myself; nevertheless, I always carry a revolver on me. Here it is. [*Shows revolver.*]

CHARLOTTA: Finished. Now I'm going. [*Slings the gun over her shoulder.*] You're a very clever man, Yepikhodov, and quite terrifying; women must be mad about you. Brrr! [*Starts to go.*] These clever people are all so stupid, there's no one for me to talk to. . . . Alone, always alone, I have no one . . . and who I am, and why I am, nobody knows. . . . [*Goes out, unhurriedly.*]

YEPIKHODOV: Strictly speaking, all else aside, I must state regarding myself, that fate treats me unmercifully, as a storm does a small ship. If, let us assume, I am mistaken, then why, to mention a single instance, do I wake up this morning, and there on my chest see a spider of terrifying magnitude? . . . Like that. [*Indicates with both hands.*] And likewise, I take up some kvas to quench my thirst, and there see something in the highest degree unseemly, like a cockroach. [*Pause*] Have you read Buckle? [*Pause*] If I may trouble you, Avdotya Fedorovna, I should like to have a word or two with you.

DUNYASHA: Go ahead.

YEPIKHODOV: I prefer to speak with you alone. . . . [*Sighs.*]

DUNYASHA [*embarrassed*]: Very well . . . only first bring me my little cape . . . you'll find it by the cupboard. . . . It's rather damp here. . . .

YEPIKHODOV: Certainly, ma'am . . . I'll fetch it, ma'am. . . . Now I know what to do with my revolver. . . . [*Takes the guitar and goes off playing it.*]

YASHA: Two-and-twenty Troubles! Between ourselves, a stupid fellow. [*Yawns.*]

DUNYASHA: God forbid that he should shoot himself. [*Pause*] I've grown so anxious, I'm always worried. I was only a little girl when I was taken into the master's house, and now I'm quite unused to the simple life, and my hands are white as can be, just like a lady's. I've become so delicate, so tender and ladylike, I'm afraid of everything. . . . Frightfully so. And, Yasha, if you deceive me, I just don't know what will become of my nerves.

YASHA [*kisses her*]: You little cucumber! Of course, a girl should never forget herself. What I dislike above everything is when a girl doesn't conduct herself properly.

DUNYASHA: I'm passionately in love with you; you're educated, you can discuss anything. [*Pause*]

YASHA [*yawns*]: Yes. . . . As I see it, it's like this: if a girl loves somebody, that means she's immoral. [*Pause*] Very pleasant smoking a cigar in the open air. . . . [*Listens.*] Someone's coming this way. . . . It's the masters. [DUNYASHA *impulsively embraces him.*] You go home, as if you'd been to the river to bathe; take that path, otherwise they'll see you and suspect me of having a rendezvous with you. I can't endure that sort of thing.

DUNYASHA [*with a little cough*]: My head is beginning to ache from your cigar. . . . [*Goes out.*]

[YASHA *remains, sitting near the chapel.* LYUBOV AN-DREYEVNA, GAYEV, *and* LOPAKHIN *enter.*]

LOPAKHIN: You must make up your mind once and for all—time won't stand still. The question, after all, is quite simple. Do you agree to lease the land for summer cottages or not? Answer in one word: yes or no? Only one word!

LYUBOV ANDREYEVNA: Who is it that smokes those disgusting cigars out here? [*Sits down.*]

GAYEV: Now that the railway line is so near, it's made things convenient. [*Sits down.*] We went to town and had lunch . . . cue ball to the center! I feel like going to the house first and playing a game.

LYUBOV ANDREYEVNA: Later.

LOPAKHIN: Just one word! [*Imploringly*] Do give me an answer!

GAYEV [*yawning*]: How's that?

LYUBOV ANDREYEVNA [*looks into her purse*]: Yester-day I had a lot of money, and today there's hardly any left. My poor Varya tries to economize by feeding every-one milk soup, and in the kitchen the old people get nothing but dried peas, while I squander money foolishly. . . . [*Drops the purse, scattering gold coins.*] There they go. . . . [*Vexed*]

YASHA: Allow me, I'll pick them up in an instant. [*Picks up the money.*]

LYUBOV ANDREYEVNA: Please do, Yasha. And why did I go to town for lunch? . . . That miserable restaurant of yours with its music, and tablecloths smelling of

soap. . . . Why drink so much, Lyonya? Why eat so
much? Why talk so much? Today in the restaurant again
you talked too much, and it was all so pointless. About
the seventies, about the decadents. And to whom? Talking to waiters about the decadents!

LOPAKHIN: Yes.

GAYEV [*waving his hand*]: I'm incorrigible, that's
evident. . . . [*Irritably to* YASHA] Why do you keep twirl-
ing about in front of me?

YASHA [*laughs*]: I can't help laughing when I hear
your voice.

GAYEV [*to his sister*]: Either he or I——

LYUBOV ANDREYEVNA: Go away, Yasha, run along.

YASHA [*hands* LYUBOV ANDREYEVNA *her purse*]: I'm
going, right away. [*Hardly able to contain his laughter.*]
This very instant. . . . [*Goes out.*]

LOPAKHIN: That rich man, Deriganov, is prepared to
buy the estate. They say he's coming to the auction
himself.

LYUBOV ANDREYEVNA: Where did you hear that?

LOPAKHIN: That's what they're saying in town.

LYUBOV ANDREYEVNA: Our aunt in Yaroslav promised to send us something, but when and how much, no
one knows.

LOPAKHIN: How much do you think she'll send? A
hundred thousand? Two hundred?

LYUBOV ANDREYEVNA: Oh . . . ten or fifteen thousand, and we'll be thankful for that.

LOPAKHIN: Forgive me, but I have never seen such frivolous, such queer, unbusinesslike people as you, my friends. You are told in plain language that your estate is to be sold, and it's as though you don't understand it.

LYUBOV ANDREYEVNA: But what are we to do? Tell us what to do.

LOPAKHIN: I tell you every day. Every day I say the same thing. Both the cherry orchard and the land must be leased for summer cottages, and it must be done now, as quickly as possible—the auction is close at hand. Try to understand! Once you definitely decide on the cottages, you can raise as much money as you like, and then you are saved.

LYUBOV ANDREYEVNA: Cottages, summer people— forgive me, but it's so vulgar.

GAYEV: I agree with you, absolutely.

LOPAKHIN: I'll either burst into tears, start shouting, or fall into a faint! I can't stand it! You've worn me out! [*To* GAYEV] You're an old woman!

GAYEV: How's that?

LOPAKHIN: An old woman! [*Starts to go.*]

LYUBOV ANDREYEVNA [*alarmed*]: No, don't go, stay, my dear. I beg you. Perhaps we'll think of something!

LOPAKHIN: What is there to think of?

LYUBOV ANDREYEVNA: Don't go away, please. With you here it's more cheerful somehow. . . . [*Pause*] I keep expecting something to happen, like the house caving in on us.

GAYEV [*in deep thought*]: Double rail shot into the corner. . . . Cross table to the center. . . .

LYUBOV ANDREYEVNA: We have sinned so much. . . .

LOPAKHIN: What sins could you have——

GAYEV [*puts a candy into his mouth*]:   They say I've eaten up my entire fortune in candies. . . . [*Laughs.*]

LYUBOV ANDREYEVNA: Oh, my sins. . . . I've always squandered money recklessly, like a madwoman, and I married a man who did nothing but amass debts. My husband died from champagne—he drank terribly—then, to my sorrow, I fell in love with another man, lived with him, and just at that time—that was my first punishment, a blow on the head—my little boy was drowned . . . here in the river. And I went abroad, went away for good, never to return, never to see this river. . . . I closed my eyes and ran, beside myself, and *he* after me . . . callously, without pity. I bought a villa near Mentone, because he fell ill there, and for three years I had no rest, day or night. The sick man wore me out, my soul dried up. Then last year, when the villa was sold to pay my debts, I went to Paris, and there he stripped me of everything, and left me for another woman; I tried to poison myself. . . . So stupid, so shameful. . . . And suddenly I felt a longing for Russia, for my own country, for my little girl. . . . [*Wipes away her tears.*] Lord, Lord, be merciful, forgive my sins! Don't punish me any more! [*Takes a telegram out of her pocket.*] This came today from Paris. . . . He asks my forgiveness, begs me to return. . . . [*Tears up telegram.*] Do I hear music? [*Listens.*]

GAYEV: That's our famous Jewish band. You remember, four violins, a flute and double bass.

LYUBOV ANDREYEVNA: It's still in existence? We ought to send for them some time and give a party.

LOPAKHIN [*listens*]:   I don't hear anything. . . . [*Sings softly.*] "The Germans, for pay, will turn Russians into

Frenchmen, they say." [*Laughs.*] What a play I saw yesterday at the theater—very funny!

LYUBOV ANDREYEVNA: There was probably nothing funny about it. Instead of going to see plays you ought to look at yourselves a little more often. How drab your lives are, how full of futile talk!

LOPAKHIN: That's true. I must say, this life of ours is stupid. . . . [*Pause*] My father was a peasant, an idiot; he understood nothing, taught me nothing; all he did was beat me when he was drunk, and always with a stick. As a matter of fact, I'm as big a blockhead and idiot as he was. I never learned anything, my handwriting's disgusting, I write like a pig—I'm ashamed to have people see it.

LYUBOV ANDREYEVNA: You ought to get married, my friend.

LOPAKHIN: Yes . . . that's true.

LYUBOV ANDREYEVNA: To our Varya. She's a nice girl.

LOPAKHIN: Yes.

LYUBOV ANDREYEVNA: She's a girl who comes from simple people, works all day long, but the main thing is she loves you. Besides, you've liked her for a long time now.

LOPAKHIN: Well? I've nothing against it. . . . She's a good girl. [*Pause*]

GAYEV: I've been offered a place in the bank. Six thousand a year. . . . Have you heard?

LYUBOV ANDREYEVNA: How could you! You stay where you are. . . .

[FIRS *enters carrying an overcoat*.]

FIRS [*To* GAYEV]: If you please, sir, put this on, it's damp.

GAYEV [*puts on the overcoat*]: You're a pest, old man.

FIRS: Never mind. . . . You went off this morning without telling me. [*Looks him over*.]

LYUBOV ANDREYEVNA: How you have aged, Firs!

FIRS: What do you wish, madam?

LOPAKHIN: She says you've grown very old!

FIRS: I've lived a long time. They were arranging a marriage for me before your papa was born. . . . [*Laughs*.] I was already head footman when the Emancipation came. At that time I wouldn't consent to my freedom, I stayed with the masters. . . . [*Pause*] I remember, everyone was happy, but what they were happy about, they themselves didn't know.

LOPAKHIN: It was better in the old days. At least they flogged them.

FIRS [*not hearing*]: Of course. The peasants kept to the masters, the masters kept to the peasants; but now they have all gone their own ways, you can't tell about anything.

GAYEV: Be quiet, Firs. Tomorrow I must go to town. I've been promised an introduction to a certain general who might let us have a loan.

LOPAKHIN: Nothing will come of it. And you can rest assured, you won't even pay the interest.

LYUBOV ANDREYEVNA: He's raving. There is no such general.

[*Enter* TROFIMOV, ANYA, *and* VARYA.)

GAYEV: Here come our young people.

ANYA: There's Mama.

LYUBOV ANDREYEVNA [*tenderly*]: Come, come along, my darlings. [*Embraces* ANYA *and* VARYA.] If you only knew how I love you both! Sit here beside me—there, like that.

[*They all sit down.*]

LOPAKHIN: Our eternal student is always with the young ladies.

TROFIMOV: That's none of your business.

LOPAKHIN: He'll soon be fifty, but he's still a student.

TROFIMOV: Drop your stupid jokes.

LOPAKHIN: What are you so angry about, you queer fellow?

TROFIMOV: Just leave me alone.

LOPAKHIN [*laughs*]: Let me ask you something: what do you make of me?

TROFIMOV: My idea of you, Yermolai Alekseich, is this: you're a rich man, you will soon be a millionaire. Just as the beast of prey, which devours everything that crosses its path, is necessary in the metabolic process, so are you necessary.

[*Everyone laughs.*]

VARYA: Petya, you'd better tell us something about the planets.

LYUBOV ANDREYEVNA: No, let's go on with yesterday's conversation.

TROFIMOV: What was it about?

GAYEV: About the proud man.

TROFIMOV: We talked a long time yesterday, but we didn't get anywhere. In the proud man, in your sense of the word, there's something mystical. And you may be right from your point of view, but if you look at it simply, without being abstruse, why even talk about pride? Is there any sense in it if, physiologically, man is poorly constructed, if, in the vast majority of cases, he is coarse, ignorant, and profoundly unhappy? We should stop admiring ourselves. We should just work, and that's all.

GAYEV: You die, anyway.

TROFIMOV: Who knows? And what does it mean—to die? It may be that man has a hundred senses, and at his death only the five that are known to us perish, and the other ninety-five go on living.

LYUBOV ANDREYEVNA: How clever you are, Petya!

LOPAKHIN [*ironically*]: Terribly clever!

TROFIMOV: Mankind goes forward, perfecting its powers. Everything that is now unattainable will some day be comprehensible and within our grasp, only we must work, and help with all our might those who are seeking the truth. So far, among us here in Russia, only a very few work. The great majority of the intelligentsia that I know seek nothing, do nothing, and as yet are incapable of work. They call themselves the intelligentsia, yet they belittle their servants, treat the peasants like animals, are wretched students, never read anything serious, and do absolutely nothing; they only talk about science and know very little about art. They all look serious, have grim expressions, speak of weighty matters, and philosophize; and meanwhile anyone can see that the workers eat abominably, sleep without pillows, thirty or forty to a room, and everywhere there are bedbugs, stench, dampness, and immorality. . . . It's obvious that all our fine talk is merely to delude ourselves and others. Show me the day nurseries they are always talking about—and where are the reading rooms? They only write about them in novels, but in reality they don't exist. There is nothing but filth, vulgarity, asiaticism. . . . I'm afraid of those very serious countenances, I don't like them, I'm afraid of serious conversations. We'd do better to remain silent.

LOPAKHIN: You know, I get up before five in the morning, and I work from morning to night; now, I'm always handling money, my own and other people's, and I see what people around me are like. You have only to start doing something to find out how few honest, decent people there are. Sometimes, when I can't sleep, I think: "Lord, Thou gavest us vast forests, boundless fields, broad horizons, and living in their midst we ourselves ought truly to be giants. . . ."

LYUBOV ANDREYEVNA: Now you want giants! They're good only in fairy tales, otherwise they're frightening.

[YEPIKHODOV *crosses at the rear of the stage, playing the guitar.*]

LYUBOV ANDREYEVNA [*pensively*]: There goes Yepikhodov . . .

ANYA [*pensively*]: There goes Yepikhodov . . .

GAYEV: The sun has set, ladies and gentlemen.

TROFIMOV: Yes.

GAYEV [*in a low voice, as though reciting*]: Oh, Nature, wondrous Nature, you shine with eternal radiance, beautiful and indifferent; you, whom we call mother, unite within yourself both life and death, giving life and taking it away. . . .

VARYA [*beseechingly*]: Uncle dear!

ANYA: Uncle, you're doing it again!

TROFIMOV: You'd better cue ball into the center.

GAYEV: I'll be silent, silent.

[*All sit lost in thought. The silence is broken only by the subdued muttering of* FIRS. *Suddenly a distant sound is heard as if from the sky, like the sound of a snapped string mournfully dying away.*]

LYUBOV ANDREYEVNA: What was that?

LOPAKHIN: I don't know. Somewhere far off in a mine shaft a bucket's broken loose. But somewhere very far away.

GAYEV: It might be a bird of some sort . . . like a heron.

TROFIMOV: Or an owl . . .

LYUBOV ANDREYEVNA [*shudders*]: It's unpleasant somehow. . . . [*Pause*]

FIRS: The same thing happened before the troubles: an owl hooted and the samovar hissed continually.

GAYEV: Before what troubles?

FIRS: Before the Emancipation.

LYUBOV ANDREYEVNA: Come along, my friends, let us go, evening is falling. [*To* ANYA] There are tears in your eyes—what is it, my little one?

[*Embraces her.*]

ANYA: It's all right, Mama. It's nothing.

TROFIMOV: Someone is coming.

[A STRANGER *appears wearing a shabby white forage cap and an overcoat. He is slightly drunk.*]

STRANGER: Permit me to inquire, can I go straight through here to the station?

GAYEV: You can. Follow the road.

STRANGER: I am deeply grateful to you. [*Coughs.*] Splendid weather. . . . [*Reciting*] "My brother, my suffering brother . . . come to the Volga, whose groans . . ." [*To* VARYA] Mademoiselle, will you oblige a hungry Russian with thirty kopecks?

[VARYA, *frightened, cries out.*]

LOPAKHIN [*angrily*]:   There's a limit to everything.

LYUBOV ANDREYEVNA [*panic-stricken*]: Here you are—take this. . . . [*Fumbles in her purse.*] I have no silver. . . . Never mind, here's a gold piece for you. . . .

STRANGER: I am deeply grateful to you. [*Goes off.*]

[*Laughter*]

VARYA [*frightened*]: I'm leaving . . . I'm leaving. . . . Oh, Mama, dear, there's nothing in the house for the servants to eat, and you give him a gold piece!

LYUBOV ANDREYEVNA: What's to be done with such a silly creature? When we get home I'll give you all I've got. Yermolai Alekseyevich, you'll lend me some more!

LOPAKHIN: At your service.

LYUBOV ANDREYEVNA: Come, my friends, it's time to go. Oh, Varya, we have definitely made a match for you. Congratulations!

VARYA [*through tears*]: Mama, that's not something to joke about.

LOPAKHIN: "Aurelia, get thee to a nunnery . . ."

GAYEV: Look, my hands are trembling: it's a long time since I've played a game of billiards.

LOPAKHIN: "Aurelia, O Nymph, in thy orisons, be all my sins remember'd!"

LYUBOV ANDREYEVNA: Let us go, my friends, it will soon be suppertime.

VARYA: He frightened me. My heart is simply pounding.

LOPAKHIN: Let me remind you, ladies and gentlemen: on the twenty-second of August the cherry orchard is to be sold. Think about that!—Think!

[*All go out except* TROFIMOV *and* ANYA.]

ANYA [*laughs*]:   My thanks to the stranger for frightening Varya, now we are alone.

TROFIMOV: Varya is so afraid we might suddenly fall in love with each other that she hasn't left us alone for days. With her narrow mind she can't understand that we are above love. To avoid the petty and the illusory, which prevent our being free and happy—that is the aim and meaning of life. Forward! We are moving irresistibly toward the bright star that burns in the distance! Forward! Do not fall behind, friends!

ANYA [*clasping her hands*]:   How well you talk! [*Pause*] It's marvelous here today!

TROFIMOV: Yes, the weather is wonderful.

ANYA: What have you done to me, Petya, that I no longer love the cherry orchard as I used to? I loved it so tenderly, it seemed to me there was no better place on earth than our orchard.

TROFIMOV: All Russia is our orchard. It is a great and beautiful land, and there are many wonderful places in it. [*Pause*] Just think, Anya: your grandfather, your great-grandfather, and all your ancestors were serf-owners, possessors of living souls. Don't you see that from every cherry tree, from every leaf and trunk, human beings are peering out at you? Don't you hear their voices? To possess living souls—that has corrupted all of you, those who lived before and you who are living now, so that your mother, you, your uncle, no longer perceive that you are living in debt, at someone else's expense, at the expense of those whom you wouldn't allow to cross your threshold. . . . We are at least two hundred years behind the times, we have as yet absolutely nothing, we have no definite attitude toward the past, we only philosophize, complain of boredom, or drink vodka. Yet it's quite clear that to begin to live we must first atone for the past, be done with it, and we can atone for it only by suffering, only by extraordinary, unceasing labor. Understand this, Anya.

ANYA: The house we live in hasn't really been ours for a long time, and I shall leave it, I give you my word.

TROFIMOV: If you have the keys of the household, throw them into the well and go. Be as free as the wind.

ANYA [*in ecstasy*]: How well you put that!

TROFIMOV: Believe me, Anya, believe me! I am not yet thirty, I am young, still a student, but I have already been through so much! As soon as winter comes, I am hungry, sick, worried, poor as a beggar, and—where has not fate driven me! Where have I not been? And yet always, every minute of the day and night, my soul was filled with inexplicable premonitions. I have a premonition of happiness, Anya, I can see it . . .

ANYA: The moon is rising.

[YEPIKHODOV *is heard playing the same melancholy song on the guitar. The moon rises. Somewhere near the poplars* VARYA *is looking for* ANYA *and calling: "Anya, where are you?"*]

TROFIMOV: Yes, the moon is rising. [*Pause*] There it is—happiness . . . it's coming, nearer and nearer, I can hear its footsteps. And if we do not see it, if we do not recognize it, what does it matter? Others will see it.

VARYA'S VOICE: Anya! Where are you?

TROFIMOV: That Varya again! [*Angrily*] It's revolting!

ANYA: Well? Let's go down to the river. It's lovely there.

TROFIMOV: Come on. [*They go.*]

VARYA'S VOICE: Anya! Anya!

Act III

[*The drawing room, separated by an arch from the ballroom. The chandelier is lighted. The Jewish band that was mentioned in Act II is heard playing in the hall. It is evening. In the ballroom they are dancing a grand rond. The voice of* SEMYONOV-PISHCHIK: *_*"Promenade à une paire!" *They all enter the drawing room:* PISHCHIK *and* CHARLOTTA IVANOVNA *are the first couple,* TROFIMOV *and* LYUBOV ANDREYEVNA *the second,* ANYA *and the* POST-OFFICE CLERK *the third,* VARYA *and the* STATIONMASTER *the fourth, etc.* VARYA, *quietly weeping, dries her tears as she dances.* DUNYASHA *is in the last couple. As they cross the drawing room* PISHCHIK *calls:* "Grand rond, balancez!" *and* "Les cavaliers à genoux et remercier vos dames!" FIRS, *wearing a dress coat, brings in a tray with seltzer water.* PISHCHIK *and* TROFIMOV *come into the drawing room.*]

PISHCHIK: I'm a full-blooded man, I've already had two strokes, and dancing's hard work for me, but as they say, "If you run with the pack, you can bark or not, but at least wag your tail." At that, I'm as strong as a horse. My late father—quite a joker he was, God rest his soul—used to say, talking about our origins, that the ancient line of Semyonov-Pishchik was descended from the very horse that Caligula had seated in the Senate. . . . [*Sits down.*] But the trouble is—no money! A hungry dog believes in nothing but meat. . . . [*Snores but wakes up at once.*] It's the same with me—I can think of nothing but money. . . .

362

TROFIMOV: You know, there really is something equine about your figure.

PISHCHIK: Well, a horse is a fine animal. . . . You can sell a horse.

[*There is the sound of a billiard game in the next room.* VARYA *appears in the archway.*]

TROFIMOV [*teasing her*]: Madame Lopakhina! Madame Lopakhina!

VARYA [*angrily*]: Mangy gentleman!

TROFIMOV: Yes, I am a mangy gentleman, and proud of it!

VARYA [*reflecting bitterly*]: Here we've hired musicians, and what are we going to pay them with? [*Goes out.*]

TROFIMOV [*to* PISHCHIK]: If the energy you have expended in the course of your life trying to find money to pay interest had gone into something else, ultimately, you might very well have turned the world upside down.

PISHCHIK: Nietzsche . . . the philosopher . . . the greatest, most renowned . . . a man of tremendous intellect . . . says in his works that it is possible to forge banknotes.

TROFIMOV: And have you read Nietzsche?

PISHCHIK: Well . . . Dashenka told me. I'm in such a state now that I'm just about ready for forging. . . . The day after tomorrow I have to pay three hundred and ten rubles . . . I've got a hundred and thirty. . . . [*Feels in his pocket, grows alarmed.*] The money is gone! I've lost the money! [*Tearfully*] Where is my money? [*Joyfully*] Here it is, inside the lining. . . . I'm all in a sweat. . . .

[LYUBOV ANDREYEVNA *and* CHARLOTTA IVANOVNA *come in.*]

LYUBOV ANDREYEVNA [*humming a* Lezginka]: Why does Leonid take so long? What is he doing in town? [*To* DUNYASHA] Dunyasha, offer the musicians some tea.

TROFIMOV: In all probability, the auction didn't take place.

LYUBOV ANDREYEVNA: It was the wrong time to have the musicians, the wrong time to give a dance. . . . Well, never mind. . . . [*Sits down and hums softly.*]

CHARLOTTA [*gives* PISHCHIK *a deck of cards*]: Here's a deck of cards for you. Think of a card.

PISHCHIK: I've thought of one.

CHARLOTTA: Now shuffle the pack. Very good. And now, my dear Mr. Pishchik, hand it to me. *Eins, zwei, drei!* Now look for it—it's in your side pocket.

PISHCHIK [*takes the card out of his side pocket*]: The eight of spades—absolutely right! [*Amazed*] Think of that, now!

CHARLOTTA [*holding the deck of cards in the palm of her hand, to* TROFIMOV]: Quickly, tell me, which card is on top?

TROFIMOV: What? Well, the queen of spades.

CHARLOTTA: Right! [*To* PISHCHIK] Now which card is on top?

PISHCHIK: The ace of hearts.

CHARLOTTA: Right! [*Claps her hands and the deck of cards disappears.*] What lovely weather we're having today! [*A mysterious feminine voice, which seems to come from under the floor, answers her: "Oh, yes, splendid weather, madam."*] You are so nice, you're my ideal. . . . [*The voice: "And I'm very fond of you, too, madam."*]

STATIONMASTER [*applauding*]: Bravo, Madame Ventriloquist!

PISHCHIK [*amazed*]: Think of that, now! Most enchanting Charlotta Ivanovna . . . I am simply in love with you. . . .

CHARLOTTA: In love? [*Shrugs her shoulders.*] Is it possible that you can love? *Guter Mensch, aber schlechter Musikant.*

TROFIMOV [*claps* PISHCHIK *on the shoulder*]: You old horse, you!

CHARLOTTA: Attention, please! One more trick. [*Takes a lap robe from a chair.*] Here's a very fine lap robe; I should like to sell it. [*Shakes it out.*] Doesn't anyone want to buy it?

PISHCHIK [*amazed*]: Think of that, now!

CHARLOTTA: *Eins, zwei, drei!* [*Quickly raises the lap robe; behind it stands* ANYA, *who curtseys, runs to her mother, embraces her, and runs back into the ballroom amid the general enthusiasm.*]

LYUBOV ANDREYEVNA [*applauding*]: Bravo, bravo!

CHARLOTTA: Once again! *Eins, zwei, drei.* [*Raises the lap robe; behind it stands* VARYA, *who bows.*]

PISHCHIK [*amazed*]: Think of that, now!

CHARLOTTA: The end! [*Throws the robe at* PISHCHIK, *makes a curtsey, and runs out of the room.*]

PISHCHIK [*hurries after her*] The minx! . . . What a woman! What a woman! [*Goes out.*]

LYUBOV ANDREYEVNA: And Leonid still not here. What he is doing in town so long, I do not understand! It must be all over by now. Either the estate is sold, or the auction didn't take place—but why keep us in suspense so long!

VARYA [*trying to comfort her*]: Uncle has bought it, I am certain of that.

TROFIMOV [*mockingly*]: Yes.

VARYA: Great-aunt sent him power of attorney to buy it in her name and transfer the debt. She's doing it for Anya's sake. And I am sure, with God's help, Uncle will buy it.

LYUBOV ANDREYEVNA: Our great-aunt in Yaroslav sent fifteen thousand to buy the estate in her name—she doesn't trust us—but that's not even enough to pay the interest. [*Covers her face with her hands.*] Today my fate will be decided, my fate . . .

TROFIMOV [*teasing* VARYA]: Madame Lopakhina!

VARYA [*angrily*]: Eternal student! Twice already you've been expelled from the university.

LYUBOV ANDREYEVNA: Why are you so cross, Varya? If he teases you about Lopakhin, what of it? Go ahead and marry Lopakhin if you want to. He's a nice man, he's interesting. And if you don't want to, don't. Nobody's forcing you, my pet.

VARYA: To be frank, Mama dear, I regard this matter seriously. He is a good man, I like him.

LYUBOV ANDREYEVNA: Then marry him. I don't know what you're waiting for!

VARYA: Mama, I can't propose to him myself. For the last two years everyone's been talking to me about him; everyone talks, but he is either silent or he jokes. I understand. He's getting rich, he's absorbed in business, he has no time for me. If I had some money, no matter how little, if it were only a hundred rubles, I'd drop everything and go far away. I'd go into a nunnery.

TROFIMOV: A blessing!

VARYA [*to* TROFIMOV]: A student ought to be intelligent! [*In a gentle tone, tearfully*] How homely you have grown, Petya, how old! [*To* LYUBOV ANDREYEVNA, *no longer crying*] It's just that I cannot live without work, Mama. I must be doing something every minute.

[YASHA *enters.*]

YASHA [*barely able to suppress his laughter*]: Yepikhodov has broken a billiard cue! [*Goes out.*]

VARYA: But why is Yepikhodov here? Who gave him permission to play billiards? I don't understand these people. . . . [*Goes out.*]

LYUBOV ANDREYEVNA: Don't tease her, Petya. You can see she's unhappy enough without that.

TROFIMOV: She's much too zealous, always meddling in other people's affairs. All summer long she's given Anya and me no peace—afraid a romance might develop. What business is it of hers? Besides, I've given no occasion for it, I am far removed from such banality. We are above love!

LYUBOV ANDREYEVNA: And I suppose I am beneath love. [*In great agitation*] Why isn't Leonid here? If only I knew whether the estate had been sold or not! The disaster seems to me so incredible that I don't even know what to think, I'm lost. . . . I could scream this

very instant . . . I could do something foolish. Save me,
Petya. Talk to me, say something. . . .

TROFIMOV: Whether or not the estate is sold today—
does it really matter? That's all done with long ago;
there's no turning back, the path is overgrown. Be calm,
my dear. One must not deceive oneself; at least once in
one's life one ought to look the truth straight in the eye.

LYUBOV ANDREYEVNA: What truth? You can see
where there is truth and where there isn't, but I seem
to have lost my sight, I see nothing. You boldly settle
all the important problems, but tell me, my dear boy,
isn't it because you are young and have not yet had to
suffer for a single one of your problems? You boldly
look ahead, but isn't it because you neither see nor expect anything dreadful, since life is still hidden from your
young eyes? You're bolder, more honest, deeper than
we are, but think about it, be just a little bit magnanimous, and spare me. You see, I was born here, my
mother and father lived here, and my grandfather. I love
this house, without the cherry orchard my life has no
meaning for me, and if it must be sold, then sell me with
the orchard. . . . [*Embraces* TROFIMOV *and kisses him on
the forehead.*] And my son was drowned here. . . .
[*Weeps.*] Have pity on me, you good, kind man.

TROFIMOV: You know I feel for you with all my
heart.

LYUBOV ANDREYEVNA: But that should have been
said differently, quite differently. . . . [*Takes out her
handkerchief and a telegram falls to the floor.*] My heart
is heavy today, you can't imagine. It's so noisy here, my
soul quivers at every sound, I tremble all over, and yet
I can't go to my room. When I am alone the silence
frightens me. Don't condemn me, Petya . . . I love you
as if you were my own. I would gladly let you marry
Anya, I swear it, only you must study, my dear, you
must get your degree. You do nothing, fate simply tosses
you from place to place—it's so strange. . . . Isn't that

true? Isn't it? And you must do something about your beard, to make it grow somehow. . . . [*Laughs.*] You're so funny!

TROFIMOV [*picks up the telegram*]: I have no desire to be an Adonis.

LYUBOV ANDREYEVNA: That's a telegram from Paris. I get them every day. One yesterday, one today. That wild man has fallen ill again, he's in trouble again. . . . He begs my forgiveness, implores me to come, and really, I ought to go to Paris to be near him. Your face is stern, Petya, but what can one do, my dear? What am I to do? He is ill, he's alone and unhappy, and who will look after him there, who will keep him from making mistakes, who will give him his medicine on time? And why hide it or keep silent, I love him, that's clear. I love him, love him. . . . It's a millstone round my neck, I'm sinking to the bottom with it, but I love that stone, I cannot live without it. [*Presses* TROFIMOV's *hand.*] Don't think badly of me, Petya, and don't say anything to me, don't say anything. . . .

TROFIMOV [*through tears*]: For God's sake, forgive my frankness: you know that he robbed you!

LYUBOV ANDREYEVNA: No, no, no, you mustn't say such things! [*Covers her ears.*]

TROFIMOV: But he's a scoundrel! You're the only one who doesn't know it! He's a petty scoundrel, a nonentity——

LYUBOV ANDREYEVNA [*angry, but controlling herself*]: You are twenty-six or twenty-seven years old, but you're still a schoolboy!

TROFIMOV: That may be!

LYUBOV ANDREYEVNA: You should be a man, at your age you ought to understand those who love. And you ought to be in love yourself. [*Angrily*] Yes, yes! It's not purity with you, it's simply prudery, you're a ridiculous crank, a freak——

TROFIMOV [*horrified*]:　What is she saying!

LYUBOV ANDREYEVNA:　"I am above love!" You're not above love, you're just an addlepate, as Firs would say. Not to have a mistress at your age!

TROFIMOV [*in horror*]:　This is awful! What is she saying! . . . [*Goes quickly toward the ballroom.*] This is awful . . . I can't . . . I won't stay here. . . . [*Goes out, but immediately returns.*] All is over between us! [*Goes out to the hall.*]

LYUBOV ANDREYEVNA [*calls after him*]:　Petya, wait! You absurd creature, I was joking! Petya!

[*In the hall there is the sound of someone running quickly downstairs and suddenly falling with a crash.* ANYA *and* VARYA *scream, but a moment later laughter is heard.*]

LYUBOV ANDREYEVNA:　What was that?

[ANYA *runs in.*]

ANYA [*laughing*]:　Petya fell down the stairs! [*Runs out.*]

LYUBOV ANDREYEVNA:　What a funny boy that Petya is!

[*The* STATIONMASTER *stands in the middle of the ballroom and recites A. Tolstoy's "The Sinner." Everyone listens to him, but he has no sooner spoken a few lines than the sound of a waltz is heard from the hall and the recitation is broken off. They all dance.* TROFIMOV, ANYA, VARYA, *and* LYUBOV ANDREYEVNA *come in from the hall.*]

LYUBOV ANDREYEVNA: Come, Petya . . . come, you pure soul . . . please, forgive me. . . . Let's dance. . . . [*They dance.*]

[ANYA *and* VARYA *dance.* FIRS *comes in, puts his stick by the side door.* YASHA *also comes into the drawing room and watches the dancers.*]

YASHA: What is it, grandpa?

FIRS: I don't feel well. In the old days we used to have generals, barons, admirals, dancing at our balls, but now we send for the post-office clerk and the stationmaster, and even they are none too eager to come. Somehow I've grown weak. The late master, their grandfather, dosed everyone with sealing wax, no matter what ailed them. I've been taking sealing wax every day for twenty years or more; maybe that's what's kept me alive.

YASHA: You bore me, grandpa. [*Yawns.*] High time you croaked.

FIRS: Ah, you . . . addlepate! [*Mumbles.*]

[TROFIMOV *and* LYUBOV ANDREYEVNA *dance from the ballroom into the drawing room.*]

LYUBOV ANDREYEVNA: *Merci.* I'll sit down a while. [*Sits.*] I'm tired.

[ANYA *comes in.*]

ANYA [*excitedly*]: There was a man in the kitchen just now saying that the cherry orchard was sold today.

LYUBOV ANDREYEVNA: Sold to whom?

ANYA: He didn't say. He's gone. [*Dances with* TROFIMOV; *they go into the ballroom.*]

YASHA: That was just some old man babbling. A stranger.

FIRS: Leonid Andreich is not back yet, still hasn't come. And he's wearing the light, between-seasons overcoat; like enough he'll catch cold. Ah, when they're young they're green.

LYUBOV ANDREYEVNA: This is killing me. Yasha, go and find out who it was sold to.

YASHA: But that old man left long ago. [*Laughs.*]

LYUBOV ANDREYEVNA [*slightly annoyed*]: Well, what are you laughing at? What are you so happy about?

YASHA: That Yepikhodov is very funny! Hopeless! Two-and-twenty Troubles.

LYUBOV ANDREYEVNA: Firs, if the estate is sold, where will you go?

FIRS: Wherever you tell me to go, I'll go.

LYUBOV ANDREYEVNA: Why do you look like that? Aren't you well? You ought to go to bed.

FIRS: Yes. . . . [*With a smirk*] Go to bed, and without me who will serve, who will see to things? I'm the only one in the whole house.

YASHA [*to* LYUBOV ANDREYEVNA]: Lyubov Andreyevna! Permit me to make a request, be so kind! If you go back to Paris again, do me the favor of taking me with you. It is positively impossible for me to stay here. [*Looking around, then in a low voice*] There's no need to say it, you can see for yourself, it's an uncivilized country, the people have no morals, and the boredom! The food they give us in the kitchen is unmentionable, and besides, there's this Firs who keeps walking about mumbling all sorts of inappropriate things. Take me with you, be so kind!

[*Enter* PISHCHIK.]

PISHCHIK: May I have the pleasure of a waltz with you, fairest lady? [LYUBOV ANDREYEVNA *goes with him.*] I really must borrow a hundred and eighty rubles from you, my charmer . . . I really must. . . . [*Dancing*] Just a hundred and eighty rubles. . . . [*They pass into the ballroom.*]

YASHA [*softly sings*]: "Wilt thou know my soul's unrest . . ."

[*In the ballroom a figure in a gray top hat and checked trousers is jumping about, waving its arms; there are shouts of "Bravo, Charlotta Ivanovna!"*]

DUNYASHA [*stopping to powder her face*]: The young mistress told me to dance—there are lots of gentlemen and not enough ladies—but dancing makes me dizzy, and my heart begins to thump. Firs Nikolayevich, the post-office clerk just said something to me that took my breath away.

[*The music grows more subdued.*]

FIRS: What did he say to you?

DUNYASHA: "You," he said, "are like a flower."

YASHA [*yawns*]: What ignorance. . . . [*Goes out.*]

DUNYASHA: Like a flower. . . . I'm such a delicate girl, I just adore tender words.

FIRS: You'll get your head turned.

[*Enter* YEPIKHODOV.]

YEPIKHODOV: Avdotya Fyodorovna, you are not desirous of seeing me . . . I might almost be some sort of insect. [*Sighs.*] Ah, life!

DUNYASHA: What is it you want?

YEPIKHODOV: Indubitably, you may be right. [*Sighs.*] But, of course, if one looks at it from a point of view, then, if I may so express myself, and you will forgive my frankness, you have completely reduced me to a state of mind. I know my fate, every day some misfortune befalls me, but I have long since grown accustomed to that; I look upon my fate with a smile. But you gave me your word, and although I——

DUNYASHA: Please, we'll talk about it later, but leave me in peace now. Just now I'm dreaming. . . . [*Plays with her fan.*]

YEPIKHODOV: Every day a misfortune, and yet, if I may so express myself, I merely smile, I even laugh.

[VARYA *enters from the ballroom.*]

VARYA: Are you still here, Semyon? What a disrespectful man you are, really! [*To* DUNYASHA] Run along, Dunyasha. [*To* YEPIKHODOV] First you play billiards and break a cue, then you wander about the drawing room as though you were a guest.

YEPIKHODOV: You cannot, if I may so express myself, penalize me.

VARYA: I am not penalizing you, I'm telling you. You do nothing but wander from one place to another, and you don't do your work. We keep a clerk, but for what, I don't know.

YEPIKHODOV [*offended*]: Whether I work, or wander about, or eat, or play billiards, these are matters to be discussed only by persons of discernment, and my elders.

VARYA: You dare say that to me! [*Flaring up*] You dare? You mean to say I have no discernment? Get out of here! This instant!

YEPIKHODOV [*intimidated*]: I beg you to express yourself in a more delicate manner.

VARYA [*beside herself*]: Get out, this very instant! Get out! [*He goes to the door, she follows him.*] Two-and-twenty Troubles! Don't let me set eyes on you again!

YEPIKHODOV [*goes out, his voice is heard behind the door*]: I shall lodge a complaint against you!

VARYA: Oh, you're coming back? [*Seizes the stick left near the door by* FIRS.] Come, come on. . . . Come, I'll show you. . . . Ah, so you're coming, are you? Then take that—[*Swings the stick just as* LOPAKHIN *enters.*]

LOPAKHIN: Thank you kindly.

VARYA [*angrily and mockingly*]: I beg your pardon.

LOPAKHIN: Not at all. I humbly thank you for your charming reception.

VARYA: Don't mention it. [*Walks away, then looks back and gently asks.*] I didn't hurt you, did I?

LOPAKHIN: No, it's nothing. A huge bump coming up, that's all.

[*Voices in the ballroom: "Lopakhin has come! Yermolai Alekseich!"* PISHCHIK *enters.*]

PISHCHIK: As I live and breathe! [*Kisses* LOPAKHIN.] There is a whiff of cognac about you, dear soul. And we've been making merry here, too.

[*Enter* LYUBOV ANDREYEVNA.]

LYUBOV ANDREYEVNA: Is that you, Yermolai Alekseich? What kept you so long? Where's Leonid?

LOPAKHIN: Leonid Andreich arrived with me, he's coming . . .

LYUBOV ANDREYEVNA [*agitated*]: Well, what happened? Did the sale take place? Tell me!

LOPAKHIN [*embarrassed, fearing to reveal his joy*]: The auction was over by four o'clock. . . . We missed the train, had to wait till half past nine. [*Sighing heavily*] Ugh! My head is swimming. . . .

[*Enter* GAYEV; *he carries his purchases in one hand and wipes away his tears with the other.*]

LYUBOV ANDREYEVNA: Lyonya, what happened? Well, Lyonya? [*Impatiently, through tears*] Be quick, for God's sake!

GAYEV [*not answering her, simply waves his hand. To* FIRS, *weeping*]: Here, take these. . . . There's anchovies, Kerch herrings. . . . I haven't eaten anything all day. . . . What I have been through! [*The click of billiard balls is heard through the open door to the billiard room, and* YASHA's *voice: "Seven and eighteen!"* GAYEV's *expression changes, he is no longer weeping.*] I'm terribly tired. Firs, help me change. [*Goes through the ballroom to his own room, followed by* FIRS.]

PISHCHIK: What happened at the auction? Come on, tell us!

LYUBOV ANDREYEVNA: Is the cherry orchard sold?

LOPAKHIN: It's sold.

LYUBOV ANDREYEVNA: Who bought it?

LOPAKHIN: I bought it. [*Pause*]

[LYUBOV ANDREYEVNA *is overcome; she would fall to the floor if it were not for the chair and table near which she stands.* VARYA *takes the keys from her belt and throws them on the floor in the middle of the drawing room and goes out.*]

LOPAKHIN: I bought it! Kindly wait a moment, ladies and gentlemen, my head is swimming, I can't talk. . . . [*Laughs.*] We arrived at the auction, Deriganov was already there. Leonid Andreich had only fifteen thousand, and straight off Deriganov bid thirty thousand over and above the mortgage. I saw how the land lay, so I got into the fight and bid forty. He bid forty-five. I bid fifty-five. In other words, he kept raising it by five thousand, and I by ten. Well, it finally came to an end. I bid ninety thousand above the mortgage, and it was knocked down to me. The cherry orchard is now mine! Mine! [*Laughs uproariously.*] Lord! God in heaven! The cherry orchard is mine! Tell me I'm drunk, out of my mind, that I imagine it. . . . [*Stamps his feet.*] Don't laugh at me! If my father and my grandfather could only rise from their graves and see all that has happened, how their Yermolai, their beaten, half-literate Yermolai, who used to run about barefoot in winter, how that same Yermolai has bought an estate, the most beautiful estate in the whole world! I bought the estate where my father and grandfather were slaves, where they weren't even allowed in the kitchen. I'm asleep, this is just some dream of mine, it only seems to be. . . . It's the fruit of your imagination, hidden in the darkness of uncertainty. . . . [*Picks up the keys, smiling tenderly.*] She threw down the keys, wants to show that she's not mistress here any more. . . . [*Jingles the keys.*] Well, no matter. [*The orchestra is heard tuning up.*] Hey, musicians, play, I want to hear you! Come on, everybody, and see how Yermolai Lopakhin will lay the ax to the cherry orchard, how the trees will fall to the ground! We're going to build summer cottages, and our grandsons and great-grandsons will see a new life here. . . . Music! Strike up!

[*The orchestra plays.* LYUBOV ANDREYEVNA *sinks into a chair and weeps bitterly.*]

LOPAKHIN [*reproachfully*]: Why didn't you listen to me, why? My poor friend, there's no turning back now. [*With tears*] Oh, if only all this could be over quickly, if somehow our discordant, unhappy life could be changed!

PISHCHIK [*takes him by the arm; speaks in an undertone*]: She's crying. Let's go into the ballroom, let her be alone. . . . Come on. . . . [*Leads him into the ballroom.*]

LOPAKHIN: What's happened? Musicians, play so I can hear you! Let everything be as I want it! [*Ironically*] Here comes the new master, owner of the cherry orchard! [*Accidentally bumps into a little table, almost upsetting the candelabrum.*] I can pay for everything! [*Goes out with* PISHCHIK.]

[*There is no one left in either the drawing room or the ballroom except* LYUBOV ANDREYEVNA, *who sits huddled up and weeping bitterly. The music plays softly.* ANYA *and* TROFIMOV *enter hurriedly.* ANYA *goes to her mother and kneels before her.* TROFIMOV *remains in the doorway of the ballroom.*]

ANYA: Mama! . . . Mama, you're crying! Dear, kind, good Mama, my beautiful one, I love you . . . I bless you. The cherry orchard is sold, it's gone, that's true, true, but don't cry, Mama, life is still before you, you still have your good, pure soul. . . . Come with me, come, darling, we'll go away from here! . . . We'll plant a new orchard, more luxuriant than this one. You will see it and understand; and joy, quiet, deep joy, will sink into your soul, like the evening sun, and you will smile, Mama! Come, darling, let us go. . . .

Act IV

[*The scene is the same as Act I. There are neither curtains on the windows nor pictures on the walls, and only a little furniture piled up in one corner, as if for sale. There is a sense of emptiness. Near the outer door, at the rear of the stage, suitcases, traveling bags, etc., are piled up. Through the open door on the left the voices of* VARYA *and* ANYA *can be heard.* LOPAKHIN *stands waiting.* YASHA *is holding a tray with little glasses of champagne. In the hall,* YEPIKHODOV *is tying up a box. Offstage, at the rear, there is a hum of voices. It is the peasants who have come to say good-bye.* GAYEV'*s voice: "Thanks, brothers, thank you."*]

YASHA: The peasants have come to say good-bye. In my opinion, Yermolai Alekseich, peasants are good-natured, but they don't know much.

[*The hum subsides.* LYUBOV ANDREYEVNA *enters from the hall with* GAYEV. *She is not crying, but she is pale, her face twitches, and she cannot speak.*]

GAYEV: You gave them your purse, Lyuba. That won't do! That won't do!

LYUBOV ANDREYEVNA: I couldn't help it! I couldn't help it! [*They both go out.*]

LOPAKHIN [*in the doorway, calls after them*]:   Please, do me the honor of having a little glass at parting. I didn't think of bringing champagne from town, and at the station I found only one bottle. Please! What's the matter, friends, don't you want any? [*Walks away from the door.*] If I'd known that, I wouldn't have bought it. Well, then I won't drink any either. [YASHA *carefully sets the tray down on a chair.*] At least you have a glass, Yasha.

YASHA: To those who are departing! Good luck! [*Drinks.*] This champagne is not the real stuff, I can assure you.

LOPAKHIN: Eight rubles a bottle. [*Pause*] It's devilish cold in here.

YASHA: They didn't light the stoves today; it doesn't matter, since we're leaving. [*Laughs.*]

LOPAKHIN: Why are you laughing?

YASHA: Because I'm pleased.

LOPAKHIN: It's October, yet it's sunny and still outside, like summer. Good for building. [*Looks at his watch, then calls through the door.*] Bear in mind, ladies and gentlemen, only forty-six minutes till train time! That means leaving for the station in twenty minutes. Better hurry up!

[TROFIMOV *enters from outside wearing an overcoat.*]

TROFIMOV: Seems to me it's time to start. The carriages are at the door. What the devil has become of my rubbers? They're lost. [*Calls through the door.*] Anya, my rubbers are not here. I can't find them.

LOPAKHIN: I've got to go to Kharkov. I'm taking the same train you are. I'm going to spend the winter in Kharkov. I've been hanging around here with you, and I'm sick and tired of loafing. I can't live without work,

I don't know what to do with my hands; they dangle in some strange way, as if they didn't belong to me.

TROFIMOV: We'll soon be gone, then you can take up your useful labors again.

LOPAKHIN: Here, have a little drink.

TROFIMOV: No, I don't want any.

LOPAKHIN: So you're off for Moscow?

TROFIMOV: Yes, I'll see them into town, and tomorrow I'll go to Moscow.

LOPAKHIN: Yes. . . . Well, I expect the professors haven't been giving any lectures: they're waiting for you to come!

TROFIMOV: That's none of your business.

LOPAKHIN: How many years is it you've been studying at the university?

TROFIMOV: Can't you think of something new? That's stale and flat. [*Looks for his rubbers.*] You know, we'll probably never see each other again, so allow me to give you one piece of advice at parting: don't wave your arms about! Get out of that habit—of arm-waving. And another thing, building cottages and counting on the summer residents in time becoming independent farmers—that's just another form of arm-waving. Well, when all's said and done, I'm fond of you anyway. You have fine, delicate fingers, like an artist; you have a fine delicate soul.

LOPAKHIN [*embraces him*]: Good-bye, my dear fellow. Thank you for everything. Let me give you some money for the journey, if you need it.

TROFIMOV: What for? I don't need it.

LOPAKHIN: But you haven't any!

TROFIMOV: I have. Thank you. I got some money for a translation. Here it is in my pocket. [*Anxiously*] But where are my rubbers?

VARYA [*from the next room*]:   Here, take the nasty things! [*Flings a pair of rubbers onto the stage.*]

TROFIMOV: What are you so cross about, Varya? Hm. . . . But these are not my rubbers.

LOPAKHIN: In the spring I sowed three thousand acres of poppies, and now I've made forty thousand rubles clear. And when my poppies were in bloom, what a picture it was! So, I'm telling you, I've made forty thousand, which means I'm offering you a loan because I can afford to. Why turn up your nose? I'm a peasant—I speak bluntly.

TROFIMOV: Your father was a peasant, mine was a pharmacist—which proves absolutely nothing. [LOPAKHIN *takes out his wallet.*] No, don't—even if you gave me two hundred thousand I wouldn't take it. I'm a free man. And everything that is valued so highly and held so dear by all of you, rich and poor alike, has not the slightest power over me—it's like a feather floating in the air. I can get along without you, I can pass you by, I'm strong and proud. Mankind is advancing toward the highest truth, the highest happiness attainable on earth, and I am in the front ranks!

LOPAKHIN: Will you get there?

TROFIMOV: I'll get there. [*Pause*] I'll either get there or I'll show others the way to get there.

[*The sound of axes chopping down trees is heard in the distance.*]

LOPAKHIN: Well, good-bye, my dear fellow. It's time to go. We turn up our noses at one another, but life goes on just the same. When I work for a long time without stopping, my mind is easier, and it seems to me that I, too, know why I exist. But how many there are in Russia, brother, who exist nobody knows why. Well, it doesn't matter, that's not what makes the wheels go round. They say Leonid Andreich has taken a position in the bank, six thousand a year. . . . Only, of course, he won't stick it out, he's too lazy. . . .

ANYA [*in the doorway*]:   Mama asks you not to start cutting down the cherry orchard until she's gone.

TROFIMOV: Yes, really, not to have had the tact . . . [*Goes out through the hall.*]

LOPAKHIN: Right away, right away. . . . Ach, what people. . . . [*Follows* TROFIMOV *out.*]

ANYA: Has Firs been taken to the hospital?

YASHA: I told them this morning. They must have taken him.

ANYA [*to* YEPIKHODOV, *who is crossing the room*]:   Semyon Panteleich, please find out if Firs has been taken to the hospital.

YASHA [*offended*]:   I told Yegor this morning. Why ask a dozen times?

YEPIKHODOV: It is my conclusive opinion that the venerable Firs is beyond repair; it's time he was gathered to his fathers. And I can only envy him. [*Puts a suitcase down on a hatbox and crushes it.*] There you are! Of course! I knew it! [*Goes out.*]

YASHA [*mockingly*]:   Two-and-twenty Troubles!

VARYA [*through the door*]:   Has Firs been taken to the hospital?

ANYA: Yes, he has.

VARYA: Then why didn't they take the letter to the doctor?

ANYA: We must send it on after them. . . . [*Goes out.*]

VARYA [*from the adjoining room*]:   Where is Yasha? Tell him his mother has come to say good-bye to him.

YASHA [*waves his hand*]:   They really try my patience.

[DUNYASHA *has been fussing with the luggage; now that* YASHA *is alone she goes up to him.*]

DUNYASHA: You might give me one little look, Yasha. You're going away . . . leaving me. . . . [*Cries and throws herself on his neck.*]

YASHA: What's there to cry about? [*Drinks champagne.*] In six days I'll be in Paris again. Tomorrow we'll take the express, off we go, and that's the last you'll see of us. I can hardly believe it. *Vive la France!* This place is not for me, I can't live here. . . . It can't be helped. I've had enough of this ignorance—I'm fed up with it. [*Drinks champagne.*] What are you crying for? Behave yourself properly, then you won't cry.

DUNYASHA [*looks into a small mirror and powders her face*]:   Send me a letter from Paris. You know, I loved you, Yasha, how I loved you! I'm such a tender creature, Yasha!

YASHA: Here they come. [*Busies himself with the luggage, humming softly.*]

[*Enter* LYUBOV ANDREYEVNA, GAYEV, CHARLOTTA IVANOVNA.]

GAYEV: We ought to be leaving. There's not much time now. [*Looks at* YASHA.] Who smells of herring?

LYUBOV ANDREYEVNA: In about ten minutes we should be getting into the carriages. [*Glances around the room.*] Good-bye, dear house, old grandfather. Winter will pass, spring will come, and you will no longer be here, they will tear you down. How much these walls have seen! [*Kisses her daughter warmly.*] My treasure, you are radiant, your eyes are sparkling like two diamonds. Are you glad? Very?

ANYA: Very! A new life is beginning, Mama!

GAYEV [*cheerfully*]: Yes, indeed, everything is all right now. Before the cherry orchard was sold we were all worried and miserable, but afterward, when the question was finally settled once and for all, everybody calmed down and felt quite cheerful. . . . I'm in a bank now, a financier . . . cue ball into the center . . . and you, Lyuba, say what you like, you look better, no doubt about it.

LYUBOV ANDREYEVNA: Yes. My nerves are better, that's true. [*Her hat and coat are handed to her.*] I sleep well. Carry out my things, Yasha, it's time. [*To* ANYA] My little girl, we shall see each other soon . . . I shall go to Paris and live there on the money your great-aunt sent to buy the estate—long live Auntie!—but that money won't last long.

ANYA: You'll come back soon, Mama, soon . . . won't you? I'll study hard and pass my high school examinations, and then I can work and help you. We'll read all sorts of books together, Mama. . . . Won't we? [*Kisses her mother's hand.*] We'll read in the autumn evenings, we'll read lots of books, and a new and wonderful world will open up before us. . . . [*Dreaming*] Mama, come back. . . .

LYUBOV ANDREYEVNA: I'll come, my precious. [*Embraces her.*]

[*Enter* LOPAKHIN. CHARLOTTA IVANOVNA *is softly humming a song.*]

GAYEV: Happy Charlotta: she's singing!

CHARLOTTA [*picks up a bundle and holds it like a baby in swaddling clothes*]: Bye, baby, bye. . . . [*A baby's crying is heard, "Wah! Wah!"*] Be quiet my darling, my dear little boy. [*"Wah! Wah!"*] I'm so sorry for you! [*Throws the bundle down.*] You will find me a position, won't you? I can't go on like this.

LOPAKHIN: We'll find something, Charlotta Ivanovna, don't worry.

GAYEV: Everyone is leaving us, Varya's going away . . . all of a sudden nobody needs us.

CHARLOTTA: I have nowhere to go in town. I must go away. [*Hums.*] It doesn't matter . . .

[*Enter* PISHCHIK.]

LOPAKHIN: Nature's wonder!

PISHCHIK [*panting*]: Ugh! Let me catch my breath. . . . I'm exhausted. . . . My esteemed friends. . . . Give me some water. . . .

GAYEV: After money, I suppose? Excuse me, I'm fleeing from temptation. . . . [*Goes out.*]

PISHCHIK: It's a long time since I've been to see you . . . fairest lady. . . . [*To* LOPAKHIN] So you're here. . . . Glad to see you, you intellectual giant. . . .

Here . . . take it . . . four hundred rubles . . . I still owe
you eight hundred and forty . . .

LOPAKHIN [*shrugs his shoulders in bewilderment*]: I
must be dreaming. . . . Where did you get it?

PISHCHIK: Wait . . . I'm hot. . . . A most extraordinary
event. Some Englishmen came to my place and discovered some kind of white clay on my land. [*To* LYUBOV
ANDREYEVNA] And four hundred for you . . . fairest,
most wonderful lady. . . . [*Hands her the money.*] The
rest later. [*Takes a drink of water.*] Just now a young
man in the train was saying that a certain . . . great
philosopher recommends jumping off roofs. . . . "Jump!"
he says, and therein lies the whole problem. [*In amazement*] Think of that, now! . . . Water!

LOPAKHIN: Who were those Englishmen?

PISHCHIK: I leased them the tract of land with the
clay on it for twenty-four years. . . . And now, excuse
me, I have no time . . . I must be trotting along . . . I'm
going to Znoikov's . . . to Kardamanov's . . . I owe
everybody. [*Drinks.*] Keep well . . . I'll drop in on
Thursday. . . .

LYUBOV ANDREYEVNA: We're just moving into town,
and tomorrow I go abroad . . .

PISHCHIK: What? [*Alarmed*] Why into town? That's
why I see the furniture . . . suitcases. . . . Well, never
mind. . . . [*Through tears*] Never mind. . . . Men of the
greatest intellect, those Englishmen. . . . Never mind. . . .
Be happy . . . God will help you. . . . Never mind. . . .
Everything in this world comes to an end. . . . [*Kisses*
LYUBOV ANDREYEVNA'*s hand.*] And should the news
reach you that my end has come, just remember this old
horse, and say: "There once lived a certain Semyonov-
Pishchik, God rest his soul." . . . Splendid weather. . . .
Yes. . . . [*Goes out greatly disconcerted, but immediately*

returns and speaks from the doorway.] Dashenka sends her regards. [*Goes out.*]

LYUBOV ANDREYEVNA:　Now we can go. I am leaving with two things on my mind. First—that Firs is sick. [*Looks at her watch.*] We still have about five minutes. . . .

ANYA:　Mama, Firs has already been taken to the hospital. Yasha sent him there this morning.

LYUBOV ANDREYEVNA:　My second concern is Varya. She's used to getting up early and working, and now, with no work to do, she's like a fish out of water. She's grown pale and thin, and cries all the time, poor girl. . . . [*Pause*] You know very well, Yermolai Alekseich, that I dreamed of marrying her to you, and everything pointed to your getting married. [*Whispers to* ANYA, *who nods to* CHARLOTTA, *and they both go out.*] She loves you, you are fond of her, and I don't know—I don't know why it is you seem to avoid each other. I can't understand it!

LOPAKHIN:　To tell you the truth, I don't understand it myself. The whole thing is strange, somehow. . . . If there's still time, I'm ready right now. . . . Let's finish it up—and *basta,* but without you I feel I'll never be able to propose to her.

LYUBOV ANDREYEVNA:　Splendid! After all, it only takes a minute. I'll call her in at once. . . .

LOPAKHIN:　And we even have the champagne. [*Looks at the glasses.*] Empty! Somebody's already drunk it. [YASHA *coughs.*] That's what you call lapping it up.

LYUBOV ANDREYEVNA [*animatedly*]:　Splendid! We'll leave you. . . . Yasha, *allez!* I'll call her. . . . [*At the door*] Varya, leave everything and come here. Come! [*Goes out with* YASHA.]

LOPAKHIN [*looking at his watch*]:   Yes. . . . [*Pause*]

[*Behind the door there is smothered laughter and whispering; finally* VARYA *enters.*]

VARYA [*looking over the luggage for a long time*]:   Strange, I can't seem to find it . . .

LOPAKHIN: What are you looking for?

VARYA: I packed it myself, and I can't remember . . . [*Pause*]

LOPAKHIN: Where are you going now, Varya Mikhailovna?

VARYA: I? To the Ragulins'. . . . I've agreed to go there to look after the house . . . as a sort of housekeeper.

LOPAKHIN: At Yashnevo? That would be about seventy versts from here. [*Pause*] Well, life in this house has come to an end. . . .

VARYA [*examining the luggage*]:   Where can it be? . . . Perhaps I put it in the trunk. . . . Yes, life in this house has come to an end . . . there'll be no more . . .

LOPAKHIN: And I'm off for Kharkov . . . by the next train. I have a lot to do. I'm leaving Yepikhodov here . . . I've taken him on.

VARYA: Really!

LOPAKHIN: Last year at this time it was already snowing, if you remember, but now it's still and sunny. It's cold though. . . . About three degrees of frost.

VARYA: I haven't looked. [*Pause*] And besides, our thermometer's broken. [*Pause*]

[*A voice from the yard calls: "Yermolai Alekseich!"*]

LOPAKHIN [*as if he had been waiting for a long time for the call*]:   Coming! [*Goes out quickly.*]

[VARYA *sits on the floor, lays her head on a bundle of clothes, and quietly sobs. The door opens and* LYUBOV ANDREYEVNA *enters cautiously.*]

LYUBOV ANDREYEVNA: Well? [*Pause*] We must be going.

VARYA [*no longer crying, dries her eyes*]:   Yes, it's time, Mama dear. I can get to the Ragulins' today, if only we don't miss the train.

LYUBOV ANDREYEVNA [*in the doorway*]:   Anya, put your things on!

[*Enter* ANYA, *then* GAYEV *and* CHARLOTTA IVANOVNA. GAYEV *wears a warm overcoat with a hood. The servants and coachmen come in.* YEPIKHODOV *bustles about the luggage.*]

LYUBOV ANDREYEVNA: Now we can be on our way.

ANYA [*joyfully*]:   On our way!

GAYEV: My friends, my dear, cherished friends! Leaving this house forever, can I pass over, in silence, can I refrain from giving utterance, as we say farewell, to those feelings that now fill my whole being——

ANYA [*imploringly*]:   Uncle!

VARYA: Uncle dear, don't!

GAYEV [*forlornly*]:   Double the rail off the white to center table . . . yellow into the side pocket. . . . I'll be quiet. . . .

[*Enter* TROFIMOV, *then* LOPAKHIN.]

TROFIMOV: Well, ladies and gentlemen, it's time to go!

LOPAKHIN: Yepikhodov, my coat!

LYUBOV ANDREYEVNA: I'll sit here just one more minute. It's as though I had never before seen what the walls of this house were like, what the ceilings were like, and now I look at them hungrily, with such tender love . . .

GAYEV: I remember when I was six years old, sitting on this window sill on Whitsunday, watching my father going to church . . .

LYUBOV ANDREYEVNA: Have they taken all the things?

LOPAKHIN: Everything, I think. [*Puts on his over-coat.*] Yepikhodov, see that everything is in order.

YEPIKHODOV [*in a hoarse voice*]:   Rest assured, Yermolai Alekseich!

LOPAKHIN: What's the matter with your voice?

YEPIKHODOV: Just drank some water . . . must have swallowed something.

YASHA [*contemptuously*]:   What ignorance!

LYUBOV ANDREYEVNA: When we go—there won't be a soul left here. . . .

LOPAKHIN: Till spring.

VARYA [*pulls an umbrella out of a bundle as though she were going to hit someone;* LOPAKHIN *pretends to be frightened*]:   Why are you—I never thought of such a thing!

TROFIMOV: Ladies and gentlemen, let's get into the carriages—it's time now! The train will soon be in!

VARYA: Petya, there they are—your rubbers, by the suitcase. [*Tearfully*] And what dirty old things they are!

TROFIMOV [*putting on his rubbers*]: Let's go, ladies and gentlemen!

GAYEV [*extremely upset, afraid of bursting into tears*]: The train . . . the station. . . . Cross table to the center, double the rail . . . on the white into the corner.

LYUBOV ANDREYEVNA: Let us go!

GAYEV: Are we all here? No one in there? [*Locks the side door on the left.*] There are some things stored in there, we must lock up. Let's go!

ANYA: Good-bye, house! Good-bye, old life!

TROFIMOV: Hail to the new life! [*Goes out with* ANYA.]

[VARYA *looks around the room and slowly goes out.* YASHA *and* CHARLOTTA *with her dog go out.*]

LOPAKHIN: And so, till spring. Come along, my friends. . . . Till we meet! [*Goes out.*]

[LYUBOV ANDREYEVNA *and* GAYEV *are left alone. As though they had been waiting for this, they fall onto each other's necks and break into quiet, restrained sobs, afraid of being heard.*]

GAYEV [*in despair*]: My sister, my sister. . . .

LYUBOV ANDREYEVNA: Oh, my dear, sweet, lovely orchard! . . . My life, my youth, my happiness, good-bye! . . . Good-bye!

ANYA'S VOICE [*gaily calling*]:   Mama!

TROFIMOV'S VOICE [*gay and excited*]:   Aa-oo!

LYUBOV ANDREYEVNA: One last look at these walls, these windows. . . . Mother loved to walk about in this room. . . .

GAYEV: My sister, my sister!

ANYA'S VOICE: Mama!

TROFIMOV'S VOICE: Aa-oo!

LYUBOV ANDREYEVNA: We're coming! [*They go out.*]

[*The stage is empty. There is the sound of doors being locked, then of the carriages driving away. It grows quiet. In the stillness there is the dull thud of an ax on a tree, a forlorn, melancholy sound. Footsteps are heard. From the door on the right* FIRS *appears. He is dressed as always in a jacket and white waistcoat, and wears slippers. He is ill.*]

FIRS [*goes to the door and tries the handle*]:   Locked. They have gone. . . . [*Sits down on the sofa.*] They've forgotten me. . . . Never mind . . . I'll sit here awhile. . . . I expect Leonid Andreich hasn't put on his fur coat and has gone off in his overcoat. [*Sighs anxiously.*] And I didn't see to it. . . . When they're young, they're green! [*Mumbles something which cannot be understood.*] I'll lie down awhile. . . . There's no strength left in you, nothing's left, nothing. . . . Ach, you . . . addlepate! [*Lies motionless.*]

[*A distant sound is heard that seems to come from the sky, the sound of a snapped string mournfully dying away. A stillness falls, and nothing is heard but the thud of the ax on a tree far away in the orchard.*]

1903

Afterword

> "In spite of all my attempts at being serious, the result
> is nothing; with me the serious always alternates with
> the trivial."
> —Letter to Yakov Polonsky, 22 February 1888

We usually used to go to the theater together. We
would get tickets for the amphitheater . . . and Anton
Pavlovich and I would turn up two hours before the
beginning of the show in order to get seats at the
front. . . . When we went into the theater we never
knew what we were going to see—we had no idea
what a play or an opera or an operetta was—but it
was all interesting to us. Another passionate theater
buff who would often join us was our uncle Mitrofan
Georgievich Chekhov. In Taganrog he was nicknamed
"Mr. Pilgrim" because he was so religious, but in fact
he was just as fanatical about the theater as we
were. . . . When we left the theater we would walk
down the streets all the way home remembering viv-
idly what we had seen, never noticing the weather or
the bumpy pavement. And the next day Anton Pavlovich would act everything out. . . .

This is how Ivan Chekhov recalled his elder brother's earliest theatrical expeditions. What Chekhov saw when he
went to the theater for the very first time (this was in the
autumn of 1873, when he was thirteen years old) was an
uproarious operetta by Jacques Offenbach. A big hit all

over Europe, *La belle Hélène* was being performed for the first time in Taganrog that season, and Chekhov was absolutely entranced. The world of Offenbach's irreverent take on Greek mythology, brimming with exuberant waltzes, witty jokes and parodies of "straight" opera, might seem a long way from that of Chekhov's late plays, in which most of the characters seem to take themselves dreadfully seriously and the outlook is generally bleak, but in various subtle ways, it actually informed his whole approach to drama. A closer look at the circumstances of Chekhov's early theatergoing can help us understand why that should be so. We tend to see Chekhovian drama through the prism of the four plays written toward the end of his life, but it is helpful to keep in mind that his previous stage reputation was largely based on a string of hilarious one-act farces.

It would have been hard for Chekhov not to have been drawn to the theater when he was growing up. Until the end of the nineteenth century, being born into a typical merchant family meant growing up in a very conservative, inward-looking environment in which secular entertainments like the theater were frowned upon. In Chekhov's case it was worse because his father was not only more disciplinarian than other merchants—he was more devout as well. Thus the days of Chekhov's childhood were filled with long hours serving in his father's shop or singing in the choir at interminable church services. He was lucky to be educated at the Taganrog Classical Gymnasium, but as a state-run school in Tsarist Russia, this institution too was stiflingly conservative. Pupils had to obtain special permission to go to the theater, and were expressly forbidden from sitting up in the amphitheater, where the seats were cheapest. It is not surprising, then, that this is where schoolboys from the Gymnasium were often to be found, having donned false beards and mustaches to avoid detection. Nor is it surprising that they were far more interested in seeing "melodrama" in action, rather than learning about it in a dry, academic way from their teachers; the theater was the most exciting place in town. Among the many colorful reminiscences to be found in the 2003 book *Taganrog and the Chekhovs*, published in Russia, there is one by Anton's aunt Marfa: "When going to the theater, Antosha would come to us in his school uniform and then change out of it, pulling a workman's cap over his eyes before setting off for the theater with his friends, and choosing poorly lit backstreets in order not to be seen by the school authorities. We would ask Antosha to tell us what he had seen in the theater and he would mimic both the actors and the audience. He was particularly good at the comic scenes. We used to split our sides laughing."

Still a busy trading port in the 1870s, Taganrog was cosmopolitan for a Russian town, and while its theater was small, both its repertoire and the quality of its performances were superior to the usual provincial fare, owing to the patronage of the wealthy Greeks and Italians in town. The latter were responsible for creating the lively and sometimes unruly atmosphere in the auditorium, the most popular artists inspiring fanatical devotion from their young fans in the amphitheater, some of whom would still be shouting, "Bravo," long after the sounds of the carriages taking their idols home at the end of the season had died away. It was no doubt with Taganrog in mind that Chekhov much later in his life described the provincial theater in his story "The Lady with the Little Dog," not forgetting to include schoolboys smoking on the landing outside the amphitheater:

> Like in most provincial theaters there was mist above the central chandelier and the people in the amphitheater were making a lot of noise. The local Romeos stood in the front row with their hands clasped behind their backs before the performance started; in the governor's box the governor's daughter was sitting in the front row in a boa, with the governor himself modestly hiding behind the partition, so that only his hands were visible. . . .

The theatrical education that Chekhov received by seeing the Russian classics, dramas and operettas on the Taganrog stage soon inspired amateur dramatics at home, where he naturally assumed the roles of both producer and director. As actor, meanwhile, his most noted role was that of the Mayor in Gogol's *The Government Inspector*, for which he wore his smartest school uniform with shiny buttons and a lot of carefully applied makeup.

It was only when Chekhov went to some shows while visiting Moscow for the first time in 1877 that he realized quite how provincial his local theater was. Nevertheless, by the time he moved to Moscow permanently two years later, to join his destitute family and enter medical school, Chekhov was able to add theater criticism and reportage to his portfolio as a writer of sketches and comic stories—a career he initially entered in order to help make ends meet. Over the course of the 1880s, he ranged very widely, writing about everything from the low life who frequented Moscow's Salon de Varieté to the regrettable closure of one of the city's early private theaters, which he praised as being one of the few institutions that had been keen to explore serious repertoire. And signs of the future iconoclast are detectable in his unsparing review of the legendary French actress Sarah Bernhardt, who began a season at the Bolshoi Theater in November 1881. Certainly not lacking in confidence, the twenty-one-year-old Chekhov found her acting style far too mannered and self-absorbed. All the while, of course, he was mentally squirreling away ideas about the nature of drama that would later come to fruition in the creation of his deliberately unhistrionic play *The Seagull* and the character of the brittle and egocentric actress Arkadina.

The passion Chekhov had for the theater was bound to find an outlet in his own writing, and his earliest extant drama, a one-acter with the typically playful title of *A Forced Declaration or The Sudden Death of a Horse or The Magnanimity of the Russian People*, was written when he was sixteen years old. Soon after writing this short skit, Chekhov started conceiving a full-blown serious pay. *Platonov* was completed in 1881, but never staged in his lifetime, not least because of its excessive length. It had all the ingredients of melodrama: a couple of attempted suicides, a murder, a hero with three romantic entanglements—all the sorts of things in fact that Chekhov would carefully remove from center stage in his later plays. It was a process he began with *Ivanov*, the play with which he made his stage debut in 1887.

In *Ivanov* Chekhov paid lip service to contemporary dramatic convention, but the play contains clear signs of the iconoclasm that was to bring him notoriety with *The Seagull* a decade later. In passing, it is worth remarking on the fact that Chekhov began his career as a dramatist at an extremely interesting time in Russian theatrical history. Until 1882 all theaters in Moscow and St. Petersburg were directly controlled by the Russian government, which meant not only was there no chance of audiences being exposed to subversive ideas, but that bureaucracy often prevailed over creativity. The abolition of the state monopoly suddenly made private initiative and experiment possible, and it was in Moscow, which was both the country's industrial heartland and also a long way from the officialdom of St. Petersburg, that private theaters took off first. This was good for Chekhov, who was sought out by the owner of the newly established Korsh Theater; he wanted this promising writer of comic stories to write a funny play for him that would be a sure box-office draw. But this is not quite what he got. And the audience, who also looked forward to an evening of light entertainment, were equally nonplussed. There were no clear heroes and villains, and they could not work out who they should be identifying with (which was all part of Chekhov's plan). Ambiguity was not really a viable category in Russian theater yet.

After the furor surrounding *Ivanov*, Chekhov seemed to revert to type by writing the two one-act comedies *The Bear* and *The Proposal*, which became smash hits as soon as they were premiered, in 1888 and 1889, respectively. As a prose writer, Chekhov had by this time scaled the heights by responding to a commission from a serious literary journal in 1888 with his groundbreaking story "The Steppe." This was a meteoric ascent, bearing in mind his humble beginnings as a contributor to lowbrow comic weeklies only a few years earlier. With his versions of French vaudevilles, Chekhov now became a household name in Russia, feted in Moscow and St. Petersburg alike. A command performance of *The Bear* was even given before Alexander III at his summer dacha. Both became staples of Russian amateur-dramatic societies, and it is in these two effervescent, artistically unadventurous vaudevilles that we can see most clearly the hand of Offenbach, composer of musical vaudevilles, who together with his inspired librettist, Halévy, had instilled in Chekhov a lasting affection for wit and bright, fast-paced, seamless action all those years back when he was a teenager in Taganrog. With exceptions made for works like *Eugene Onegin*, Chekhov never quite got into opera as much as operetta, its irreverent sister. And the zest and frivolousness common to the best operettas also find their way, albeit transmuted, into Chekhov's four late dramatic masterpieces, where they are sometimes given a more sardonic tone (as in the comic asides in the otherwise elegiac *Three Sisters*), but more often provide a vein of absurd humor to act as a counterpoint to the gloomy introspection of characters like Uncle Vanya. The slapstick becomes more pronounced in *The Cherry Orchard*, which Chekhov least of all wished to be perceived as a tragedy, having fought against such oversimplifying polarizations throughout his career. The strange alternation of the comic and tragic is a typically subversive Chekhovian touch.

None of the handful of one-act plays Chekhov wrote subsequent to *The Bear* and *The Proposal* were destined to be as successful, although some of them were certainly original: the action of *Tatyana Repina* (1889), which continues a play his friend Alexei Suvorin had written, takes place during a wedding service. Chekhov certainly never seemed at a loss for ideas. In December 1888, he wrote to Suvorin: "When I've written myself out, I'm going to write vaudevilles and live off them. I think I could write about a hundred of them a year. Vaudeville subjects gush out of me like oil from the wells of Baku." Six years later, in January 1894, he confessed to Suvorin: "It is much easier to write about Socrates than about a young lady or a cook. From this you can draw the conclusion that I take the writing of one-act plays seriously."

Chekhov's path as a serious dramatist certainly was not straight. He did not move directly from *Ivanov* to his four great plays. In between came *The Wood Demon*, which he wrote in 1889 without a commission, and which was considerably more unconventional than *Ivanov*, and definitely less "dramatic." After it was turned down for production by the Imperial Theaters, Chekhov handed it over to a Moscow theater, a move he soon regretted when the production opened underrehearsed and was quickly taken out of the repertoire after a very poor reception. *The Seagull*, which he completed in 1896, was an even more unorthodox play, and its author made a fatal error by letting it be performed at the Imperial Alexandrinsky Theater, to an audience looking forward to a traditional comedy. This was a play that seemed to combine every single dramatic genre going, but also flouted them. Its characters were neither heroic nor villainous, and they did not seem to do much. The juggernaut of the Imperial Theaters could not cope with the delicate nuances and sophisticated parody Chekhov was championing, and the first-night fiasco is now the stuff of theater history legend.

Hardly surprisingly, Chekhov was very discouraged by the misunderstanding that greeted *The Seagull*, but it did not stop him pillaging *The Wood Demon* in 1897 to create *Uncle Vanya*, which was successfully produced in provincial theaters. It was at this point that Vladimir Nemirovich-Danchenko, who along with Konstantin Stanislavsky had founded the Moscow Art Theater in 1897, started to persuade Chekhov to let them stage *The Seagull*. Nemirovich-Danchenko and Stanislavsky belonged to a different generation of theatrical impresarios, who took the staging of drama seriously, understood the refined theater of mood that Chekhov was developing in his plays, and worked closely to train an ensemble of actors who would be governed by a director who would for the first time take a leading role in interpreting works performed. They followed their historic production of *The Seagull* in 1898 with a production of *Uncle Vanya* in 1899, and premieres of *The Three Sisters* in 1901 and *The Cherry Orchard* in 1904. They were not all definitive productions, and indeed, Chekhov grew increasingly dissatisfied with the emphasis on veri-

similitude, by which Stanislavsky in particular placed
much store. With their proto-existentialist themes, and
their subtle stylization, Chekhov was gradually becoming
more abstract, but his symbolism was largely lost on
Stanislavsky. Not even being married to one of the company's leading actresses helped. Olga Knipper (whom
Chekhov met at the company's first reading of *The Seagull* in 1898 and finally married in 1901, insisting on the
part-time relationship remaining part-time) created the
roles of Elena, Masha and Ranevskaya.

All of Chekhov's four last plays are set on a country
estate, and the first two were actually written at Meli-
khovo, the modest country estate that Chekhov himself
finally managed to acquire in 1892, fulfilling a long-held
dream, albeit at a time when the great era of the Russian
country estate was already in terminal decline. The last
two plays were written in Yalta, which became Chekhov's new place of enforced residence in 1898, following the belated diagnosis of the tuberculosis that would
finally kill him in 1904. *The Three Sisters* reflects Chekhov's longing to be back in Moscow, while *The Cherry
Orchard* looks nostalgically back to the cherry trees he
had planted in the garden he had had to leave at Meli-
khovo. If, from a sociocultural point of view, his last
plays are about the forces of change and the disintegration of the old way of life of which the country estate
was the fulcrum, they are also about the gradual extinc-
tion of his own life, and are highly lyrical. They are
elegiac poems writ large. Peter Brook was right when
he said in his book *The Shifting Point* (1988, p. 157)
that "it is construction that counts, rhythm, the purely
theatrical poetry that comes not from beautiful words,
but from the right word at the right moment." This poetry
is dependent on a careful observation of the "coded mes-
sages" represented by Chekhov's punctuation, "which re-
cord characters' relationships and emotions, the moments
at which ideas come together or follow their own course,"
enabling us "to grasp what the words conceal."

The late plays certainly reflect Chekhov's life and his
preoccupations, but the allusions are predictably either
highly diffuse or deeply buried. Thus the motif of the

killing of a seagull most probably has its antecedent in the wounded woodcock shot by Chekhov's friend Levitan in 1892, and Dr. Astrov in *Uncle Vanya* was inspired in part by a socially committed physician of his acquaintance. The Pushkin quotation at the beginning of *The Three Sisters* seems to have been triggered by associations between the mulberry tree he found at his Crimean dacha and the one in Taganrog, which was said to have inspired those lines from *Ruslan and Lyudmila* that Masha quotes. The ominous sound of the breaking string in *The Cherry Orchard*, meanwhile, which seems in retrospect such a prescient symbol of sudden and violent social collapse, first appears in his 1887 story "Fortune." There it relates to a bucket breaking loose in a mine shaft deep in the southern steppes near to where Chekhov grew up. It was a landscape he loved, and it was where he had his first adventures. In 1904, he knew he would never see the steppe again, and the oblique reference to it in his final work can be seen as a kind of leave-taking of one of his greatest sources of lyrical inspiration (it was not by chance that he made his fictional debut in a literary journal with a story called "The Steppe"), and also a poignant recollection of his youth, when he had everything ahead of him, and so much to look forward to.

With his untheatrical plays of contained emotion, muted climaxes, tensions and silences, their pathos leavened by burlesque, Chekhov turned his back on all the dramatic conventions of his day, which called for clear-cut characters, action, and a recognizable plot. He was also in a strange way rebelling against the theatricality he had grown up with—that of the Russian Orthodox Church, whose lengthy, highly ritualized services he had been forced to participate in as a chorister when he was a child. But it was a rebellion that was very subtle. Not for nothing did Simon Karlinsky call Chekhov the "gentle subversive" in a seminal article that prefaces his 1973 edition of the writer's letters in English translation. And it is telling that while Chekhov wrote many more stories than he wrote plays, his last play was also his very last work.

—Rosamund Bartlett

Selected Bibliography

WORKS BY ANTON CHEKHOV

Don Juan in the Russian Manner, also known as *Platonov*, 1881   Unfinished Play
The Tales of the Melpomene, 1884
On the Highway, 1885   Play
Motley Stories, 1886
In the Twilight, 1887   Stories
The Kiss, 1887   Story
Ivanov, 1887   Play
The Steppe, 1888   Short Novel
The Name-Day Party, 1888   Short Novel
The Bear, 1888   Play
The Proposal, 1889   Play
Ward Six, 1892   Short Novel
Sakhalin Island, 1893   Story
The Black Monk, 1894   Story
The Sea Gull, 1896   Play
Peasants, 1897   Short Novel
Uncle Vanya, 1897   Play
In the Ravine, 1900   Short Novel
The Three Sisters, 1901   Play
The Betrothed, 1903   Story
The Cherry Orchard, 1904   Play

SELECTED BIOGRAPHY AND CRITICISM

Avilova, Lydia. *Chekhov in My Life*. Trans. David Magarshack. London: Methuen, 1989.

Bartlett, Rosamund. *Chekhov: Scenes from a Life*. London: Free Press, 2004.

———, ed. *Anton Chekhov, A Life in Letters*. Trans. Rosamud Bartlett and Anthony Phillips. London: Penguin Classics, 2004.

Clayton, J. Douglas, *Checkhov Then and Now: The Reception of Chekhov in World Culture*. New York: Peter Lang, 1997.

Clyman, Toby, ed. *A Chekhov Companion*. Westport, CT: Greenwood Press, 1985.

Eekman, Thomas A., ed. *Critical Essays on Anton Chekhov*. Boston: G. K. Hall, 1989.

Gilman, Richard. *Chekhov's Plays: An Opening into Eternity*. New Haven, CT: Yale University Press, 1995.

Gottlieb, Vera and Paul Allain, eds. *The Cambridge Companion to Chekhov*. Cambridge: Cambridge University Press, 2000.

Hackett, Jean. *The Actor's Chekhov*. Lyme, NH: Smith & Kraus, 1992.

Howe, Irving. "What Can We Do with Chekhov?" in *Pequod: A Journal of Contemporary Literature and Literary Criticism* 34 (1992), pp. 11–15.

Jackson, Robert Louis, ed. *Checkhov: A Collection of Critical Essays*. Englewood Cliff, NJ: Prentice-Hall, 1967.

Karlinsky, Simon, ed. *Anton Chekhov's Life and Thought: Selected Letters and Commentary*. Trans. Michael Henry Heim and Simon Karlinsky. Evanston, IL: Northwestern University Press, 1973.

Kirk, Irina. *Anton Chekhov*. Boston: Twayne, 1981.

Pitcher, Harvey. *The Chekhov Play: A New Interpretation*. New York: Barnes & Noble, 1973.

Pritchett, V. S. *Chekhov: A Spirit Set Free*. New York: Random House, 1998.

Rayfield, Donald. *Anton Chekhov: A Life*. New York: Henry Holt, 1988.

———. *Understanding Chekhov: A Critical Study of Chekhov's Prose and Drama*. Madison: University of Wisconsin Press, 1999.

Senelick, Laurence. *The Chekhov Theatre: A Century of the Plays in Performance*. Cambridge: Cambridge University Press, 2000.

Simmons, Ernest J. *Chekhov: A Biography*. Boston: Little, Brown, 1962.

Troyat, Henri. *Chekhov*. New York: Fawcett Columbine, 1986.

Turkov, Andrei, compiler. *Anton Chekhov and His Times*. Cynthia Carlile, translator of memoirs; Sharon McKee, translator of letters. Fayetteville: University of Arkansas Press, 1995.

Wood, James. "No More Mr. Nice Guy: The Brutal Comedy of Anton Chekhov" in *The New Republic* (February 5, 1996), pp. 32–39.

Signet Classics

Russia's Greatest Short Fiction

ANTON CHEKHOV: SELECTED STORIES

Anton Chekhov, a master of both the sentimental
and ironic, is a writer of broad scope and
thoughtful insight. These tales, whether sadly
sentimental or pensively bitter, are the equal of
his plays. Included in this volume are:
*The Confession, A Nincompoop, Ninochka—A Love
Story, A Cure for Drinking, The Milksop, In Spring,
The Kiss*, and many more.

THE DEATH OF IVAN ILYCH
AND OTHER STORIES by Leo Tolstoy

Leo Tolstoy combined detailed physical
description with perceptive psychological insight
to sweep aside the sham of surface appearances
and lay bare man's intimate gestures, acts, and
thoughts. Murder and sacrifice...greed and
devotion...lust and affection...vanity and love—
one by one, in this volume of great stories,
Tolstoy dissects the basic drives, emotions, and
motives of ordinary people searching for self-
knowledge and spiritual perfection.

Available wherever books are sold or at
signetclassics.com